SWEET CHAOS

ALSO BY CAROL BRIGHTMAN

Between Friends: The Correspondence of Hannah Arendt and
Mary McCarthy, 1949–1975 (editor)

Writing Dangerously: Mary McCarthy and Her World

Larry Rivers: Drawings and Digressions (coauthor)

The Venceremos Brigade: Young Americans Sharing the Life and
Work of Revolutionary Cuba (coeditor)

SWEET CHAOS

THE GRATEFUL DEAD'S
AMERICAN ADVENTURE

CAROL BRIGHTMAN

CLARKSON POTTER/PUBLISHERS
NEW YORK

Grateful acknowledgment is made for permission to reprint quotations from the lyrics of Robert Hunter, used by permission of Ice Nine Publishing Company. Excerpts from "Closing Time" and "The Future" by Leonard Cohen, copyright © 1993 Sony/ATV Songs LLC; "Waiting for the Miracle" by Leonard Cohen and Sharon Robinson, copyright © 1992 Sony/ATV Songs LLC, MCA Music Publishing, Geffen Music and Robinhill Music; "Take This Waltz" by Leonard Cohen, based on a poem by Federico García Lorca, copyright © 1990 Sony/ATV Songs LLC and Estana Srl. All rights on behalf of Sony/ATV Songs LLC administered by Sony/ATV Music Publishing, 8 Music Square West, Nashville, TN 37203. All rights reserved. Used by permission. Lyric excerpt from "You and Me" by Neil Young. Copyright © 1992 by Silver Fiddle Music. All rights reserved. Reprinted by permission of Warner Bros. Publications U.S., Inc., Miami, FL 33014. "Visions of Johanna" copyright © 1966 by Dwarf Music. All rights reserved. International copyright secured. Reprinted by permission. Reprinted by permission of Viking Penguin: excerpts from Robert Hunter's "An American Adventure," in *Sentinel*, and "Holigomena," in *Night Cadre*. From *Conversations with the Dead: The Grateful Dead Interview Book* by David Gans. Copyright © 1991 by David Gans. Published by arrangement with Carol Publishing Group. A Citadel Press Book. Reprinted by permission of HarperCollins: excerpt from a poem by Allen Ginsberg, "First Party at Ken Kesey's with Hell's Angels," in *Collected Poems: 1947–1980*. Acknowledgment is made for permission to quote material from Tom Wolfe, *The Electric Kool-Aid Acid Test* (New York: Bantam, 1978); Robert Greenfield, *Dark Star: An Oral Biography of Jerry Garcia* (New York: Morrow, 1996); the Editors of *Rolling Stone, Garcia* (Boston: Little, Brown, 1995); John W. Scott, ed., *DeadBase VI* (Hanover, NH: DeadBase, 1992); Rock Scully with David Dalton, *Living with the Dead* (Boston: Little, Brown, 1996). Grateful acknowledgment is made to Paul Grushkin, coauthor, *Grateful Dead: The Official Book of Deadheads* (New York: William Morrow, 1983), author, *The Art of Rock: Posters from Presley to Punk* (New York: Abbeville, 1987) for access to photo and poster archives.

Published by Clarkson N. Potter, Inc., 201 East 50th Street, New York, New York 10022. Member of the Crown Publishing Group.
Random House, Inc. New York, Toronto, London, Sydney, Auckland
www.randomhouse.com
CLARKSON N. POTTER, POTTER, and colophon are trademarks of Clarkson N. Potter, Inc.

Printed in the United States of America

Design by Lauren Monchik

Library of Congress Cataloging-in-Publication Data

Brightman, Carol.
    Sweet chaos : the Grateful Dead's American adventure / by Carol Brightman.
    Includes bibliographical references and index.
        1. Grateful Dead (Musical group)   I. Title.
    ML421.G72B75 1998
    782.42166′092′2—dc21   98-11826
                                                                                     MN

ISBN 0-517-59448-X

10 9 8 7 6 5 4 3

First Edition

FOR SARABINH AND SIMON

CONTENTS

PART IV REAPING THE WHIRLWIND

I'm Uncle Sam/That's who I am
Been hidin' out/in a rock-and-roll band
Shake the hand/that shook the hand
Of P. T. Barnum/and Charlie Chan

ROBERT HUNTER, "U.S. BLUES"

SWEET CHAOS

in crowds ran to parades and political demonstrations. The political was molting into the personal, but music was music, as far as I was concerned, and dance was play, not worship. With the Grateful Dead, it was as if the music had been spoken for by a secret society of lotus-eaters, and now the musicians, having slipped into the hair shirts of prophets and holy men, were no longer available to the casual listener.

At the same time, the Dead kept reaching out and making new conquests, especially on college campuses. The enormity of the following they amassed over the next twenty-odd years raises the question of agency. How much is the vaunted Grateful Dead *phenomenon* an expression of the yearnings of the vast audiences they tapped? To understand the Dead's place in American history, don't we need to take a closer look at how history shaped them? And what was the band's role in creating a subculture that, three years after Jerry Garcia's death, remains surprisingly intact?

"We don't have any real plans," Garcia told *The Greening of America*'s author Charles Reich in 1972. "Everything's kinda hashed out. It stumbles, then it creeps, then it flies with one wing and bumps into trees, and shit, you know, we're committed to it by now . . ."—which was the nonleader leader speaking. For Mickey Hart, however, forging the new culture was a crusade. "We went on a head-hunting mission for twenty-five years," he exclaims. "We went out there and got this army in tow." It started around 1969, when the band dispatched its first power object, the image of a skeleton walking on stilts across *The Tibetan Book of the Dead*, dragging a ball and chain. The work of a forgotten artist, it was the original Mr. Bones, a Grateful Dead icon; and Hart remembers it as a code that "let you see in the windows of people in San Francisco who were Deadheads before there were Deadheads."

In any event, it was this former jug band from Palo Alto, alone among the collapsing stars of the '60s, that gathered unto itself the free-floating energy of a disenchanted generation, and carried it through three decades. Nobody else did it. No other bands; no communes, peace groups, political factions or tendencies, art movements or experimental film groups—though one might argue that durability and longevity are not necessarily virtues in a counterinstitution whose job it is to challenge the way things are on behalf of alternate arrangements not (yet) in place. Nobody wants to become trapped in The Slough of Decayed Language or The Museum of Leftover Ideologies (as the artist Robert Smithson, writing in 1968, called the cul-de-sacs of "the crumbling world mind"). And you still hear people, rock critics mainly, contend that if the Grateful Dead had died a timely death, say, sometime in the middle '70s when disco and alternative pop were on the rise, their substantial contribution to American music would have been assured; whereas today—partly because, in one form or another, the musicians *keep playing*—the judgment remains open.

In critical circles, the nervousness about this band with a past, whose audiences have created their own world, complete with fan magazines, radio shows, and endless chat rooms and conferences on the Internet, is a story in itself. You don't hear "Sugaree," "Ramble on, Rose," or "Truckin' " on Classic Rock. Nor do you read about the Grateful Dead or the Jerry Garcia Band in ceremonial roundups of '60s rock 'n' roll in the national media. With a ready-made audience, beholden to Grateful Dead Productions, there never was much incentive for the music industry to make collateral investments.

Even before the band launched its MTV video of the hit tune "Touch of Grey" in 1987, when the big money poured in, the Grateful Dead was the top concert draw in the United States for several years with no advertising and very little press. Ticketmaster sold the leftover tickets after the band processed direct-mail orders from Deadheads, which included "tour booklets" reserving blocks of tickets for every show. After 1983, the Dead never played to an empty seat (or almost never); and they did it without studio recordings, for the most part, and without ever reviving the songwriting spree of 1970.

As in the 1970s, so in the 1980s: While the band quietly brought in bumper crops of new customers from multiseason tours that crisscrossed the country, nobody outside the fanzines and the "merchandising books" (as fan books are called in the trade) investigated the phenomenon. In a mass culture whose marketing system is geared to annual turnovers of product, the Grateful Dead were dismissed as a "sixties band," a relic, *something that had already happened.* From this, it followed that they were playing to *cult* audiences, which, like the musicians, were out of touch with the latest trends in music, fashion, even drugs. With their celebration of themselves as a community, and their intricate rituals of mutual aid,

Deadheads, moreover, were out of touch with the "go for it" values of the 1980s and 1990s.

Among critics, the Dead acquired a pariah status for another reason: the deification of Jerry Garcia. In Robert Smithson's Grand Guignol, there is a "Room of Great Artists," in which a continuous film shows "the artist alienated from society," with sections titled "Suffering, discovery, fame, and decline." As in the classic literature of the misunderstood genius, the movie delves into the artist's private torment, and shows his conflicts as he struggles to make the world understand his vision.

Jerry Garcia need not apply. This cliché was not for him. Having situated himself in what he called "the Grateful Dead universe"—quite happily, it seems, until, perhaps, the end—he removed himself from the camera eye, and slipped into another cliché: the guru, the man who can do no wrong. A more dangerous one by far, it damaged his personal life and shut him off from a creative give-and-take with a larger world, although not from other musicians, ranging from Branford Marsalis to James Cotton, who played with the Dead. Nor did it keep Garcia from the struggle he valued most, which was to bring his musicianship into line with the sacred vision he nourished of his craft.

You don't have to be a fan of the Grateful Dead to recognize that the traveling road show tapped into something deeper in American life than nostalgia for the '60s. Perhaps it's more accurate to see the "geo-gypsies," as a poet friend of mine calls Deadheads, as a site-specific response to the anomie of everyday life. They have borrowed somebody else's past as a cover for what they're actually doing. This has little to do with what led the gypsies of the 1960s to gather in large numbers, whether to protest public wrongs or to celebrate the birth of a new nation, kicking and screaming its way free of the old. Deadheads are simply doing a piece of the road together. They're doing it with music; and many are doing it with a little help from psychedelic drugs, which function not unlike the helper figure in a fairy tale.

This is the fox, hunchback, or the jack-of-all-trades in the ancient story "The Water of Life," where the helper is a reincarnated corpse, grateful to the hero for having buried him. The figure materializes by the side of the road with a magic potion to aid the adventurer in the fulfillment of a task: to outwit an ogre in order to unite with a maiden, or to rescue a dying king and restore the poisoned land. When the goal is achieved, the helper departs, and the hero moves on. The tale alludes to a youth's departure from home, and the need for a mentor to aid in the transition from adolescence to adulthood. In our day, the transition may be fraught with peril. Wayfarers get stuck with their helpers for years, drifting from one magic potion to another, forgetting they have a task. You may find them traveling with a band, the same band, summer after summer; partaking of the "magic" until the "magic" becomes the life and the life (for a few) becomes a ragged claw scuttling across the parking lot for a fix. Deadheads have a joke about the lingering. Question: How do you know if somebody is a Deadhead? Answer: He's still there.

The Grateful Dead's music, meanwhile, is encoded with allusions to the twists in life's road, as in "Stella Blue," where "it all rolls into one / and nothing comes for free / There's nothing you can hold / for very long . . ." The musical journey repeats itself endlessly; the lyrics, especially Robert Hunter's lyrics, are like mushrooms that are nibbled again and again and keep springing back. The delivery of the songs by Jerry Garcia, in the tent-sized black T-shirt of later years, could break the hardest heart on a good night: the long, fluid guitar solos, swooping and soaring, sometimes sounding like a violin; the dreamy tremolo voice caressing the words, feeling their weight, as if they have a life of their own. Even an off night—and many of the shows I saw between 1992 and 1995 were off nights—could be retrieved by a moment of exploration and discovery on the part of the musicians that was as unexpected as a Mozart sonata in the subway.

On tour, this was a house band whose "house" changed from city to city. The party was always the same, and resembled a family reunion, "a family reunion of the world's misfits," insiders say. And yet there is nothing particularly eccentric about the Grateful Dead's followers, who come in all ages and classes, though most are white, and a majority are male. Misfit consciousness is a very American state of mind. Everybody has a friend, a sister or brother, child or parent, nephew or grandson who is or was a Deadhead. There's so-and-so in the mail room, your seatmate on the plane, the governor of a New England state, the clerk in the bookstore, the inmates of a medium-security prison in Oregon, an astrophysicist in Colorado Springs, a dulcimer player in Denver, students everywhere, a famous chef in Chicago, a Stealth bomber pilot with Dead stickers on his wing (who died in 1996), a cohort of lawyers in San Francisco, a minion of brokers on Wall Street, a handful of young actors in Hoboken, middle-aged bikers in Vermont, a string of carpenters and fishermen along the Maine coast, shipbuilders at the Bath Iron Works, a Child Protective Services supervisor in Lewiston, Bar Harbor yachtsmen whose J boats are named after Dead songs, a distinguished novelist's son, a famous actress's daughter, the coach of the Chicago Bulls, the deliveryman from the florist—a fair number of whom I met during the six years of researching this book.

Deadheads are everywhere and nowhere, so much a part of American life as to appear almost invisible. This invisibility, in fact, is a curious aspect of the phenomenon; as if the subculture surrounding the Grateful Dead had become a piece of Americana before anyone had a chance to plumb its roots or ponder its chameleonlike character. The Grateful Dead have probably played to more people over the years than any other performing group in American history, and yet this "little society out there," as Jerry Garcia called the Dead's world—whose invisibility surprised him, too—remains largely ignored by students of American culture.

Why? I wondered when I sat down with bassist Phil Lesh in the spring of 1996, thinking of the writers I knew who had raised their eyebrows at the project I began in 1992. "What's there to write about?" they asked; and I'd say, *Are you kidding?* not sure myself at the beginning, so overwhelmed was I by the enormity of what I'd taken on. This was to identify the elements of the drama the Grateful Dead enacted for its fans as it crossed the continent year after year for thirty years. Lesh pondered the question. "It may be that it's a little too weird. It's slippery," he said of the Grateful Dead. "There's nothing you can get a handle on. It seems like it's too tough a nut for them to crack, or it's like looking at a mirrored ball: There's nothing to grasp, because all you're seeing is what's reflected. All you're seeing is yourself."

This last is certainly true. Students of religion will see a religious movement in the fervor of the congregation; and they will not be wrong. A religious note is touched almost every time Jerry Garcia speaks of psychedelics, as when he discourses (in 1993) on how acid allowed him to go beyond ordinary experience; to probe an alternate reality that as a child he believed existed but that he could never find. "Everything on the other side was really okay, and even fun," he discovered. The acid world was "shadowy, ambiguous and half-concealed," not unlike the spiritual world of Catholicism, which he inherited from his Spanish father and Irish mother. He was sure he had "received direct instruction about his life while high," Garcia told the interviewer, and he swore that once he had "ridden up into the heavens and had been shown the face of God."

When I ask Lesh why he used to say that "every place we play is church," he explains that improvisation is a form of worship. "When we play, we're prayin'. . . . And then you have to hope that the dove descends." "High" theory merges with a kind of crazy sociology when Lesh speaks of how dropping acid together week after week, month after month, created a kind of group mind for the band. "Merged thoughts," he says, "have greater meaning than we do as individuals."

Perhaps I risk seeing myself when I return in these pages to the 1960s and early '70s to examine not just the Dead's world but the community they shunned across the Bay in Berkeley, as well. Along with Vietnam in 1967 and Cuba in 1970, Berkeley is revisited to rattle memory's cage and remind the contemporary reader of the political events that influenced young radicals. One cannot re-create the era out of which the Grateful Dead emerged without recalling civil rights and the Free Speech Movement, Vietnam, the Cuban Revolution, and Weatherman. But reviewing this history also reminds us that when this "sixties band" lifted off into the 1970s, '80s, and '90s, it left a good deal behind.

Looked at more closely, the Grateful Dead's family—patriarchal, secretive, anarchy-loving, communal, suspicious of outsiders and sometimes of insiders—suggests a throwback to a cranky nineteenth-century dystopia. California sets the stage for the Dead's formation—not just Haight Ashbury's saturnalia but old San Francisco, the San Francisco of the Gold Rush, which drew Jerry Garcia's ancestors on his mother's side. This was when "the spirit of chance prevailed in the town," as historian Van Wyck Brooks writes, "where the topsy-turvy was almost the rule, though the golden stream from the mines flowed over all."

The spirit of chance would always rule the Grateful Dead, even after 1987 when the band acquired a whole new crowd, a younger set, who stayed on and brought their kid brothers and sisters. Scanning the history of the brigand band—its early brushes with the drug law, its on-again, off-again tie to the Hell's Angels, its susceptibility to shamans and medicine men of dubious repute—one senses that this kinship with the frontier ruffians of the 1850s, and the actors, musicians, and fandango dancers who crossed the plains to amuse them, might be the real one. And the much ballyhooed descent from the 1960s is but a prelude to the tale.

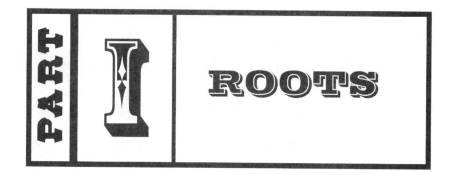

PART I ROOTS

PROLOGUE

We were doing the Acid Tests, which was our first
response to formlessness. Formlessness and chaos lead
to new forms. And new order. Closer to, probably, what
the real order is.

JERRY GARCIA

The Captain has just informed me that we're going into Operation Crystal-
lization, announces a hidden voice. *The chief engineer has left his station*
at the TV console to go down to the engine room to prepare the engine fuel to
enter this new configuration [cut to Prankster Ken Babbs sipping from a
tiny cup]. *Cassady, however, will remain at his post in the projection booth in*
order to keep driving this ship. . . .

IT's JANUARY 8, 1966, and the Merry Pranksters, a boys' gang with girl
pals, steeped in the sci-fi argot of Captain Marvel and EC comics from the
1950s, are staging a party inside a cavernous second-floor auditorium in
San Francisco called the Fillmore. The "Captain" is Ken Kesey, known outside the group for his psychic thriller *One Flew Over the Cuckoo's Nest*
(1962). Neal Cassady, celebrated teddy boy of the Beat Generation, re-
puted to be able to retread tires with his thumbnails, has attached himself
to the Pranksters as a mechanic/hipster of the old school. The "engine
fuel" is LSD, known as acid; and this is an Acid Test, which is another motif
from the sci-fi hero tales: *Can You Pass the Acid Test?* The future has arrived
wearing the robes of the past.

Everybody's dancing a herky-jerk dance, with heads bobbing back
and forth and invisible wires tying shoulders and knees to an invisible

puppeteer. Cassady dances and clutches his hair at the same time, as if holding his own strings. The women, who are pretty, wear short cocktail dresses—all but the one in jeans and an oversized striped T-shirt, who stomps and spins in a pool of righteous abandon. This is Kesey's young sidekick Mountain Girl, née Carolyn Adams, from Hyde Park, New York. A few men, including Stanley Owsley, the mad chemist behind the "engine fuel," wear crewneck sweaters and owlish glasses and look like graduate students from the late 1950s and early 1960s, which some of them are. Others, such as Page Browning, wear space-age costumes. With his harlequin-painted face and teased sequin-studded silver hair, Browning looks like a David Bowie character, or like Blueboy, the catlike villain Jack Webb introduced on *Dragnet* later in the '60s, an acidhead gone bad.

It just seems to be orderly chaos, YES, crackles a second voice over the loudspeaker. *In the end, nothing but mindless chaos, that same old dude, good old Mindless Chaos, hassling, ever hassling.*

But wait a minute. How can chaos be both "orderly" and "mindless"?

In these harum-scarum scenes from Kesey's videotape, which is a pastiche of the Fillmore Acid Test and another one in Los Angeles, the stray remark from the control tower is our first clue that there may be method to the madness. That isn't to say that the mix of music, liquid light projections, and weird sound effects, filtered through hallucinogenic drugs, has been doctored to produce a desired effect. Or that the mind, swooping like a heat-seeking missile toward the flash of form in the swarm of new sensations, has construed an order more pleasing to itself—which is what the mind usually does. The overture to chaos, "hassling, ever hassling," is the "ripple in still water / when there is no pebble tossed" (as the song goes), which tells us that the action, whatever it is, is happening *beneath* the surface of reality and not on the face of it.

Acid trips, in any event, are far from mindless; and they sometimes repeat themselves, as if with LSD the subject taps into a hidden chamber of the brain that is linked by underground circuitry to a cosmic zoo. Thus an Oakland Hell's Angel, Skip Workman, who was turned on to LSD by the Pranksters in 1964, and attended some of the Acid Tests, always saw the same huge fire-breathing dragon, heaving against a field of American flags. "The dragon was keeping time with the music," he recalls, "and sometimes the dragon would be blowing a bugle and the notes would be coming out of the bugle." And all he could think of on the morning of a trip was, *"I gotta see the dragon again."*

At the Fillmore, the Pranksters' house band stands off in a corner, playing the blues. The musicians appear oddly disconnected from one another, and from the dancers—which is not how the musicians read it, but the viewer doesn't know that. There's a chubby biker dude in leather mouthing a harmonica and singing "I'm a Hog for You"; a bass player with a blond Fauntleroy hairdo; the boy—or is it a girl?—playing rhythm guitar; a straight-looking kid on drums; and the lead guitarist, whose thick black crinkly pageboy wobbles like a dime-store wig as he rocks over his strings. Wearing a polka-dot shirt and a palomino vest, he sings the refrain of a Reverend Gary Davis song over and over:

> Death
> don't have no mercy
> in this world

These are the Warlocks—Ron "Pigpen" McKernan, Phil Lesh, Bobby Weir, Bill Kreutzmann, and Jerry Garcia—who have just renamed themselves the Grateful Dead. Like the Merry Pranksters, who include Stanford University dropouts, along with Ken Kesey's Oregon friends, they have come up to San Francisco from Palo Alto. Unlike the Pranksters, who are theatrical, mischief-making, messianic, a little older, the Warlocks have been influenced by the more cabalistic mentality of the Beats, whom Lesh and Garcia, in particular, revere.

Their gang—whose Palo Alto birthplace, not far from Kesey's former digs on Perry Lane, was a dilapidated mansion known as the Chateau—was first called the "love scene." The "love scene" is what a young friend from London, Alan Trist, christened the core group in 1960–1961, which included Robert Hunter, later the Grateful Dead's principal lyricist, Garcia, Garcia's childhood friends Laird Grant and Willy Legate, Phil Lesh, Lesh's Beat poet friend Bob Petersen, and Trist. While the name had worn off by the mid-'60s, it stamped the little circle from the beginning as a *scene*.

There was no doubt who the leader was. "It was easy with Jerry as part of your crew to feel that you were going to amount to something," says

Hunter, who doesn't want to talk about Jerry Garcia, although he keeps returning to him. "I'll say it—he had what it took," he exclaims. A sense of destiny mainly; a belief that the world, and not just the musical world, was his oyster.

At the Acid Tests, Jerry's Palo Alto gang was entering a new configuration, as American in its aching for transcendence as it was in its early search for musical roots in the American past. Operation Crystallization had begun.

~CHAPTER~
1

THE MAGIC ART OF THE GREAT HUMBUG

Rather than write, I will ride buses, study the insides of
jails, and see what goes on.

KEN KESEY

*G*o with the flow! was the watchword in 1964, when Ken Elton Kesey, ex-wrestler, "Most Likely to Succeed" at Springfield (Oregon) High, star attraction in the Stanford University writing program, and, at twenty-nine, the author of a hugely successful first novel, lay down his pen for a more direct raid on the consciousness game. The "flow" was acid's undertow, which grabbed at the ankles like a deep current welling up from a distant shore.

"I'd rather be a lightning rod than a seismograph," Kesey told Tom Wolfe, who celebrates Kesey in *The Electric Kool-Aid Acid Test* as "the Sun King, looking bigger all the time, with that great jaw in profile against the redwoods. . . ." With *One Flew Over the Cuckoo's Nest,* Kesey was a seismograph, recording vibrations from deep within the culture. The novel's mental hospital, presided over by Nurse Ratched, is a supple metaphor for the politics of adjustment, which dominated the 1950s. Anything that fouled the smooth workings of the "Combine," as Kesey calls the tyranny of consensus—with its impersonal, clinical face, not so different from the 1990s—was crushed.

Now he was messing with the vibrations themselves. "Tootling the multitudes," he called his early raids on the cultural mainstream, which included, on one occasion, turning up in Phoenix, Arizona, during the 1964 presidential campaign decked out in American flag regalia and waving a huge placard saying, A VOTE FOR BARRY [Goldwater] IS A VOTE FOR FUN.

Nineteen sixty-four was the year Kesey took to the road in the 1939 International Harvester bus, which today lies moldering like a giant turnip in a ravine on his Oregon ranch. The gaily painted 1948 replica stands in the Rock and Roll Hall of Fame in Cleveland, next to Janis Joplin's Mercedes-Benz. In the summer of 1964, speed freak Neal Cassady was the designated driver of the original bus, as he had been for Kerouac and his gang in the 1940s and '50s, when the long-distance vehicle of choice was usually an old jalopy. Cassady, who was famous for streaking through the night as his companions slept—the car's left-front wheel cleaving the median line while the chassis shimmied at ninety miles per hour—was useful for another reason. He tied the new hipsters not only to the glorious past but also to a blue-collar Dionysian fantasy (which is where the Hell's Angels come in) that winds like a holding stitch through American bohemianism. Packed with Pranksters like a fun house on wheels, the magic bus, Furthur (as it was called), circumnavigated the country in a slipstream of lysergic acid, dispensing more roadside mayhem in that breakaway year than a circus on the run.

In 1964, the ground the Pranksters shook was already heaving underfoot. The summer of 1964 was when the rebel '60s can be said to have parted company with the '50s. The New Left broke away from the old Left, and from liberals—first at the Democratic National Convention in Atlantic City, where liberal Democrats sold the Mississippi Freedom Democratic Party downriver (or so the rebels believed), thus ending a brief but historic alliance between blacks and whites. The second turning point came with the shelling of an American destroyer in the Gulf of Tonkin by a North Vietnamese PT boat, followed by massive U.S. air attacks on North Vietnamese bases in reprisal. Almost overnight, President Lyndon Johnson parlayed the Tonkin Gulf encounter into a major incident, and sailed a de facto declaration of war through a largely liberal Congress. The third turning point arrived with the triumph of the Free Speech Movement (FSM) on the University of California's Berkeley campus in the fall of 1964.

It was this trio of prophetic events that social historian Todd Gitlin suggests gave birth to the "[radical] movement's expressive side," along with "the politics of going it alone, or looking for allies in revolution . . .

[and] the idea of 'liberation'; the movement as a culture, a way of life apart." Here is when the seeds of what would later be called "identity politics" were sown; also the idea of the personal as political. At the same time, the very notion of "a way of life apart" was intensified by the arrival of psychedelics.

Kesey and the Pranksters were soon to demonstrate that, as Berkeley's Free Speech organizers feared, drugs could divorce the will from political action. But LSD produced other, more ambiguous effects. Once ingested, "the force of acid itself could not be denied, or forgotten, or assimilated. It hung there, apart from the rest of experience, *terra incognita,* a gaping hole in [the] mental maps," writes Gitlin, an early president of Students for a Democratic Society (SDS), who couldn't have made this observation without having tasted the forbidden fruit.

While street acid turned up on college campuses around 1965, it would be a few more years before it found its entry point into the student movement. But when LSD did work its "magic" on radical political consciousness, it fed on a vision of change not so different *in form* from the one that gripped Kesey's crowd. "Change was seen as survival," another former SDS president, Carl Oglesby, recalls. And "nothing could stand for that overall sense of going through profound changes so well as the immediate, powerful and explicit transformation you went through when you dropped acid." Just as breaking through the barricades redefined you as a new person, so, too, might taking LSD.

Meanwhile, it's funny how the psychedelic bus trip is never mentioned in the same breath with the year's climactic political occurrences, as if culture and politics run on separate (tenured) tracks, which by and large they do. (The proliferation of black, feminist, and "queer" studies, which view "politics" altogether differently, offer no exception.) In popular history, headlines are reserved for the arranged event: not the magic bus, but the Beatles' 1964 appearance on *The Ed Sullivan Show.* Political milestones mark the triumph of law, like the passage of 1964's Civil Rights Act, rather than landmark steps toward political change, such as the formation of the Mississippi Freedom Democratic Party.

In *The Electric Kool-Aid Acid Test,* Tom Wolfe mythologizes the Merry Pranksters in prose that is irradiated by the gee-whiz wonder of a big-time acid trip. But he also makes the shrewd observation that with their Day-Glo-painted, superstereo'd bus, the Pranksters, far from dropouts, were scouting the perimeters of postwar America's "Neon Renaissance." "It was a fantasy world *already,* this electro-pastel world of Mom& Dad&Buddy&Sis in the suburbs," he writes:

> There they go, in the family car, a white Pontiac Bonneville sedan—*the family car!*—a huge crazy god-awful powerful fantasy creature to begin with, 327-horsepower . . . [S]o why not move off your snug-harbor quilty-bed dead center and cut loose—go ahead and say it—Shazam!—juice it up to what it's already aching to be: 327,000 horsepower, a whole superhighway long and *soaring, screaming* on toward . . . Edge City, and ultimate fantasies, current and future . . .

"You're either on the bus or off the bus," said Kesey. (Or "you're either *on* the bus, *off* the bus, or *under* the bus," *fixing* it, a veteran of the 1964 trip recalls.) And the party bus, for that's what it was, just as pre-prohibition LSD was mainly a party drug, was actually the Pranksters' Bonneville sedan. It was the *extended*-family car (like the painted vans that would later follow the Grateful Dead). " 'Better Living Through Chemistry,' is how we were brought up," remembers Gene Anthony, the photographer who memorialized the Summer of Love in *Newsweek* in 1967. "Mind expansion, you say? Sure, I'll take a pill."

For Kesey, the early trips were travel on a grand scale. "I took these drugs as an *American,*" he tells me, speaking not of the Acid Tests but of the government experiments administered at the VA hospital in Menlo Park in 1959–1960. And he likens himself and his fellow travelers to Lewis and Clark heading west. "Jefferson," he says, "wanted to know what's goin' on out here. We were the same kind of people. Like Lewis and Clark, we were trying to go into this unknown land, chart it and come back and report it as clearly as we could." Their explorations took place in weekly sessions where they were paid between twenty and seventy-five dollars a day—"more each time to keep you coming back," says Robert Hunter, who also signed up—to test-drive a batch of what the government called "psychotomimetic [madness-mimicking] drugs."

Psilocybin was the first hallucinogen Kesey was administered. Mescaline and LSD followed, interspersed with other psychotropic drugs. Their tendency to turn household objects into monsters sometimes toppled the subject into his own horror movie. Hunter, however, a lover of horror comics who takes his hat off to anyone who can scare him, responded to this portion of the menu with gusto. "I was beset by monsters," he says happily, remembering the day a locker door flew open inside the VA hospital and Dracula stepped out. "I knew I was hallucinating," he says, and wondered, "What can you do with this?" He fantasized a crystal dagger, and "plunged it into my heart. I pulled it out, dripping with blood. . . . And that's not all," he says. "I saw an elevator shaft. I jumped down it. This was great fun. I was never, ever frightened of psychedelics," Hunter assures me; at least when he was alone and free to hobnob with demons from his subconscious. "It's entertaining," he says, "to have them out there."

When he was in a crowd of people, it was a different story; and Hunter remembers a "horror trip" he had in 1966 at the Trips Festival, which was a two-day Acid Test minus the acid (though everybody brought their own), beefed up by the involvement of crusader Stewart Brand and the budding impresario Bill Graham. Sitting in a cold sweat in the vortex of a churning sea of costumed freaks, wondering why he had dropped acid in such a setting, he was drawn to a sentence forming on the wall: OUTSIDE IS INSIDE. HOW DOES IT LOOK? Kesey, who was adept at steering beginners away from paranoid trips, had inscribed it on an overhead projector. Suddenly, everything was okay. If outside was inside, inside could be outside—and the awful trip was only a projection.

Hunter doesn't want me to think his visions were all horror stories, because they weren't. Even in the clinical setting of the VA hospital, he went "all the way," seeing "God and all that good stuff." The VA interviewers wanted to know whether any of the drugs increased his susceptibility to hypnosis, and so they tried to hypnotize him—before, during, and after the doses, never successfully. During one session, tears had poured out of his eyes, and the clinician asked why he was crying. "I'm not crying," Hunter explained. "I'm in another dimension. I'm inhabiting the body of a great green Buddha and there's a pool that is flowing out of my eyes."

Kesey had nothing but contempt for the government people in their white coats, carrying clipboards and asking inane questions, "who didn't have the common *balls* to take the stuff themselves. So they hired students. All the other guinea pigs, not just me," he asserts, "knew that what was happening was as important as anything that's happened this century, and maybe in the last five hundred years." "*What* was happening?" I ask. And Kesey shifts into the present tense, as if what I'm after is a piece of the action, which, in a way, I am. (The gin and tonics on the kitchen table between us are a poor substitute for the chemicals we're discussing.)

A kind of tartar builds up over your consciousness, and you think this is the world. This isn't the world; this is just tartar, a wall, a buildup of scum and shit. People come along who have great power and they knock a hole in that. And through that hole comes this blinding bolt of light, and you see it and you remember, Oh, I FORGOT about that. I keep being drawn back into this Procter and Gamble world.

Who punched the hole through the wall?

Kesey doesn't miss a beat. *Garcia opened the hole. Cassady kept punching this hole,* he says, naming the heavenly choir; *and the light that comes through it makes you realize that we're not trapped in the Newtonian Pat Buchanan world. There's another thing that's happening. And the only way to survive as a nation is to become HEALTHY in this way, to not be hung up in the flesh, and with all this stuff that Buddha and Mohammed and Christ and everybody always warns you against—*

Stop, I say, unsettled by all these Names. *I've just figured out the connection between Lewis and Clark and the men in white coats. They were testing you, and you were testing IT!*

Kesey nods. *Yeah,* he says. *These people are members of the establishment, all the way back to the twelfth century. These were doctors, government people. It took us about two trips to realize, THEY DON'T KNOW SHIT! . . . Then at a certain point the government says, I don't like the looks of these kids after they've been taking this stuff. Let's make it illegal. We were in the midst of an experiment,* he finishes. *We still are.*

The initial experiments had been launched by the Central Intelligence Agency, which began to investigate mind-altering drugs and parapsychology in 1953 under the auspices of a James Bondish program called MK-ULTRA. MK-ULTRA, in turn, had its roots in the Office of Strategic Services's (OSS) wartime fascination with so-called truth drugs like mescaline, scopolamine, and liquid marijuana. The first of the government's Acid Tests were carried out on workers at the Manhattan Project, whose security was deemed sufficiently dense to ensure the secrecy of the new mind-control program. Later, MK-ULTRA's drug research was conducted mainly at prisons and mental hospitals.

By 1959–1960, when Kesey was dosed with psilocybin, mescaline, and LSD, the CIA had started farming its research out to VA hospitals and the Army Chemical Corps. In university cities like Palo Alto and Boston, where both the CIA and the Army carried out testing programs at institutions connected to Stanford and Harvard, volunteering for an LSD trip became the hip thing to do. By 1965, over two hundred research studies were under way throughout the country, many involving military personnel (not always knowingly), and some whose investigators were engaged in a good deal of self-experimentation.

A few months before my trip to Oregon to see Kesey and Mountain Girl, *The New Yorker* had run an item about a visit Kesey and Ken Babbs had paid their old pal Timothy Leary in Beverly Hills. Leary, who was dying of prostate cancer, had turned his customary Sunday-afternoon drop-in into an Irish wake, with the Departed One receiving. Kesey, whose birthday it was, toasted his "great mentors": Neal Cassady, Allen Ginsberg, Jerry Garcia—and Leary. "We were all ringside while you made history," he told the frail old hoofer. Then he offered a second toast, to the CIA.

I asked Kesey whether he was referring to the Menlo Park experiments—which he was—and whether he knew then that the CIA was behind them. No, he said. Allen Ginsberg used to tell them this, but nobody believed him until the Freedom of Information Act unlocked the evidence. How did Ginsberg know? I asked. "Ginsberg was one of those little ferrets," Kesey said, "and he had a lot of other little ferrets under him, and they ferreted out a lot of this stuff." When the proof arrived, Kesey had said, "Of course, of course." Now, he submits, "that's how you know there are angels and other beings, because irony suggests a humor from above." His mind caterwauls ahead. "And when you see something like the Grateful Dead spreading acid around that the CIA has brought into the country [which isn't exactly what happened, but Kesey's not a stickler for detail], you can feel the irony, and can get a little giggle out of it yourself."

Hunter appreciates the irony, too. *"You betcha,"* he says when I marvel over the unexpected creativity of government military research. "They created *me* for one thing. And Kesey and the Acid Tests."

With his traveling road shows, Ken Kesey was a genuine trailblazer. An interesting American type, he belongs to the frontier, albeit a frontier of literature and vaudeville, like Paul Bunyan or the Medicine Man. He reminds one of the Wizard of Oz—and *is,* in fact, in a video he produced a few years ago called *Twisters,* which is modeled on *The Wonderful Wizard of Oz. Twisters* borrows liberally from Grateful Dead lyrics, and it treats what Kesey calls "end-of-the-millennium angst," though he himself abides by happy endings. *"Sometimes the light's all shining on me,"* the Wizard belts out in a finale, scored after Jerry Garcia's death:

> Other times I can barely see
> Lately it's occurred to me
> What a glorious trip it still do be, do be, do be, do be!

With the magic bus and the Acid Tests, Kesey cut a spur in America's open road. Travel, psychedelics, music, lights, costume, dance, and the *gang*—together they begat the magic bundle that the Grateful Dead would carry through ballrooms and old vaudeville halls, gyms, sports arenas, and giant coliseums over the next thirty-odd years. His fateful move was to have introduced LSD, via the Acid Tests, to San Francisco's rock 'n' roll community, rather than keep it within Prankster circles, or drop it on the politically charged community across the Bay.

There, on the University of California's flagship campus, another path was being cut through the increasingly bureaucratized routines of college life in the 1960s. After U.C. chancellor Clark Kerr enforced his September 1964 gag order against politicking on the Berkeley campus, four hundred student protesters seized Sproul Hall and turned it into a "liberated zone," projecting Chaplin movies on the walls, smoking grass in the stairwells, and listening to folksingers in the halls. The next day, helmeted riot police dragged the students from the building, thus anointing the Free Speech Movement with the power of dangerousness.

Berkeley's movement was led by students who had worked with the Student Nonviolent Coordinating Committee (SNCC) in the Mississippi voter-registration projects of the summer of 1964. There, among unlettered sharecroppers who were regularly terrorized by Ku Klux Klan night riders, these middle-class kids had acquired a respect for the moral and political power of resistance that was not easily forgotten when they returned to school. An echo of the struggle being waged in the South can be heard in FSM leader Mario Savio's words:

> There is a time when the operation of the machine becomes so odious, makes you so sick at heart, that you can't take part; you can't even passively take part, and you've got to put your bodies upon the gears and upon the wheels, upon the levers, upon all the apparatus and you've got to make it stop. And you've got to indicate to the people who run it, to the people who own it, that unless you're free, the machine will be prevented from working at all.

Addressing an audience of eighteen thousand in Berkeley's Greek Theater in October, Chancellor Kerr put forth his vision of the academic community as a "knowledge factory," designed to create socially productive individuals. It was not a vision destined to win favor with his listeners, but Kerr's real mistake came afterward, when Savio, a philosophy major who had worked with SNCC in Lowndes County, stepped to the rostrum to invite everyone to a rally where the speech could be debated. Before he finished a sentence, he was grabbed by two cops and wrestled to the floor. The next day, the faculty senate voted overwhelmingly to accede to the FSM's demands, which centered on the campus community's right to organize support for the civil rights movement.

One of those collective peak experiences had been reached—Columbia University SDS's takeover of Fayerwether Hall four years later would be another—when students were seized by the exhilaration that came from mass rebellion to imagine they had broken through the ivy wall into a wider world, where anything was possible. It was a "frame-breaking experience," recalls the FSM's self-styled "mystical propagandist," Michael Rossman—not unlike an acid trip. Only in this case, the "frameworks of individual perception" were broken "by willfully and collectively changing social reality." And Rossman, referring to the spontaneous decision of a crowd of students to prevent the police from hauling off a manacled protestor, summons up the "transcendent hours around the police car which crystallized a new consciousness among us." Out of that had emerged "an entity, a *thing* distinct from our selves": the Free Speech Movement. Thus had they been relieved of some of the "terrible and naked responsibility" for all that was happening, "as if to say, 'it's not me doing this, it's the FSM.' "

Like the hole punched in Kesey's wall of "scum and shit," the confrontation with authority enlightened and empowered the Berkeley students to undertake hitherto-undreamed-of tasks. FSM's Free University, hammered out by students sitting cross-legged on civil defense drums in the basement of Sproul, was one result of the Berkeley strike. A counterinstitution born of revolt—of chaos—it was the first of many Free Universities and Alternate U's to emerge in the wake of protests during the years ahead. But the more important effect of the uprising was the transformative power of civil disobedience.

Berkeley's wasn't the era's first successful political confrontation. The demonstrations on the steps of San Francisco's City Hall in May 1960, opposing the House Un-American Activities Committee (HUAC) investigations, broke the ice. Nationally, the Greensboro, North Carolina, sit-ins in February of that year sparked the dynamo that turned a portion of the younger generation's sense of alienation, of *differentness,* into the opposition politics of a committed minority. But the direct action of Berkeley students in the fall of 1964—the year the first cohort of baby boomers reached college age en masse—cast a long shadow over the 1960s.

For the community grouped around Kesey in what Mountain Girl calls "our little island in La Honda," it was a shadow to be reckoned with; and it was, in a confrontation the following year. What happened when U.C. Berkeley's Vietnam Day Committee invited Ken Kesey to address an all-day antiwar teach-in on October 16, 1965, is reported in *The Electric Kool-Aid Acid Test* (an account Kesey confirms in its essentials). He had arrived late in the afternoon in the bus, accompanied by a dozen Pranksters wearing scraps of Army surplus, tooting horns and twanging guitars. Awaiting his turn behind the platform, Kesey had contemplated the speakers; "shock workers of the tongue," Tom Wolfe calls them, who addressed the crowd (about fifteen thousand filling Sproul Plaza) "while the PA loudspeakers boomed and rabbled and raked across them." For Wolfe, the political rally is a farce: "toggle coats, Desert Boots, civil rights, down with the war in Vietnam"—it's all one cigar. Kesey, in his big orange highway worker's coat and Day-Glo-painted World War I helmet, is the nitty-gritty.

Among the "workers of the tongue" is M. S. Arnoni, who wears a prison uniform to commemorate the family he lost in a concentration camp in World War II. If the dead "could call out to you from their graves or from the fields and rivers upon which their ashes were thrown," he tells the crowd, "they would implore this generation of Americans not to be silent in the face of the genocidal atrocities committed on the people of Vietnam." Bay Area radical Paul Jacobs is next, and from where Kesey stands, only his voice is heard "rolling and thundering, powerful as Wotan, out over that ocean of big ears and eager faces. . . ."

Wolfe delivers a cool, deflating slap to the *cheek* of '60s radicalism, and then, driving in deeper, draws forth from an antiwar teach-in, via counterrhetoric, a fascist rally. Kesey is joined by Paul Krassner, *The Realist's* editor, who is a fan. Together, they take in Paul Jacobs: "omnipotent and more forensic and orotund and thunderous minute by minute—*It is written, but I say unto you . . . the jackals of history—ree-ree-ree-ree . . .*" They don't know what he's saying, but they "can hear the crowd roaring back and baying on cue, and they can see Jacobs, hunched over squat and thick into the microphone, with his hands stabbing out for emphasis, and there, at sundown, silhouetted against the florid sky, is his jaw, jutting out, like a cantaloupe."

Krassner plays Horatio to Kesey's Hamlet: "You could not help being drawn, almost physically, toward him," he says; "like being sucked in by a vast, spiritual vacuum cleaner."

Nodding toward Jacobs, Kesey says:

> "Look up there," . . . "Don't listen to the words, just the sound, and the gestures . . . who do you see?"
>
> And suddenly Krassner wants very badly to be right. . . .
>
> "Mussolini . . . ?"

Yep.

"You're playing their game," Kesey drawls into the microphone when it's his turn to speak. *"We've all heard all this and seen all this before, but we keep*

doing it," he says, honking on a harmonica in between lines. "It" is *"the cry of the ego,"* which is *"the cry of this rally! . . . Me! Me! Me! And that's the way wars get fought,"* he continues, because of *"ego . . . because enough people want to scream pay attention to Me. . . . Yep, you're playing their game."* As for Vietnam, *"There's only one thing to do. And that's everybody just look at it, look at the war, and turn your backs and say . . . Fuck it."*

It was a strange performance; and the message, given the time and the place, was about as far from the brute actuality of the fighting in Southeast Asia, and the concerns of the rising antiwar movement, as one could get without falling off the grid. For the Pranksters, however, it was a coup. "The whole reason to go to Vietnam Day was more to participate in an event where a lot of people would be than to actually protest the war," Mountain Girl contends. "We weren't thinking about the war," she says. "We were mostly interested in getting our piece of the turf where we could get in there and maybe get some of these poor antiwar maniacs over here and have some fun." In Berkeley, the Pranksters were on a recruiting mission: "The idea," says Mountain Girl, "was really to subvert people to our way of thinking."

The *anti*-antiwar sentiment had its own roots. Ken Babbs had recently returned from Vietnam, where he flew helicopters high on psilocybin, according to Kesey, who had kept him supplied. "He didn't want to line up and take a shot at the military he had just served," Mountain Girl states. Nor were the Pranksters ready to go up against the Hell's Angels, those weird centurions who provided them, and later the Grateful Dead, with a kind of instant karma of outlawry in the Bay Area. Many of the Angels had also been in the service, she points out, and were passionate about believing *"the United States shall rule the world."* Skip Workman, who had arrived in Oakland on the USS *Ranger,* an aircraft carrier out of Norfolk, Virginia, in 1957, was one of them. In 1965, when he was vice president of the Oakland club, he and a half-dozen Oakland Angels "took on ten thousand demonstrators" who were marching from Berkeley to the Oakland Army Terminal—which they never reached, until another march in 1967.

When Berkeley radicals came to the Pranksters' compound in La Honda, Mountain Girl remembers sitting there "in amazement," listening to them talk politics. "It was all so *serious.* . . . We were busy studying LSD with the party God," she says, "trying to learn how to do it really right, how to have incredible parties." The Pranksters operated in a different force field, one that flowed from their sense of themselves as embattled artists, "creative, sensitive, crazy people," she maintains, who knew "America was a very thorny environment" for what they wanted to do. To sow riot? I ask, thinking of Johnny Appleseed (and of Berkeley). Yes, she says, but "a riot of color, a jungle, a garden. I mean, it was just like, *God,* we gotta get somethin' *goin'* here!" And she grins in remembered anticipation.

∽

~CHAPTER~
2

ENTER COSMIC FORCES

That motley drama—oh, be sure
It shall not be forgot!
With its Phantom chased for evermore,
By a crowd that seize it not . . .
EDGAR ALLAN POE, "THE CONQUEROR WORM"

L A HONDA WAS the base camp for that other committed minority, just girding its loins:

> in the huge
> wooden house, a yellow chandelier
> at 3 AM the blast of loudspeakers
> hi fi Rolling Stones Ray Charles Beatles
> Jumping Joe Jackson and twenty youths
> dancing to the vibration through the floor
> a little weed in the bathroom, girls in scarlet
> tights, one muscular, smooth skinned man
> sweating dancing for hours, beer cans
> bent littering the yard, a hanged man
> sculpture dangling from a high creek branch,
> children sleeping softly in bedroom bunks,
> And 4 police cars parked outside the painted
> gate, red lights revolving in the leaves

And beside the gate, a mailbox painted red, white, and blue.

This was the bread-and-butter poem Allen Ginsberg sent to Ken Kesey after a visit to La Honda with Peter Orlovsky in August 1964. It was the weekend the Pranksters invited the Hell's Angels down for an experiment in intergalactic living. Skip Workman remembers filing into the house and sitting down to a little introduction from Kesey about what to expect from LSD, which none of them had ever tried. " 'You might see things expanding and shrinking and stretching and you may have hallucinations' and, uh—we couldn't wait," he says. The music he remembers "vibratin' and bouncin' off the trees" was Bob Dylan's "Mr. Tambourine Man."

LSD had begun to interest Allen Ginsberg for one of the reasons it had first attracted the CIA: its apparent ability to wipe the slate clean of conditioned reflexes. For the CIA, this raised the possibility of reprogramming enemy agents, as well as of embarrassing enemy leaders in public appearances via covert acid attacks. Ginsberg, on the other hand, wondered if the phenomenon would permit the inebriant brief flashes of insight into the categories in which he ordinarily deposited his experience. What if the categories were disposable, and life (love, even death) could be embraced in the buff? It was the antique Rousseauian fantasy, ever new, which Timothy Leary revived when he argued, around the same time, that psychedelics reveal the games we unconsciously adopt to play our parts in society's roundelay. Oh, to command such knowledge at the drop of a pill!

Health depended on punching holes in the pseudoworld, in order to embrace the light emanating from the real world, which is the sacred, invisible world. What distinguishes the Ginsberg/Leary/Kesey vision from Rousseau's, however, and makes it quintessentially American, is that the return to the innocence of the unconditioned life—to what Aldous Huxley, in *The Doors of Perception,* calls "the miracle, moment by moment, of naked existence"—is achieved with the aid of technology. To see what Adam saw on the morning of creation is a gift of chemistry—most commonly, via the compound accidentally synthesized in 1938 in the research laboratories of a pharmaceutical house in Switzerland: the twenty-fifth batch of d-lysergic acid diethylamide, or LSD-25. If ever a company achieved consumer loyalty of the deepest dye, it was with the discovery of that mystic substance, known round the world by its mystic name, Sandoz.

With LSD, Ginsberg rejoiced, "technology has produced a chemical which catalyzes a consciousness which finds the entire civilization leading up to that pill absurd." And here was another variation on the traditional Romantic theme, one touched by the millenarian passions of the 1960s. This was the belief, promoted by the Pranksters, that LSD was a change agent with radical implications for the transformation of consciousness, if not of society—more radical than the protests and prophesies cranked out on campus mimeograph machines. Which is where the "incredible parties" came in. They were organizing tools.

And the organizers? One was the eighteen-year-old girl with the trucker's drawl who had turned up at La Honda on a black motorcycle just as the bus had returned from the east. Workman remembers her hanging out with a Hell's Angel known as "Terry the Tramp," who later became the Angels' drug contact with Owsley Stanley. "She was gutsy. She said what was on her mind," Sara Ruppenthal, Jerry Garcia's first wife, recalls of Mountain Girl, then still known as Carolyn Adams: "Like a big kid, a big beautiful girl who had somehow escaped being squelched as a teenager." Sara, who saw herself as "Wendy, sewing on the buttons [for] the Lost Boys"—Jerry, and the gang from the Chateau—couldn't help but admire this tall brown-eyed girl, the house electrician, who scampered around patching wires together for the Pranksters. Her Prankster name had originated with Neal Cassady, who had run into her in a Palo Alto café and told Kesey he had met a girl who was a little wild, "like she was kind of a mountain girl."

A high school beatnik who was expelled for excessive deviltry six weeks before graduation, Carolyn was a tomboy who imagined herself running along the old Mohawk Trail, chasing deer or making buckskin clothes and cooking wild plants like an Indian. She was an avid reader of fantasy and science fiction. "Good books" included Homer, Kazantzakis, and Victor Hugo. She was horrified by J. D. Salinger. When she got to *The Catcher in the Rye,* she thought, "This is the worst book I've ever read! Nothing ever happens in this book! Big deal! Does the guy even get laid?" She liked *The Electric Kool-Aid Acid Test,* including the theoretical parts. "Wolfe and I kind of hit it off," she says, which is evident from the book.

Tom Wolfe had dressed out his antic narrative of the Pranksters' adventures (drawn in part from tapes Kesey had given him) with quotations from a German sociology of religion:

> Following a profound new experience, providing a new illumination of the world, the founder, a highly charismatic person, begins enlisting disciples. These followers become an informally but closely knit association, bound together by the new experience,

whose nature the founder has revealed and interpreted. . . . A growing sense of solidarity . . . differentiates them from any other form of social organization. . . . Ties of family and kinship and loyalties of various kinds were at least temporarily relaxed or severed.

The shoe fit, and neither Kesey nor Mountain Girl have disowned it. The "founder," meanwhile, according to the sociologist Joachim Wach, writing in 1944, has "visions, dreams, trances, frequent ecstasies. . . . There is something elemental about [him], an uncompromising attitude and an archaic manner and language . . . He appears as a renewer of lost contacts with the hidden powers of life," and emerges from "simpler folk," to whom he remains true in speech and manner, even in the changed environment. Kesey exactly. (Though this kind of categorizing is slippery; Wach could be describing Hitler.)

Mountain Girl, on the other hand—"MG" to friends and family, or simply "Mountain"—is a more complicated piece of work. With her middle-class background, one imagines that the Hell's Angelic speech she perfected in Palo Alto was a social adaptation. Not so different in form from the adaptation her mother made when she converted to atheism and brought her children up as Unitarians, having been raised herself by American missionaries in India. Her mother "*loathed* any thought of organized religion," Mountain Girl relates, "so we were raised to not believe in anything and make up our own minds." It was a comfortable arrangement, which gave them "the idea of the human experience as the peak experience. But as soon as I started taking psychedelics," she notes, "I got the . . . sense that there was far, far more out there." And presto chango, she went from being "a complete skeptic, an agnostic, to a believer in divine force."

Listening to Mountain Girl tell a now-familiar tale, I sense I'm in the presence of a folk genre, also typically American. It's the story of the Trip, the "fat trip"—as Jerry Garcia called any unexpected experience that rearranges the brain cells, like running into Charlie Mingus drinking martinis out of a thermos in Central Park, or meeting William Burroughs in a hotel in Amsterdam. But Mountain Girl's acid trip has a surprising twist when she brings it up-to-date.

What you're doing is dropping all your filters and beginning to sense the bio-

logical network, and the biological network is so vast. It's just EE-NOR-MOUS. You put out a thought and you hear it echoing back and across . . . it's so gigantic. And we have many many filters to keep us from noticing that. To retain our individuality, we keep those very tightly zipped up most of the time. Once you start taking that stuff off, boy, you start lookin' for a name to hang it on. That larger experience.

I'm more of a skeptic again than I used to be, she says suddenly. *Because somehow it almost seems as if the universe is on automatic.*

What a thought! I exclaim.

Well, she says, *inherent in matter is thought. It's not really any specific one cosmic being tinkering around with us. It's just cosmic being itself and it doesn't have a personality or form or voice or dwelling. It's just the inherent thought-matter connection.*

So when you say "automatic," you mean it's just happening the way a physical law might happen?

Yes, she says. *It's sort of like the Internet: When you log on, you get somewhere. There's a network, and we are all part of it, whether we're consciously engaged in it or not.*

So why, I wonder, *have you become a skeptic again?*

For a long time there, I felt we were being manipulated by cosmic forces. And maybe I don't feel that way anymore, she responds. *Or perhaps I've just—*

You and "cosmic forces" are on a—

On an equal footing. Yes.

You don't have to embrace it or run away—

Right. So maybe I've come to rest with all that stuff. And I'm not in a process of discovery.

(So there it is, a new maxim for our generation: If we're not in a process of discovery, maybe we're in recovery.)

Wolfe drops a few more hints about Kesey and his flock from Joachim Wach. The founder "speaks cryptically, with words, signs, gestures, many metaphors, symbolic acts. . . . [He] illuminates and interprets the past and anticipates the future in terms of the *kairos* (the supreme moment)" —Mountain Girl's *larger experience:* the Trip. But you don't need a German sociologist to recognize the role Kesey played as the interpreter of a new religious experience. Precedents may be found among the born-again revivalists of the American frontier, who were themselves emissaries of a

"blinding bolt of light" (albeit a chem-free one). "The Holy Spirit descended upon me in a manner that seemed to go through me body and soul," the celebrated circuit rider Charles Finney testified in 1821, after a brush with the divine in the forest near his cabin. "Indeed it seemed to come in waves and waves of liquid love. . . . It seemed like the very breath of God." Finney, like Kesey, was drawn to take his visions to a larger world that had suddenly grown strange, teetering, as post-Revolutionary America was—mid-'60s America, too—on the brink of change.

But Kesey was not a founder of churches. More like a scoutmaster, he and Prankster Ken Babbs were good at leading trips into the wilderness, starting fires in the rain, reading sermons in stone, books in babbling brooks. "We talked about being astronauts of inner space," Babbs recalls; "we had to be as well-trained, in as good a shape and as mentally powerful as an astronaut in outer space, so as not to be thrown by any of the accidents or the unexpected we'd run into."

Kesey's god, or the god broadcast in the mid-'60s, was impersonal, a force that discloses an underlying order. "Go with the flow" has a more complex etymology than, say, "Go for it," or Leary's "Tune in, turn on, drop out." It reveals a deeper dimension of the psychedelic experience: the manifestation, during a high-octane trip, of a transcendent purposefulness to the universe. "Cosmo," Kesey called the flash of a higher order lying behind the riot of color and form that marked the first stage of the psychedelic journey. Cosmo was a superior intelligence, to which the rest of the world remained blind. Against this orderliness, one's personal identity appeared as fixed and immutable as a blade of grass—furthering perhaps that strange passivity the '60s drug culture shares with the Beats.

"In the wildest hipster, making a mystique of bop, drugs, and the night life," Beat novelist John Clellon Holmes observed in the 1950s, "there is no desire to shatter the 'square' society in which he lives, only to elude it. To get on a soapbox or write a manifesto would seem to him absurd." The wildest Prankster behaved the same way—unless he stepped forth, as Kesey had at the Berkeley teach-in, to kick over the soapbox. Why strive to change the structure of the puny environment in which you're stuck when you can see the big picture? The point is to accept it, and then rise above your environment, or alter your perception of it, by accepting the larger pattern.

Movement, in other words, lies in the unfurling of consciousness—

sometimes a titanic affair wherein "universes dissolve and reappear," which is how Jerry Garcia described his "last transcendental acid trip" (in contrast to more ordinary ones). It took place at a Grateful Dead base camp called Rancho Olompali, in Marin County, later in the 1960s. "I lay down and closed my eyes—but I could see . . . this pattern," he told interviewer David Gans. At first, he could see only a part of it; then, suddenly, his vision began "to open like an old-time coffee can with a key," until it reached 360 degrees, revealing the word *ALL*. In the fabric of the letters, in their design, "every kind of thought form" was unveiled, and he entered "some kind of totally 'otherly' dimension beyond time and beyond physical reality. . . . Things happened that I've never recovered from," he said. "It was definitely one of those 'before and after' experiences," mainly because the trip (fueled by a cocktail of mescaline and LSD) took on "a curious sort of purposefulness, like there was something making an effort to communicate with me, and really had a teacherly attitude toward me."

"Were you under Kesey's tutelage?" Gans asked. "I was getting high with these guys, but it wasn't coming from them," Garcia replied; "it was coming from 'it,' whatever 'it' is. . . . [A] lot of it came in the form of a big voice saying, 'Now do you get it?' . . . You get moments of that, 'Oh yeah, right,' where everything settles down and you realize you're doing just exactly what you were supposed to be doing, everything's the way it's supposed to be. . . ."

It's when I mention the Rancho Olompali trip to Mountain Girl (who wasn't there) that she describes her encounter with "cosmic forces." Or Cosmic Forces, as I begin to picture him. And the more I hear the tale, the more it seems that Cosmic Forces may be saying one thing to the boys and another to the girls.

> *It was probably a couple of years before I really enjoyed getting all the way out there,* Mountain Girl tells me. *I liked to fool around with smaller dosages and work through it. Work and joke and carry on . . . have projects going— painting, building. I wouldn't just lay there with the blankies pulled over me and trip out. That was not for me. I was far too physically active. . . . My whole thing was, you-gotta-get-up-and-be-useful* [old lady's voice]*, you can't-just-lay-there. So . . . I'd go racing up to the top of the hill, go paint a tree stump, you know, SOMETHING. I didn't understand that there were other ways—*

Jerry, like Kesey, is reassured by the orderliness of Cosmic Forces.

"There's something about the coherence of that persona, whatever it is, that's so much more than the me which is this sort of cringing, ineffectual, completely powerless dumbshit—yeah, a human," he says. "Consciousness goes a quantum step further than just life, you know," he ventures:

> I think consciousness has a place in the cosmic game, the atoms-and-universe game, the big game. I can't imagine that it's mindless—there's too much organization, and the organization is too incredible. It has that huge, vast wisdom—
>
> Gans: But yet it's random—
>
> Garcia: Is it? When you take psychedelics, the way your mind spins information to you, does it have that thing of synchronicity, and all that sort of miraculous quality?
>
> Gans: Sometimes.
>
> Garcia: Wouldn't you say that that suggests organization of an extremely sophisticated nature, somehow?

Reading such passages, which are not uncommon in interviews with Jerry Garcia, one is reminded of a Russian intellectual or a rabbinical student, mulling over the nature of History or Divine Will while his wife busies herself in the kitchen. But the "big voice saying, 'Now do you get it?' " spoke to Hell's Angels, as well. Tripping on Skip Workman's roof, an Oakland club member called "Freewheelin' Frank" saw rows of chariots wheeling across the sky, whereupon a trapdoor slowly opened in the heavens, and a deep voice thundered, *"You're not ready yet!"* before slamming shut.

The women I've talked to about psychedelics sound more like Mountain Girl. "Acid made you think you could do anything," my sister, Candace, told me a few years ago when I visited her in California. She remembered a time in the early '70s, not long after she became the Grateful Dead's full-time lighting designer, when she and some friends were tripping on a beach in Mendocino after a show, and they raced to the top of an almost-perpendicular beach cliff. The next day, they came back to try it again and couldn't get halfway up.

LSD puts you in tune with nature, she explains. You are a part of it, not apart from it. I know, I say, recalling one of the few times I dropped acid, when I climbed over a fence somewhere in Marin County in 1970,

sat down, and began talking with a horse and a couple of cows, who talked back, naturally. Cosmic Forces was nowhere in evidence (perhaps because I had taken a modest dose). Nor was it a journey into inner space, or a space so *outer* as to turn the traveler's earthly habitat into a shimmering orb of translucent sensations—like the tiny spinning planet the dying man glimpses from above as he rockets through the heavens, his spirit temporarily detached from a body that is not quite ready to give up the ghost. "Cows are always part of an acid trip," my sister observes sagely. And so, I suspect, is the desire for contact with transcendental reality, a "craving," LSD analyst Stanislav Grof proposes, that "can be more powerful than the sexual urge."

After Carolyn Adams was expelled from the Quaker-run Oakland School in Poughkeepsie, she accompanied her brother, a graduate student at Stanford, to Palo Alto. It was the fall of 1963, and she got a job in Stanford's organic chemistry lab, working the graveyard shift, which included running a huge machine known as a mass spectrometer. "I had to learn it from scratch," Mountain Girl says, "but I was sharp and picked it right up."

It was a talent, this ease with machines, which came in handy at the Acid Tests when she became the wire tech. "I did the microphones," she tells me. "I soldered, I coiled, I uncoiled, I wrapped, I rolled, I changed tapes, I spliced. . . . *'How come this plug isn't working? Take it apart and solder it RIGHT NOW!'* and you've just taken a hundred mikes of acid, and [warped voice] *s o l d e r r r t h e w i r r r e . . .*" And thus she learned how to work under stress, another talent.

How did she hook up with Kesey? I asked, sensing, even before my visit with him, that, whatever else they had in common, this large, raw-boned woman with long iron gray hair and dancing eyes and the wizard who tells loopy stories shared a prodigious appetite for play. "I was there at Stanford, and he lived right over the hill," she said. It was inevitable; everybody gravitated toward Kesey. The literary circle he had presided over in 1961—when he reminded Malcolm Cowley, then lecturing in Stanford's writing program, of the young Hemingway in Paris, "the man whom the other young rebels tried to imitate"—had morphed into a funny farm. But Kesey, with his ten-gallon hat, quiet speech, curly blond hair, and lonesome-cowboy good looks, was still the man of the hour: a darling of the media, whose newfound taste for outrageousness enhanced his notoriety. To Mountain Girl, theirs was "an intellectual companion-ship"; the sexual attraction was brief, "a minor note," she informs me—though it had produced her eldest daughter, Sunshine, born in Mexico in the summer of 1966, when Mountain Girl joined Kesey in his flight from a California drug charge. She remembers how "very connected [he was] in the world of literature," and how "we were constantly being visited by graduate students or writers or people doing interviews. . . . He had a very bright, engaging repartee going all the time," she says, which she loved.

Palo Alto, meanwhile, was the magic carpet. It was where everything happened.

> *That's where all the music was . . . Jerry was there and Hunter was there, Page was there, all the characters were there. Palo Alto was the beautiful golden bas-ket that this all came out of. Palo Alto was INCREDIBLE in those days. I'm coming from out of upstate New York, a gloomy place, there's nothing going on there—terrible poverty and despair. And you get to Palo Alto and it's this GORGEOUS place, golden, wide streets, houses set way back, that interesting California architecture and weird plants and palm trees. . . . The oranges are FALLING off the trees—WOW!*

No wonder the acid trips remembered from this time and place re-mind people of Disneyland ("It was the first-time realization that we could go to Disneyland any time, man," Garcia's folk-musician friend David Nel-son says; "[i]t was great . . . no hangover"). Or that the flowers in Huxley's *The Doors of Perception* were "shining with their own inner light and all but quivering under the pressure of the significance with which they were charged"—not unlike the flowers in his own garden in the Hollywood Hills. This shining and quivering, incidentally, is a quality they share with the scarlet poppies nodding at Judy Garland in *The Wizard of Oz*. They are California flowers. And psychedelics, in their salad days, when Cary Grant told *Look* magazine that LSD had made a new man out of him, were Cali-fornia drugs. Imagine the flora and fauna—and the music—LSD might have left in its wake had the long, strange trip commenced in Sitka, Alaska.

Jerry and Hunter, meanwhile, had set up shop in Palo Alto in the early '60s as itinerant artists. Too green for Kesey's early parties on Perry Lane—where they were once thrown out for being underage—they had the sure instinct of hipsters for rooting themselves in a *place*. Kepler's

Bookstore, with its tiny alcove for coffee and music in the back, and its shelves bulging with Kerouac, Joyce, and J. R. R. Tolkien, was a far cry from the Café Flore in Paris or the San Remo in New York, but it was a magnet for young off-the-street intellectuals. Among the latter, the Chateau boys had managed to make a reputation for themselves as rebels. They were not "hippies." Not yet. "*Hippie,*" says Hunter, "was a perjorative term for high school kids trying to pass for intellectuals." As part of the burgeoning folk movement, "we were an interim movement that helped spawn the hippie generation," he says. "We were lost in the middle some-where, but we knew that we had *amazing* potential, and that something was going to come of it."

Shortly before Mountain Girl arrived, Jerry had married Sara Rup-penthal when she became pregnant with Heather Garcia in 1963. He had moved out of the Chateau, but the funky old house on Skyline Drive still served as a base. Drugs, as always, were an accoutrement of hip bohemia. Not heroin, as in New York in the 1950s, or peyote buttons from the Ex-otic Plant Company in Laredo, Texas—not even acid (until the end of 1964)—it was mainly marijuana and speed that Jerry and Bob's circle con-sumed with the abandon of young people whose systems are wide open.

Hemp, cocaine, opium, and hooch had always flourished in San Francisco's bohemia, with its century-old ties to Europe and the Orient, but LSD en-tered the Bay Area mainly through L.A. psychiatrists, whose pioneer re-search, in many instances, was financed by the CIA. Timothy Leary and Richard Alpert's clinical investigations at Harvard in 1960–1961 grew out of the healing experiments of Oscar Janiger, Sidney Cohen, Betty Eisner, and Aldous Huxley in Los Angeles in the late '50s, along with a band of Beverly Hills LSD therapists whom Aldous Huxley viewed with embar-rassment (Cary Grant's doctor, for example).

In the summer of 1963, after Leary and Alpert had been fired from Harvard for holding "drug parties" with students, Hollywood buzzed with the news that the Mexican government had expelled them and their In-ternational Federation for Internal Freedom (an LSD resort) from Mex-ico. And soon the two men had resurfaced in Los Angeles at the psychedelic community's evening salons, where Christopher Isherwood, Alan Watts, and Anaïs Nin, among other gurus and disciples, were in attendance. Leary and Alpert's next stop was Billy Hitchcock's four-thousand-acre estate in Millbrook, New York, a more enduring home, which is where the Pranksters descended on them in the psychedelic bus, thereby inscribing a circle of sorts.

In Los Angeles, as in Bay Area rock 'n' roll circles later, a taste of the forbidden fruit aroused in the subject a longing to spread the forbidden knowledge. LSD was heady stuff: what its discoverer, Albert Hofmann, describes as the "truly cosmogonic power" of hallucinogens to "shift the wavelength setting of the receiving 'self,' and thereby to evoke alterations in reality consciousness." In the LSD state, "the boundaries between the experiencing self and the outer world more or less disappear. . . . A portion of the self overflows into the outer world, into objects, which begin to live, to have another, a deeper meaning."

Hence, the palpable significance of every leaf and twig. *Things* are flooded with the ambient energy of an ego that is no longer obligated to maintain the fiction (phenomenologically speaking) of a subject's separateness from the object world. From this dissolution of boundaries came the LSD user's widely reported sense of what Jay Stevens, in *Storming Heaven,* describes as knowing how it felt "to be one with the universe, to know that you existed on a multitude of levels, and not just on the puny one called I."

For L.A. psychiatrist Sidney Cohen, who regularly reported his findings at symposia that the CIA funded and monitored through the Josiah Macy, Jr. Foundation, this inflation of consciousness produced what he called an "integrative experience." Its chief perceptual component consisted of "looking upon beauty and light. Affectually there is a feeling of great relaxation and hyperphoria," he noted. "The patients describe an insightfulness into themselves, an awareness of their place in the environment, and a sense of order in life." Alas, the redemptive light might be followed the next month by a reunion with the noisy family of neuroses that had brought the client to the doctor in the first place. But this caveat hadn't prevented Cohen from offering his treatments to colleagues, mainly shrinks, but also influential writers and scientists, such as a group of analysts from the Rand Corporation, a think tank in Santa Monica. Among the latter was the famous author of *On Thermonuclear War,* Herman Kahn—who had reportedly stretched out on the floor, murmuring, *"Wow."* Afterward, Kahn told Cohen that he had been busy reviewing bombing strategies against mainland China.

Herman Kahn developed a real taste for LSD. In the mid '60s, when the Rand Corporation expanded its counterinsurgency research on Vietnam to embrace domestic unrest among disaffected youth at home, it was Kahn who urged Rand to examine the effects of LSD on personality change, including "changes in dogmatism" and political affiliations. His own personal investigations continued throughout the '60s and took him to Millbrook and Saint Mark's Place in New York, where he was, if not a familiar figure (all 325 pounds of him), then an unforgettable one. By the year 2000, Kahn predicted—in an instance of psychedelic hubris typical of heavy users—there would be an alternative "dropped-out" country inside the United States.

Acid trips, one notices, never seem to take their subjects very far from home. And when they do, *home*—a heightened *alternative* "reality consciousness"—is simply projected outward. Given spheres, like empires, are enlarged. When Henry Luce, the founder of *Time, Life,* and *Fortune,* took LSD with Huxley and Christopher Isherwood in the late '50s, he saw a vision of God on a golf course; later he professed to "hear" heavenly music in a cactus garden—not an uncommon experience with psychedelics. Synesthesia, it's called. If, as Albert Hofmann noted after first dosing himself in 1943, "every sound generated a vividly changing image, with its own consistent form and color," why couldn't every cactus and flower play its tune?

Henry Luce had been introduced to LSD by Sidney Cohen. LSD's early adepts were always trying to turn on "opinion leaders" and "change agents." What the world needed was what Terrance McKenna later called "a deputized minority—a shamanic professional class [McKenna would probably have excluded Luce], whose job is to bring ideas out of the deep, black water and show them off to the rest of us." Leary and Alpert's "children's crusade," when it arrived, horrified such men. As did Prankster Ken Kesey's program of "tootling the multitudes," and of "getting people to ask questions by getting them high."

Something of the social class, education, or the immediate circumstances of the tripper can also be deduced from firsthand accounts of the experience. When Luce gave a J. P. Morgan vice president, R. Gordon Wasson, seventeen pages in the May 27, 1957, issue of *Life* to narrate a virtual love affair with "magic mushrooms" in Mexico, he treated the magazine's readers to a Cook's tour of medieval antiquities. Wasson's visions "began with art motifs . . . such as might decorate carpets or textiles or wallpaper . . . [which] evolved into palaces with courts, arcades, gardens." Not surprisingly, his interest in Mexican fungi fascinated the CIA, who had arranged for an MK-ULTRA contract chemist named James Moore to attach himself to the expedition. (The lure was foundation support via a CIA conduit, the Geschickter Fund for Medical Research, in Washington, D.C.)

In the wrong set and setting, however, as a few Pranksters discovered on the bus, psychedelic experiences could be positively nightmarish. An object might wash up on one's perceptual shore stripped of all meaning, naked, yet bearing an important message. This sometimes happened to Jerry Garcia when he was tripping at the Fillmore Auditorium; with a troubled expression, he would stare down at his hand on the neck of the guitar, as if to say, *What the hell is this?* What is it *doing?* It certainly happened to a young set designer who was a friend of Candace. On his way to an acidhead's "Pink Party" later in the '70s, he suddenly realized he was holding something in his hands. He looked down and saw it was a steering wheel, which is how he knew he was driving. He and his friends, high on LSD, had painted themselves pink and stuck feathers to their skin, but when they reached the party, there was cocaine spilling out of little trays on the tables. Not a "Pink Party" at all, it was a *blow* party, full of people arguing in sharp, flinty voices over board games. Thus did drugs influence fashion and dictate props, rearranging the outer world to conform to alterations in the inner one.

In 1964, the Day-Glo-painted bus was a case in point. Here was an object that embodied an inner world electrified by subcurrents *not* from the 1960s but from the 1950s. These included not only the government's early LSD experiments but also the bold stroke and spatter of Abstract Expressionism, as well as the road-running fantasies of the Beats. David Nelson remembers Page Browning, who lived in the Chateau in Palo Alto in 1961, coming over to score some pot at the place on Gilman Street that Nelson shared with Jerry, Sara, and Phil Lesh early in 1965. "Have you heard about the Bus?" Page asked them; and he told them about how the Pranksters had "painted this bus just like a Jackson Pollock painting and then they got Neal Cassady to drive it." Nelson, Jerry, and Phil were all ears. Page said the Pranksters had gone east to meet Kerouac, and to make contact with Leary at Millbrook—neither of whom had welcomed them with open arms. They had gone to a nearby army-navy store to buy surplus smoke bombs, the kind that release red and green smoke on impact, and then lobbed them over Hitchcock's wall.

But the story that amazed Nelson, Garcia, and Lesh the most was Page's account of Neal Cassady barreling through the heartland high on acid and being stopped by cops, "and the cops just being completely nonplussed and straight people across the nation being totally nonplussed by this outrageous bus and this guy with headphones on driving," he recalls. " 'God,' " they all said, " 'you mean Neal was taking acid and driving, too? . . . How do you drive when you're hallucinating?' " And Page said, "We asked him about that too and Neal said, 'You just pick out the hallucinations from the real stuff. Then you drive right through the hallucinations!' "

Leary and his colleague Ralph Metzner were then politicking for the establishment of something called the Commission of Psychochemical Education, a "blue-ribbon panel" of neurologists, psychologists, educators, and religious leaders that they hoped would propose guidelines for further research. Leary, too, had courted opinion leaders—"influentials," he called them—before later presenting himself to mass society as a guru. It was Leary who had said, at Harvard, "We'll turn on [Arthur] Schlesinger and then we'll turn on [Jack] Kennedy," and Allen Ginsberg who had replied, "Why not begin by turning artists on?" And it was through Ginsberg, according to Jay Stevens, that "Leary was introduced into that curious milieu wherein wealth and avant-garde art find each other mutually amusing."

At Millbrook, meanwhile, when the Pranksters arrived, Dick Alpert, Ralph Metzner, and the other "Millbrookies" (as Mountain Girl calls them) were busily engaged in what they called the "mapping of consciousness" and hadn't wanted to be disturbed. Mountain Girl, who wasn't on the bus, visited Millbrook the following year when she was home for Thanksgiving. "They had a heavy Buddhist overload," she recalls. "We've never had a clue as to what Buddhists might be up to," she says, switching to Pranksterese: "the brain-mind connection—*huh . . . duh*. Very 'East Coast,' you know—lah-de-dah, we're all going to meditate now. Ring the little silver bells—*ding-ding-ding*. Millbrook!" "The crypt trip," other California visitors called the psychedelic investigations at Hitchcock's mansion, which were structured around Leary's adaptation of *The Tibetan Book of the Dead*.

Metzner, who left soon after, when it became clear that Millbrook was never going to be the quiet research center he had envisioned, relates a dream he had during the early period. In it, "the three of us, Tim, Dick and myself, were vaudeville artists, doing a song and dance routine, with exciting music and chorus girls, to try to present something that was deeply serious and even sacred." That was it in a nutshell—or would be soon enough. However, the opposite was also true. In spiritual matters, seriousness was never so shallow as when it was *deep*. Or so a Prankster might think.

It was not until late 1964 or early 1965 that Jerry Garcia and his wife, Sara, had started taking LSD themselves—the pure pharmaceutical stuff, Sandoz—with Nelson, Phil Lesh, Jerry's old buddy Laird Grant, Bob Weir, and Sue Swanson, a teenage classmate of Weir's from Menlo-Atherton High School. Bob Hunter, who knew all about it, wasn't part of these early group ventures—partly because he preferred tripping alone, and partly because he had pulled away from the "love scene" to shake a se-rious addiction to speed. Sara Ruppenthal remembers the early acid trips as wonderful times, when the earth, a rock or gnarled tree branch, might rear up, reminding them, literally, of the *force* of nature. It was usually benevolent (as in "May the Force be with you," a Hollywood gloss on an acid trip), but not always.

LSD could be dangerous when the hallucinations merged with the "real stuff" and it was no longer possible to tell the difference. Rooftop trippers often had to remind themselves, when climbing down, that the ground, which seemed to have risen to the level of the eaves, was actually a long way off. Sometimes when the Merry Pranksters orchestrated a "test," it seemed as if they deliberately probed this ambiguity, as when they invited Beat poet and filmmaker Kenneth Anger and the San Francisco "di-abolists" out to La Honda for a Mother's Day party in 1965. Kesey recalls that the Pranksters had taken a lot of acid and had dressed up in long robes and played "dolorous music" as they led their guests up the hill to a little amphitheater they had made in the redwoods. In the center was Ron Boise's Thunder Machine, a hollow metal sculpture depicting nude figures embracing. Hooked up to the ever-present sound system, it roared and boomed when you banged it, producing a tremendous echo. Also in the middle of the clearing was a glowing tree stump, lit by a spotlight hidden in the trees.

What followed was a scene out of the Brothers Grimm gone Dada:

> The stump was painted gold and sitting on the stump was a golden ax. After banging and clanging we lowered a bird cage from the redwoods. In the bird cage was a big hen. We got everybody out and spun this little pointer on what was called the "toke board." We spun it around and whoever it pointed at, it was obvious they were going to take that hen out and chop its head off. The thing pointed at Page Browning. Page went in there and picked the chicken out and the chicken had laid an egg. On the tape . . . you can hear . . . *"Stomp that egg!"* So he got the hen out of there and put its head on the stump and chopped the head off. Page threw the chicken still alive and flopping right into the audience. Feathers and blood and squawking and people running and screaming and all these diabolists and Kenneth Anger got up and left. . . . We out-eviled them. Kesey adds: "It all had that acid edge to it, of, 'This is something that might count.'"

For Jerry Garcia, such parties were *not* fun. Both Sara and Jerry's older brother, Clifford ("Tiff"), remember him grousing about "these people . . . up in the woods getting ripped and doing these weird things," though Sara was initially more threatened by the wild scenes than Jerry was. After she went to a Palo Alto Acid Test and saw Cassady juggling his sledgehammer and everybody dancing to the Warlocks' music, she was torn "between being the mom and the student and tending the home fires, and going off to participate in something extraordinary that had never happened before. There was really a sense of history to it all," she recalls; and for a while, she had tried to do everything.

"Was there a big initial flash between Jerry and Ken?" Mountain Girl asks rhetorically. Not really, she says. At that point, there was more of a professional rivalry. "Jerry was always interested in what Ken was doing but . . . they all felt kind of overpowered by the Prankster scene. Because it was so well developed and so loony and unpredictable. The Warlocks . . . were almost voyeuristic. They would come through, perform, and take off again," leaving drummer Bill Kreutzmann—the "straight guy," who organized gigs and acted as manager—to stomp his feet when there wasn't any money to collect. Nor was there much space to start friendships. As the Saturday-night parties at La Honda and elsewhere got larger and more unruly—particularly after the Hell's Angels became regular visitors—the Pranksters started getting busted, and spending more and more time in court.

Years later, Jerry Garcia presented a different picture. "We were younger than the Pranksters . . . wilder," he said. He was speaking perhaps of a slightly earlier period, before both the Warlocks and its predecessor, Mother McCree's Uptown Jug Champions, when Kesey was still living in Palo Alto and loosely connected to Stanford, and Jerry and his pals were "on the street." "We were definitely Dionysian as opposed to Apollonian. It was like we were celebrating life," he said. Drugs were part of a continuous search for "that explosion. . . . When the Pranksters took acid, they fucked with each other really. In a big way. We just got high and went crazy."

This was true, especially in the first year (before the "transcendental" trips began); but the Warlocks were not exactly Dionysian. It was six months to a year before they all tripped openly at parties in Palo Alto. At first, it was "really secretive," Laird Grant remembers. "People were feeling, 'Should we let other people know about this?' " Then, suddenly— about the time the Pranksters' parties outgrew La Honda—it was " 'Yeah. Everybody should do it.' " Before 1965 was over, the Warlocks had dropped out of the straight music scene—where they had played at roadhouses and clubs—and become Ken Kesey's house band. And for the next six months, Pigpen McKernan, Phil Lesh, Bob Weir, Bill Kreutzmann, and Garcia performed only at the Acid Tests, immersing themselves in a sensorium of sound, light, and mind-altering drugs that transformed their music, and the expectations of their audiences, forever.

⌒✍⌒

CHAPTER 3

FLASHES OF RECOGNITION

But for our project it were best
That each should go the road of fire
And seek adventure matching his desire.

GOETHE, *FAUST, PART TWO*

"ONE DAY THE idea was there," said Jerry Garcia, speaking of the first Acid Test at a roadhouse called Big Nig's in San Jose, on December 4, 1965. It was the night the Rolling Stones were playing the Cow Palace in San Francisco. " 'Why don't we have a big party,' " Jerry remembered Kesey saying a few weeks before, " 'and you guys bring your instruments and play, and us Pranksters will set up all our tape recorders and bullshit, and we'll all get stoned.' " As if the Chief was just horsing around at La Honda, and the lure of new turf on the peninsula had not aroused the proselytizer in him, which of course it had.

"The idea was of its essence formless," said Garcia. "There was nothing going *on*. We'd just go up there and make something of it. . . . It was not a gig." And this was true enough. With the harum-scarum sound effects and primitive light shows, the Acid Tests were far too casual for that. "The really neat thing," he reflected later, referring to the accidental quality of the early happenings, "was that we didn't have to be responsible." Not only did the drugs absolve the band of predictability but the camaraderie with which the acid was consumed (in paper cups of Kool-Aid, ladled from trash cans, or sipped from eggshell teacups) turned every performance into a collaboration.

The lines between performer and audience were dissolved, also those

49

between bandleader and band. The former happened not because the per-formers had stepped outside the proscenium but because everybody was busy reinventing themselves out of the materials at hand. ("Bring your own gadgets," said the invitation to the Trips Festival at the Longshore-man's Hall on January 22–23, 1966, meaning everything from tape decks to projectors; "A.C. outlets will be provided.") The formlessness of which Garcia spoke, however, was only skin-deep. Or rather, as one's acid-drenched consciousness began to molt, disclosing first one, then another plane of consciousness, new forms took shape, verging on what he called "ordered chaos or some *region* of chaos. The Test would start off and then there would be chaos," he explained. "Everybody would be high and flash-ing and going through insane changes during which everything would be *demolished,* man, and spilled and broken . . . and after that, another thing would happen, maybe smoothing out the chaos. . . ."

Over the years, in concert, the experience never wholly left the band. "It opened the doors and left them open," long after the group stopped dropping acid together, Phil Lesh declares. "You've heard about flash-backs," Lesh says when we talk about this history. "Onstage was one con-tinual flashback." I mention Candace's remark about LSD making her feel she could do anything. Did it have a similar effect on the band? What *did* come through the doors so many years ago?

"It had a lot to do with telepathy," Lesh begins, setting forth an image of the first apostleship that might serve as a microcosm for the larger con-gregation that grew around the band in years to come. "We were one or-ganism. We used to describe ourselves as the limbs of a drummer, or the fingers of a fingerpicking guitarist. We tried to interlock rhythmically or tonally. We'd interlock our playing so it would form this continuous iri-descent kind of map or maze."

What if somebody started taking off in a new direction and got caught up in his own trip, I ask. "Either everyone would go with him, or—" Lesh stops. What usually happened was that Garcia changed the tempo in the middle of a song. "He'd slow it down with a couple of chords [makes chord sounds] and everybody would go [repeats sounds]. New tempo. Or some-times it wouldn't be quite that slick. Sometimes we'd stumble along, and somebody would grind some gears."

I had been hearing gears grinding in the concerts I attended in the 1990s. Weir and Garcia, and maybe Lesh, would throw out a few phrases, and they would hang there, and when they didn't go anywhere, the music died out, occasionally with a little help from Candace. "I have to say I have seen my sister bring down the lights at points when it did seem the right thing to do," I said, hoping I wasn't putting my foot in my mouth. Lesh laughed. "It's totally legitimate," he said. "It diffuses everyone's attention. Everyone relaxes and takes a deep breath because there's nothing really to focus on. It just dissolves into silence, and then something else will come out."

At least that was true in the best of times. In the 1990s, however, the momentum faded, in Lesh's opinion. "We became more predictable," he says. The improvisational interludes that kept the music fresh were themselves curtailed. I was lucky to hear the gears grind at all; though Deadheads who prefer the singalong ballads were not to be disappointed. Speaking of the moments when the band broke into another realm of creation, weaving out of bits and pieces a musical whole cloth—the "iridescent maze"—Phil can't remember many. For him, the Grateful Dead "didn't really catch the flame again after '91 or '92."

The sudden eruption of harmony in the midst of chaos is, of course, a leitmotif of the Grateful Dead's music. Very likely, it grew out of the primal exchange experienced at the Acid Tests, which Bob Weir calls our "baptismo del fuego." It remained a signature of the band; and when it was missing from a set or failed to incite wonder, the performance fell flat. If the listener didn't know such lapses were inevitable—were, indeed, part of a ritual of transcendence the Grateful Dead executed again and again— he or she might dismiss the music out of hand. Because the musicians hadn't delivered the goods; and the listeners emerged with their emotions slung in the same old racks. There were no sudden flashes of insight into one's relationship with one's father or the cosmos—which might be memorialized in the line of a favorite song but originated in these moments.

When he wasn't playing at the Acid Tests, Garcia, meanwhile, was intrigued by the microphones that Kesey, with Mountain Girl's help, stationed around the hall. If you wandered by, you might stop and talk into one, and somebody wearing earphones at the end of the wire, listening in on the mikes with a tape recorder and a mixing board, would seize on what you said, tape it, and toss it out to the assembled throng. Suddenly, you heard your words booming back at you; and of course they were *just*

right, their meaning enhanced by having been appropriated by a hidden au-
ditor. What was significant about such experiences was that they didn't
happen to one person alone. "Nobody was doing *something,*" is how Garcia
put it; "it was everybody doing bits and pieces of something, the result of
which was something else."

This and another reflection, about the "magic" of thousands of people,
"all helplessly stoned, all finding themselves in a roomful of other thousands of people, *none of whom any of them were afraid of,*" bring us to another
aspect of the Grateful Dead's debt to the Acid Tests. The urge to merge,
to shuck the ego's straitjacket for a coat of many colors—an impulse that
lies not far beneath the surface of America's vaunted individualism—was
stimulated in these rough-and-tumble halls as it was nowhere else.

"I know that if the Acid Tests had never happened we would have been
just another band," Phil Lesh told an interviewer in the 1980s. And Garcia, speculating along with him about how the Dead's "incredible myth"
began, recalled playing at the Tests stoned, "and you'd look out there and
you'd see that guy and he'd look up and go, 'Yeah, I know what you
guys are doing. I know what you guys are up to!' and you knew that they
knew. It was like one on one," he said: "Recognition, it was flashes of
recognition."

Recognition of the trip that electrified the band is what it was, when
more seemed to happen during a midnight ride (day trips, too) than happened in a thousand lifetimes. Speaking of the flash, Lesh thought it was
"as close as you can come to being somebody else." This nod of an altered
consciousness toward another is something "deep," Garcia agreed: "a moment of true knowing." Not the high but the communion, bathed in drugs,
and in the afterglow of drugs, bound the musicians to one another and to
their fans.

In the smile of a turned-on stranger, there was another kind of recognition: a glimpse of something words had trouble catching. This was a
sense of *promise,* which Hunter Thompson recalls as a "sense that what we
were doing was *right,* that we were winning . . . that sense of inevitable
victory over the forces of Old and Evil. Not in any mean or military
sense," he hastens to add; "we didn't need that. Our energy would simply
prevail. There was no point in fighting. . . . We were riding the crest of a
high and beautiful wave."

"What the Acid Tests did was help us see another dimension," says

Gene Anthony, whose *Newsweek* photographs of the Trips Festival launched a media bath that would swamp the Haight Ashbury scene before the following year was out. "Just knowing that dimension existed changed us," he declares, speaking of an "us" that included Stewart Brand, the former biologist who helped organize the Trips Festival. Brand, who founded America Needs Indians after discovering peyote cults in Arizona and New Mexico, went on to publish the *Whole Earth Catalog* in 1972, and cofound the computer conference system called the Whole Earth 'Lectronic Link, or the WELL, in 1985. Working with Brand on the Trips Festival's sideshows—the God Box, the Congress of Wonders, among them—were some of the pioneers of the personal computer revolution, including Apple's cofounder Steve Jobs. Acid's tendency to "[make] us think that anything was possible, that we could do far-out things" (Anthony), was hardly limited to musicians or the Pranksters.

If the Acid Tests planted the seeds from which the Grateful Dead grew like Jack's beanstalk, Jerry Garcia's attachment to traditional American music provided the seedbed. Garcia's fondness for old-time music possessed an urgency that speaks of past lives. Bluegrass, for instance, may have recalled the years after his father drowned, when Jerry and his brother, Tiff, lived with their maternal grandmother at 87 Harrington Street in San Francisco.

While their mother worked long hours at José's, her late husband's bar down by the docks, it was Tillie Clifford (a "stern lady . . . with a twinkle in her eye," who liked Jerry "a whole bunch," remembers a friend) who looked after the boys. A radical in her youth, Jerry's grandmother had helped found the Laundry Workers Union, later absorbed by The Amalgamated Clothing and Textile Workers Union, and was still serving as its secretary-treasurer in 1950. Her favorite radio program was Nashville's "Grand Ole Opry"; and while Jerry and Tiff sat around the kitchen table drawing on shirt cardboards (Jerry already showing a "creative passion," according to Tiff), they listened to jug bands that had performed in the 1920s, and to "talking bluesmen" whose tradition harkened back to minstrel shows. If Harrington Street was "Jerry's psychic home," as Laird Grant suggests, this music, during a painful time, may have offered a kind of spiritual refuge.

During the folk revival of the early '60s, Garcia collected the music of

Virginia miners, Negro jug bands, Delta bluesmen, and Child ballads (the antique story songs gathered by Francis James Child in the nineteenth century). He was influenced, as Bob Dylan was, by musicologist Harry Smith's compilation of "hillbilly" and "race" recordings from the 1920s and '30s in the *Anthology of American Folk Music*. That, and Alan Lomax's field recordings, along with folk music from the Riverside, Vanguard, and Tradition labels, offered young musicians like Garcia, Dylan, Phil Ochs, and Joan Baez a range of voices from outside the melting pot that were dazzling in their variety. (Folkways, which brought out Harry Smith's *Anthology* in three boxed sets of 78s in 1952, reissued it on CDs under the Smithsonian/Folkways label in 1997.)

A record-collecting maven with an anthropological sensibility, Smith preferred studio to field recordings. But he would probably be uneasy with the dichotomy that critic Greil Marcus suggests between "the old, weird America" of "Smithville" (good), and "the old, free America" of Kenneth Rexroth and Woody Guthrie (bad). In the folk music of the 1940s, '50s, and '60s that relied on the Lomax recordings, Greil Marcus argues, revivalists such as Guthrie, Pete Seeger, and the Weavers perpetuated New Deal–era pieties about the struggles of the workingman that ignored both the varied artistry and the orneriness of the original musicians. Given his love for the odd and the low-down, Garcia might have agreed. There are traces of the *Anthology*'s lyrics—with their hangings, supernatural visions, swindles, and endless wandering—in the songs that he and Bob Hunter later composed for *Workingman's Dead* (1970) and *American Beauty* (1970). The very idea of an "invisible" world, hidden inside the official one, came naturally to Jerry. But Marcus's argument that it was the idiosyncratic truth of the studio recordings—the "founding document," he calls Smith's collection—that inspired the folk revival ignores the actual listening habits of musicians.

Along with hundreds of young folkies in the early '60s, Garcia and Hunter started by listening to the Weavers, the Kingston Trio, and the Limelighters, because it was what they heard first. "This stuff was entertaining and fun to play," says Hunter. "We weren't dead serious at this point. Dead seriousness came when Jerry and Dave Nelson discovered the New Lost City Ramblers and the old-timey stuff, which directed them back to the roots that the Ramblers knew so well."

When young folk musicians split among themselves, it was along more practical lines. Some were reconfiguring the music to express the passions for political change at large in the land. Others apprenticed themselves to backcountry voices whose restlessness spoke affectingly to their own sense of homelessness. And there were crossover figures, such as Bob Dylan, who did both. As a folk musician hanging out in Palo Alto's coffeehouses, Jerry Garcia—jamming with fellow pickers Dave Nelson, Bob Hunter, Eric Thompson, Jorma Kaukonen, John "Marmaduke" Dawson, and occasionally Sara Ruppenthal (who played an autoharp and a rosewood Martin guitar)—stood with the second group. But it wasn't the content of the old-time music so much as the virtuoso playing of the guitars, mandolins, and five-string banjos that drew him to the party.

The folk movement was led by protest singers like Phil Ochs and Joan Baez—whom Garcia disdained for not being a purist, and for a success (undeserved, he thought) that put her on the cover of *Time* in 1963. "He was jealous of her because her [second] record had just come out," suggests Ruppenthal, who was invited to accompany Baez, a friend, on her first European tour, but who declined, having thrown her lot in with Jerry.

At first, Garcia and Joan Baez, who went to Palo Alto High School (as did Sara, Bill Kreutzmann, and Ron McKernan), had performed some of the same songs, such as "Long Black Veil" and "Fennario." In the spring of 1960, right after Jerry got out of the Army, Barbara Meier, an early girlfriend (also a late one) remembers him wooing her with Joan Baez songs in the backseat of a car. She was fifteen and had already read *On the Road,* "and fallen in love with that world and somehow connected on a very deep level with the whole Kerouac/Buddhist vision. . . ." Jerry Garcia, at nineteen, "the archetypal beatnik with his goatee and black hair—singing these songs and looking up from under those eyebrows," perfectly "embodied and manifested that world." (After her first encounter with Jerry the following year, Sara Ruppenthal, a film student at Stanford, felt like she had put on "some new piece of clothing," that made her feel "wild and ready for action," which she "got.")

Bob Hunter, who had invited Pete Seeger to play at the University of Connecticut when Hunter was president of the Folk Music Club, remembers walking into the Chateau in 1961 when Jerry was playing a Joan Baez record. "He was absolutely *smitten* by it," Hunter says. A month or two later, Garcia was onto something else. As his guitar playing improved, "Jerry would be inclined to dive into the more ethnic versions," Hunter recalls. And within a month of absorbing Joan Baez, they were all off into bluegrass music. One thing led to another. "Mississippi John Hurt was important to us because he's such a fingerpicker, and that would lead us right to [blues singer] Elizabeth Cotten, and then [country singer] Merle Travis. But nobody in our particular scene followed Merle Travis's virtuoso route," he notes. "The boys were mostly into slavish imitations"—which, Hunter informs me, he was not.

Hunter was "not that interested in rendering other people's music accurately"; and so there developed "a schism" between him and "the ethnic purist crowd": Nelson, Garcia, Eric Thompson, and Marshall Leicester, a childhood friend of Jerry's from Menlo Park, who played banjo. At the same time, there was a willful impetuousness on Garcia's part that may have contributed to the schism. After Jerry "diversified" into bluegrass, Hunter had absorbed it by osmosis, just by living in the same house. He and Jerry and Nelson were performing publicly (Nelson and Hunter on guitar, Jerry on banjo) as the Wildwood Boys. But when one weekend Jerry picked up a mandolin and said, "Do you think you could learn this in a day, because we don't have a mandolin player?" Hunter backed off.

Like Garcia, Hunter had come home to Palo Alto straight from the Army, after lasting only a year at the University of Connecticut. Like Jerry, too, he played folk music in service clubs on brand-new Martin guitars. When they first met, Hunter tells me, they went to a party together where there was a guitar. They both dived for it, and Bob got it first. He did a song or two, "and when Garcia got it, he obviously played the guitar better than I could," he says, "and so he wouldn't give it back, and never did." By 1962, Hunter thought of himself as "a novelist, a writer. That was serious," he says. "Music was not serious; it was fun." A bit later, when Garcia was starting up another band, Mother McCree's Uptown Jug Champions, he asked Hunter if he'd like to play jug. "I couldn't get a tone out of the jug, and I handed it back to him and said, 'No. That's not for me.' "

While Garcia zigged, Hunter zagged. When the Acid Tests started at the end of 1965, Bob, who by then was doing a lot of speed, got stuck in "a downward-headed drug culture" in Palo Alto. He also got stuck in the Scientology movement for a while; and as a member of the National Guard he was called into action to help put down the Watts riots during the summer of 1965. It was, he says, "a very high and very low point in my life." The high came when he sat down for the first time to write songs. He loved what the Beatles were doing and what Dylan was doing, and thought, I can do this, and wrote "Saint Stephen," "China Cat Sunflower," and "Alligator." Among the Dead's most famous songs, they were written and performed without any connection with the band. "I played those songs," Hunter declares; "those were my songs." In March and October of 1997 and again in 1998, he hit the road on a solo tour to sing them again.

By the end of 1963, Jerry Garcia was playing Scott Joplin rags on the piano. He had teamed up for "wet gigs," as the new bar jobs were called, with Ron McKernan (not yet "Pigpen") in an R & B band called the Zodiacs. Formerly Dr. Don and the Interns, after the leader, a black musician named Don Dee Great, the Zodiacs also played at Bay Area fraternity houses and stripper joints.

Garcia had already performed in several bluegrass bands, most of which he had formed himself. He sang and played guitar, banjo, even fiddle and autoharp, an occasion, in a club in nearby San Jose where Jorma Kaukonen played the songs of the Reverend Gary Davis. On his very first gig, with Hunter in 1960, the odd couple had taken home five dollars each. Since then, Garcia had played in local nightspots like the Tangent (which is where Mountain Girl first saw him), St. Michael's Alley, Magoo's Pizza Parlor, and the Boar's Head café at the Jewish Community Center. It was in such halls, and in the back room of Dana Morgan's Music Store, where both Jerry and McKernan worked, that a handful of young musicians who helped create the "San Francisco Sound"—not just Garcia and the boys but also Kaukonen and Paul Kantner (Jefferson Airplane), Dave Nelson and Marmaduke Dawson (New Riders of the Purple Sage)—took this roots music and carried it into rock 'n' roll.

By 1963, meanwhile, folk music had found its niche in the recording industry. Old bluesmen who had recorded in the 1920s and '30s, such as Mississippi John Hurt, Lightnin' Hopkins, and Sonny Terry and Brownie McGhee, were drawing huge crowds in college towns. More blues records turned up on pop-music charts in the early '60s than in any decade before or since; although the proportion of hard-core blues in the R & B hit lists, tunes like "Hard to Handle" and "Searchin'," which Ron McKernan liked to sing, had dropped since the 1950s. Pop audience–response pendulums had settled on the Kingston Trio, Peter, Paul and Mary, and Joan Baez—whose continuing success, in Garcia's view, "just didn't seem right. . . . 'Ah, she picks her nose,' " Sara Ruppenthal remembers him muttering. Jerry, she says, "wanted to do something big—but there was no show business niche for him."

In Robert Greenfield's oral-history biography *Dark Star,* there is a striking image of Jerry Garcia "walk[ing] around the house with a guitar on." It speaks to the singular intensity of this early ambition. The house was the Chateau. "[Jerry] could be so intent on what he was doing," a Palo Alto friend recounts, "that he would come and stand in front of people the way you stand in front of somebody you're going to have a conversation with." But when you said something, he made no response. His fingers kept darting over the strings, often repeating a phrase or passage, as if by duplicating the sounds, he might retrieve the emotion he was after.

Years later, Garcia told an interviewer that when he first heard the five-string banjo of Bill Monroe on a Folkways recording, he thought, " 'God, what is that sound? I gotta make that sound.' It became an obsession," and he "learned how to learn something difficult." It took a long time because he had to listen to the record over and over, slowing it down at times to hear the individual notes. "I got a lot of respect for the individual note," he declared, observing that "[w]hen you're blasting along straight eighth notes at a quick tempo, it requires a lot of control and a lot of practice. The root of my playing," Garcia added, "is that every note counts, every note has a personality, every note has a little spirit." Later, in his own music, this attentiveness became "the familiar slick lick with the up-twist at the end," which Ken Kesey memorialized after Garcia's death: "that merry snake twining through the woodpile, flickering in and out of the loosely stacked chords." Yet even at the end of his life he returned to certain American classics that taught him to listen with his fingers, to bend and slide a note exactly as Mississippi John Hurt does in "Louis Collins." Garcia's rendition of Hurt's valedictory to a murdered friend, released posthumously in a Jerry Garcia–David Grisman CD entitled *Shady Grove,* is Garcia's Rosebud (not to be confused with his guitar of the same name). "Louis Collins" and "Stealin'," another *Shady Grove* gem, originally played by the Memphis Jug Band and released on a 78 "race" record in the 1930s (along with "I Whipped My Woman with a Single Tree" and "Feed Your Friend with a Long-Handled Spoon"), stand out in the mountainous discography of Jerry Garcia's musical career as paeans to an old love—like the little wooden sled at the end of *Citizen Kane*.

During the early 1960s, long before the Acid Test, Jerry Garcia was "learning how to learn." He was matching his masters note by note in order to assimilate the formal elegance that underlay their seemingly effortless access to feeling. He had entered a period of apprenticeship, which was not uncommon among young people burning to express themselves in one medium or another. Movies, for example. At the University of Chicago, where I was a graduate student, I used to gather around the editing machine in the Documentary Film Group's office with my filmmaker friends, who were doing the same thing as Garcia. Their "notes" were the frames they froze over and over in order to study the lighting that bathed a scene in darkness, or the wide-angle photography that created the illusion of vast spaces, or the floor shot that made a man look menacing, all techniques that Orson Welles used in *Citizen Kane*.

That movie was a primer for young cineastes at Chicago, one of whom, Gordon Quinn, would go on to make award-winning documentaries in years to come. So was the work of Josef von Sternberg, at whose feet we sat when he arrived to present a Marlene Dietrich series at the university. On the face of it, nothing connected von Sternberg's lingering dissolves, tricky lighting, and artfully constructed settings, much less the heavy narration and sparse dialogue of Orson Welles's work, with the free-form cinema verité documentaries the Chicago students were making. But these passages illuminated the elements of filmmaking. And the artifice, strangely enough, or not so strangely, when you think about Brecht, kept one's attention on the *play* at the heart of emotion, the *act* of creation.

"Technique is the test of our sincerity," a friend said at the time, speaking for the young and talented who have nothing (yet) to say. Filming live-action events with a handheld camera was not so different from Jerry Garcia's experience in the early '60s of "blasting along . . . at a quick tempo" on a guitar or banjo. If you were not careful—if you weren't on intimate terms with the elements of the craft—the results could be a blur. Garcia, however, who soon had a good deal to say, never lost his obsession with technique.

His fondness for traditional music was informed by a curiosity that slipped underground in years to come but which never left him. In the beginning, as in the end, he was drawn to tangled tales of loss, separation, and death, and to comeback tunes, like "Stealin'," rueful and self-mocking:

> Stealin', stealin', pretty mama don't you tell on me,
> I'm stealin' back to that same old used to be

Sara Ruppenthal speaks for the beginning, when Jerry and his cronies immersed themselves in field recordings and Folkways albums: "those tunings and turns of phrase and story lines were so American—and also peculiar and haunting in a way that spoke to the imagination and the heart," she reflects. "We were just barely into our twenties, all fired up with a sense of possibility. We idealized these traditional musicians as our chosen roots—our adopted family; we wanted to become part of this lineage."

They were like the "coo-coo bird" Clarence Ashley sings about in the nonsense verses collected in the *Anthology of American Folk Music,* beset by what Greil Marcus terms "displacement, restlessness, homelessness." Marcus finds Oliver Wendell Holmes recommending in 1872 that the cuckoo, an American motif, be installed as a national symbol. "We Americans are all cuckoos. We make our homes in the nests of other birds," writes Holmes—which isn't quite right. The cuckoo, Marcus points out, "lays its eggs in the nests of other birds, leaving its progeny to be raised by others, to grow up as imposters in another's house."

Something like this displacement was imposed on the African slaves and indentured servants from Europe who were the ancestors of many of the musicians represented in the *Anthology.* Palo Alto's minstrels, and their counterparts across the country, were displaced persons of a different sort. Their flights toward alien nests were voluntary. Their own roots seemed problematic; or were severed by death, as they were for Jerry Garcia, who grew estranged from his mother after his father died and she remarried. His father, José, or Joe, who played clarinet in the jazz and dance bands he also led, was the black sheep in a family of middle-class Spaniards who had emigrated to California before World War I. Jerry, who early on fell out of contact with the Spanish side of his family, believed he had inherited the mantle.

Bob Hunter was born Robert Burns in Arroyo Grande, California. His father, a Scot, was an itinerant electrician, a drinking man who was once thrown in jail in Montana with Hunter's grandfather for cattle rustling. He died when Bob was a boy. When his mother remarried, she chose a Scotsman of a different stripe, a sales manager at McGraw-Hill who was the son of a Presbyterian minister from Scotland. Bob took his stepfather's name, but he remains Robert Burns at heart. "All through my life," he says, "I've had a great identification with the bard of Scotland"—which is certainly evident in the stanzas he wrote for his stepfather, Norman MacPherson Hunter, and read on the occasion of his death in 1996. Among them:

> The rapture of death must equal
> And exceed the pain of leaving
> Or God, if God there be,
> But toys with men
> Upon this ancient ground of grieving.

In "An Elegy for Jerry," which Hunter read at Garcia's funeral service, the identification with Burns is also evident. Speaking of the muse that served them both, he writes:

> How should she desert us now?
> Scars of battle on her brow,
> bedraggled feathers on her wings,
> and yet she sings, she sings!
>
> May she bear thee to thy rest,
> the ancient bower of flowers
> beyond the solitude of days,
> the tyranny of hours—
> the wreath of shining laurel lie
> upon your shaggy head,
> bestowing power to play the lyre
> to legends of the dead.

For these young folksingers thirty-five years ago, as for young people generally, family relationships were subject to flare-ups between generations that stood in starker contrast to one another than they do today. The generational tensions were exacerbated by the rift between the 1950s and the increasingly chaotic '60s. In this regard, it is interesting to note that during the polarizing year of 1963—when hundreds of civil rights demonstrators were bloodied in Birmingham, Alabama, and afterward 200,000 people marched on Washington; when a president was assassinated, and his assassin murdered *on television;* while on the cultural front, folk music started to go electric—Jerry Garcia and his friends clung to the receding shore. When Bob Dylan first plugged his guitar into an amplifier at the Monterey Folk Festival in the summer of 1963 (before going electric with the Band at Newport two years later), Jerry and Sara walked out. They were "stern traditionalists" who eschewed "modernization and want[ed] to imitate and preserve the old forms," Sara recalls; though naturally for Jerry, this changed "in that ongoing tension between preservation and innovation."

Jerry Garcia, like Bob Dylan, would become adept at navigating the dialectic between tradition and invention. Roots music served them each as stepping-stones for individual talents whose output would come around again to replenish tradition. Thus, the Hunter/Garcia classic, "Truckin'," is under consideration by the Library of Congress for investiture as a National Treasure. And Bob Dylan's "basement tapes" from the late '60s, which reinterpreted American traditional song from the Folkways *Anthology,* are now icons. Bob Dylan himself has long been a human icon—a discomfiting experience that once led him to exclaim, "God, I'm glad I'm not me."

"It [tradition] cannot be inherited, and if you want it you must obtain it by great labor," writes T. S. Eliot, in "Tradition and the Individual Talent." If you would be an artist beyond your twenty-fifth year, he adds, you need a "historical sense"—"a perception not only of the pastness of the past, but of its presence." You must write your music, in other words, and play and sing it, not only with your own generation's cri de coeur in your bones but with the cris de coeur that preceded you, as well. For Eliot, it was a "sense of the timeless and the temporal together [that] makes a writer traditional," and at the same time, "acutely conscious . . . of his own contemporaneity."

Dylan and Garcia both understood this paradox. When they broke with tradition, it was after they had explored and internalized it thoroughly; yet each would come around again to reinterpret it. In Dylan's case, rebellion, overall, was joyous: a building on the ruins of the past that posited a future. One after another, the breakaway albums of the mid-'60s—*The Freewheelin' Bob Dylan* (1963), *The Times They Are A-Changin'* (1964), *Another Side of Bob Dylan* (1964), *Bringing It All Back Home* (1965), *Highway 61 Revisited* (1965), and *Blonde on Blonde* (1966)—mark the sudden twists and turns in consciousness that set his generation apart from any other. The madness, the achievement, was in the method—as in the long allegorical narratives of *Highway 61 Revisited,* which are not sung so much as spoken, in the southern tradition of "talking blues," over the furious guitar tracks laid down by Mike Bloomfield.

"Like a Rolling Stone" conveys the in-your-face bravado of the student movements, albeit with a hook. "How does it *FEEL* / to be on your own with no direction home" is sung with a snarl—both angry and triumphant, but laced with a nagging bitterness. Dylan's voice grazes the melody line; words bunch up in the interstices of the beat, so that you have to *think* about the words, not just feel them—something unusual in a song. The tension between anger and fear, between going it alone and loneliness, is the fever of youth. The howl of rage and frustration is a musical equivalent of Ginsberg's "Howl," with its undercurrent of anguish over the loss of dreams, American dreams, which were largely founded (when you think about the Indians) on other people's nightmares. The lyrics, driving *against* the melody, open an uneasy space between singer and listener. Dylan draws you in and pushes you away simultaneously, creating an emotional frisson that is immensely moving, realer than real.

Hunter's and Garcia's relation to tradition is different. More backward-looking, it is no less engaged with contemporary longings. Acquiescence to events over which you have no control, or *feel* you have no control, not rebellion, is the leitmotif of many a Grateful Dead song. So, too, is the shrug at the sphinx, the sheriff, the wolf, the girl (or boy) who's left behind, even if it's you. Acquiescence, however, is not necessarily surrender—not, at any rate, *dog-faced* surrender of the type that some folks (myself included) associate with inaction in the face of entropy, banality, hypocrisy, or crimes against the people. Acquiescence, in Deaddom, is first of all a strategy for achieving a desired state of consciousness. *Loving* acquiescence is the watchword.

In *The Lazy Man's Guide to Enlightenment,* Thaddeus Golas offers an experience from a bad acid trip to make a point with which many Dead-heads would agree. "One of my psychedelic excursions had gotten off to a bad start, and I was sinking into a really satanic bummer," Golas relates. "As I looked about me at people turning evil, shrunken, colorless, old, and weird, I suddenly thought, *'Well, what did you think it was that needed to be loved?'* And just like that, the doors opened and I was in paradise."

Not that Bob and Jerry harbored such therapeutic thoughts back in Palo Alto—though acid had introduced them to the power of a thought. Nor did they see themselves as philosophes or gurus, God forbid, but as artists—artists, however, who "were something new under the sun," Hunter informs me, to my surprise. "I remember how back in the 1960s we thought that we were going to change the world, we really did!" he ex-claims. "There were no more Beats around and whatever was coming next hadn't really declared itself."

While Garcia was the sterner traditionalist, Hunter "was writing post-modern." He was dipping into old ballads mainly for atmosphere. What the two men shared was a fondness for innuendo and indirection that led them to treasure a murky line from an old folktale, such as "ten thousand got drowneded that never was born," in "The Mummer's Song." "It was the power of the almost-expressed, the resonant," that mattered most, Garcia once proposed. "It seemed to speak at some level other than the most ob-vious one, and it was more moving for that reason." Such lines had the "scary power that the Mass used to have in Latin."

Alan Lomax's *Folk Songs of North America* introduced them to an oral tradition that, over centuries, might strip a ballad of narrative verses that were extraneous to its core, and leave a stray line traveling through time, like "black eels and eel broth, mother," or "I fain would lie doon," in "Lord Randal." They were tag lines, with bits of flesh still clinging to them, alert-ing anyone who paid attention that something momentous had happened long, long ago. For Hunter and Garcia, these fragments were a passport to a wider, deeper pool of allegory than was available to most up-and-coming rockers—one that might nourish them when the acid-induced flashes of recognition wore thin.

For them both, the half-told tale, "rich in weirdness," was a folk tradi-tion they admired in any tune that had survived what Garcia referred to as "the telephone game through several generations," and what Hunter called the "as-if-by-ear-tradition." This last was indispensable to Hunter, who employed it in the lyrics for *Workingman's Dead*, *American Beauty*, and *Wake of the Flood* (1973) to catch the voice of a drifter's ironic lament, or a gambler's requiem, to wit:

> The wolf came in, I got my cards
> We sat down for a game
> I cut my deck to the Queen of Spades
>   but the cards were all the same
>
>   Don't murder me
>   I beg of you, don't murder me
>   Please
>   don't murder me

There's a mournful, soughing tone to the narrator's voice in "Dire Wolf," a tone that doesn't change much from one song to the next. "Cumberland Blues," for example:

> Lotta poor man got the Cumberland Blues
> He can't win for losin'
> Lotta poor man got to walk the line
> Just to pay his union dues
>
> I don't know now
> I just don't know
> If I'm goin' back again. . . .

The best compliment Hunter ever got for a lyric was from an old man who had actually worked in the Cumberland mine. "I wonder what the guy who wrote this song would've thought," the fellow said, "if he'd ever known something like the Grateful Dead was gonna do it."

"But the loneliness and the lost stuff that so informs these songs, that was my life," Hunter tells me. The out-of-luck gambler staggering about in a haze of red whiskey is an extended metaphor for the chemical excesses and romantic losses he suffered throughout the '60s. And he corrects me when I comment on the folk themes that seem to shimmer through the lines. "They came out of my imagination," Hunter insists; he challenges me to name a song he's done that is based in any specific way on traditional ballads. "Even 'Casey Jones' only takes the character of Casey Jones and the train wreck and puts it in an entirely different context, with an entirely different rhythm." Dupree in "Dupree's Diamond Blues" is a folk character; as is Stagger in "Stagger Lee" (who appears in songs that Ma Rainey, Furry Lewis, and John Hurt sang in the '20s). But in "Stagger Lee," Hunter asserts, he "turned the traditional character and situation on its head, and introduced the character of Delia from an entirely different song. And threw these things together and stirred the soup up."

The lyrics carry "a *sense* of tradition; if you go into it more deeply, it's going to disappear," he explains. What Dave Van Ronk said of Bob Dylan—"He was always a sponge, picking up whatever was around him"—applies to Hunter, as well. When you're cookin', *everything* goes into the pot. As for the western drapery, that, too, is an expression of personal identity, one that was reconstructed, however, in the writing of the songs. "I became more aware of myself as a westerner the more I *wrote* as a westerner," Hunter says. But it wasn't until he started visiting England in the early '70s, interestingly enough, that he began to define himself as a westerner "in a really comprehensive sense."

The attachment to odd locutions from Anglo-Saxon tradition, on the other hand, is bred in the bone, and can be troublesome, maybe for that reason. When I ask him about the lines from "Lord Randal," Hunter nods his head vigorously, happy that I've noticed. "Oh God, yes," he says; "wonderful language, vaguely Elizabethan. I got to *watch* that. I can fall into that real quick. . . . I have to keep my writing from being too literate, [I] really do, because I *am* literate!" he exclaims, poking another cigarette in his aquafilter. "It can be a cross in rock 'n' roll." Especially with the blues. "If you're going to sing the blues, you shouldn't have any education. You should drink a lot, and that should be about it. And have a good sense of rhythm. . . . I got into writing blues," he relates, "because Jerry loved the blues and wanted some blues—specifically, twelve-bar blues. They're easy enough to write, and I'd give him some, but," he says, hitching his voice into a drawl, *"It's not mah thing ta write the blues.* I have the wrong cultural background."

"What is your thing?" I ask him (reminded, suddenly, of former road manager Rock Scully's depiction of Hunter as "a fifties collegiate hipster, basically"). "Hopefully, I don't repeat it," he answers. "I keep looking for other forms . . . which is what gives the Dead's music such an eclectic feel. . . . If I've done it well, I want to move on to something else."

Robert Hunter's specialty, I decide later, is his sixth sense for the tag lines of a buried culture. It's a popular Anglo-Saxon culture, whose topographical features have been largely molded by the appetites and fantasies of Jerry Garcia—even if much of the emotion derives from the strife, first in Hunter's personal life and then, later, in the band's life. There are innumerable examples of this allusive power in the songs, but one that comes immediately to mind, probably because I heard it so often at concerts in the 1990s, is "Ramble On, Rose":

> Just like Jack the Ripper
> Just like Mojo Hand
> Just like Billy Sunday
> In a shotgun ragtime band
> Just like New York City
> Just like Jericho
> Pace the halls and climb the walls
> Get out when they blow
>
> Did you say your name was
> Ramblin' Rose?
> Ramble on, Baby
> Settle down easy
>   Ramble on, Rose
>
> Just like Crazy Otto
> Just like Wolfman Jack
> Sitting plush with a royal flush
> Aces back to back
> Just like Mary Shelley
> Just like Frankenstein
> Clank your chains and count your change
> Try to walk the line
>
> Good-bye, Mama and Papa
> Good-bye, Jack and Jill

> The grass ain't greener, the wine ain't sweeter
> either side of the hill

The gang's all there: the names and faces from a dozen "postmodern creations," as Hunter calls his songs. Jack the Ripper, Mojo, New York City, redolent of a hundred and one plots used and abused; drug references; private jokes about dealers and newspapermen; literary tributes; references to L.A.–Frisco spats—viz, the Mamas and the Papas, and to the ambiguities of fame ("Clank your chains and count your change"). Audiences returned again and again to feast on this banquet of allusions to a transcendent world. What Hunter's lyrics created for Jerry Garcia—"a mythos or alternate universe that's got a lot of interesting stuff in it," Garcia once said—was not so different from what the lyrics create for fans.

Over time, Garcia and Hunter wove together strands of bluegrass, English and American folk motifs, California country and western, gospel, blues, the Beatles, Dylan, and the Band into a Whitmanesque sampler that was Greek to prime-time DJs accustomed to the three-minute song bite. But like no other popular music before or since, it spoke to the dailiness of experience, the experience of *getting by,* which is largely overlooked in the lyrics of other bands; and it satisfied a longing for songs that *come* from somewhere, that have a past, if only a *sense* of the past.

~CHAPTER~
4

HOW THE BALLOON WAS LAUNCHED

Time's a stripper
Doing it just for you
ROBERT HUNTER, "CATS UNDER THE STARS"

ON NEW YEAR'S Eve of 1963, fifteen-year-old Bob Weir was wandering the back streets of Palo Alto with his high school friend Bob Matthews. Too young to get into the clubs, their ears pricked up when they heard banjo music coming from the rear of Dana Morgan's Music Store. It was Jerry Garcia who let them in when they knocked. Weir, the adopted son of a well-to-do family in the Palo Alto suburb of Hillsborough, knew him only as "the local hot banjo player." Unaware of the holiday, Jerry was waiting for his students to show up, and the two boys easily persuaded him to unlock the showroom. As Weir tells it, "we grabbed a couple of guitars—the ones we'd always wanted to play [and] had a good time playing and singing and kicking stuff around all night, and by the end of the evening . . . we decided we had enough second-rate talent there to throw together a jug band."

Bob Hunter and Dave Nelson named it Mother McCree's Uptown Jug Champions. For Garcia, the new band was an attempt to bridge the gap between bluegrass and the blues. A few days later, rehearsals began in his and Sara's garage with some more people, including Nelson and Ron McKernan. They pulled together the jugs, washboard, washtub, broom handle, and string, then figured out how to use them by listening to old jug band records that Jerry had worn thin. "A few of us sort of struck a chord together," says Weir, who "really couldn't play at all," he admits, "but they figured if anybody's got to start from scratch it probably ought to be me." He was assigned the washtub bass. Dave Nelson remembers that "Weir was the most unabashed to give it a try. He was up there making fart noises. To play jug? What an offer. In a band? To go, 'Uhh phoooo. Boooo.' And that was your instrument?" In a few weeks they were all ready. And thanks to Garcia's (lifelong) knack for inspiring other musicians, if sometimes by a ferocious perfectionism they could not risk themselves, and to Ron McKernan's audience appeal, Mother McCree's Uptown Jug Champions soon had work nearly every weekend.

McKernan, who acquired the name Pigpen at this time, after the "Peanuts" character with the snarly hair and sooty cheeks, was the performer who, according to Nelson, made the band "legitimate beyond belief." Like Blind Lemon Jefferson or Howlin' Wolf, "Pigpen," they all thought, was a great stage name. This son of a popular Bay Area DJ known as "Cool Breeze," who had grown up in a predominately black neighborhood in East Palo Alto, gave them something their competitors on the East Coast, the Kweskin Jug Band, didn't have: a genuine down-and-dirty blues singer who did the harmonica part exactly right. "He didn't copy it note for note," Nelson remarks. "He had perfect feeling."

When Garcia and his friend Sandy Rothman left on a cross-country musical pilgrimage to hear bluegrass music in the summer of 1964, Bob Weir, who had started studying acoustic guitar with Jerry in January, took over his teacher's beginning and intermediate students. His confidence soared: Sue Swanson, a former classmate at Menlo-Atherton High School, where Weir was an indifferent student—in part, because of an undiagnosed dyslexia so severe that he could barely read—remembers how proud he sounded when he turned around in his seat on the first day of world history class and said, "I have a band." Sue and a friend had been whispering excitedly about the Beatles concert they had gone to that summer, and how they had snuck into the hotel where the Beatles were staying.

"Weir was very cute. Still is," says Swanson, who helps run Grateful Dead Merchandising in Novato and remains a member of the Dead's first family. (Bob Weir has good press with the Dead's women. "He was this adorable, soft young man," reports Mountain Girl. "He doesn't have any thorns in his personality, anywhere.") Word of the new band, along with his larky good looks—and a reputation for weirdness—endeared him to them immediately. And he *was* weird. On tests, he filled in the True/False boxes to form the shape of a plane. When he refused to stand for the Pledge of Allegiance, Swanson and her friend hissed, "Traitor! Traitor!" out of the corners of their mouths.

The following year, when the Beatles returned to San Francisco, Weir drove with Sue Swanson and another friend to the Cow Palace in Daly City to see them. It was September 2, 1965, and the media had been trumpeting the big event for days. Sue and Sara Ruppenthal had gone to see the Beatles' latest movie, *Help!,* about twelve times and had memorized every line. *A Hard Day's Night,* the Beatles' first film, had brought a reluctant Jerry Garcia around, after an initial distaste. Early hit tunes like "I Want to Hold Your Hand" left him unimpressed; although from the beginning he was less critical than other folk musicians of the Beatles' appropriation of '50s rock 'n' roll, having sniffed out the pivotal presence of pot, then acid, in their magic. "They were a trip," Ruppenthal recalls, "and there was something inspiring about these smart adorable talented guys our own age getting to make a movie about themselves being very silly. We could identify with that kind of irreverent off-the-wall zaniness"—especially once she and Jerry had started dropping acid: "That changed everything."

By the second San Francisco concert, the impact of LSD and the Beatles had effected a sweeping transformation of consciousness. Looking back, Hunter remembers it happening all at once: "Out of the blue sky appeared the Beatles, the Rolling Stones, and [the electrified] Bob Dylan. Add a little acid to all of that and your orientation changed very quickly." The old-time music, however, stayed "at the roots of our rock and roll, more than pop music. . . . All that good stuff went into the music from that point on," starting with the featured song on the Grateful Dead's first record, "Viola Lee Blues."

No one from the band describes the impact of the Beatles with the same enthusiasm that Garcia did. "When the Dead started out, did you have a sense that it would last this long?" he was asked by an interviewer in 1993. "We had big ideas," he answered, referring to a time when suddenly his own passion for bluegrass appeared a little overzealous, even to him. "I mean, as far as we were concerned, we were going to be the next Beatles. . . . [W]e were on a trip, definitely. We had enough of that kind of crazy faith in ourselves." For Mother McCree's, which by New Year's Eve of 1964 had turned into an electric rock 'n' roll band called the

Warlocks, the arrival of the Beatles joined two critical ideas: the idea of the *group* and the idea of fun. Big fun. And a third: fame.

On the way to the September 1965 concert, meanwhile, Sue Swanson (who wanted to support the new band and make it famous, she told me, "so that then we might meet the Beatles") thought she spotted the Fab Four's limousine up ahead. She floored the car and raced up behind it, and sure enough it was. Swerving into the breakdown lane, she slipped in beside it, ignoring the frantic waves of construction workers; and together the two cars roared up to a back entrance of the Cow Palace, where an iron gate opened long enough to let the limo shoot in before snapping shut. The tagalongs were left outside. Weir, who was high on acid, sat between the two girls. "Don't let them get away! *Catch 'em! Catch 'em!*" they shouted, and he leapt out, scaled the chain-link fence, and sprinted down the concrete ramp after the disappearing car.

This was the Beatles concert that spooked Ken Kesey, and according to Tom Wolfe, it set him up for the *"cry of the ego"* dirge he delivered at the antiwar rally in Berkeley the following month. The Cow Palace appears to Kesey as a "roaring hell," an arena packed with "a writhing, seething mass of little girls waving their arms in the air . . . a single colonial animal with a thousand waving pink tentacles . . . vibrating poison madness and filling the universe with the teeny agony torn out of them." The Beatles, hardly mentioned, "are the creature's head. The teeny freaks are the body. But the head has lost control of the body and the body rebels and goes amok and that is what cancer is."

The Pranksters, not merry at all, though "stoned out of their gourds," are led by a terrified Kesey out of the maze of concrete tunnels and cyclone fences to the safety of the bus. Mountain Girl, who digs the scene, lags behind, ruing the day she went to see the Beatles " 'with a bunch of old men who never saw a rock 'n' roll show before.' " And one wonders: Is this horror of the mass crowd—"baying on cue" at Berkeley—really Kesey's? The answer, it seems, is yes.

Thirty years after the Beatles concert, Kesey can still summon the moment: "I saw power like I never imagined it before," he says. "When George [Harrison] would turn his head, you'd hear the screaming wave follow his head like this"—and he dips to the right, pointing an invisible guitar. "What the Beatles were saying was, Come closer, come closer. 'Love me do.' And the people were pressing closer and closer. But they didn't know how to sing that moment. And the moment needed to say, *Don't* come closer. Stay *back*. Stay *back*."

At the height of their own power, it was a moment that the Grateful Dead mastered well. Kesey allows as how only the Grateful Dead were "supple enough to read the notes written on the wall that are changing all the time"—the notes, presumably, that tell the head what the body needs. And what is that? Kesey rambles on about "that crack that lets in all the light," a "split-second thing that happens when the Dead are playing," which leads the audience to say, " 'Wow! Did you see that?' That's it, that's the moment."

But what *did* keep sixty thousand people dancing in place at a Grateful Dead concert—arms waving overhead, singing and whooping in unison, show after show, year after year, decade after decade, but calm, *becalmed*, bemushroomed (sometimes), taking it *all* in—as if the power of the stage, far from tearing them out of themselves, flooded them with grace? So that, as Kesey remarks, "the kids [would] watch five hours of mediocre music to have that one click happen, for that puts them in touch with the invisible."

With the Warlocks, the little family expanded to take in drummer Bill Kreutzmann, then working at the post office, which was the California musician's (also poet's) traditional employer. Kreutzmann, who had performed in a band at Palo Alto High called the Legends, whose members wore red jackets and did "At the Hop," was into rock 'n' roll, period. Jerry tapped him because he had heard good things about him as a drummer, not because he was a friend. Kreutzmann, in fact, was the first recruit who was not already a buddy. "I'd rather do things with friends," Garcia once said, " 'cause you want to turn your friends on—"

Garcia had first met Kreutzmann when he went to his house in 1963 to buy a banjo from his father, "Big Bill." Later, young Bill ended up working at Dana Morgan's, but he never heard Mother McCree's Uptown Jug Champions. With Bill Kreutzmann—who looked like "a surly, juvenile delinquent" to road manager Rock Scully when he first saw the band—the Warlocks got rhythm. Now, when he looked out at the audience, Garcia could see something new. People were dancing, really dancing, dancing to a beat.

For the first few months, Dana Morgan, Jr., little Dana, whose father supplied the Warlocks with their instruments, sat in on bass. After debuting at Magoo's, and playing Rolling Stones covers, also Jimmy Reed and Muddy Waters tunes (a preference that led many to see the Warlocks as Pigpen's band), the group started getting out-of-town gigs in Hayward, Redwood City, and at Family Dog shows at the Longshoreman's Hall in San Francisco. This last came about after Phil Lesh—an "arrogant youth, a composer of modernist music," Garcia once described him—replaced Dana Morgan early in 1965.

Phil Lesh's incorporation into the group marked a small but telling departure from the embryonic pattern of growth that Garcia's stewardship had followed until then. "When Lesh came along, it was a great deal more than a question of just replacing one musician with a better musician," Jerry's old Menlo Park pal Marshall Leicester observes. "Because Jerry took a real leap there"; and Leicester remembers "some of us chicken bourgeois types being afraid he'd lose his job at Morgan's by firing his boss's son." Dana Morgan, Sr., was, in effect, Jerry Garcia's first promoter.

When a few friends asked Phil to back off, he said, " 'No way, I've waited too long for this.' Phil," says Leicester, "was really ambitious and could be really hard-nosed in a way that was always difficult for Jerry." (When he first met Jerry Garcia, he hated him, Lesh once told Grateful Dead manager Jon McIntire, because, he said, "This guy has too much power.") But the edginess was useful, as time would tell, especially when Lesh's willfulness was directed outward, at getting the band's way. Garcia, who found confrontation of any kind distasteful, much preferred to deputize an unpleasant task to someone else. His seeming detachment from mundane issues of hiring and firing was often a ruse; and even in those early years, as Leicester, who teaches English literature at the University of California, Santa Cruz, recalls, "what often looked like a kind of narcissism on Jerry's part was in fact him being more intense and in a certain way much more ruthless than others." As for the "leap" he took with Lesh, that happened when "something which was partly being done as a concession to grown-up bourgeois life and the need to make money"—working for Dana Morgan and playing with his son—turned "into the possibility of making something greater. . . ."

Berkeley-born Phil Lesh hadn't come out of nowhere. Jerry had first met him at the Palo Alto Peace Center in 1961 when he and Bob Hunter were playing together in East Palo Alto. "Me and Phil . . . we were just in the same social world, really," Garcia said in 1983. He always knew that musically Phil was involved in "some amazing things." A couple of years older, and a friend of Page Browning, Lesh had made his way to the Chateau, and is remembered as a kind of mad scientist whose grand orchestral scores baffled even his musician friends. Once stuck in Las Vegas with his buddy Tom Constanten—another whiz kid who had a symphony performed when he was seventeen and later played with the Grateful Dead—Lesh had composed a piece, called "Foci," for four orchestras surrounding an audience. He had done this while working as a keno marker at the Horseshoe Club, after Constanten's father, the headwaiter at the Sands, had failed to find him and Tom better jobs. Before he was twenty-one, Lesh had written three symphonies and a few concertos (unproduced) for polytonal and atonal orchestras: "Conceptual music," one might call such fanfares, which need not be heard—and rarely are—to win a certain recognition.

In a sense, Garcia was returning a favor when he chose Phil Lesh. In 1962, after being impressed by Jerry's banjo playing when he heard it at a party, and by his ability to play acoustic guitar and sing, Phil had introduced him to the host of KPFA's "The Midnight Special" in Berkeley, where Lesh worked as engineer. After listening to a tape they made, she had engaged Jerry on the spot, and soon he became something of a KPFA regular.

The radio gig was prophetic. By 1966, when the Grateful Dead had settled in Haight Ashbury, FM radio, liberated from the lockstep programming of AM's three-minute songs, had become the new rock 'n' rollers' lifeline. Its nocturnal transmissions played the latest music and carried the community's news. "Our tribal drum," Rock Scully calls it. "Without FM," he contends, speaking of the takeoff years in San Francisco, there wouldn't have been "an audience large enough to sustain the Dead."

With Phil Lesh, there also arrived a new set of musical influences: jazz, mainly Ornette Coleman and Miles Davis, along with contemporary classical music—most notably the modernist compositions of Charles Ives, Karlheinz Stockhausen, Pierre Boulez, and Luciano Berio, with whom Lesh studied electronic music at Mills College. With the Grateful Dead, "I just saw myself as the bass player, essentially," he says today, while pointing out that the role of bass player in the Dead is very different from that in other outfits, in that (theoretically) he doesn't repeat himself. Because the Grateful Dead "evolved with collective improvisation," Lesh explains, "that means every voice is adding to the musical dialogue, or trialogue, or quadrilogue—moving the music while keeping it fresh, keeping it *changing*. Nobody in the band would just sit there and play the same thing over and over, which is what bass players mostly do."

Everybody in the band speaks with passion and precision about this business of improvisation, which is rarely the triumph of instinct over mind it's commonly believed to be, and which is no more mindless than talk that goes somewhere is thoughtless. Lesh and Garcia, speaking different tongues, endow it with a special intensity. In time, Lesh's familiarity with avant-garde music and musique concrète, along with his orchestral consciousness, helped set the Grateful Dead apart from better-known peers like the Lovin' Spoonful, Quicksilver Messenger Service, Big Brother and the Holding Company, and the Jefferson Airplane. But it would take a few years before such influences kicked in; and he could say (as he did in 1972, on the Dead's first European tour), "I've always thought of the music we play as 'electric chamber music,' which has been called the music of friends."

In 1965, he had never even played bass. " 'Here, Phil, here's a bass,' " Marmaduke Dawson remembers saying: "And Phil said, 'What do I do with it?' And I said, 'This is the A string, this is the E string and you get to make the E string be the same as the A string by pushing on the fifth fret. . . . The basic beat is boom boom boom and then you need to go up to here, boom boom, boom boom.' "

Lesh, who had played trumpet in the Berkeley High School jazz band and was said to have perfect pitch, even if his musical experience was mainly composition, mastered the basics in a few weeks. Still, it has been fairly said that both he and Bob Weir continued learning on the job throughout the 1960s, and that in the case of Weir, whose inability to read included sheet music, the apprenticeship continued through the 1970s. (As for Lesh's perfect pitch, it didn't always extend to his singing voice.) Even Jerry Garcia, who once told a Grateful Dead manager that he believed he was one of the best banjo players in the United States, was a relative newcomer on electric guitar (though he had briefly played one in high school). In 1965, only Pigpen impressed everyone as a pro; not only as a blues singer, playing harmonica, and as a backup musician on the electric organ but also as a beatnik, which was almost as important. Someone who partied with black hookers and drank Ripple, and led Jerry Garcia to say, "If you're going to hang out with Pigpen, you're taking your life in your hands." "Pigpen was the real beatnik," says Dawson. "Everybody else was imitation beatniks."

What really set the Warlocks apart from other bands, aside from their miscellaneous musical abilities, and a certain ragged edge—"A sorrier-looking bunch you never saw," writes Scully in *Living With the Dead;* you *knew* "they're never going to amount to anything"—was the sense these young men had of themselves as a gang. One sees them as a sort of refugee family, caught between the generations: less sixtyish than people think, more fiftyish. The romance with the Beats, for example, persisted long after Kerouac's star had burned out for many others their age. In 1960–1961, when Bob Hunter, Jerry Garcia, and their new English friend Alan Trist were devouring Kerouac, Ginsberg, and Henry Miller in Kepler's Bookstore, the Beat Generation had already been gobbled up by the media and fed back in bite-sized chunks in *Life* and *Time,* or so it seemed to me. A beatnik was a suburban kid, girl or boy, who dressed in black, listened to folk music or jazz, and carried a book, which was read and reread but remained on one's person, like Mountain Girl's "blankie." Such books were not likely to include *Howl,* Phil Lesh's favorite (he wanted to set it to music), which was already cropping up on college reading lists. Ginsberg's "I have seen the best minds of my generation destroyed by madness, starving hysterical naked, / dragging themselves through the negro streets at dawn looking for an angry fix . . ." struck the wrong declamatory note in an age of affluence tripping toward war. It was a cri de coeur of the '50s. (And has been again for restless youth in the '90s, along with *On the Road.*) Henry Miller's *Sexus, Nexus,* and *The Tropic of Capricorn,* which had just arrived in their cryptic green wrappers, and which fascinated Lesh and his friend Bob Petersen, as well as Alan Trist, were actually émigré products from the '30s.

I had my own rendezvous with bohemia in the summer of 1961, working as a waitress at the Wreck Club in Provincetown, and doing some painting, after graduating from college. In miniature, Provincetown carried something of San Francisco's sense of inhabiting the edge. In San Francisco's case, it was the western edge of a landmass across whose broad back countless pilgrims traveled in search of pleasure and enlightenment. Edge City, Kesey's name for the outer limits of consciousness visited on acid, couldn't have flourished anywhere else but on California's north coast. The Last Resort might be a better name for P'town, the fist of a brawny arm jutting out into the Atlantic, which, sociologically speaking, was an extension of New York's bohemia.

The diminutive *P'town* conveys a fall from grace, a terminal condition, it seemed when I was there, about which everybody was always talking. "You should have been here last summer . . . or the year before . . . or the year before that, when Hans Hofmann was still teaching in the East End," people would say after Hofmann's departure in 1961, when Franz Kline, Milton Avery, Jack Tworkov, and Seong Moy were still painting in town. Provincetown's Valhalla was dominated by the ghosts of the Provincetown Players, especially Eugene O'Neill, from the exciting years before World War I. Well-known writers had followed: John Dos Passos in the 1930s, Norman Mailer more recently, along with the Abstract Expressionists from New York. Jazz musicians like Zoot Sims and Mose Allison came and went while I was there; but the day-trippers had multiplied.

Provincetown's bohemia, however, still bristled with "the odd and the queer," as Mary Vorse, a founder of the Provincetown Playhouse, once called the town's eccentrics. In 1961, they were people of indeterminate occupation, with funny names, who seemed to come in pairs like animals off the Ark: Buster and Baby Elephant, Dot and Dutch. Others, like the Hat Lady, who danced upstairs at the Atlantic House, traveled alone; as did Wanda, Fat Frances, Popeye, and Crypto Terry, a literary impersonator who drove a yellow sports car and pretended to be the writer Terry Southern.

The Provincetown Players, more than a legendary theater group, had been that rare thing: a genuine community of artists, which, not unlike the Grateful Dead, saw itself as a "clan," one that had initially included the audience. As the preamble stated: "If there is nothing to take the place of the common religious purpose and passion of the primitive group, out of which the Dionysian dance was born, no new vital drama can arise in any people." Like the Dead, who wanted their clan to control *everything* (viz, All Our Own Equipment Company, and All Our Own Record Company, in the early '70s), the Provincetown Players had been driven by an instinct for self-sufficiency. "Why not write our own plays and put them on ourselves," they said, "giving writer, actor, designer a chance to work together without the commercial thing imposed from without?" As a matter of course, the plan would "furnish the kind of audience that will cause new plays to be written."

What united the original Provincetown bohemians, playwrights and painters both, was the idea "that Art was the great universal refreshment." Curiously, for such dissimilar folk, this is what united the founders of the Grateful Dead. "What we were interested in was art," recalls Alan Trist, who was nineteen when he and his father, Eric Trist, a Visiting Fellow at Stanford who founded the Tavistock Institute in London, arrived in Palo Alto in 1960. "It was the business of being an artist that totally captured Jerry and Hunter," he states, pointing out to me, when we meet at a bagel shop near the Dead's office in San Rafael, that it was "art in the sense in which art is free of the political frame of reference."

Trist, who runs the Grateful Dead's publishing company, Ice Nine, is a curious figure. In American folklore, he would be the fair Englishman who pops up on the frontier to go adventuring with the ruffians. In real life, he was the intellectual of the gang, whose fascination with the Beats was kindled in Paris before he came to California, when he worked briefly at Shakespeare and Company's bookstore near the Boulevard Michelin. In Palo Alto, he "got this feeling that the whole bohemian tradition that I was soaked in in Paris and London had just jumped the Atlantic." He remembers 1960–1961 as "a very literary year."

"A large part of our conversation was based on what we had been reading," Trist relates. "Or it was Jerry learning those folk songs. Or it was Hunter writing in his journal," or reading Dylan Thomas. "Or it was John the Poet who had an incredible collection of classical music"—mainly Bach. Early in 1961, when the Vatican's organist came to Grace Cathedral in San Francisco and played the complete organ works of Bach, Alan and Jerry had gone to hear him. Trist remembers looking up at the vaulted ceiling of the cathedral during a concert and "having a very psychedelic experience" (though LSD was still a few years away). In the patches of light and dark concrete, he saw faces, including D. H. Lawrence's, with whom he "carried on a silent conversation."

"Alan," according to Hunter, "was a heavy prime mover in getting us together to recognize ourselves as a *group*." But of them all, he adds, "Jerry was the only one who "always knew what he was doing; he was going to be a professional musician." Hunter wanted to be a novelist. But even Garcia, whose vision of himself as an artist was first kindled in the third grade by a pretty teacher who taught ceramics and papier-mâché, had originally thought of becoming a visual artist.

A high school dropout when he entered the Army in 1959—in part to escape both high school and home—Garcia had first trained to be a painter, before turning to music. The only formal schooling he ever had was at the California School of Fine Arts (now the San Francisco Art Institute), where, according to Barbara Meier, he connected with "action painting, abstract expressionism, and the jazz underpinnings of it all. The whole mix of Kerouac, Joyce, painting, poetry, and jazz" was grist for his mill. Meier's Jerry Garcia "was already [at nineteen] an incredible intellect, very well read," brimming over with "literary references" that included *Finnegans Wake*: "a psychedelic vision of reality" (beloved by Hunter), which he "got" long before he took psychedelics. "Very early on," she contends, "Jerry got the essential random nature of the art that James Joyce and John Cage represented." And he assimilated it, presumably, alongside the mysteries of Tolkien's *The Hobbit*—another favorite, which David Grisman remembers Jerry and Hunter reading a little later.

In 1965, The Hobbits was one of a dozen monikers that the Warlocks—whose name another band was already using—had considered before choosing the Grateful Dead. Others were Vanilla Plumbego, after an Edward Gorey book that Bob Weir liked, and Jerry's choice: Mythical Ethical Icicle Tricycle. The name Grateful Dead, as every Deadhead knows, chose itself when Garcia flipped open an old dictionary at Phil's house, "and there it was. . . . It was one of those moments," he told *Rolling Stone*, "like everything else on the page went blank, diffuse, just sorta *oozed* away, and there was *grateful dead. Big* black letters *edged* all around in gold, man, blasting out at me, such a stunning combination." A veritable fat trip. "So I said, 'How about Grateful Dead,' and that was it." In this version, the band was smoking the superpsychedelic DMT. In another, later account, Garcia didn't like the name at first but felt it was too powerful to ignore. Weir and Kreutzmann didn't like it, either, but "people started calling us that and it just started, *Grateful Dead, Grateful Dead*. . . ."

An entry from the 1955 *Funk and Wagnalls Dictionary* is cited by Deadheads:

GRATEFUL DEAD—The motif of a cycle of folk tales which begins with the hero's coming upon a group of people ill-treating or refusing to bury the corpse of a man who had died without paying his debts. He gives his last penny, either to pay the man's debts or to give him decent burial. Within a few hours he meets with a traveling companion who aids him in some impossible task. . . . The story ends with the companion's disclosing himself as the man whose corpse the other had befriended.

Tolkien was part of a fascination with the shadowy world of the Illuminati and Grail seekers, with cryptic medieval texts about the Philosopher's Stone and Dagobert the Horrible, which so interested the Warlock's manager Hank Harrison, as well as Lesh and Garcia. Such literature mirrors the altered states of an acid trip, as do certain folktales, with their merging of visible and invisible worlds. Trist, who read social anthropology at Cambridge after he returned to England in 1961, has retold the hero tale called "The Water of Life." Subtitled *A Tale of the Grateful Dead, The Water of Life* incorporates the folk motif of the Grateful Dead:

> "You have shown me kindness," the beggar said, "and the way to the Water of Life is long and hard. You must pass through the Dark Wood then climb high into the Mountains of the North where stands the castle of a fierce ogre. The object of your quest can be found there. In order to succeed you must defend yourself against enemies and give of yourself when no one asks."

What can one say about such fantasies, whose antiquated figures, dressed out with allusions to Sir Gawain and Dante, appear so simple and childlike? Except for the challenge: "give of yourself when no one asks," which taps out a code esteemed by Deadheads. And this passage?

> The prince pressed the petal to his lips and soon fell into a blissful slumber, dreaming of a golden road which wound through the mountains, down, down through a gorge of diamond waterfalls to the banks of a sweetly singing river, where he drank deeply and bathed as though cradled in its arms.

It's all there, all the mystic *stuff:* the *petals* and *diamonds* from "Dark Star," the first of Hunter's lyrics written with Jerry Garcia, and treasured by fans; the *golden road,* the *mountains* and *rivers* from a dozen Grateful Dead anthems. And the echoes of ballads from the British Isles known and admired by Jerry, Bob, and Alan. *The Water of Life* is what the tired Grail seeker, home from the office, might read to his or her children. Between it and *Howl* there would seem to exist an unbridgeable chasm. Yet such texts coexist in the Grateful Dead's arcanum in a way they do not anywhere else in American culture.

In Deaddom, the dreamy, folkish romanticism occupies the imagination's inner tract while the Beat sensibility patrols the perimeters. Quite early, the Grateful Dead moved from its original karma of defiant bohemianism to become a kind of sanctuary for audiences who were moved alternately by the music, the drugs, the dance, the *scene,* but who took comfort, in the end, in belonging to one another as much as to the band. It was Phil Lesh who once said, "I've always felt . . . that we could do something that was not necessarily extramusical, but something where the music would be only the first step, something even close to religion, not in the sense that 'the Beatles are more popular than Jesus,' but in the sense of the actual communing." Perhaps it was the flashes of recognition first experienced at the Acid Tests that led the band "to say that every place we play is church." The perception faded in the 1970s, according to Lesh, when a certain rigidity set in with the group's increasing reliance on the ballad material that inspired *Workingman's Dead* and *American Beauty.* The band's drugs changed, too, something Lesh didn't mention then but does when we talk in San Rafael. The openhanded experimental groping for new musical forms that psychedelics encouraged was supplanted by a harsher sensibility driven by cocaine.

From the Beats of the 1950s, Garcia, Lesh, and Hunter inherited their social cynicism and political indifference, also the romance of the hip, the cool. Being *cool* was no small part of Jerry Garcia's power. Being cool was not letting it hurt, or not letting anyone know it hurt. Keeping it light. "Well, I just see us as a lot of good-time pirates," he told a *Rolling Stone* reporter when "the missionaries of bliss" (as the reporter called the Dead's fans) started closing in on the band toward the end of the 1960s. "I'd like to apologize in advance to anybody who believes we're something really serious. The seriousness comes up as lightness, and I think that's the way it should be."

Plunked down in the midst of Palo Alto nearly forty years ago, Alan Trist thought he saw a resurgence of the bohemian traditions he had discovered on the Left Bank. Palo Alto, however, was where Beat poets Gary Snyder, Allen Ginsberg, and speed freak Neal Cassady passed the baton to California's hippies. If the Dead were singled out for special attention by Cassady, and they were, it was partly because of the Prankster tie, and the band's inexhaustible drug connections, but also because Cassady—a non-stop talker and "the ultimate sight gag" (Garcia)—found a stage with the Grateful Dead that nobody else supplied him. The remarkable ingathering Trist discovered was, in reality, the last hurrah for American bohemianism. Before the '60s were out, Ginsberg, Snyder, and others had taken cover in the sheltering arms of Tibetan Buddhism, in ashrams and later in multiplex arts centers, such as the Naropa Institute in Boulder, Colorado. Neal Cassady was found dead beside a railroad track outside San Miguel de Allende, Mexico, in 1968—cause of death (other than a superfluity of tequila and drugs) unknown.

Nothing like Palo Alto's changing of the guard was happening in Provincetown. What remained from the original bohemia was the street culture, the improvisatory rhythms of hipsters, which was also an element of the Dead's early culture. Acid, in fact, gave the tradition of *hanging out* new life, slowing down the clocks, shutting off alarms, phones, and opportunity's hard knocks, so that the moment's wonder might be explored in its plenitude. But acid also dissolved the cerebral, talky, disputatious edge of Beat culture. People rarely read books when they're high on acid, or write them. With exceptions, of course. Kesey turned out portions of *One Flew Over the Cuckoo's Nest* while working in the VA hospital in Menlo Park as a psychiatric aide, where he had continued his chemical investigations on his own. And Hunter wrote the song "What's Become of the Baby?" under the influence: "Panes of crystal / Eyes sparkle like waterfalls / lighting the polished ice caverns of Khan / But where in the looking-glass fields of illusion / wandered the child who was perfect as dawn?"

Deadheads are still hanging out. But one thing Deadheads are not is *cool.* At least not in the Beat sense. They lack the hipster's cynicism, with its occasional odor of idealism gone bad.

Provincetown's survivors were gentle people for the most part, like Buster, who had suffered a head injury playing football for Minnesota, which left him a little slow; he made papier-mâché death masks for tourists on Commercial Street. Some of my waiter friends were painters, or they were professional waiters who migrated to Key West or Martinique in the wintertime, and were excellent if fussy cooks. Other summer regulars dabbled in art heists and drug deals; although the only drug I saw besides pot was amyl nitrate, popped beneath the nose for an erotic buzz. A good many people were on their way to becoming drunks. Most were older than I, and this added to the thrill of living among them.

There was nothing of the "sense of awakening minds" that Alan Trist recalls about Palo Alto, as if it were yesterday. "We were all nineteen years old. We were just coming into adulthood, so the sense of discovery and adventure was strong. We were in the shadow of the bomb, the shadow of apartheid in South Africa. All those issues made our generation really questioning," he adds. Bertrand Russell was one of his great heroes. In 1958, Trist participated in the first Aldermaston march (from London to Aldermaston), which gave birth to the Campaign for Nuclear Disarmament. "We had a very intense experience of all that together," he asserts; and, like Bob Hunter, he "knew that something was going to come out of this," though not necessarily a rock band. Even after spending the rest of the '60s in England, he says, "I always had the sense that that year [1960–1961] was the roots of my consciousness."

In Provincetown, the sense of something *gone* was as strong as Palo Alto's sense of awakening. There was no youth culture, for one thing. The concept didn't exist, although the reality was gestating in California. There was nothing of what keyboardist Tom Constanten, referring to the counterculture's commercial edge, calls "the cult thing, which is really overlapping markets," such as "galvanized the 'sixties, cliques that are both cross-pollinating and secretive." There were no networks of buddiehoods, band families, tribes; of dealers and dealt, of pathbreakers and caretakers, such as attended the birth of the Grateful Dead.

Provincetown was on its way to becoming the day-tripper's mecca it is today, awash in ice cream, fudge, and candles—its summer landlord class dominated by graying homosexuals who started arriving in the '50s. It might not be worth recalling but for an extraordinary event that briefly stemmed the tide. This was an obscenity trial, the result of a sting operation engineered by the town's Portuguese police chief, known as "Cobra," against *The Provincetown Review*. A teenager was set up to buy the summer 1961 issue with Hubert Selby Jr.'s story of a gang rape, "Tralala"; and the editors, Bill Ward and Harriet Sommers, were charged with corrupting the morals of a minor. The magazine was temporarily shut down; and for a few weeks the bars emptied as the town packed the courtroom in Town Hall to watch the show.

Obscenity trials were to the Beats what defense trials later became for the antiwar movement: ceremonies of renewal in which virtue, the right of free expression in this case, mustered her patrons in time of battle. For the defendants, the trick was to maintain the offensive while protecting the injured party; to consolidate, perhaps extend, the virtuous cause. More often than not, victory for the defendant brought the cause to a standstill. That is, the new territory that had been opened up by the artist/activist was ploughed under in the effort to defend principles (the rule of law), rather than the new ideas under attack. So it was in Provincetown.

Summoned to the defense were the decidedly un-Beat writer and critic Allen Tate, poet Stanley Kunitz, and townie Norman Mailer. Together, they argued that "Tralala" was protected by her illustrious forebears, *Ulysses* and *Lady Chatterley's Lover,* whose First Amendment rights had already been won in court. Not much was heard from Harriet Sommers or Bill Ward. Hubert Selby Jr. wasn't there. Mailer kept the audience laughing at his back-and-forth with the curmudgeonly Yankee judge, and with Cobra, with whom he'd tilted before. For a while, it was as if the scandal-ridden Provincetown of old, with its lust for controversy (LEWD AND STEWED versus RUDE AND PRUDE proclaimed a two-sided sandwich board spoofing rival playhouses in the '20s), was back in business. Too young to experience a time warp, I did nonetheless.

But this was show business, with the drip-drip of celebrity poisoning the well, and nothing came of it. I don't remember the verdict; guilty, I see now, with the prosecutor's case later overturned on appeal down the Cape in Barnstable. The summer of 1961, meanwhile, turned out to be a turning point for me. The business of being an "artist" no longer interested me as much as the larger world of politics that was opening up outside my window. When I went to the University of Chicago in the fall, it was to get an M.A. in literature so I could teach, which I did, but already one foot was out the door.

In the summer of 1964, another obscenity trial opened to a packed hall in San Francisco Municipal Court. The outsized metal sculptures of Ron Boise, creator of the Pranksters' Thunder Machine, was the cause célèbre. *Set* and *setting,* the acid-tripper's compass, couldn't have been more different from that on the outer Cape, and so, naturally, was the outcome. As in Provincetown, famed experts testified for the defendant: a gallery owner selling Boise's *Kama Sutra*–inspired renderings of couples making love. There the parallel ended. The trial, which attracted all manner of concerned hipsters, including the Merry Pranksters and Jerry's gang— "Boise was one of us," Hank Harrison recalls, "so it was like we were all on trial"—was widely touted as an art seminar. By its close, everyone knew enough about art, from the Greeks through modern times, to understand why Ron Boise's sculptures did not violate contemporary standards; also why they had redeeming social importance, and were thus protected by the First Amendment.

Inside the Municipal Court building, another drama was playing itself out, one that happened whenever the tribes converged to defend their own. This was the swarming of the neo-Beats in search of a new queen. By 1967, they would find one in Jerry Garcia. When the Haight was a "big anarchistic family, with the bands as a sort of primal father and we as happy, naive children," Jerry Garcia, a participant wrote at the time, "was the archetypical mayor. . . ." Sometimes he even talked like one. "We're a nation of outlaws," Garcia proclaimed after a much-publicized pot bust at Grateful Dead headquarters on October 2, 1967. "A good outlaw makes a new law, makes it okay to do what he's doing." But more often his influence lay in the quiet power he exercised within his own charmed circle. That, and a musical ambition that fed on itself, alongside the peculiar sense he always conveyed of having a role to play in the larger culture, drew people to him.

PART II TAKEOFF

~CHAPTER~
5

COURTING THE STRANGE

ENTHUSIASM. It furthers one to install helpers
And to set armies marching.

Thunder comes resounding out of the earth:
The image of ENTHUSIASM.
Thus the ancient kings made music
In order to honor merit,
And offered it with splendor
To the Supreme Deity,
Inviting their ancestors to be present.

I CHING

"MOST BANDS HIT a song fast, then stretch out for a while, ending up with a bang," writes Greil Marcus. "The Dead go into a song slowly, tentatively, and build up an atmosphere until everyone is inside the music. Then they take off, exploring the figures over and over again with that super rhythm section. If you're outside it, it can be boring," he observes from his perch at the Santa Clara County Fairgrounds on May 18, 1968. "But when they get to you, it's incredible and hypnotic, as if the music was happening inside you."

The Fairgrounds' crowd in San Jose, California, was a little green—not a Haight Ashbury audience, but country cousins, and young, very young. "These kids came from the Scouts, from Sunday School, mowing the lawn for chores and maybe getting a pony for Christmas. And they're going straight out of that world toward the world of Pigpen and Janis. It's a big jump," Marcus comments. Even with a hard-driving lineup that included the Doors, Big Brother and the Holding Company, Jefferson

89

Airplane, Country Joe and the Fish, and Taj Mahal, the bands were having trouble warming the kids up. It was the Grateful Dead playing "Alligator" that "blew the place wide open." After the remarkable middle section had gone on for half an hour, the music trailed off into percussion sounds, then the *clang-clang* of a cymbal, then silence. The audience stood transfixed, barely clapping, as if some fundamental musical experience—the transformation of sound into emotion—was working its way through the collective psyche.

A telling scene. Not Lucy in the Sky with Diamonds, but Dick and Jane on the Yellow Brick Road, it stands apart from the flash of paisley images that usually adorn the tale of the glory days of the Grateful Dead. The Acid Tests were over. No more "room games" when rolls of toilet paper were hurled back and forth, trailing beautiful streamers, and (as Mountain Girl recalls) "there was lots of crawling on your hands and knees on the floor, laughing." No more exhortations to GET NEKKID! FREAK FREELY! KISS YOUR BRAINS GOOD-BYE! with Kesey's voice inviting everyone to *"Stay in your own movie."* Or Ken Babbs playing electronic pinball with the house sounds from the Tower of Power. The movie had jumped the Pranksters' closed-circuit television screens, which had helped train the audience to see *themselves* as performers. The magic show was on the road.

It was the Acid Tests that had created the audience for the San Francisco ballrooms. These were funky dance halls such as the Carousel on the corner of Market and Van Ness, which was owned by the League of Irish Voters, and briefly leased by the Dead and the Airplane; and the Fillmore Auditorium, formerly used by the Fillmore District's black community, where people could sit or stand or dance as they wished, and the bands played from the floor. Union headquarters like California Hall and the Longshoreman's Hall, also the Avalon Ballroom, were brought into the new era by a commune called the Family Dog, after their own dances on Waller Street spilled out on the sidewalks.

In October 1965, the Family Dog's Chet Helms, who later managed Big Brother and the Holding Company, produced the first "dance concert" at the Longshoreman's Hall. Called "A Tribute to Dr. Strange," after the comic book character Doctor Strange, the music was supplied by Jefferson Airplane and the Great Society. Two months later, the San Francisco Mime Troupe's business manager, Bill Graham, staged a benefit at the Fillmore Auditorium to raise money for the defense of Ronnie Davis, the Mime Troupe founder, who had been arrested for performing in a city park without a permit. Both events were huge successes, and the ballroom fever spread. Along with the old Straight Theatre, which was brought back to life when the Grateful Dead played there in June 1967, they were all places where Jerry Garcia's father might have worked. Playing them a dozen times a year in the middle '60s, Jerry, a fifth-generation San Franciscan on his mother's side, had come home.

Music critic Joel Selvin, who started working for the *San Francisco Chronicle* as a copyboy around this time, remembers the halls, as do others, via the senses. The liquid light images weren't projected onto screens; they "*covered* the end of the room," along with flashing strobes. The smell of incense was mixed with pot, and with the odors of bodies twisting and bobbing to music that seemed very loud at the time, and was. It was a case of "sensory envelopment," Selvin says, "an overload."

At the *Chronicle,* by early 1967, the popular columnist Ralph J. Gleason had already singled the Grateful Dead out as "hippier and happier than any almost any group that comes to mind." Along with the Charlatans, Country Joe and the Fish, and Big Brother and the Holding Company, Gleason wrote, the Dead had "plugged San Francisco into a rock movement which now exerts a nationwide influence on pop music." A principal force behind all this, he added, was "Jerry (Captain Trips) Garcia . . . regarded by some critics as one of the best guitarists in the country." As for the nickname, Jerry earned it, his friends told Gleason, "because 'everything is a trip with him.' "

For the Dead, the San Francisco ballrooms created the audience for Winterland; for the Fairgrounds in San Jose, the Dream Bowl in Vallejo, and beyond. When they began touring in 1967, Rock Scully and comanager Danny Rifkin, a former U.C. Berkeley student from the Bronx, booked similar halls in other cities: the Grande Ballroom in Detroit, the American Legion Hall in Lake Tahoe, the Eagles Auditorium in Seattle, the Stanley Theater in Pittsburgh, the Capitol Theater in Port Chester, New York, and in Manhattan, two former vaudeville halls in a nest of appetizing stores in the East Village, the Anderson Theater and the Fillmore East.

At home, the ballrooms served the Bay Area bands as induction centers for a scene whose vibrancy sprang from the music, the dancing, the light shows and posters. All these art forms were products of a community in the process of fashioning a culture. Especially was this true of the Grateful Dead, whose shoestring productions were the work of a loose network of friends and family. "Acid networks," Garcia called them: "the old line of communication . . . one or two guys that go back and forth," sometimes dealers, sometimes musicians. An original liquid light show producer, Bill Ham, did the lights for the early shows; he was followed by Jerry Abrams and Glen McKay, whose team called itself Headlights, and by Mary Ann Mayer (now a Carmelite nun) and her "traveling light show." The band's dealer Owsley Stanley financed the equipment and ran the sound system until his tabbing factory in Orinda was raided in late 1967, and he was sentenced later to three years in prison (one served). Owsley also conceived the original skull and lightning bolt logo, used on the jacket of the 1976 album known as *Steal Your Face.* The rendering was done by artist Bob Thomas.

During the Acid Tests, an entire show at the Fillmore Auditorium might cost $350, with $200 going to rent the hall. Tickets were $1.50 or $2, slightly more for benefits, which were frequent. By 1967, with Bill Graham running the Carousel, which was renamed the Fillmore West, and Chet Helms the Avalon, the bands were paid flat fees—not yet percentages—of from five hundred to two thousand dollars a gig. More popular groups like the Airplane, Big Brother, Quicksilver, and the Dead got the higher amounts. The scene was pretty woolly. "Fellini on stage," remembers Warner Bros. executive Joe Smith, who was sent in his "Bank of America blue suit with striped tie" to check out the Grateful Dead. "People lying on the floor. Body painting. Light shows. Incense. And this droning set from the Dead." But what did he know? As soon as he started talking to the band, he got calls from colleagues around the country: "Wow. You're going to have the Dead? Okay!" In 1967, the Grateful Dead's equipment weighed thirteen hundred pounds and fit into Laird Grant's van. By the Santa Clara Fairgrounds show, it weighed around six thousand pounds and still fit in a van, a much larger one.

In the mid-'60s, the Dead were still one of dozens of Bay Area bands mutating out of high schools, colleges, and coffeehouses, and, in the case of Country Joe McDonald (my favorite), out of the Berkeley political scene. Another group, the Charlatans, who billed themselves as "the first psychedelic band," had also been the first to land a grown-up gig, at a saloon in Virginia City in the summer of 1965. Led by San Francisco State student George Hunter, the Charlatans had pioneered the outlaw motif. In publicity pictures, they look like a cross between Mississippi riverboat gamblers and cowboys dressed in their Sunday best. They were showmen who enjoyed parading around hotels and the San Francisco Airport with empty instrument cases under their arms. Probably this, along with too much extracurricular talent, marked their musical career for an early demise.

Charlatan Mike Ferguson went on to open the Magic Theatre for Mad Men Only, San Francisco's first head shop, which sold dope along with pipes and papers, antiques and old books. And George Hunter, who admired the work of Maxfield Parrish, is credited by some for introducing the Victorian aesthetic into Haight Ashbury graphics. Wes Wilson, no relation to the Charlatans, originated the basic psychedelic type style known as "24 pt. Illegible," which had infuriated Bill Graham when he couldn't read the posters he ordered for the Fillmore. (He was mollified when he learned he could sell them afterward for a dollar each.) The undulating Art Nouveau lettering in the famous dance hall posters of Rick Griffin, Stanley Mouse, and Michael Bowen owes a debt in part to George Hunter and Wes Wilson.

There were other bands, such as the Jefferson Airplane, that lived together like the Dead did, "but never in the embryonic state where you were working together, living together, dealing with each other's day-to-day shit," the Airplane's Jorma Kaukonen recalls. This is what the Dead did, first in Palo Alto and then in Los Angeles, where Owsley set them up after the Trips Festival in late January 1966. That was the two-day multiband carnival, organized by Stewart Brand, which grossed twelve thousand dollars, alerting Bill Graham to the Grateful Dead's draw. It was the Trips Festival, with its huge banners, flags, and cascading lights, that gave Bay Area artisans a chance to strut their stuff on a common stage. After six months in Owsley's L.A. laboratory, meanwhile, where the Dead honed their skills for a takeoff they all sensed was coming, the band moved into a rooming house that Danny Rifkin managed at 710 Ashbury, installing Pigpen first to flush out the tenants.

By then, Mountain Girl had returned from Manzanillo, Mexico, where she and a string of Pranksters had holed up with Kesey during his flight from a San Mateo, California, drug charge. In Mexico, she had given birth to the baby she named Solano, or Sunshine (which was close enough—*solano*, she soon discovered, means "sunporch"). To ensure the baby's U.S. citizenship, she had married the blond Prankster with the foxy epaulets, George Walker. Kesey already had a wife, Faye, who had returned to Oregon with their three small children.

From Manzanillo, where they stayed six months, Kesey, anticipating his return, had been in touch with Rock Scully and Danny Rifkin—or "Rockinrifkin," as he called the Dead's managers, thinking they were a single person—to line up the Grateful Dead for the next-to-last Acid Test. This took place on October 2, 1966, at San Francisco State University (where Rock and Rifkin were then enrolled as part-time students), a few days before the government made possession of LSD by ordinary citizens a federal crime. The last Test was the Acid Test Graduation on October 31, 1966, a dry run three weeks after LSD was declared illegal. There Kesey had not exactly sworn off the drug but spoke vaguely of "a life beyond acid."

It was at the San Francisco State gig that Rock Scully's then-girlfriend, Valerie Steinbrecher, known as "Tangerine," remembers watching Mountain Girl and Jerry Garcia "connect. As far as I know, it went boom! He played to her all night. You could feel it," she says. It was a *coup de foudre*. Mountain Girl had cut her long dark hair and dyed it blond. Sunshine was two or three months old, and her mother carried her around in a little straw basket. "She's an R. Crumb hippie-chick vision, swinging her bright orange bleached hair . . . her kid with Kesey bouncing in the basket on her back, and just *beaming* at Jerry," Scully recalls. Jerry had pursued this celebrated young Prankster with an intensity that was almost, but not quite, as fierce as the intensity with which he worked on a new song or chord change.

And Kesey? It wasn't that Jerry "got her away" from him, Sue Swanson remarks. "She was fascinated with Jerry and the Dead's trip. And perhaps the Prankster thing had gotten a little stale for her at that point." Kesey's charisma, in fact, would sink after the Acid Test Graduation, when it was perceived that he had buckled under the combined pressures of LSD's criminalization and the jail sentences pending against him.

"The Acid Tests were over. . . . [T]he Pranksters had split up and everybody went their separate ways. That's when Jerry and I moved together," declares Mountain Girl when we talk. It's the "spiraling up" of energy in San Francisco at the time that interests her more than the lightning transition. "The whole city," she says, "was *buzzing* with young people's energy wanting stuff to happen, and the Haight was starting to boil over." Confrontations with cops were not yet the order of the day; nor had hard drugs and their capos implanted themselves in the soft loamy soil of the youth culture. "The energy out there on the street was so friendly and warm and sort of excited. It was extremely pleasant, and it really went to your head," she says, grinning and inhaling deeply, as if it were still wafting about.

Inside 710 Ashbury, the energy had imploded. The big Victorian row house with the gingerbread porch and sky blue stoop was packed with people whose faces changed from week to week. Some lived out of closets, others in the basement or up in the attic, where Neal Cassady briefly camped. Dozens of toothbrushes sprouted in the bathrooms. At first, Jerry, Mountain Girl, and Sunshine burrowed into a tiny bedroom. Nobody ever saw them, Scully recalls, because they never came out—theirs being "a great big love." Mountain Girl remembers it all as a "wonderful scene." It possessed that elemental chaos that drew forth her best managerial efforts.

Plaster was falling from the ceilings; and the house was usually filthy, with musical instruments stacked along the wainscoting, and ashtrays overflowing with cigarettes and joints. A huge American flag covering one wall—against which Gene Anthony first photographed the Grateful Dead—comprised the most notable interior decoration. Skip Workman recalls another: a long oak trestle table with silver candelabra that melted before his eyes into pools of liquid silver while he was tripping during a visit. Nobody cleaned or cooked, and only Bob Weir knew where the nearest grocery store was. So Mountain Girl took charge, planning meals, getting the boys to shop, shaming Scully into vacuuming—until Jon McIntire, another former manager, arranged for a couple of friends to help with housekeeping.

Talking to a young woman reporter from the *San Francisco Examiner* in 1997, Mountain Girl concedes that she wasn't happy about being relegated to caretaker status. "Not at all. It was sort of the unfortunate consequences of my . . . procreative act"; and "this concentration on the domestic side [was] certainly not intentional on my part. But God," she exclaims, "if somebody didn't cook, do you know what they would eat? . . . Chips and

Twinkies. Ratburgers." Besides, she wasn't a musician, she adds. She tried to run the soundboard for a while, but with Sunshine in tow, she was distracted and missed too many cues, and so she was dismissed.

Gone were the days when she would crouch in an old Chevy the Pranksters used as an isolation booth, trying to record a hit record with Neal Cassady. When the Grateful Dead started touring in 1967, there was no more room for amateur electronics. "I didn't really have a role [in the band], and Jerry didn't seem to want me to have a role," Mountain Girl said. This is proffered without rancor. Nor does she blame Jerry for being upset over a book she published in 1970 about organic gardening and marijuana growing—"my revolutionary text"—entitled *The Primo Plant*. He believed it would make him an easier bust. She felt exposed by it, too, but believed she knew how to avoid getting busted—by not sticking her neck out. Never selling, never buying. Being self-sufficient. "I was a mom with kids," she reminds me; having had a daughter, Annabelle, with Jerry in 1970, who was followed in 1974 by Theresa.

Mountain Girl is no feminist, at least not in the popular sense of the term. She doesn't make an easy victim. Jon McIntire relates that when she met Jerry, MG told him "she recognized in him that his music was the stuff of greatness. And she wanted to help that greatness." It's what Sara Ruppenthal remembers feeling, too: "that he was destined for greatness, and that I had a role to play. To help him." Like Mountain Girl, who says that if Jerry went for a few days without playing, he'd be afraid he'd never be able to play again, Sara recounts how he might work for two or three days on a single phrase. She would make him coffee, keep him in cigarettes, and sometimes scold him for spending his Dana Morgan's paycheck on grass—all the while keeping house and taking care of baby Heather. "His real relationships were in the music [scene]," she reflects, "not his family." Mountain Girl would agree. Jerry Garcia acknowledged as much himself when, years later, in that roundabout fashion in which public figures reach out to their families—through interviews with the press—he thanked all his daughters for putting up with his vagabond ways. (After his death, twenty-five-year-old Annabelle Garcia ventured a reply. "He was a cool father," she said, "but a shitty dad.")

"Jerry loved his work," says Mountain Girl, recalling a period when they lived in Marin County. "His whole thing was to drive to San Francisco, play a gig, go home, go to sleep, get up, have breakfast, drive to San

Francisco, play a gig . . . that was it for him. That was the world. That was his happiest space. He was a pro," and nothing could interfere with this routine. "It would have been like a ballplayer missing a game. How could you do that? And that level of his dedication," she notes, "really fired everybody."

The division of labor that left her in solitary charge of hearth and home was broken once in July 1968, after they had moved out of 710 Ashbury. They had bought a little TV and a secondhand Plymouth station wagon and settled into a semblance of domestic life. When the Dead had a gig in a bowling alley called Kings Beach Bowl in Lake Tahoe, and the ticky-tacky motel was fouler than most, Jerry had proposed they camp out. Mountain Girl made her checklist, shopped for food, and assembled the gear and sleeping bags. With Jerry at the wheel, they headed down a logging trail in the Sierra Mountains to a little clearing off the road. Jerry slammed the station wagon over a rock or stump, and Mountain Girl thought (unnecessarily, as it turned out), "Oh, hell. We're going to be stuck here forever." The sun set and the mosquitoes came out, but it was a beautiful spot, and Jerry surprised her. "He bustled all around and built a little fire and he cooked some steak and potatoes in tinfoil. . . . We spent the night looking at the stars and it was as sweet as it could possibly be," she says; "the only time we ever did anything like that and it was completely on his whim."

Jerry and Mountain Girl lived together unmarried from 1967 to early 1975, during which time Mountain Girl was still technically married to George Walker. By 1975, she and Jerry had separated and Mountain Girl was living most of the time in Oregon. After she divorced Walker, she and Jerry were married in a perfunctory ceremony, largely for tax reasons, at a New Year's Eve concert in Oakland Coliseum in 1981. They gave their address as the Grateful Dead's office on the corner of Lincoln and Fifth in San Rafael, and continued to live apart.

Mountain Girl is the matriarch of the golden age of the Grateful Dead. To thousands of Deadheads, the much-publicized court battle in the winter of 1996–1997 between "Dark Deborah," as MG's partisans called Jerry Garcia's third wife, Deborah Koons Garcia, and Carolyn Adams Garcia (MG) had the quality of a morality play. On the docket was not only the formal question of whether wife number three had to pay off wife number two, per her late husband's agreement. (Answer: yes.) Nor was it Mountain Girl's on-again, off-again relationship with Jerry Garcia, the legal status of which Deborah Koons Garcia contested, albeit unsuccessfully. On trial also was the romantic bohemianism of the 1960s, whose sole surviving standard-bearer, in the opinion of many fans, is the Grateful Dead.

"The problem is that mom and dad had a real hippie relationship," observes Annabelle Garcia, "and you cannot explain a '60s relationship in legal terms." And it's true: The "spiraling up" of youthful energies that Mountain Girl evokes is hard to convey in the context of today's culture, which is *anti*romantic, fearful of upheaval, and suspicious, especially of the young. Deborah Koons Garcia's courtroom remark—that "the thing about the whole communal deal in the '60s [was that] you couldn't get rid of anybody"—perfectly expresses our bureaucratic soul. A middle-aged culture is what we have, and in ten or fifteen years it will probably be a geriatric one, for the baby boomers are still driving the train. Everywhere, we'll read about growing older, nearer to God or self. We are like a "rat moving through the body of a python," journalist Andy Kopkind once wrote, "intact and isolated from everything before and behind it, still self-conscious and undigested."

Death, which is already being turned into a *good,* a *good* death, something to work for and possess, will become the great subject of the age. When that happens, another side of the Grateful Dead's legacy, evident in Robert Hunter's lyrics, may acquire new luster. This is the romance with death and loss that one finds in the songs, an undertow of resignation that kicks in especially with *Workingman's Dead* and *American Beauty* in 1970—which is when the energies out there on the street, once so friendly and excited, turned mean.

In 1966–1967, meanwhile, the communal experience, with Jerry and Mountain Girl at the helm, had bonded the Grateful Dead in a most extraordinary way. It seemed to Jorma Kaukonen as if "their band family almost superseded their personal lives." The band family, starting with Mother McCree's, *was* family. The family that lived together and dropped acid together would play together, through the death of three key-boardists, until the death of the leader parted them (temporarily).

Looking back, one might think the communalism that infused the Dead with its air of collective ecstasy put the band family ahead of its time. Thus, the Grateful Dead anticipated the communes and cooperatives that spread across the land in the late '60s—those eccentric establishments that lent the political movement of which I became a part the air of another country: labile, unpredictable, subject to influences from beyond the pale. It's true that the band was part of the original wave of communards whose domestic arrangements constituted a point of departure from the bohemians of the '50s. But the notion of alternative lifestyles didn't interest the Dead. Within the group, attention centered on the work, the gigs. Music was the product. Fun was the by-product, when possible. The shared experience, the bonding agent, was often worry.

"Every day you'd wake up and there was always some kind of psychodrama going on. One person was disagreeing with another or they were going to fire Weir," Sue Swanson remembers. "Pig was not playing right or somebody was being a motherfucker or Billy was pulling some maneuver with the money." For many years Swanson "lived and breathed by what was happening" in the band. Later, living apart, she and others found themselves still caught in a collective drama that snuck into conversations, invading thoughts and erupting into dreams, as if a group mind were bottom-feeding inside one's innermost self.

The Grateful Dead's family was not rooted in either the radical or separatist impulses that inspired some of the well-known communes of the period, like the Red Family in Berkeley or Red Clover and Total Loss Farm (aka Packer Corners) in Vermont. But it was hardly immune to utopian fantasies about drugs, and it embodied these fantasies more persuasively and persistently than any other group in the 1960s. "We used to believe *sincerely* that marijuana was going to be legalized 'next year.' We were so sure that common sense would prevail," Mountain Girl relates. Legalization of pot had almost won on a couple of California ballots. In the Psychedelic Shop near the intersection of Haight and Ashbury, where the shelves were stacked with esoterica, smoking paraphernalia, dance hall posters, paisley fabrics, and Indian bells, owner Ron Thelin hoped the Haight might become "a world famous dope center." There would be fine tea shops with big jars of Acapulco Gold, and drugstores with unadulterated LSD. About acid, however, the Dead nurtured fewer illusions and grander dreams.

With the criminalization of LSD on October 6, 1966, acid slipped deeper into a subculture that was fully equipped to supplant former pharmaceutical and government supplies. The first big surge of street acid had hit colleges and youth communities in the fall of 1965, after another eventful summer. President Johnson had increased U.S. troop strength in Vietnam to 125,000, and had sent 20,000 marines to the Dominican Republic on a "police action." Malcolm X had been assassinated in February, and rioting broke out in Watts that August. The second half of the 1960s was pervaded by a sense of daily apocalypse, as countless testimonies have shown, so that one may be excused if, in retrospect, the years weigh in like decades. Augustus Owsley Stanley III, the grandson of a Kentucky senator, had begun supplying LSD to the California market in 1965 out of an underground lab he ran with a University of California chemistry major, Melissa Cargill, on Virginia Street in Berkeley, and then from a larger one in nearby Richmond with a second partner, Tim Sculley. Allen Cohen, who edited the Haight's psychedelic paper *The Oracle,* and who later helped organize the Human Be-In in Golden Gate Park, sold the stuff on the street. In the Bay Area, and in New York, *Owsley,* as in "Owsley Blues," spoken with a lift of the eyebrow, carried the same weight as *Sandoz.* (Owsley Blues, with an image of Batman on the blotter paper, marked a 500-microgram hit, a big one.)

By 1966, Owsley and Cargill had stockpiled over eight hundred grams of the base material, lysergic acid monohydrate, from chemical supply houses in Southern California. After the ban, Owsley and Tim Sculley found new sources in Israel and Switzerland. Eight hundred grams yielded approximately 2,500,000 doses of LSD, which sold for one to two dollars a dose wholesale. Volume, not markup, determined the enormous profits reaped by this operation—a substantial portion of which helped launch the Grateful Dead. The mom-and-pop production figures for the band in the mid-'60s, reported in the *Grateful Dead Family Album,* skirt the hidden costs of the insatiable appetite for new gadgets that Owsley (or "Bear," as he was called) stimulated in the band—synthesizers that could make music out of any sound and a stereo PA system years ahead of its time. "It was Bear who turned a set of speakers around one day and let the band hear themselves," says Joel Selvin, "thus inventing stage monitors." With this mad scientist of sound ("Gyro Gearloose" was another nickname), Jerry Garcia and Phil Lesh were in their element.

Owsley had been drawn to the Dead at the Muir Beach Acid Test on

December 18, 1965, when he experienced a dazzling "gestalt." It was as if the music and drugs had burned away the psychic insulation that kept one person apart from another: "like a hymen," he said in 1991, "a mental hymen. And then the connection would be made, and all the people would be linked up and start sharing thoughts and images and ideas." Garcia's guitar sounded like "the claws of a tiger." It scared him and thrilled him at the same time. "You can't talk about this stuff," he thought to himself, but he could "subvocalize a revelation"—namely, that this band was "going to be greater than the Beatles. . . ."

At the Watts Test a few months later, Owsley *saw* the sound coming out of the speakers; and the experience joined two passions: a reverence for LSD as "a pathway to another place," which "seemed to give you access to mental powers" known to ancient alchemists, Rosicrucians, and Freemasons, whose literature he read as science. And it focused a talent for manipulating sound on a worthy subject: the band. Following the Watts Test, which took place six months after the Watts riots, Owsley no longer saw himself as the electrical engineer he had trained to be, nor as a chemist, but as an *artist*. After *seeing* sound, he would accept whatever psychedelics disclosed to him as real, "more real, perhaps, than my everyday life," which was governed by a "restricted consciousness. . . ."

There was but a hop and a skip between Owsley's fevered imagination, wired for sound and hungry for a recognition that his secret trade denied him, and the Grateful Dead's inexhaustible appetite for drugs, amps, and synthesizers, not to mention its expanding charisma, available to anyone who could serve its growing need for logistical support. The Dead's own evolving metaphysic, meanwhile, or at least Jerry Garcia's, was remarkably similar to Owsley's.

Owsley on alchemy, for instance, sounds like Garcia on the mindfulness of "consciousness." To David Gans, Owsley explains that the "basic tenet of alchemy is that the universe is mental, that there's a being which is nothing but mind, pure mind, and that all that we experience is the creation of this mind." This is proffered to account for why his experience with psychedelics has led him to regard *plants* as highly conscious entities, possibly because they aren't troubled by having an ego and making decisions. Gans, a rationalist, wonders if perhaps Owsley isn't "construing consciousness rather broadly"—a question not unlike the mild objection he raised in 1981 to Jerry Garcia's attribution of "vast wisdom" to a higher consciousness. As he got deeper into psychedelics, Garcia, too, construed consciousness rather broadly, suggesting that "[i]t might be that consciousness is the whole reason there is a universe." For him (as for Owsley), "we're just like other animals on this planet. We're fuckin' around is all." What psychedelics revealed was "that the operating system is more wise than what we are able to stick into our consciousness."

The vernacular is California crude, but the vision, with its objectification of *consciousness*—apprehended on acid and refined in sobriety—is of a piece with the divinations of nineteenth-century American transcendentalists. In the exaltation of "pure mind" and the purposefulness of consciousness, one hears Emerson discoursing on the Oversoul, which permeates creation and is present in all living things. Substitute the word *consciousness* for *Nature* in the lines from Emerson's poem "Experience," and you have an ode to Garcia's "me which is this sort of cringing, ineffectual, completely powerless dumbshit. . . ."

> Little man, least of all,
> Among the legs of his guardians tall,
> Walked about with puzzled look.
> Him by the hand dear Nature took

"Nature" rescues mere mortals from the chaos and meaninglessness of unreflected experience, just as "consciousness" or "mind" (cum LSD) lends order and meaning to the indignities of personal life. In Garcia's and Owsley's vision, however, "little man" is lost; "the butt of a cosmic joke," Garcia calls a human being. Gone is the nineteenth-century optimism that urges the free citizen of a newly independent nation to reach for the stars. In its place is a kind of pantheism, profoundly pessimistic, almost medieval in its evocation of personal limits: as if the "powerless dumbshit" is a sinner crawling on wounded knees to kiss the hem of his Savior.

Owsley's pantheism embraced inanimate objects, as well. After noting that the powerful psychedelic DMT (another product of Bear Research) made music sound louder, more strident, he proceeded to measure the amps with and without someone smoking the compound, in order to determine whether output increased in its presence. It did, he said: fourfold.

"Believe it's real," Melissa Cargill had always insisted of such phenomena. "Don't assume that this is an illusion caused by the substance." *Test* it. *Test* it. A faith worth having is a faith worth testing.

Owsley saw the Grateful Dead as among the "smartest people" he had ever met. It was "the art of the scene" that impressed him: "doing something that was right out on the edge, the edge of consciousness, the edge of social, the edge of magic, the edge of music. . . ." There is no doubt that he was a player in the band's formative years, even if he was something of "a magic wolf in sheep's clothing." More crank than genius as the years wore on, Owsley, according to Hank Harrison, "was a monumental paranoic personality, with elaborate delusions of grandeur," who screamed at people as if he was the owner of the band, and glared at women who refused to bend to his will.

In the 1980s and '90s, he made jewelry and sold it at concerts, where he was a familiar figure—usually barefoot, wearing shorts and a tank top, the better to display a carefully tended body. "Geez, you know, besides everything else everyone has gone through, Bear would be there flexing his muscles," comments a second-generation member of the Dead's family, Cassidy Law, who was asked to "feel his muscles" once too often. "He's into Chinese astrology and talkin' to young girls," a young actress in New York, Carla Murray, reports. When she encountered Owsley at concerts in later years, "he seemed a little burnt," she says gently. "You're the rat. You were born in '65? You're the rat," he would say, whenever he saw her; and he could never stop talking about the album *Bear's Choice,* which the Grateful Dead named after him. But there is little question that the L.A. interlude Owsley made possible in 1966, coming as it did before the Acid Tests were over, bonded the Dead during a peak experience in their lives.

For the Lost Boys, Owsley made a better Wendy than either Sara Ruppenthal or Mountain Girl, though one might question the strict carnivore's diet of red meat, eggs, and milk—no fruit or vegetables—that he enforced in the communal house on Laffler Road where they lived for a few months. It wasn't a tidy shop. The German pill-making machine that stamped out the drugs upstairs dusted everything, as in a psychedelic bakery, with a thin purple powder. But he paid the bills. The band made their per diems hustling "samples" with other musicians and supplying the gofers from Hollywood with Owsley's latest. "Bear bought us time and space," says Lesh. "It was patronage in the finest sense; he never once thought about the money."

After April 1966, Sandoz had stopped shipping lysergic acid to anyone in the United States but the CIA and the Pentagon's Chemical and Bacteriological Warfare (CBW) labs. Once the miracle drug had burst the confines of academe and the doctor's office—not to mention the research facilities of MK-ULTRA—LSD had fallen afoul of a drumbeat of bad press notices. It was almost as if an understanding had been reached between government and media that maybe it was time to batten down the hatches.

Scare headlines—A MONSTER IN OUR MIDST: A DRUG CALLED LSD! and THRILL DRUG WARPS MIND, KILLS—replaced the earlier blessings that *Life* and *Look* gave the famous experimenters of previous years. In March 1966, a *Life* cover story, "LSD: The Exploding Threat of the Mind Drug That Got Out of Control," called the experience a "chemical Russian roulette" in which players gambled with their sanity. LSD, no longer the plaything of a deputized elite, was depicted as "a one-way trip to an asylum, prison, or grave." LSD-related admissions to New York's Bellevue Hospital ballooned, as if fulfilling a curse. Bad trips, which did accompany the spread of the drug, were reported as the norm; and false information, such as the assertion that LSD causes chromosome damage, slipped into the news stream.

As an instrument of social control, the "LSD Madness" story now occupied the place "Reefer Madness" held in the 1930s, with a significant difference. The madness-mimicking properties ascribed to hallucinogens had originally been a construct of the Clandestine Services. Working in independent laboratories, therapeutically oriented researchers had reached quite different conclusions. In their view, LSD was not psychotomimetic, but *psychedelic:* meaning "mind-manifesting," with all the possibilities for clinical investigation that implied. The neutral term had been coined by Dr. Humphrey Osmond, a young British psychiatrist working in Saskatchewan, Canada, in the mid-'50s. In a letter to Aldous Huxley, he accompanied his choice with a couplet:

> To fathom hell or soar angelic,
> Just take a pinch of psychedelic.

Huxley had proposed *phanerothyme,* meaning "to render the soul visible," with this jingle: *"To make this trivial world sublime / Take half a gramme of phanerothyme."* In the mid-'60s, however, by advancing the "madness" paradigm in the public arena, the medical establishment and the media breathed new life into the CIA's operational definition, which, strangely enough, had *lost* its demonic cachet for the MK-ULTRA crowd.

Not only was the "madness" fixation contested by youthful revelers in hippie enclaves across the country, but LSD had proved to be an unreliable weapon in the Cold War. Foreign revolutionaries and Left-leaning political leaders abroad were now less likely to be targeted for surprise acid attacks—as Fidel Castro was in the early '60s—for the simple reason that the disorienting effects of LSD outside the laboratory proved impossible to predict. It was after repeated failures to dose Castro that the CIA, under Richard Helms, had concocted a scheme to dust his shoes with thallium salts to make his beard fall out. When that didn't work, the focus shifted to eliminating him altogether; and during the final years of the Kennedy administration, MK-ULTRA's chief "medical officer," Dr. Sidney Gottlieb, was ordered to prepare biochemical poisons for a series of assassination attempts that allied the Agency with anti-Castro mercenaries and the mob, an effort first documented in the *Congressional Record* of November 20, 1975.

Historians no longer need debate whether Kennedy knew of the assassination attempts against Castro after the failure of the Bay of Pigs invasion in 1961. Thanks to the recent publication of classified documents concerning the CIA's botched attempts to end Castro's rule in the early '60s, the president's awareness can no longer be doubted. In *The Dark Side of Camelot,* meanwhile, Seymour Hersh quotes a former CIA official from clandestine operations, Samuel Halpern, as saying of both JFK and Bobby Kennedy: "You don't know what pressure is until you get those two sons of bitches laying it on you. We felt we were doing things in Cuba because of a family vendetta and not because of the good of the United States." No wonder Lyndon Johnson was convinced that Castro was behind the assassination of Kennedy.

In the meantime, the CIA proceeded to establish listening posts in Haight Ashbury, even helping underground chemists set up acid factories during 1967's Summer of Love. MK-ULTRA had been reorganized into MK-SEARCH in 1964, and the following year the new program phased out a San Francisco safe house that MK-ULTRA had run since 1956 under a former FBI narcotics officer named George Hunter White. Called Operation Midnight Climax, White's directives had included paying drug-addicted prostitutes to pick up men and bring them back to a house on Telegraph Hill, where they were given drinks laced with LSD and their reactions monitored through two-way mirrors. Now that the Haight furnished the CIA with what one agent referred to as "a human guinea pig farm," such establishments were no longer needed.

How strange it must have been for these old spooks to watch hippies playing with the chemicals they had once believed would transform the cloak-and-dagger trade. No wonder they were curious. "Drugs and covert operations go together like fleas on a dog," CIA analyst David MacMichael observed at the time; and soon government watchdogs were swarming all over the Haight—though you wouldn't know it from the popular histories of the '60s. In book after book, the Summer of Love occurs in a political vacuum, and LSD is but an ornament to the scene.

After he retired, George White bid farewell to Sidney Gottlieb in a letter that might stand as Exhibit A in the unwritten history of the CIA as America's true counterculture: its longest-running underground and the repository of some of its enduring fantasies. "I was a very minor missionary, actually a heretic, but I toiled wholeheartedly in the vineyards because it was fun, fun, fun," wrote White, who also helped train American spies for the OSS during World War II. "Where else could a red-blooded American boy lie, kill, cheat, steal, rape, and pillage with the sanction and blessing of the All-Highest?"

In 1967, old MK-ULTRA hands such as Dr. Louis Joylon ("Jolly") West, expert at testing LSD "under threat conditions," were enlisted to probe the remarkable convergence of thousands of young people eager to sample nearly any experimental drug set before them. And there was no doubt about it: Starting with the Pranksters, who were the first to take LSD out of the war labs and hospitals, hippies were mixing drugs as if there were no tomorrow.

"There was a brew going on," says Mountain Girl, which included the superpotent DMT when they could get it, though DMT she associates with Millbrook. "It is, to LSD, as 198-proof rum is to hot milk with a few drops of brandy," reports Robert Hunter. (When I ask him if he knows whether DMT was used in the MK-ULTRA experiments, he doesn't, but doubts it. "Too intense," he says. "That would be a pretty scary thing to do to someone." I don't know, either, but suspect it was.) LSD, mescaline, peyote tea, LSD-like analogues, methedrine—all were part of the brew. Pot was readily available and pot was the most troublesome, Mountain Girl relates, because it was hard to conceal and busts were frequent. In the beginning, she didn't know the difference between some of these drugs, but she soon learned to stay away from LSD with downers or uppers mixed in, and not to take anything with speed.

Such purism wasn't shared by the menfolk; least of all by Jerry, Phil, and Hunter. In the early 1960s, after Lesh had returned from Las Vegas and moved to San Francisco with Tom Constanten, getting a job at the post office, where Danny Rifkin also worked (along with Kreutzmann), he was shooting up methedrine nearly every day. Racing the postal truck up Market Street at rush hour, picking up the mail, he terrified the MUNI bus drivers. Hunter remembers a lost year in 1964–1965, when he was so strung out on meth that he cut himself off from everybody. "You could only do this stuff for so long before you drove yourself nuts and had to get off. I got psycho behind it," he says. Hard drugs, speed especially, had been part of the coffeehouse scene in Palo Alto, and they were embedded in the group's veneration of the Beats. For the band, the Acid Tests may have been where the "incredible myth" began, but LSD, viewed over the thirty-year haul, was a tiny atoll in a roiling sea of harder stuff.

Cocaine and opiates kicked in during the 1970s, part of their appeal being the lack of needles. The heroin was high-grade, like the "skag" American troops were introduced to in Vietnam—pure enough to smoke, and readily available; for the Grateful Dead, however, at prices that ate into personal profits. GIs in Southeast Asia got it almost for free. Mountain Girl couldn't go on the warpath as she had at 710 Ashbury, when she sometimes threw the boys up against the wall, rolling up their sleeves to check for tracks.

LSD stayed on as an elixir, a break from work; or a prank, as when an unsuspecting friend or foe was dosed. DMT admitted serious psychedelic explorers like Hunter and Owsley to a higher realm, whose power to command submission to Cosmic Forces was irresistible. When the going got rough, you couldn't stop to remind yourself that this was a *subjective* experience. With DMT, you didn't drive through the hallucinations. "You're inside it. It's *objective*," says Hunter, who took the drug intravenously a few times before a DMT voice he calls "the BOSS" told him to stop.

It's a reality, Hunter says of the experience, *not a hallucination at all, but the key to another dimension. It's as if you were suddenly to lose your color vision and you could only see in black and white.*

I look puzzled.

This is a DIFFERENT REALITY, he tries again. *It is the same as when you take up scuba diving and you understand that there is part of a creature of the sea in you, and it's been there in your back wing all along.*

I still don't get it, not having taken up scuba diving.

It's a separate reality. It doesn't impinge on this reality. It doesn't RELATE even to this reality. It's just a different place, he repeats, *willing* the idea into my skull. *The laws of time and space and consecutiveness and probability . . . are simply suspended and we get to see a different world. And this can't help but be edifying in a deep way.*

Skip Workman, who never missed a drug—only heroin was off-limits to Hell's Angels—remembers shaving a piece of DMT from a waxy ball and smoking it in a pipe with pot. With one toke, he fell against the wall "and slid down to the floor and went right down the Nile River. I saw the Egyptians and the pharaohs and the water buffalos, the pyramids and the Sphinx—it was beautiful," he tells me. Then I get it.

William Burroughs, I notice, cast a cold eye on the use of psychedelics as psychic thrill drugs, though he might have relished the dimensional distortions of DMT. At Harvard in the early 1960s, checking out Leary's experiments with LSD, he found a "semipermanent cocktail party with a band of starry-eyed intellectuals talking some half-assed jive about brotherly love." Psychedelics, he believed, would be used to control rather than liberate the vision-starved masses, a position he argues in a passage in *Nova Express* written after the Harvard visit. "Stay out of The Big Store—Flush their drug kicks down the drain—*They are poisoning and monopolizing the hallucinogen drugs—learn to make it without any chemical corn—*"

Cocaine was a work drug, and heroin, for Garcia and Scully especially, became, over time, a blessed escape from the Grateful Dead. It protected them from a scene the fans rarely saw—one that had "a juggernaut energy all its own . . . just kind of rolling around," Mountain Girl recalls. It was a scene that left Jerry "in resistance not infrequently," she says delicately, referring, mainly, to the grinding predictability of having to play in the same old places almost every night.

Do you know where you're going to be on September twelfth? You're going to be sweating on some stage in Akron. And there's no way to get out of it. There's no way. What if you woke up that day and didn't want to play. And Jerry did . . . those days happened to him, and he would, you know, plod out there and play, but he didn't like it. And his energy was not always there for it.

Jerry, she adds, *was also in a state of resistance to being pushed around all the time by the scene. And the scene itself was hungry, and it wanted to go out and make money because people have needs and demands. And so he did the best he could with that and he always went and played when he could. And he sort of made that a discipline. But this was not a person who appreciated discipline.*

That's probably where the heroin came in. It gave him a private life, I suggest.

Oh, God, she says, *I think the heroin was like the latest cool thing, and it was just—that stuff really gets you.* She *felt so sorry for him once he got involved in it. And [looking] at him on the cover of the* Go to Heaven *album, that photograph of him—Oh, Jesus, he looks so bad.* She sighs. *Poor baby!*

This Grateful Dead, of course, which "just kind of rolled along as an entertainment industry all its own," was not yet in sight in the mid-'60s. The seeds were there, if you're looking backward; but who could have imagined the hungers down the road that would separate the Mythical Ethical Dead from the pack, and infuse it with extraterrestrial powers of survival? Who could predict the seriousness with which the band would go after live audiences in the early 1970s? Or the depth of its commitment to music that could be renewed and extended, stretched and bent, without losing its signature? Or the sucking sound of a retreating wave of interest from professional rock critics, such as Greil Marcus and Robert Christgau, who generally ignored the Grateful Dead after 1973, when Deadheads began to stake their claim?

Critic Joel Selvin remembers the Dead's original San Francisco audiences as different from their tie-dyed successors; and different, too, from the audiences of other bands, such as Quicksilver Messenger Service, with whom it was often paired. Both groups were dance bands, but the Dead attracted "hard-core hippies" of whom it was said, "they came out of the woodwork." They were the people "who macraméd their own clothes, who had to hustle to scrape up the three bucks for a show, who didn't have much of a job," according to Selvin. "They turned out for the Grateful Dead because of the dance thing"—which suggests more than a passing resemblance to an enduring core of Deadheads in the 1970s, '80s, and '90s.

In 1966, acid remained the drug of choice. On October sixth, the day of the anti-LSD law, the Grateful Dead had joined other bands in a Love Pageant Rally organized by the Psychedelic Shop's Ron Thelin, artist Michael Bowen, and *The Oracle*'s editor, Allen Cohen, in the Panhandle of Golden Gate Park. It marked the debut of the song "Alice D. Millionaire" before thousands of hippies in high costume, chanting, ringing bells, dancing—a modern, drug-soaked version of a Victorian garden party, where diaphanous young ladies trip the light fantastic to the sinuous notes of flutes and mandolins. Kesey's bus stood by glowing in the sunlight. ("Alice D. Millionaire," after a *Chronicle* headline "LSD MILLIONAIRE ARRESTED" commemorated Owsley's first bust.) Golden Gate pageants like this were seed events whose magic ingredients would crop up in Dead shows for decades to come.

LSD's sudden embrace by the young caught the old guard by surprise. Albert Hofmann, the proper Swiss chemist whom thousands celebrated on the fiftieth anniversary of his first acid trip, in San Francisco in 1993, never expected that lysergic acid "would ever find worldwide use as an inebriant. . . . [W]ith its unfathomably uncanny, profound effects, so unlike the character of a recreational drug," he was sure it would follow a path that mescaline had taken when it was written up in science journals earlier in the century. Mescaline's use had been properly confined to medicine, and to artistic and literary circles. When both it and LSD were embraced by the masses, Hofmann, like other commentators, cited "deep-seated sociological causes" for the drugs' appeal: modern man's "alienation from nature . . . a mechanized, lifeless working world, ennui, purposelessness, the lack of a religious, nurturing and meaningful philosophical foundation of life." Only artists and writers, living outside the sociological law, it seemed, qualified for the higher uses of the drug.

What is remarkable about such views, apart from the stale elitism, is how ignorant they were of what was really going on. The CIA knew better, as did analysts from the Rand Corporation and the Stanford Research Institute (SRI), which also established listening posts in the Haight during the Summer of Love. All three set out to observe the voluntary use of mind-altering drugs by young people, some of whom—the real targets of these operations—were becoming increasingly involved in militant political activities.

The Rand Corporation's objectives had largely been shaped by the intrepid Herman Kahn, who wanted to measure the impact of LSD on political activism and political thinking generally. SRI, which, like Rand, was heavily engaged in Vietnam-related military research, had plucked OSS veteran Capt. Al Hubbard, an early LSD advocate, out of Canadian retirement as a "special investigative agent." Hubbard's job was to gather data "regarding student unrest, drug abuse, drug use at schools and universities, causes and nature of radical activities, and similar matters, some of a classified nature." It was Captain Hubbard, hater of hippies and radicals, and supposedly no friend of the CIA, either, who first reported that most underground LSD factories were funded by the Mafia. Given the record of Mafia–MK-ULTRA ties in the Caribbean, it seems probable that these were the operations that offered CIA agents their entry points into the Haight. In the "drugs and covert operations go together like fleas on a dog" formula, the mob, in other words, was the scratch.

Nineteen sixty-seven was the summer when an essential raw ingredient of LSD, ergotamine tartrate, was in short supply; and perhaps partly for that reason, the CIA's Technical Services staff released the formula for a psychoactive agent called STP into the scientific community. ("STP, oh God, it was awful," Kesey tells me. "It was invented to weaken the person so that he could be interrogated.") Here was another experimental drug that would surely find its way to "the human guinea pig farm," which it did, with Owsley himself putting it into production in the summer of 1967. STP (Serenity, Tranquility, Peace) was first developed in 1964 by an experimental chemist at the Dow Chemical Company. Dow had sent samples to the headquarters of the Army Chemical Corps in Edgewood, Maryland, a common practice; and the Edgewood Arsenal had passed them on to the Agency. MK-SEARCH's researchers had used STP in behavioral-modification studies, along with a related compound in which it had a deeper interest, a powerful psychoactive incapacitating agent called BZ.

A buzzy hallucinogen that was far from tranquil, STP enjoyed a brief vogue, aided no doubt by the free advertising it got from STP Motor Oil, whose oval stickers suddenly appeared everywhere. But the drug was never very popular; and in 1969, when I first visited San Francisco, it traveled with a little cloud over its head; not as dark as the cloud hanging over the acid the Mafia peddled, which was fortified with speed and sometimes strychnine—SYNDICATE ACID STINKS! proclaimed Haight Ashbury graffiti—but suspect nonetheless. (*Very* suspect, when one learns that STP was held responsible for the worst drug trips at the Altamont festival in December 1969.) STP seems to have found its natural habitat at rock festivals in the early '70s, such as at the Atlanta Pops Festival in July 1971, where it appeared cut with 10 percent strychnine in pills called "pinkies," and combined with LSD in tabs called "orange sunshine."

BZ swam into my screen in the spring of 1966, after I had left Chicago for New York, where I was swept up in the infant antiwar movement. I was working on the magazine *Viet-Report,* whose June–July issue contained a special bulletin on chemical warfare in Vietnam. BZ, whose disabling effects reportedly included temporary paralysis and loss of muscular coordination for ten days, was a little-known player, mainly because it had not yet been authorized for use. This, from a *Wall Street Journal* account of a "proposal to dig more deeply into Uncle Sam's bag of exotic weapons . . ." That BZ had already been used we knew from the French press, often a more reliable source of military news in the early years of the war than our own.

After the effects wear off, the *Wall Street Journal* reporter noted, the victim "won't recall being drugged." And this was echoed by a March 1966 report in *L'Express* that BZ, used in a First Cavalry (Airmobile) attack on a Vietcong battalion at Bong Son, South Vietnam, was "a lethargic gas which causes one to lose his memory." In 1970, the CIA, citing "trends in modern police action and warfare indicat[ing] the desire to incapacitate reversibly and demoralize, rather than kill, the enemy," pressed for BZ's use in domestic peacekeeping. A hideous prospect, it was apparently not acted upon.

In fact, BZ was a spin-off of MK-SEARCH's bag of tricks; a psychochemical that, according to documents obtained by Senator Frank Church's investigation of the CIA in 1977, causes "trips" lasting a week or more, "and tends to induce violent behavior." The target victim usually had to be hospitalized, and thus bore "the social stigma of mental problems." The Church committee confirmed that BZ had been used "to assassinate a target's character." An MK-SEARCH veteran said, "It's an old technique. You neutralize someone by having their constituency doubt them."

Agents had become leery of such drugs; and even after MK-ULTRA's original "medical director," Sidney Gottlieb, was kicked upstairs to supervise "scientific matters" for counterintelligence operations, he was unable to overcome the view from the field that psychotomimetic drugs didn't work, or that they worked too well (sometimes precipitating an unintended "executive action," i.e., death), or "that their operational use leads to laziness and poor tradecraft." Thus (in my view) did BZ, the CIA's monster acid, a mutant, find its way to the military front, where it doesn't seem to have proved any more reliable. At home, meanwhile, the Army stockpiled fifty tons of the stuff, enough to turn the whole world into raving lunatics. I didn't pay much attention to this new type of weapon in 1966. How important, after all, were psychochemical explosives alongside incendiary bombs weighing from five hundred to two thousand pounds, guided missiles, and fragmentation bombs with their evil little bomblets, all of which (and more) were hurled at North and South Vietnam at a rate two times the tonnage that Allied forces dropped on all of Europe and Asia in World War II?

Nor had I connected the research on psychochemicals that kept turning up in *Viet-Report*'s investigations of the military-academic complex with the burgeoning acid culture at home. Psychedelics were not yet part of our experience; not even pot, in my case—until New Year's Eve of 1967, when somebody gave me and my associate editor some first-class reefer, which we smoked while listening to the *Sgt. Pepper's Lonely Hearts Club Band* before disappearing into the night.

Looking back at the chemical and biological warfare research *Viet-Report* published in 1968, with MK-ULTRA/SEARCH in mind, I see that the command chain was longer than I had thought. It wound its way through CIA and military laboratories, VA hospitals, think tanks, and university science departments—including UCLA's medical school, which began pursuing "a rational approach to the search for new Chemical Warfare lethal and incapacitating agents," specifically "types that have hallucinogenic properties"—*as early as 1961*. That the chain would lead, in 1966, to a BZ-armed helicopter attack on guerrillas in South Vietnam is what the moment demanded: a make-no-sense war but a "democratic" one, in which a great many individuals performed their separate tasks, and nobody knew the meaning of the play.

Psychoactive drugs, when all is said and done, are like Ariadne's thread. Pull it, just a little, and whole sectors of American society, unrelated but for an intense attachment to the manipulation of consciousness, neuroconsciousness, begin to unravel and merge.

∽

~CHAPTER~
6

SUMMERTIME DONE COME AND GONE

I see all of Southeast Asia
I can see El Salvador
I hear the cries of children
And the other songs of war
It's like a mighty melody
That rings down from the sky
Standing here upon the moon
I watch it all roll by
All roll by
All roll by
All roll by

ROBERT HUNTER, "STANDING ON THE MOON"

VIETNAM AMBUSHED ME during my first teaching job, at Central YMCA College ("in the heart of downtown Chicago"), in the fall of 1963. I had gotten my M.A. and was staying on in Hyde Park with a boyfriend, an undergraduate, whose apartment was not far from Elijah Muhammad's house. My English composition classes were filled with children of Muslim hierarchs, many of whom would soon be draft bait. This may explain the eagerness with which they decoded the war news in the *Chicago Tribune*, part of our study of the use and abuse of the written word.

We were reading "Politics and the English Language" and testing Orwell's famous thesis that "In our time, political speech and writing are largely the defense of the indefensible." The *Tribune*, with its glowing reports of the Strategic Hamlet program, the latest in President Kennedy's bag of counterinsurgency tricks, was our laboratory. "Defensive villages are bombarded from the air, the inhabitants driven out into the countryside, the cattle machine-gunned, the huts set on fire with incendiary bullets. This is called *pacification*," Orwell had written in 1946. "Millions of peasants are robbed of their farms and sent trudging along the roads with no more than they can carry: This is called . . . *rectification of frontiers.*" That was the Spanish Civil War, and the dénouement of World War II. In South Vietnam, the forced relocation of peasants in "New Life hamlets" behind barbed wire was still cloaked in liberal dialect, but it wasn't hard for my students to read between the lines.

No doubt the racial aspects of fortified enclaves were more vivid to them than to me. I saw reservations embedded in the cowboys-and-Indians rhetoric, with the Indians being the peasants who refused to be pacified. And behind that loomed the specter of concentration camps. Perhaps the students were reminded of the Model Cities program, which was just then demolishing poor neighborhoods in Chicago, and relocating black families to fortresslike housing projects in a no-man's-land south of the Loop. In any event, whether we knew it or not, we were engaged in antiwar research; and somewhere along the line my fascination with the *presentation* of the war shifted to a deeper interest in what was actually happening in Vietnam.

A year and a half later, in New York, I brought a proposal for an emergency news bulletin on the war to a coalition of professors who had organized an antiwar rally in Madison Square Garden in the fall of 1964. They had raised around $3,500 and were looking for a project to fund. The magazine, called *Viet-Report,* looked like a good bet, and they backed it.

"*How did we get stuck there in the first place? Why is it taking so long to get nowhere? Why are the Vietcong fighting so hard? What do they want? What do we want? . . . Is it true we're losing? Who got us into this? Who's going to get us out?*" In July 1965, these were the questions that went out with the maiden issue. A thirty-two-page magazine, subtitled *An Emergency News Bulletin on Southeast Asian Affairs, Viet-Report* was published six or seven times a year. One of many underground papers that emerged over the next few years, it was the only one devoted almost exclusively to Vietnam—until 1968, when we published special issues on Latin America, the military-academic complex, and counterinsurgency operations at home.

In 1965, we were a mix of itinerant radicals, office workers, adjunct professors, and graduate students, some of whom were recruited by the charismatic Staughton Lynd, the Yale historian who garnered the same

Neal Cassady, 1967. © *Herb Greene*

The 1939 International Harvester bus, Furthur, with Ken Kesey riding shotgun and Cassady at the wheel, takes off across the country in the summer of 1964. © *Ronald Bevirt*

Kesey tootles the guests at a party in New York organized by Allen Ginsberg to introduce the Pranksters to Jack Kerouac. © *Ronald Bevirt*

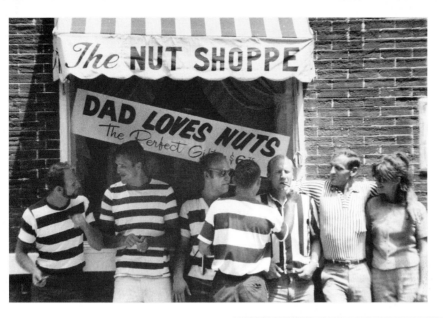

ABOVE: The Pranksters celebrate Father's Day in New York. FROM LEFT: Dale Kesey (Ken Kesey's cousin), Ken Babbs, Ken Kesey, Ken Babbs's brother John lighting cigars, Chuck Kesey (Kesey's brother), Neal Cassady, and Gretchen Fetchin'. RIGHT: Allen Ginsberg at the Prankster/Kerouac party, July 1964. BELOW: A gung-ho Ken Babbs flew helicopters in South Vietnam. © Ronald Bevirt

Jerry Garcia and Phil Lesh jamming at San Francisco's Winterland
on New Year's Eve, 1968. © *Sylvia Hamilton Clarke*

CLOCKWISE FROM ABOVE: Ron "Pigpen" McKernan; Bob Weir; Garcia; Bill Kreutzmann; and Lesh, playing in Ann Arbor, Michigan, August 13, 1967. © *Tom Copi*

The Fillmore East, New York City, 1968–1971. © *Amalie R. Rothschild*

Lighting technicians with their rigs inside the theater. The Joshua Light Show's Tom Shoesmith sits on the top platform. © *Amalie R. Rothschild*

The New Riders of the Purple Sage at the Fillmore East in 1968.
FROM LEFT: David Nelson, Jerry Garcia on banjo, and John "Marmaduke" Dawson.
© *Amalie R. Rothschild*

Bill Graham at work backstage. © *Herb Greene*

solemn respect in antiwar circles that Bob Moses did in the civil rights movement. "What is to be done?" people asked after teach-ins, and Staughton, a member of the advisory board, would sometimes say, among other things, "Go work for *Viet-Report*."

Along with the volunteers ranging in and out of the small West Seventy-second Street office were a few old friends from Cape Cod's bohemia and the University of Chicago. A jazz pianist and painter named Bud Blacklock contributed clever ink washes to plug an occasional hole in walls of type. A budding playwright from Chicago, Bernard Pomerance, steeped in classical literature, wrote about Vietnam in terms that none of us could understand. He swept the floors and emptied the wastebaskets. Along with editorial chores, I drew the cartoons that weren't lifted from other sources, and sometimes designed and illustrated the covers.

Periodically *Ramparts* staff writer Bob Scheer burst in and chastised us for wasting our time on low-grade newsprint and unprofessional distribution. You have to compete with the slicks, he argued, if you're going to have any impact. But *Viet-Report*'s goals were different. Our readers were mainly young people who were being turned on by teach-ins and demonstrations to want to know more about Vietnam and the circumstances behind U.S. involvement. Our pressruns, which occasionally reached sixty thousand, were mostly shipped out in bulk orders to campus-, church-, and community-based antiwar groups who used them as briefing papers for organizing efforts.

"To inform and not to persuade" was our initial objective. And in the first issue we quoted UN Secretary-General U Thant: "I am sure that the great American people, if only they know the true facts and the background to the developments in South Vietnam, will agree with me that further bloodshed is unnecessary. . . ." It was hardly so simple. In times of war, "truth," U Thant added, is "the first casualty"; and it was followed by other, flesh-and-blood casualties, which were beginning to come home in body bags by the thousands.

Indochina experts, such as French journalist Bernard Fall, and disillusioned American professors who worked for the U.S. Agency for International Development in South Vietnam in the early '60s, fed us damning material from the field, but none of them was committed to the political struggle against U.S. policy, and they shrank from writing it up. So we had informed ourselves in order to inform, and persuade, others—and in so doing we became, as the saying went, radicalized.

After graduating from St. John's College in Annapolis in 1966, my sister, Candace, also headed for New York, hoping to find work designing sets for theatrical productions. It was a yen kindled by working on college Shakespeare productions, and it was not to be satisfied. Instead, she found herself lighting the Manhattan Festival Ballet, then stage-managing another dance company, while running lights for theatrical productions in storefronts and churches, and driving a cab.

Her first rock 'n' roll job came by accident in January 1968 when she responded to an ad calling for a lighting designer (LD) at the Anderson Theater on Second Avenue. Expecting a theater presenting plays, she was surprised to find psychedelic posters for rock bands hanging alongside tattered hand-lettered signs in Yiddish saying DON'T SPIT ON THE FLOOR. The Anderson's LD, Chip Monck—whose name epitomized the irreality of this scene for me—offered to teach her how to run the lights for a show, but when she returned on the appointed day, he wasn't there. So she lit the show herself. Pearls Before Swine was the group, the first rock band she had ever seen.

After working with Monck at the Anderson, Candace moved across Second Avenue to the brand-new Fillmore East, next door to Ratner's delicatessen. Formerly the Loew's Commodore, another movie emporium with roots in vaudeville and the Yiddish theater, the Fillmore East, which opened in February 1968, was the sister ship of Bill Graham's Fillmore West. It was here that the Grateful Dead, sandwiched in between the Doors, Janis Joplin, the Allman Brothers, Jimi Hendrix, and the Who, among other bands, began to build their massive East Coast following. And it was at the Fillmore East, with its ancient spotlights, called "follow spots," anchored in the back of the hall, where Candace soon became the house LD, that she first met the Grateful Dead.

She and I didn't see much of each other in those years. It was as if we had slipped down different rabbit holes. We were living in the same city for the first time since childhood, but we might have been on separate planets. Between the Upper West Side of Manhattan, where politics took command, and the East Village, where the parties were, there was a gulf as deep as the Bay that separated Berkeley and the Haight.

.   .   .

Out in Golden Gate Park, California's hippies were marching to their own drummers. In January 1967, at the great San Francisco Be-In—A Gathering of the Tribes, it was called, in part, to close the gap with the politicos across the bridge—people were invited to "hang your fear at the door and join the future because the night of bruited fear of the American eagle-breast-body is over. . . ." Such press releases had a P. T. Barnum ring that made flash copy for reporters. They celebrated "the leaders, guides, and heroes of our generation": Leary, Ginsberg, Gary Snyder, Michael Mc-Clure, Lenore Kandel, Dick Alpert, Jerry Rubin, and Dick Gregory, along with the Grateful Dead, the Jefferson Airplane, Country Joe and the Fish, the Charlatans, and Quicksilver Messenger Service.

The Gathering was a triumph for the psychedelic contingent, which had indeed thrown a party the world would not forget. Owsley donated turkeys for thousands of sandwiches, along with samples of a newly minted acid called White Lightning. Halfway through the Dead's set, as if on cue, a parachutist landed at the far end of the Polo Field. Throughout the day, the political speakers were shunted off to the platform with a faulty PA system, where almost nobody listened to them. The only speaker who held the crowd was Allen Ginsberg, and he did it by conducting mass breathing exercises. At the end, he led a procession of hippies out of the park and across the highway to Ocean Beach to watch a fat red sun sink into the sea.

News of the massive Human Be-In rolled across the land, lapping into small towns and suburbs, stirring up the loose fish among the young, alerting them to the action taking place in the West. Proto-Deadheads like Peter Wigley, who lived in a small farming community in south-central Maine, and "devoured" On the Road when he was fourteen, were first reached by radio, which began playing Dylan's "Like a Rolling Stone" and songs from the Jefferson Airplane's album Surrealistic Pillow as early as 1966. In 1967, Peter Wigley tracked the hippie scene in Newsweek. He knew about City Lights Bookstore from reading Kerouac, and there it was—and there were the freaks, one step from the Beats, and the new music, and the drugs. "It was like, okay, there's a connection here," Wigley remembers thinking. And he fantasized, as many did, about stealing a car and driving cross-country to San Francisco. Thinking about it all, he didn't feel so alone at Bonny Eagle High School, where this son of a mill worker wrote his own on-the-road stories without having gone anywhere. He even had a pen name: Pierre Lablanc.

The summer of 1967 was shot through with higher contrasts than the previous one. Black ghettos in Detroit and Newark exploded under the pressure of quasi-military occupations now spreading throughout the inner cities. The war continued to escalate, and more troops were thrown on the fire. By June 20, 449,800 Americans, many of them teenagers, were stationed in Vietnam. With draft calls up and student deferments down, antiwar contingents were preparing for a giant demonstration at the Pentagon in October. *Time* gave its Man of the Year award to "Anyone Under 25." The Beatles were ballyhooed as never before. And the Monterey Pop Festival, on June fifteenth, sixteenth, and seventeenth—the first of the monster music festivals to roll across the troubled land—helped put the Grateful Dead on a larger map.

The Beatles remained the media's darlings. *Sgt. Pepper's Lonely Hearts Club Band,* which appeared in June, was a concept album, brimming over with novel sound effects and druggy allusions to "marmalade skies" and "looking-glass eyes." Structured as a musical trip, an old-timey band led listeners on a sentimental journey through the history of Anglo-American music: from ballads and folk songs to dance hall tunes, circus music, and rock 'n' roll—much as the Grateful Dead had begun to do in real time.

In the Haight, the hordes of young people streaming into town were followed by armies of tourists. Not much resistance was heard from city fathers and merchants to the "Hippie Hop Tour," whose Gray Line buses clogged the already-crowded streets. Billed as "the only foreign tour within the continental limits of the United States," the Gray Line bonanza treated gaping tourists to a running commentary on the natives' "recreational activities . . . parading and demonstrating, soul-searching," and smoking marijuana: "a household staple." The Dead's house at 710 Ashbury was a featured stop along the way.

In June, *Time,* which had been amusing its readers with similar palaver, carried a story on the San Francisco bands that indicated its reporter had been listening to the Grateful Dead and the Jefferson Airplane. "The San Francisco Sound encompasses everything from blue grass to Indian ragas, from Bach to jug band music—often within the framework of a single song. . . . The sound," the story went on, "is also the scene. With its roots in the LSDisneyland of the Haight-Ashbury district, the music is a reflection of the defiant new bohemians," which was *Time*-ese lathered over reports from the field.

The original scene, "unbelievable and like a dream," San Francisco attorney Tony Serra recalls it, was a lot more than the sound. Nor was it particularly defiant. Different, yes; exotic, theatrical, and sensuous, not unlike the flamboyant Gay Pride battalions that began surging up Castro Street in the 1970s, or the Halloween marches in New York's Greenwich Village; but never truculent and rarely confrontational. (Unless the young man who dropped his pants behind Harry Reasoner during a Summer of Love broadcast in 1967 was truculent. This happened while Reasoner, surrounded by onlookers in Golden Gate Park, was discoursing on "The Hippie Temptation" for CBS News.) "Everything was music, art, smells, fragrances, lace, beads, acting out," Tony Serra continues, adding that "everything became a form of metaphor and allegory," a perception fueled by psychedelics.

LSD immersed one in a sensorium of exotic imagery, where people sometimes looked like animals: the human version of the animal they were. To Dave Nelson, Jerry Garcia looked like a bear, a big brown bear; and Jerry's first wife, Sara Ruppenthal, had appeared as a swan or a goose. Phil Lesh told me that when he was high on acid, he used to see images of people he hadn't realized were in the area. "I'd walk around a corner and I'd see the people whose image preceded them," he says; like Pigpen, whom he associated with an angular American Indian motif. Jerry and a girlfriend named Diane broadcast their arrival with a peacock-feather logo. "It was their signature," Lesh explains, "like the identification 'friend' or 'foe' that war planes use—they get a code back; it says, Okay, this is fine, this is my wingman here."

When the whole group was working well together, not just the musicians but also the extended family of girlfriends, managers, and roadies, "you would get a composite of all . . . the other images." And Lesh remembers a time when "a huge tree with many branches" appeared to him, "[all the branches] with one of these signatures on them. Rock Scully was a little fanged creature . . . but a cute one." The creatures were generally benevolent, and the imagery mysteriously self-chosen. Today, he likens the acid-induced "signature" to the avatar he configures on a Web site, one of which is Smaug, a creature from *The Hobbit*.

On a larger scale, something like this "huge tree" had briefly spread its branches across the Haight. Thirty years later, it's not hard to see the masquerade of costumed revelers, driven by drug-inspired visions of themselves as more than human, as acting out a countercultural tableau that could only have happened in a time of war. A children's crusade of a different order than the one that rallied around presidential hopeful Eugene McCarthy the following summer, the Haight's flowering of music, dance, and psychedelic drugs marked a repudiation of politics.

"There should be some way to stop all this negative energy," the *Oracle*'s editor, Allen Cohen, told Michael Bowen in September 1966 while the two self-proclaimed "Psychedelic Rangers" sat in the Drugstore Café watching a parade of angry protesters march through the Haight. "We should be able to turn some of this bad energy into something more positive," said Cohen, thereby hatching the idea for the Love Pageant Rally, which in turn had paved the way for the Human Be-In. The Be-In, meanwhile, was a recruiting ground for the larger audience that descended on Monterey in June.

A megaevent that rubbed the Grateful Dead the wrong way, the Monterey Pop Festival was one where they turned in a lackluster performance. But it was there, folded in between the Who and Jimi Hendrix, that the musicians had become, as Scully recalls, "rock stars, sort of." After Monterey, Bill Graham went on to organize the Dead's and the Airplane's first "international tour," around an ersatz Trips Festival in Vancouver, which is when band members got a taste of the cinder-block backstage bunkers, interchangeable airport lounges, and hotel rooms that would later be home on the road. It was Bill Graham's first out-of-town promotion, the start of what would become a consuming ambition both to exploit and tame the new music.

At Monterey, meanwhile, the Grateful Dead's popularity—which still hinged on Pigpen's charisma—owed itself less to the music they played than to their eminence among the indigenous peoples of the Haight. For old-world courtiers like Andrew Loog Oldham ("Sir Fucking Andrew"), representing the Rolling Stones, and Derek Taylor, the Beatles' publicist, who was the festival's press agent, the Dead's frontier spirit burned with a gemlike flame. Jimi Hendrix and his English sidemen fell hard for Pigpen. Pete Townshend got turned on to Owsley's acid—this magical mystery drug that Liverpool and London rockers regarded as an *American* trip.

And everybody fell for Jerry, who in most reminiscences appears in peak form—not least because of Owsley's purple acid, which rained on everyone, dissolving barriers between Old World and New, and among musicians, managers, roadies, and fans. "On acid, Jerry is the Buddha," writes Scully—which is what Allen Ginsberg called him in a conversation we had about the Grateful Dead after a poetry reading in New York in 1992. With his formidable social skills intact, his boundless curiosity and amiable, outgoing nature, Jerry Garcia, in 1967, was approachable and infinitely benign.

Phil Lesh wore the black hat at Monterey. "Oh, shit! Now I *know* we're gonna get screwed!" he would say after a cloying reassurance from L.A. promoter Lou Adler that the supposedly nonprofit festival, run and financed by the artists, would not be milked for movies and recordings, and that once the bands were paid, the profits would go to worthy causes. Jerry and Rock had been swept away by the promises of co-organizer Paul Simon (over Danny Rifkin's and Phil's objections), but also by the chance to play alongside Hendrix, Otis Redding, and the Who. Their good faith was indicated by their refusal to sign the film and record releases that, sure enough, were presented to the band just before they walked onstage. It was a refusal all the more significant in that two other "people's bands," Country Joe and Big Brother, who had initially threatened to boycott the festival, had signed. The issue, as always, was control. What if the Dead's sound was poor? Who would be in the editing room to see that it was cut? And who would get the money that would most certainly be made from the film or TV special?

As a result, the Grateful Dead are neither seen nor heard in D.A. Pennebaker's exuberant documentary *Monterey Pop,* or in TV clips from the festival, or on any of the many albums that have been harvested from Monterey over the years. "People have a hard time remembering the Dead played at all," says Scully; partly, no doubt, because they absented themselves from the media loop, but also because their low-key renditions of "Viola Lee Blues" and "Cold Rain and Snow" couldn't hold their own against the stagy pyrotechnics of the Who and Jimi Hendrix, whose sets ended in orgies of smashed instruments.

When the Dead ambled on, something happened, however, which, while unrecorded, struck home with the audience. As the band warmed up, there was a mad rush for seats by people marooned without tickets outside on the fairgrounds. Somebody opened a door, and the arena suddenly overflowed with kids, many of whom believed that the Beatles were going to show up (they didn't), and others who were drawn by the dulcet sounds of their favorite Haight Ashbury band. The promoters panicked, and the Monkees' manager, wearing an Indian warbonnet, rushed onstage, grabbed Phil Lesh's microphone *while he was singing,* and exhorted the audience to cool it. "The Beatles are not coming," he said, "so all those without tickets should leave the arena *at once!*" Incensed, Lesh chased him off the stage, but not before suggesting that *everybody* without tickets should be let in.

It was an early display of an onstage ethic that in a few years would become part of the craziness of a Dead show. Citing a concert at the University of Iowa in the spring of 1971, William Burton recalls a longhaired fan, clad only in his underwear, climbing onstage with "a crazed, distant look in his eye," and clutching a key. " 'I've got to give this to Bob,' he kept saying," heading for Weir, who was busy playing. A security guard whisked him offstage; at the song break, a well-groomed young man who held some position of authority on campus "approached one of the microphones and started exhorting the audience to behave itself and have some respect for the performers." At this point, Garcia and Weir, "ostensibly tuning up for the next song, started playing loud, raucous chords on their guitars, which effectively drowned the young man out. Frustrated and a bit confused, he spoke louder into the microphone, only to be matched by consistently louder dissonance from the band, until at last he gave up and walked offstage. The Dead," Burton concludes, "had defended their own."

At the end of the Monterey festival, the Grateful Dead had taken their revenge, staging a guerrilla action that separated the goats from the sheep, and served to polish the Dead's image as rock 'n' roll Robin Hoods, dedicated to the principle of *free* music—of liberating the surplus from the rich to blow the minds of the young. To CBS and the Fender Corporation, which had lent over a million dollars' worth of equipment to the Monterey Pop Festival in return for free advertising, the band had sent a telegram on June eighteenth, with a copy duly printed by Ralph Gleason in the *Chronicle:*

> We have liberated the following amplifiers and speaker boxes, in order to provide free music to the people of San Francisco and

Northern California. They will be used three or four times for free events and returned to you at the conclusion of this week. . . .

It was incredible gear, the best they had ever encountered, nothing like the beat-up cigarette-scarred boxes Owsley had built. And seeing it unguarded after the last show Sunday night (unguarded because Rifkin and Scully had dosed the security men), the managers and roadies couldn't resist putting into action what had originally been a fantasy the band concocted backstage. They grabbed a van belonging to poster artists Stanley Mouse and Alton Kelley, backed it up to the stage, and loaded it with what they figured the musicians would need to accommodate the guitarists they wanted to jam with in Golden Gate Park. Some of them, such as Jimi Hendrix, Eric Burdon of the Animals, and Otis Redding, were already scheduled to play the Fillmore West and the Avalon Ballroom after Monterey.

The Dead had warmed up for just such a heist during the three-day festival itself when they staged two late-night surprise jams at campsites on the Monterey Peninsula College campus, across the highway from the fairgrounds. Darting about with flashlights while people slept in a pavilion used for flower shows, the crew, on the first occasion, had set up the PA with borrowed equipment from the stage, siphoning electricity from a nearby building. They even installed a projector for a light show, so that when the first chord sounded from the platform in the corner and the lights went on, people woke up to iridescent bubbles cascading across the ceiling, while the Dead, the Airplane, and Hendrix slammed into "Walkin' the Dog."

Later, the impromptu performance was repeated (with different songs) with Eric Burdon, the Byrds, and the Who playing alongside the Dead on a flatbed truck which had been smuggled onto the football field that housed the rest of the overflow crowd, comprised mainly of kids without tickets who had come in on buses from communities up and down the coast a few days earlier. The Dead had always known they would descend on Monterey ever since the Be-In, when flyers portrayed the festival as a nonprofit affair, with the slogan "Music, Love and Flowers." Danny Rifkin had been responsible for persuading the college to make the free camping available, to back up the space set aside for tents on the fairgrounds proper.

In his memoir, Scully makes much of the band's decision to stay in a nearby strip of cheap motels (along with hoi polloi like Janis Joplin, Ravi Shankar, Hendrix, and Townshend), while the L.A. promoters, led by the Mamas and the Papas, catered to the Monkees and the Rolling Stones' Brian Jones (a guest emcee) in posh hotels on the other side of town. Not much attention is given to the extraordinary pageant under way on the football field and the fairgrounds, where friends of the band set up peyote-ceremony tents glowing with Indian symbols, among tepees flying the colors of legendary communes: New Buffalo in New Mexico, Black Bear in northern California, and the Farm in Tennessee, led by Steven Gaskin.

With slim, bare-chested young men playing guitars, bongos, and harmonicas, and girl-women bending over campfires, while children and dogs scampered underfoot (and everywhere trailed the sweet smell of pot and mesquite), something like a gathering of the tribes was indeed under way. Not yet an audience—a mass assembly of strangers waiting to be entertained—it was a genuine community, or felt like one, whose center of gravity hovered somewhere in the tangle of paths running among the tents, the tepees, and the stage.

If there is another pageant in history resembling this one, it is to be found in the religious revivals of the American frontier, with their romantic circuit riders and primitive stump speakers. Speaking of the millenarian gatherings in his home territory, Kentucky preacher Richard McNemar noted, around 1800, that "it was found expedient to encamp on the ground, and continue the meeting day and night. To these encampments the people flooded in hundreds and thousands, on foot, on horseback, and in wagons and other carriages." The meetings "exhibited . . . a scene of confusion that would scarce be put into human language"; people were caught by the jerks, the shakes, the shouts. Underneath the flight from "civilized" behavior, however, *behind* the chaos, lay the quest for a religious order more appropriate to the tensions of the frontier.

In the early 1800s, this turned out to be Methodism. In 1967, it was too soon to see the new world order that would ultimately emerge from the chaos and upheavals of the '60s—a global marketplace whose citizens would commence a worldwide metamorphosis into consumers. Its center of power would be business, not government. By 1967, other communities besides the freaks and the politicos were caught up in the throes of transformation, but who noticed? In sealed boardrooms high above the streets, corporate executives, buying and selling companies, were engaged in a structural revisioning of the world economy that would be quite as radical, in its long-term effects on everyday life, as the recording of belief systems and behavior among the young.

Businessmen were also riding a wave of change, which, not unlike an acid trip, might suddenly disclose a universe devoid of familiar boundaries. What Jerry Garcia said of the Acid Tests—"Formlessness and chaos lead to new forms. And new order"—applied, as well, to the razor's edge of business. Among the West Coast heads, only the San Francisco anarchists led by Peter Berg and Emmett Grogan, who called themselves the Diggers after a revolutionary English farming group in the seventeenth century, seemed to make the connection. "Every time the tide turns, the barracuda turns," they said. "Everybody turns when the tide turns."

Planning, with half a dozen other bands, for Monterey, the Grateful Dead had sensed, as others had not, what the festival represented to the young seekers who embraced its early promise. The Dead realized that they "would have to look after them because the L.A. contingent certainly isn't going to." So they had welcomed the "lumpenhippies," as Robert Christgau calls them, making sure that people who couldn't get into the big top saw a sideshow they would never forget. Dropping Owsley's Monterey Purple and waking up late one night to Garcia, Kaukonen, and Hendrix jamming in your face was not easily forgotten. It was the sort of miracle that thrived all the better in an underground culture when there were no cameras to record it.

Looking back, Monterey may be seen as the last way station—after the Acid Tests, the Love Pageant Rally, the Be-In, and countless smaller gatherings—in a two-year ceremony of innocence that marked the flowering of the counterculture. It was America's first youth culture, and, for the twentieth century, its last.

Naturally, the impromptu flatbed shows that the Grateful Dead produced in Golden Gate were a huge success. In the Panhandle, the crew had borrowed electricity from a nearby house, patching extension cords across the street and through the trees to the makeshift stage. Seven thousand people had turned out to hear the Dead play with Burdon and Hendrix, and many more arrived a few days later for a bigger show elsewhere in the park. For this, Scully and Rifkin rented a generator, which might have alerted the cops, had they been on the warpath. They weren't; CBS, which had just acquired the Fender Corporation in a merger, decided to sit it out. Hell's Angels perched atop the purloined amps like the dogs with eyes as big as saucers that guard the treasure in Aladdin's cave. When questions were asked, the Dead played the game of looking for the one in charge: the person nobody knows or can find, who *just left* or who's *over there, Officer*—a game political organizers played all the time.

In Golden Gate, a second pageant had unfolded, an urban counterpart to the encampments at Monterey. In the Panhandle, the Diggers dispensed lettuce soup and bologna on donated Wonder bread. No health food in hippie heaven. The free-food commandos were always visible in the sea of heads, thanks to a strange contraption they hauled around, an eighteen-foot-high empty wooden "Frame of Reference," through which lost souls were invited to step in and out. The Diggers had dished out free food at Monterey, too, despite their objection to admission procedures and ticket prices that started at $3 and ended at $6.50. When Derek Taylor hinted that a portion of Monterey's profits might go to them, they warned festival organizers that they wouldn't accept the money if it was offered.

After the last show in Golden Gate Park, the Grateful Dead dispatched another telegram to CBS and Fender: "Be at the Ferry Building, Market and Embarcadero, at 12 noon. . . . So long, folks, and thanks for the loan." And the amps, speakers, and mikes were duly returned, not much worse for the wear.

Events such as these, all sharing the ethic of *free,* happened frequently during the procreative years of the Grateful Dead. They are recalled in the collective memory of Deaddom in a way that the more highly publicized, ticketed performances are not. One might see them as sidebars, lending authenticity and variety to the lead stories, which are conveyed by the familiar images of Jimi Hendrix torching his Stratocaster, or Janis Joplin erupting in a frenzy of song. But the guerrilla shows helped fuel an underground cultural movement, lasting over thirty years, while the commercial festivals did not. The festivals, especially Woodstock, two years later, sold records, millions and millions of them, which in turn helped franchise magazines and rock pundits. All together, they fueled an industry whose properties, the stars, would become nearly interchangeable so long as returns outstripped investment.

The rock festivals accomplished something else. Beginning with Monterey, where Columbia Records's Clive Davis found his Jenny Lind in Janis Joplin, they launched another, less visible subculture in which industry executives, excited by the size and warmth of the new audiences, not to mention the draw of the lead musicians, began hobnobbing with rock stars. And band members, together with managers, promoters, dealers, crew, and hangers-on, began tasting a life of flaunted privilege that set them apart from their audiences. If, at first, they hid from the fans out of embarrassment, soon the performers and their attendants would start to squabble among themselves over perks. Outside performances, they would regard the crowds of young people, who were learning how to stand in lines and wait, with abstract feelings of affection, pity, or contempt—until, years later, they barely noticed them at all.

~CHAPTER~
7

SON ET LUMIÈRE

Music, to create harmony, must investigate discord.

PLUTARCH

IN 1967, THE GRATEFUL DEAD were still filling out the team. The grinding predictability that came with more and more gigs was forcing the band to turn outward. It opened them to the musical styles of other cultures, extending Phil Lesh's and Jerry Garcia's interest in jazz at a time when the jazz world was astir with the free-form dissonance of Cecil Taylor, Ornette Coleman, and John Coltrane. Jazz musicians such as Miles Davis, who was slow to accept the new avant-garde, were assimilating rock instrumentation and rhythms into their own music. And the Dead, almost alone among rock bands, were incorporating stylistic innovations from Coltrane and Miles into their improvisational riffs. A rumor that Garcia practiced Charlie Parker tunes before going onstage still circulates in jazz circles.

The hundred flowers blooming in American music thirty years ago were not the cellophane-wrapped long-stemmed kind, but the real thing, a garden of plenty. Cross-pollination among genres was the order of the day, so it was no surprise when the Grateful Dead reached into another musical tradition to acquire its sixth member of the band. Mickey Hart, a lanky suburban cowboy from the East, who once played drums in the Air Force Band, featured himself as a big-band drummer when he was introduced to Bill Kreutzmann at a Count Basie concert at the Fillmore Auditorium in 1967. While Hart would become the Dead's percussionist, stretching the definition of a musical instrument to its breaking point with his boxed crickets and glass harp, he remained a showman whose entourage of parlor mystics and magicians once included a fire-eater. It wasn't long before his drum kit sprouted kettles and gongs onstage, culminating, in 1979, in the Beast, a giant overhead wheel from which dangled percussion instruments, chimes, and bells from around the world.

When he first met Kreutzmann, Hart had already heard the Grateful Dead, and was impressed. "It felt like some sort of force field from another planet," he recalls of his first exposure, "some incredible energy that was driving the band and pulling you in at the same time. . . . It was prayer-like music; it wasn't music that was going into the music business." Hanging out on the street with Bill after the Basie show, drinking a bottle of scotch and "playing" parked cars with the flats of their hands, Hart made a connection that quickly bore fruit. Within a month, he had left the music store he managed in San Carlos and was jamming with the band.

It was the combined energies of these two drummers, something new in rock 'n' roll—a rolling thunder of sound—that convinced Jerry Garcia to take Hart on. When Hart and I meet, he talks about the peculiar quality of this power, which is its power to heal. The rhythmic sound of two drummers, unlike the sound of two guitarists or two keyboardists, he maintains, is "trance-inducing and altered state–inducing." This is what Deadheads say; also the writer Oliver Sacks, a psychiatrist who with Hart's help brought one of his autistic patients to a Grateful Dead concert at Madison Square Garden in 1991. He wanted to see if the music the man had once loved would awaken a dormant memory and return him to consciousness. It did, for a few days; but the world that came rushing back was the world of the early '70s, when "The Last Hippie"—the title of Sacks's report in *The New York Review of Books*—had spent his final moments of consciousness before suffering the massive brain trauma that consigned him to oblivion.

In 1968, Mickey Hart was studying at the Ali Akbar College of Music in San Francisco with tabla master Shakar Gosh, learning Indian rhythm cycles on a pair of tuned hand drums, and passing the lore on to Bill Kreutzmann. In return, he and Kreutzmann instructed Shakar Gosh on traps. With a touch of scorn, Rock Scully recalls the band's assimilation of new rhythm patterns when Mickey "went tribal. We no longer had just another drummer in the band, we had an *ethnomusicologist*." "Chairman

Hart," he says, was prone to issuing statements to the press on "[t]he real role of drums in the 20th century. . . ."

I received some myself; but Mickey Hart can turn a phrase. Working on the mix of *At the Edge,* a companion CD/tape to his book *Drumming on the Edge of Magic,* "was like the ear falling in love with a new lover every time there was a playback, it was so rich and sumptuous," he says. When he speaks of how drums ceased being used for religious purposes and were taken over by the military to marshal troops, he is provocative. "Western religions didn't like the way drums were used in other cultures to induce trance and altered states," he tells interviewer Blair Jackson:

> They wanted you to be praying to that guy on the cross. . . . Re-
> ligion killed the drum in Western culture, until it made its way
> back through rock 'n' roll—the devil's music. [Laughs] Why did
> people try to suppress rock 'n' roll? Because the back beat, the
> groove, took people to the other side, and that's not considered
> acceptable in Western cultures. And where does that beat come
> from? From Africa originally. It came across with the slave trade,
> found its way to New Orleans, mutated into rhythm and blues,
> and all of a sudden you've got rock 'n' roll—check it out: they're
> dancin', they're mamboin'; they're goin' crazy! It's rhythm-
> dominated; it's got percussion galore. So it's made a tremendous
> revival, and melody and harmony are assuming their proper place
> alongside it, as part of the trinity.

Hart, whose piercing brow and pointy Spock-like ears lend him a Mephistophelian air, is the Grateful Dead's inspirational speaker—a kind of village explainer, which sometimes makes him sound like a fifth-column Deadhead inside a group that is usually more circumspect about its extramusical powers. We've got transformation going here," he said in 1984. "We don't have a popular recording group. That's what the trap-pings may look like . . . but that ain't what we have." It's like a "psy-chopomp," he declares; "an escort of the souls of the dead into the other world. . . . We're doing something else besides entertaining. People come to be changed, and we change 'em."

My own sense is that the tunes are kind of forgettable, but the music gives peo-ple a feeling that they don't get anywhere else, I say when we meet in June

1992 before a show in Albany, New York. It's my first formal interview with the band. I can barely tell one song from another, and don't try to hide it.

It gets them high. And it takes them places, Hart says.

I wonder where they go.

The Grateful Dead isn't much of a sing-along band, he begins, and contrasts it to the Steve Miller Band, which is opening the summer's shows. *Those songs you can hum. Miller is a pops tunesmith. His stuff appeals to a different level, the cognitive level. At its best, the Dead triggers other responses that aren't in the five- or six- or seven-minute song range.* For the fans, a Dead concert is *ritual. It's their connection to their past, or even the past that they don't know, or their parents' past. It makes them feel good. It's a fun thing, and there aren't that many fun things to do that you don't get arrested for. . . . They're reestablishing a community [and] the Grateful Dead is supplying the sound track. . . . It's a safe place to do battle. . . . It makes you look inside and it makes you look outside.* [At a concert] *you can see how small you are and you can see how big you are.*

Take your pick. Actually, everything Hart says applies to one or another group of Deadheads I will talk with over the next six years—except for those fans who come only for the music, a contingent that, oddly enough, he omits.

It's when I ask him how the Dead manage to keep the music interesting to one another after all these years that I hear something new to my ears. How do they decide what to play, for instance? I already know from hanging out in the lighting booth that there isn't a set-list. Even when the band sends Candace the title of an opening tune, the song may not follow. "Matter of fact, it changes more than it stays the same," Hart confirms. "More than 50 percent of the time, what we talk about backstage will not be realized." So how does the actual decision get made when they're on their feet in the middle of a set?

In different ways, he says, "but mostly it happens when someone is suggesting a song either rhythmically or melodically, with someone doing something that triggers a response from another person. And when three people are doing something that is recognizable, then the fourth person will jump on it. And then the fifth and the sixth." All this happens in the interregnums between the songs, which I resolve to listen to more carefully (along with the songs). By the following summer, I can pick out phrases from strings of tunes that bunch up together—like the " 'Playing in the Band' sandwich" that Maine Deadhead Peter Wigley describes, which moves from "Playin' " to "Uncle John's Band" to the double-drumming fantasia known as "Drumz" to the electronic interlude (no instruments) called "Space," and then back to "Uncle John's Band."

"It's playful," Hart says of the transitions between songs. "You start getting a flash, and that leads to another thing, and then you start to realize, Well, maybe we should do that. And then we do it." I ask if he ever senses himself resisting the way a flash is going, or wanting to introduce another one. "Sometimes," he says. "And then there's that ambiguity. And we have to choose collectively which way to travel. We look for the right place. Everybody's sort of wanting to do good, to do it right, you know. So we listen. Listening," he stresses, "becomes a very important feature of that particular moment in time. You *really* have to listen, and not be so involved with your personal ego and your sound. This is one of the best parts of the Grateful Dead, when we can transcend that. You can lose a bit of yourself and find the collective good stuff."

Listening is something musically trained Deadheads talk about with a similar intensity. The first time Jamie Janover heard the Grateful Dead live, he was a high school sophomore in Ridgewood, New Jersey, who listened to more traditional pop music. Like Led Zeppelin or Paul McCartney, "whatever said, *Here's* the verse. Now here comes the chorus! Here's the *g u i t a r s o l o* . . ." The Grateful Dead didn't say hello to him at all. The musicians seemed to be playing all at once, with melodies tumbling over one another, and no part weighing in more heavily than the other.

It was 1984 when some friends took him to a Dead show at the Brendan Byrne Arena in Rutherford. A hellish place, it's where a college sophomore from South Orange, New Jersey, Adam Katz, high on acid, died under mysterious circumstances at a Dead show in October 1989. Rough handling by the infamous "Yellowjackets," rent-a-cops hired by Burns Security to police the Meadowlands, was suspected, but the case was never proven. In 1984, crossing the vast parking lot was a nightmare, Janover remembers, with people leaping out to sell every conceivable drug: acid, ecstasy, mushrooms, pot. Heroin? I ask, thinking of a trio of New Jersey fans I've just interviewed, former heroin addicts who started attending Dead shows a few years after Janover. "No," he says, "that was more of an underground scene."

Jamie's friends, meanwhile, pointed out what was happening *inside* the music—how the notes of one melody might play off another, so that you had to listen to two melodies at the same time; "not to mention Phil doing some weird harmonies that were going to make you interpolate a chord differently." For Janover, who lives in Boulder, Colorado, and makes a living playing a hammer dulcimer on the streets, the Grateful Dead "were an early training in my being able to listen to more complex music." His friends also helped him notice the "vibe" that happened between the audience and the band: "how people were all so psyched, and everybody was dancing and they weren't ashamed of dancing," unlike at a heavy-metal concert, where the Yellowjackets might be more at home. "Oh this is cool," Janover thought, slipping into the feel-good groove, welcome in the 1980s; "you can do whatever you want, and it's okay. . . . But then it *really* opened up the first time I took LSD," he tells me. This was two years later, also at Brendan Byrne. Then he had clambered up to the "nosebleed seats" to take it all in.

Acid allowed him to hear so many rhythms, even during the "Space" interlude—which, following "Drumz," became a feature of every concert in the '80s—that he had to "dance really hard" to keep up with them. Dancing was another way of listening—especially dancing on the drug Ecstasy. "You not only feel every beat. You feel every impending molecule of every beat," says Peter Wigley, who used this popular aphrodisiac of the 1980s at concerts in Maine and Massachusetts. "Your body," he says, "becomes a tuning fork for the universe."

Mickey Hart speaks eloquently of the "ambiguity" that occurs when the musicians are playing overlapping themes during the "little gray areas" between the songs. "For a while nothing happens, and you stay on a pulse, and things start bubbling up and somebody makes a decision . . . and they try to push or pull the rest of the band there." It's a moment that every creative person knows, the worst and best of times, when you empty the mind to make room for the uninvited guest.

For the Grateful Dead, such moments could last seconds or many minutes. I ask Hart if the band ever loses the audience. "You might," he says, "but that's not important. The idea is to stay with it yourself." Playing for the audience is "pretty foolish. I mean, you *can't* play for the audience. You gotta play for yourself and your mates." I'm surprised by this response, which sounds like heresy coming from a band whose symbiotic relationship with its fans is nonpareil. But I will hear it again, and come to appreciate how the Dead's introversion in matters both musical and political contributed in no small way to their holding power.

Anyway, it started a long time ago, with Jerry Garcia's penchant for playing new songs in front of live audiences. Each new setting, providing an edge against which the band played, changed how a song developed, as if the listeners, seen but not heard, and treated more often than not to musical chaos, were nonetheless a necessary catalyst to the creative process. "The Jefferson Airplane certainly never went out there with anything that they didn't have down cold," Rock Scully observes. "The Dead would play stuff that they didn't even remember having written that day."

Marmaduke Dawson, the bassist for the New Riders of the Purple Sage, who toured with the Dead in 1970–1971, agrees. "None of them knew where they were going," especially during the long, three- to five-hour sets when, fortified by a good bit of LSD, they were trying for the "magic." "Garcia would be there playing around with something and Weir would be playing around with something and everybody would be doing five things together on the stage and people would still be listening and saying, 'What the hell is going on here?' . . . And sometimes they would get it. The magic of all of them seeming to think together . . ."

The "magic" could be worth waiting for, but for the fans, so, too, was the waiting—part of the existential rush of teetering on the edge of chaos when chaos is giving birth to new forms. For the musicians, finding the "good stuff" (as Hart puts it) entailed a surrender to a higher power, which was the group, the group grope. When Bill Kreutzmann speaks of his distaste for the long showy solos of drummers in the late '60s, he reflects a similar spirit. "I like playing in an ensemble," he declares; "that's the most fun for me—[to] complement the lead player, lay off a little when the vocals are going. . . . Sometimes virtuosity is lost on me—on any instrument." Kreutzmann makes a point of establishing eye contact with the others, moving cymbals around to see Garcia better (or he did until the 1990s, when, seated on the drummer's throne, with his gray head thrown back, eyes rolled up to the sky, he looked like Nero contemplating the angels while Rome burned). It was in earlier years—the Dead's last show at Winterland, for example, which is the subject of the *The Grateful Dead Movie* (1977)—that he relished the moments when "we'll be in a jam and

I'll look over at Jerry and he'll look at me and it's like, 'This is great! You havin' fun? I thought so!' "

The "conversation" is what counts, says Bob Bralove. "That's when popular music gets to be exciting, when there's a real conversation going on. Somebody's talking, somebody's listening." It's happening without any words, "and there is just the right amount of subject change, the way a beautiful conversation happens." Bralove is the young sound wizard who synthesized the Grateful Dead's instruments via the MIDI system during the band's last ten years on the road, so that guitars could play trumpets and saxophones, and drums trigger the digitalized sounds of a ten-ton glockenspiel or a train whistling through a tunnel. For better or worse— and there is sharp disagreement about these innovations, both inside and outside the band—Bralove's technology became the armature behind the instrumental segments of "Drumz" and "Space."

David Gans, meanwhile, describes a brief passage in a Grateful Dead concert in Frankfurt, Germany, on April 26, 1972, which illustrates the collective process in another way. It's in *Hundred Year Hall* (1995), a sampling from the Dead's first full-scale European tour, which Gans is reviewing on his syndicated radio show, "The Grateful Dead Hour" (since renamed "Dead to the World," and running two hours). Lesh and Weir are sitting in. Garcia is heard playing the old standby "Goin' Down the Road Feelin' Bad" at a fast clip, and then the band glides into a smoother tempo, whereupon somebody starts talking "Not Fade Away." There's a moment when half the band is playing "Not Fade Away" (another touchstone song, first done by Buddy Holly and the Rolling Stones) and the other half is playing "Goin' Down the Road." More tempo changes follow, along with some harmonic byplay, and a flash of the "bid you goodnight" refrain from "Goin' Down the Road."

Both tunes, choice bits of Americana, had already been played numerous times by the Dead. "GDTRFB," as it's known on set-lists, was originally played by Woody Guthrie, Ella Baker, Elizabeth Cotten, and Chet Atkins, among others. Roots music—and in Frankfurt, the Dead were rolling in it. "It's just this beautiful sort of telepathic thing," Gans says of the turnaround. "You get all the way into 'Not Fade Away' and then say 'the heck with it' and go straight to 'Goin' Down the Road' after all."

Lesh and Weir laugh in happy recognition. "Yes, and it's Jerry's early refrain that reenters and pulls it back in the original direction," Phil observes. "That's the stuff that we dream about. That's the stuff that we aim for," he says, "and it's the most magical, and it's the stuff that you can never predict. . . . Although there are some factors that are involved," he notes. "For instance, with only one drummer you can turn faster. You can shift gears rhythmically differently than we do with two. You're heavier and going faster with two drummers and it's hard to change direction."

The 1972 European tour, when, according to Bob Weir, "Billy played like a young god," occurred midway through a four-year period when Mickey Hart left the band. Hart's withdrawal was triggered by his father Lenny's embezzlement of some $180,000 in concert receipts during his brief tenure as the Dead's business manager. To Blair Jackson, the editor of the fan magazine *The Golden Road,* and, like Gans, a close observer of the band, it's no accident that the Dead played its freest music when there was only one drummer. This was during the Acid Tests and again in 1972–1974, when concert tapes show how effortlessly the band moved from "fat grooves to deep space and back again with just a few flicks of [Kreutzmann's] powerful wrists." Kreutzmann, Jackson believes, provided the Dead with a "rhythmic anchor" around which the guitarists could spin their webs without fear of leaving terra firma. He also contributed an "expressive current" all his own, a freewheeling mix of drum fills and splashing cymbals that had its own energy, and which made him "part of what makes the Grateful Dead first and foremost a jazz band."

This last is an opinion with which some jazz musicians, naturally, differ. "A country band with weird sound effects," jazz drummer Steve Grover calls the Grateful Dead, whose music he respects less than "the ideals of the music." The drumming, Grover finds "sort of shoddy." For rock improvisation, he prefers Cream and Jimi Hendrix, or even Phish, the current touring sensation often compared with the Dead. But he's enthusiastic about the black jazz musician David Murray, who grew up in Berkeley and "digs all those guys." Murray, a freethinker in the jazz world, "a keeper of the torch for the New York '60s jazz avant-garde," is a close friend of Bob Weir. In his most recent album, called *Dark Star,* Murray's ensemble reinterprets half a dozen Dead songs.

There's no doubt that the double drumming of the Rhythm Devils, as Hart and Kreutzmann were called, was a double-edged sword. It gave the Dead its powerful rhythm section, unmatched by any other rock band (only the Allman Brothers also had two drummers). When the "Drumz" sequence—"the crazy suite," Kreutzmann calls it, "the free space"—started to segue into the "Space" interlude in the early '80s, the door opened to experiments with digitally processed sounds previously only dreamed about. But in the late '60s, when Hart and Kreutzmann sometimes locked into long bar lengths from which they couldn't extricate themselves, the results were not so fortuitous.

The double drum work on the band's second album, *Anthem of the Sun* (1968), impresses Kreutzmann as musically less concise than he would like; turgid, even bombastic, others have said. Kreutzmann prefers the 1970 albums, *Workingman's Dead* and *American Beauty,* both for the harvest of new songs they reaped from Hunter and Garcia and for the simpler drumming. (When we meet, Hart says that the Grateful Dead "only made two good records: *Anthem of the Sun* and *Blues for Allah* [1975].") It was okay with Kreutzmann when Mickey took leave of the band for a few years after 1970, thereby ending the period of initiation—when, as Hart saw it, they were "entraining . . . beating efficiently together."

According to Mickey Hart, experimental improvs still occurred on tours in the 1990s, "from time to time, for better or worse. It's part of our style now. We make it happen. We know how to do it so well." How? I wondered, thinking of a similar process I once explored with the painter Larry Rivers, whose lively ambiguousness of line and shading was his trademark in the 1960s—an improvisational style, in another medium, not unlike the Grateful Dead's. By the end of the decade, Rivers's work, which contained the faint remains of all the artist didn't want as well as what he did, appeared to him as "the 'Larry Rivers' product.' . . . I mean, how many times can you just smudge and erase?" he fretted. "Who are you kidding?" Rivers went on to adapt to the market's preference for hard-edged multimedia collages, while retaining his autobiographical subject matter.

You might say the Grateful Dead took a similar turn when the improvisational well ran dry. First, they hired Bob Bralove to supply them with big-band sounds and an avant-garde palette of electronic color. And second, they allowed Candace Brightman to unfurl a multimedia stage set, incorporating a proscenium arch, painted scrims, live and preprogrammed video projections, and sculptural elements doubling as trusses for a vastly expanded, automated lighting system—the overall design of which changed every year. But you'd probably be missing the point. Or so

Bralove argues when I relate the mushrooming technology behind the new sounds to the move into giant coliseums that followed the hit tune "Touch of Grey" in 1986.

"You may require a broader stroke" is all he will concede. "Music satisfaction comes from the artist in us," he declares. "If I do my job well, there's music satisfaction, whether I do it with a stone and a piece of wood or I do it with the biggest computer in the world." I admit to coming from a literary convention with a bit of paranoia about technology, whereupon he asks if I "think a book is more literarily satisfying that was written on a typewriter or a word processor?" Touché. Still, I agree with Mountain Girl, who prefers Jerry's "straightforward guitar playing" to the wizardry that allowed him to step on a switch in a control mat at his feet and play "clarinet or sort of trumpety noises."

Bob Bralove relates a telling anecdote about the band's separation from its audience. When sound technician Dan Healy briefly lost the PA patch for the drums at a Cal Expo concert in the late '80s, leaving the fans to watch Kreutzmann and Hart bend and twist to a faint *tic-a-tic-a-tic-a-tic-a* sound (which was all the spectators could hear), somebody grabbed Bob by the shoulder and said, "It's not going out to the house! They've *lost* it! Should I tell 'em?" And Bralove, who was onstage with the drummers, said, "*Fuck, no!* What's that going to do? It'll just kill it." He tells me, "It was good, too," he grins, speaking of the passage the audience couldn't hear. "We were right on the groove."

The Dead, according to Hart, kept something of the improvisational spirit alive—"made it happen"—by incorporating "little minute cues inside the intricacies of the rhythm that were not available to the audience." (Or not to most.) To mark a leap into the unknown? I ask. No, he says; to signal turns in a set. It wasn't that collective leaps were no longer possible, but the band couldn't risk boring audiences of sixty thousand people. With a mass audience, it was important to provide entertainment with some degree of consistency. "Back in the '60s and '70s," critic Joel Selvin recalls, "the Dead didn't care if they were boring for hours on end. They were diving for pearls, and if they came up empty-handed, that was part of the deal." In the early '80s, Selvin noticed that the band had begun to "codify" its performances; to develop a framework to rely on: a shuffle here, an upbeat tune there; "Drumz" and "Space" in their accustomed slots midway through the second set. Gone were the long experimental jams that peaked in 1968–1970, when Tom Constanten played his "prepared piano" with the band. (This was a grand piano whose strings had been "damped" or otherwise altered by the insertion of foreign objects.)

But the uncertainty principle was honored in other ways—for example, by starting a song in one show and, after forking off into another and another, returning to finish it the next day. Or the unpredictability of Garcia's performances under the influence of drugs might suddenly open a trapdoor in the floor of an otherwise-humdrum program. Longtime fan Arthur Mack, another Mainer, who averaged twenty-five concerts a year in the '90s, could sense the shows when the musicians "probably wondered, Is this going to be a disaster?" He describes a second set at Nassau Coliseum in 1991 when Jerry was having a fit over his equipment, and Weir announced a short break so they could take care of the problem. When the band resumed playing, Jerry stood with his back to the others, strumming the same passage from "Iko Iko" over and over again. If Weir or Lesh tried to introduce a refrain or chorus, he repeated the passage, as if to say, "I'm not going to turn around and look at you and I'm going to just keep going until I feel like stopping. . . . At least that's how it appeared," says Mack. "He was having one of those nights."

But even then improvisation saved the day. The rest of the band stayed with it, "adding little nuances here and there, waiting for Jerry to decide if he wanted to do something else. Finally, he turned around, began singing the words [to "Iko Iko"], and everything was fine." Afterward, the band played a "Terrapin Station" encore for the first time in thirteen years, and did it beautifully, Mack says. An interesting story, it shows what a loose cannon Garcia could be—starting around 1980, in fact, when the seesaw of soft drugs and hard tilted toward heroin, and his withdrawal from the charmed circle he had created proceeded apace. It also shows how completely the band relied on their "nonleader leader" (as Gans calls him), even when Garcia was locked in a "no-game game."

Referring to the ensemble experience—a process that Mickey Hart, like Lesh, compares to "string quartet music, as far as how we relate to each other musically"—Joel Selvin maintains that the band used to call the "synergy that occurs when things lock up 'the seventh member. . . . Sometimes he shows up and plays the whole gig,' " they would say; " 'sometimes he comes late. Sometimes he doesn't show up at all.' " Surely the audience recognizes when the synergy is working, I suggest; but Selvin doubts it. "Deadheads," he states, "pride themselves on being a discriminating audience," but he recalls a concert at Berkeley's Greek Theater in the early '80s that suggests otherwise. Garcia played "this absolutely transcendent wa-wa solo that was like music I'd never heard before, and clearly like music *they* [the musicians] had never heard before. It had been concocted right on the spot, and it carried me away into this next movement, which was a third-rate white reggae band barely chugging along." Listening to the band play under the spell of the earlier passage was a revelation, he relates, for it dawned on him "how mundane the music was that I was now listening to." The audience, whooping and hollering, never seemed to notice the difference.

Band members have always questioned whether what Bob Weir calls "the indiscriminating and unconditional love and . . . adulation" of the fans was good for the music. Referring to the second set of a concert at the Greek Theater on September 11, 1981, which may have been the one Selvin recalls, Weir said at the time he felt "horrible when the crowd goes wild after we've just rendered a relatively dismal set. . . . They should run us out of town on a rail, and they never do."

Phil Lesh used to feel there was "information in the vibes from the audience," David Gans relates, but that early on "it became just pure energy," and therefore no longer reliable. By way of example, Gans recalls a solo Garcia performed in 1982 in Ventura, California, "that was just *awful*." The song was "Loser" and "it was full of mistakes. [Garcia] wasn't there—he was out of it at the time. And the audience went berserk." They loved it. What it said to Gans, who was interviewing band members at the time and was aware of the growing estrangement they felt from Deadheads, "was that if the fans were just as happy with a loud mistake as with a brilliant passage, no wonder these guys are feeling so alienated from the audience."

I saw the mechanics of this dilemma when Bob Bralove invited me to sit onstage, behind keyboardist Vince Welnick's speakers, during a concert at Boston Garden on September 30, 1993. It was the last show of the fall tour, "a stop-and-go, but ultimately soaring concert," according to the *Boston Globe* reviewer (the "stop-and-go" part no doubt referring to the musically uneventful first set). While the band sputtered through secondhand standbys such as "Spoonful," "El Paso," and "Broken Arrow," Bralove showed me how the headsets worked, switching us back and forth from

Weir's and Welnick's channels, "sampling" the intramural chatter, along with the musicians' instructions to sound tech Harry Popick, whose mixing station for the monitors was hidden on stage right. But I was distracted by the sea of shining faces that stretched before me.

Bobbing in a penumbra of coasting balloons and shimmering lights, the audience might have been Tom Wolfe's "writhing, seething mass of little girls waving their arms in the air" at a Beatles concert, except the majority were young men. The "vibrating poison madness" that Wolfe and Kesey picked up in 1964 was not in evidence in the aging arena, headquarters to the Home Team whose huge banners—BOSTON CELTICS 1986 WORLD CHAMPIONS—hung from the rafters. A kind of mad benevolence, tinged with ecstasy, possessed this crowd, though one must allow for variant perceptions. To an outsider, the happy faces en masse might appear anything but benevolent. Like the Talmud says, "We do not see things as they are; we see them as we are." What, I wondered, did the band see?

"For the Grateful Dead," Jerry Garcia used to say, "there is no 'Grateful Dead.' " The band stares into the vortex of a mass audience, while the "deadicated" concertgoer beholds a group of middle-aged men whose music making is the ticket to a world of dreams—one that has less to do with the actual lives of the musicians than with the hungers the fans bring to the party. Jerry, on this particular night, appeared to be molting from whatever state he had arrived in, to another, transitional zone, which he shared with no one but his instrument. When it came time for him to deliver "Candyman," the guitar was ready but the voice was not. A voice needs someone to sing to, or the memory of someone, if it's to reach the hearts of strangers. His was on hold.

Alongside Garcia's lethargy, Bob Weir scampered about like a nervous puppy, darting between Lesh and Jerry and the drummers as if to whip up a show not quite ready to get off the ground. "Garcia used to move a lot more onstage and I used to move a lot less," he told me the summer before, when we talked backstage before a concert at Soldier Field in Chicago. Mainly, he was "communicating from one part of the stage to the other," Weir explained, leading the band, in effect, though he didn't say it. "I spend a fair amount of time onstage wondering what's up," he offers instead; especially in the " 'Space' part when I haven't the foggiest idea what's coming." There's a certain "showmanship" to maintain, he adds, which the Dead had no need of until the end of the '60s, when the audiences "stopped being dancing audiences and started watching the band. And so we adapted to that"—quite happily, one senses, in his case. ("I'm the 'Mr. Show-biz' in the group," Weir said on another occasion, adding that he'd "developed the attitude over the years that by the time I start getting bored with a given number, it's a fair guess that a certain portion of the audience is getting bored, too.")

But there is a strange lassitude on the Boston stage. Not much is happening. It's like sitting in a soundproof box—or in the garage of a garage band rehearsing. It would be different if I had my own in-the-ear monitor. The monitors act as earplugs, which deaden the sound of the audience for the band members. "When we're up there pumping, there's nothing louder than us," Vince Welnick says, finding this fact "a double-edged sword." To me, the unamplified *wop-wop/tic-a-tic-a* of the double drumming sounds absentminded. Welnick's keyboard wheezes like a church organ—and my eyes rest on his little finger, which arches backward above the keys like a Cambodian dancing girl's. With his shaggy strawberry blond beard and bright Hawaiian shirts, Vince seems to fly the colors of a raunchy San Francisco bar band, which is what the Grateful Dead, at the moment, appears to be.

Lesh sings the Robbie Robertson tune "Broken Arrow," but I can barely hear him. No house sounds where I sit. Actually, there's nothing coming off the stage into the house, either. It's all in the PA. Soundman Dan Healy reconfigures the music in stereo and circulates it throughout the hall—not always evenly, I hear; for the fans at the fringe often don't get a full mix of what's happening onstage. The audience, meanwhile, roars its approval of this infrequent eruption from the Phil Zone. When I listen to the song later on a concert tape, I'm struck by the flat, uninflected phrasing; the hollow voice, straining, but not too hard, for feeling. Onstage, Bob Weir's intensity underscores the exhaustion that breaks through the surface clamor of the show like a surge of testosterone in reverse. Weir jogs through "El Paso" ("belts it out," says the *Globe*) and then comes alive—indeed, the whole stage and arena come alive, as do the lights (or is it the other way around?)—with a new tune the band introduced that year, "Easy Answers." As in "Easy answers—there're no easy answers. . . ."

.　.　.

No wonder the Wizard of Oz tries to prevent his subjects from entering
the Throne Room. The risk of exposure is too great. The gap between the
former ventriloquist from Omaha and the Great and Terrible Oz who
rules the Emerald City requires too many ropes and pulleys to animate the
enchanted forms with which he hoodwinks Dorothy and her friends: a
papier-mâché Head, a Terrible Beast patched together with animal skins,
a cotton Ball of Fire drenched in oil. Somebody is bound to tip the screen
that conceals the little man who pulls the strings. But it's in the nature of
the Wizard to be exposed. It is the way of the humbug, *the way he rules.*

In this most American of tales (which has as much to say about presi-
dents as rock bands), the little group of pilgrims from Kansas clings to the
phantom Wizard even after Toto has unmasked him. Why? Because he
alone appears capable of giving them what they need, or think they need.
It doesn't matter that he's a fraud.

> "No; you are all wrong," said the little man, meekly. "I have been
> making believe."
>
> "Making believe!" cried Dorothy. "Are you not a great Wiz-
> ard?"
>
> "Hush, my dear," he said; "don't speak so loud, or you will be
> overheard—and I should be ruined. I'm supposed to be a Great
> Wizard."
>
> "And aren't you?" she asked.
>
> "Not a bit of it, my dear; I'm just a common man."
>
> "You're more than that," said the Scarecrow, in a grieved tone;
> "you're a humbug."
>
> "Exactly so!" declared the little man, rubbing his hands to-
> gether as if it pleased him; "I am a humbug."

The Scarecrow still wants his "bran-new brains," the Tin Woodsman his
silken heart, stuffed with sawdust, the Cowardly Lion his bottle of
courage, and Dorothy wants to go home. The fact that each of them (except Dorothy) already possesses the real thing himself, something the
"good Wizard" takes pains to remind them, can no more free them from
their reliance on humbuggery than the "true facts" about Vietnam could
empower "the great American people" to bring a speedy end to the war.

So the "good Wizard" reverts to the "false Wizard" and dispenses blarney: "You must excuse me for taking your head off, but I shall have to do it in order to put your brains in their proper place." To which the Scarecrow replies, "That's all right. . . . You are quite welcome to take my head off, as long as it will be a better one when you put it on again."

With his bag of tricks, the Wizard of Oz succeeds in *realigning consciousness* so the supplicant may draw on his own resources—without, however, recognizing their origins within himself. That would entail taking responsibility for something he believes he doesn't own. Thus, he remains indebted to his liberator; and he makes a worthy successor, as the Wise Scarecrow does when Oz puts him in charge of the kingdom he himself is about to flee. The Scarecrow remains foolish, and tells them "There were wonderful thoughts in his head; but he could not say what they were because he knew no one could understand them but himself." The beauty of such wizardry in a democracy—for wizards, that is—is that while it derives from the consent of the governed, it keeps them forever in their place.

Watching the second half of the Boston Garden show from the lighting booth out front was like seeing the Great Oz in full possession of his powers. Everything was different, beginning with the trippy "Lucy in the Sky with Diamonds" that opened the set; but especially was the drumming different. While Kreutzmann and Hart pounded their back-and-forth in the "Drumz" sequence, Dan Healy bounced a stream of percussion—bongos, a xylophone, a loaflike object that went *tic-toc-tic-toc* when Hart struck it—around the arena, *rolling* it up and across the ceiling like a wave. Electronic ventriloquism, one might call the effect, it wrapped the audience in sound, so that one was hard-pressed to know where it was coming from.

Candace was leaning into the action, playing the board at the front of the booth as if it were an organ, pumping beams of color around the hall, filling the corners with tiny spinning prisms of light. The audience was her canvas, along with the stage, as it was during "Easy Answers." Then it occurred to me from my cubby behind the speakers that she was also entertaining the band—who never see the "overall picture," Bob Weir says, and only "know it's working on the audience" when they "hear people gasp at what she does." She was turning the sea of faces into a flying carpet of color for the delectation of the musicians.

Standing out in the booth, however, listening to the crowd murmur its approval of the son et lumière during the "Drumz" cycle, I see that the visual production envelops everyone, and weaves a web of color that carries the music the way the sky carries a storm. The lights, the abstract video projections on screens above the stage, and the fiber optics shimmying in the wings, are driven by the drumming, which soon tacks into "Space." But the lights create visual equivalencies to the music's atonal, antimelodic playfulness. As a second *Boston Globe* reporter enthused the next day: "During its best moments, the light show made literal the geometric structures that Dead music often implies." However that happens, the lights are doing more than accompanying the music or filling in when it stumbles—a task that, according to Weir, Candace also does well. "We can be droning on in some dismal fashion, and she can light it in such a way," he says, "that the crowd is still getting a decent show." Here, it seems, the lights dance with the music, and it's hard to tell who leads and who follows.

From where I stand, the crowd is certainly getting a better show in the second set. But how much better, and why? And what if I were back onstage, what then? It's an epistemological question, like Bishop Berkeley's tree in the forest, which cannot fall unless someone hears it. The contents of the material world are but "ideas" that only exist when they are received by a mind: "To be," the Bishop said, "is to be perceived." How is this, the idealist's view, so basic to Deaddom, to be reconciled with the presence of electronic amplification—the lighting, the rolling sounds— alongside the sensory enhancement of the drugs, and a third stimulant: the *spiritual* factor?

This last is evoked by Bob Weir's songwriting partner, John Perry Barlow, when he recalls the times "I went to a Grateful Dead concert where I thought it was just the best goddamned thing I had ever heard in my whole life, and I was happier than a pig in shit to be there." Afterward, though, when he listened to tapes of the same event, he "kept thinking, 'Wait a second. Christ. Phil's off-key. And what are all these notes where Weir's supposed to be there—was the amplifier down? I didn't hear the vocals get so out of sync at this point.'" Barlow concludes that "there's something transcendent about the experience itself that probably causes people to get into a spiritual kind of relationship to it that they wouldn't with a lot of other very fine bands."

John Barlow, a philosophe in cybernetic circles, who founded the Electronic Frontier Foundation, subscribes to a theory of "creative synergy" whereby listeners who participate intensely in a creative process modify it in some fundamental way, not just for themselves individually but also collectively, for the group. It's a popular theory among Deadheads who see themselves as the "seventh band member." Even when they discover, like Barlow, that on tape their favorite concerts sound nothing like what they remember, they collect them anyway to memorialize the larger experience. (Standing outside the spirit circle as I do, and not using drugs, I'm free to meditate on the ropes and pulleys.)

As for the music, my own limited exposure suggests that the second set is usually the better one, especially at outdoor shows, where there's no lighting during the first set. The band has warmed up, felt the pulse of the crowd, and the music has an edge. The uncertainty principle roams like a poltergeist through the dainty china country of the same old songs. "Bertha," "Good Lovin'," "Uncle John's Band," "Playing in the Band," "Attics of My Life," "Throwing Stones," "Not Fade Away": this was the second-set lineup of a Giants Stadium concert on June 6, 1993, when it seemed to me that the "Drumz"/"Space" sequence fairly exploded with the pent-up creativity of madmen—one of whom was Bralove in his bulging headphones, lurking like Dr. Caligari in the shadow of the Beast.

The Boston Garden show, however, was indoors; and the contrasts between the two sets are too extreme to owe themselves to such circumstances. Candace, moreover, who has seen *thousands* of concerts, disputes my judgment about the second sets. More often the first-set music "sailed and floated and drifted down—flying without any flying muscles," she maintains. Outdoors, before the lights, the playing was "easy, effortless"—which may be because she was freer to enjoy it. And maybe the band was more relaxed without the lights. September 30, 1993, however, was not one of those nights.

Still, had I seen the first set from the arena, I'm sure the performances wouldn't have seemed as ragged as they did from the stage. In such instances, the wizards—Bralove, Healy, and Candace—really do make the difference, I believe; and during the band's last decade, their prowess and stepped-up budgets granted the on-again, off-again energies of the musicians some respite. The huge crowds did the rest, bringing with them a core of spirit guides and music buffs (like Jamie Janover's friends), whose task has always been to break in the newcomers. Bob Bralove, however, sees it differently. The technology, in his view, remains secondary to the music, whose soul never changes.

When he and I first meet in the band's rehearsal studio in San Rafael, he talks about how Deadheads make up stories to account for what they don't understand. It's a corollary to Mickey Hart's notion that the Dead offers its fans the raw materials they need to "build their own personal mythology . . . within the Grateful Dead's larger mythos"; and it reminds me that Candace once told me that a lot of people in the audience think the lights are powered by Jerry's guitar. A funny story, I think, and I pass it on to Bralove. *"They are,"* he says solemnly. "The whole thing comes out of—" He stops, as if it's all so obvious.

In the end, it's the "collective good stuff" that remains the Grateful Dead's most influential legacy. The band's taste for ambiguity—the "fog" that makes Weir listen hard until his "fingers find what's next," and the "connection [is made] from my mind, my spirit, straight to the strings"—wears its modernity with amazing grace. The celebrated noodling of the gods, or the memory of it, is a deposit the Dead has made in the central bank of symbolic forms, along with the reinterpretation of traditional American motifs, *roots* music flying high.

"The Dead are now themselves American folklore music," Jamie Janover points out. "They're really old-style now, and there are a ton of bands that are influenced by them." These include not just well-known groups like Phish, who were informed by the Grateful Dead in the early '80s, and to a lesser extent by the Allman Brothers and Frank Zappa, but "jam bands," whose musicians have picked up the central idea of "listening to one another. The idea of a jam band," Janover explains, "is that you can take something very simple and make it into a motif, and then into a theme," which appears to emerge by accident. (A one-man band on his hammer dulcimer, Janover does it on a CD titled *Evolutions.*)

The phenomenon, he suggests, was pioneered by Jerry Garcia in jazz-like solos that came up with little melodies, which were then picked up and reflected on by somebody else, until "a call-and-answer kind of thing would happen, and that would propel itself, and work off itself, like nuclear fission." It's not unlike the search process Mickey Hart describes; and it occurs to me that what's "old-style now" couldn't be more timely for any group of musicians whose members bring to the table influences as different as those that originally fueled the Grateful Dead.

So contrary is this "intricacy of listening," as Hart calls it, to the extroversion of the political movements of the 1960s and '70s that I wonder if the Grateful Dead's original adventures with improvisation may have served the rebel years as a kind of alter ego: a counterweight to the extremities of speech and action, which helped keep the era's zeitgeist alive for later use. Thinking of the present, and not just about music, what could be more timely than the experience the Dead conveys of chaos accepted and embraced?

It's when you listen closely to the lyrics with an ear cocked to the "other songs of war" that Hunter evokes in "Standing on the Moon"—"the cries of children," the "mighty melody" rising from a troubled earth—that you sense the more ambiguous service rendered by the Grateful Dead during the exhilarating years of takeoff. This is the way in which the magic train of music, drugs, and dance, once it hit the road, offered its followers a sanctuary from the upheavals of an often scary time of change.

⌐✺⌐

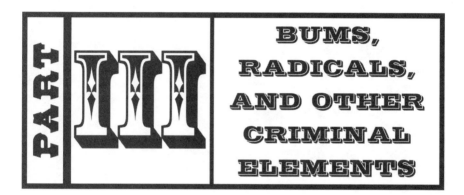

PART III

BUMS, RADICALS, AND OTHER CRIMINAL ELEMENTS

~CHAPTER~
8

THEIR SUBCULTURE AND MINE: I

There was no time like the time we
thought something was happening
which was not what we thought it was
but might as well have been considering
how little it was anything else.

ROBERT HUNTER, "AN AMERICAN ADVENTURE"

E ILEEN LAW, WHO came down the coast to San Francisco from Rionido
in 1964, fell into the dance hall scene and later became one of the Grateful Dead's right-hand women. She remembers meeting Jerry Rubin in
1966 when Berkeley's Vietnam Day Committee organized an antiwar
march in San Francisco. "It was hard for me," she says. "I saw them *stirring*
something up that I knew wasn't quite my element. I don't know if it was
stirring up anger or I was just too low-key"; but the confrontational style
of Rubin's troops ultimately sent her packing. It happened during the antiwar march down Market Street, when she experienced the sensation of a
power outside herself "amping" her—"and I remember all of a sudden just
kind of walking out, catching the MUNI, and goin' home. . . . I've never
been a marcher," she reflects, as if the same electrifying force is still at
large in the streets in 1993 when we talk, "but I sure appreciate those that
do it."

In the Haight, authority was sensed differently from how it was on the
Left. It wasn't the power of institutions, ideas, or governments to wreak
havoc in the world that came under siege but the internal checks society
exacts of an obedient citizenry. Hence, the Psychedelic Rangers'
"Prophecy of a Declaration of Independence": "When in the flow of
human events it becomes necessary for the people to cease to recognize

the obsolete social patterns which have isolated man from his consciousness. . . ." Eileen's resistance, like that of many teenagers who descended on San Francisco from outlying towns, took the form of sudden and dizzying changes in lifestyle. At seventeen, she found a job with an insurance company and moved in with an aunt and uncle in the Sunset District. A month later, she moved out to join a girlfriend who lived with her parents in Westlake. Within weeks, she hooked up with a North Beach crowd who hung out at Aquatic Park, where Santana was just going public, and announced that she was getting an apartment with three other girls.

Each step took her farther from home and closer to a kind of "outlaw life." She held on to her day job, but soon the pot she was smoking and the psychedelics she took during the Acid Tests loosened her grip on the necessity of the work. She found a part-time job making belts in the basement of a leather shop on Haight Street, where the owner, Bobby Bowles, played the Dead's first single, "The Golden Road (to Unlimited Devotion)" (1967), over and over. Eventually, she gravitated to 710 Ashbury. It was party time, when "everyone had looked like diamonds."

Her mother was aghast, but her father (divorced) still sent her sixty dollars a month. Eileen had made her move, one she says she has never regretted. When Jerry Garcia, speaking to an interviewer in the 1980s, defended the "leap of faith," which says, "Hey, the hell with the world. I'm gonna do what I wanna do and I'm willing to go for it," he might have been speaking for her and many like her. "If you get caught up in reality or society or any of the rest of those illusions," he added, "you're definitely gonna get nowhere."

"Our trip was never to go out and change the world," Garcia pointed out. "I mean, what would we change it to? Whatever we did would probably be worse than the way it is now." Besides, on the other side of reality's wall lay a secret garden of indescribable delight, where the long arm of lawfulness appeared helpless to intervene. Inside the ballrooms and union halls, musicians and dancers comprised a world unto themselves. "It became very telepathic," Eileen Law remembers, referring to the way LSD seemed to open everyone's mind to one another, creating, in effect, a group mind. The experience is mirrored in Robert Heinlein's *Stranger in a Strange Land,* a favorite in Prankster circles, where an American on Mars acquires mystic powers, lands on earth, and assembles a "nest" of followers who are inducted into a supermind via an arcane rite called "water-sharing." Personalities merge; people no longer talk, they "grok" each other, itself a form of telepathy. So it was with the Dead's first family. "When you saw each other," Eileen says, "it was like you had this secret over everybody else." Being with them, Phil Lesh's then-girlfriend, Florence Nathan, suggested later, was like living on a block where all the kids are like you.

Best approached at the midnight hour of a Grateful Dead jam, when the mix of sound and light, brought to a boil by the drugs, turned the body into a receiving instrument for messages from Beyond ("Magic is what we do," Garcia told the press, "music is how we do it"), the psychedelic garden served as a kind of Eden. It was a retreat from the tedium of day-to-day existence, and from the harsh political battles being fought outside in the streets. The garden had its counterpart in the real one, which was Golden Gate Park, where the Dead sometimes led their audiences after playing on a flatbed truck at the corner of Haight and Cole. For Jerry (Hunter, too), Golden Gate Park, "a beautiful work," embodied an idea that was important to his music, the idea of the "odyssey," of journeys and trips, with adventures along the way. One might step over a hill and be in a rhododendron dell, a world full of huge prehistoric-looking ferns, which gave way to open fields and tangled madrona, yielding, in turn, to a cloistered lagoon, with waterfalls and sculpted plants surrounding a teahouse. Walking through the park stoned, Garcia said, was to experience "the work of an artist." And this was so not just because it *was* the work of an artist (Scottish-born John McLaren) but also because one's heightened senses gave access to the beauty and complexity of the noble forms that lay embedded in the landscape.

This sensitivity to the natural world, a strand in the culture that's grown up around the Grateful Dead, is expressed with special force by a former molecular biologist, Alan Kapuler, a Deadhead who today runs a seed exchange in Corvallis, Oregon. The perception that human beings don't exist apart from nature, and are conditioned to some degree by the circumstances of their relation to it, is not new. Nor is it exclusive to Deadheads, but Kapuler, known as "Mushroom," a science whiz who graduated summa cum laude from Yale in 1963 and then received his doctorate from the Rockefeller Institute, takes the perception further. "We need interaction with a breadth of organisms," not just other human beings but "pine trees and apple trees and worms, fruit flies, salamanders, and fish . . . to be complete psycho-emotionally."

Psycho-what? I ask, not sure I've heard him right. *"Psycho-emotionally,"* he repeats: relating to "our own fabric of feeling and sensitivity," by which he means an *actual* fabric, a background, like radiation—not neutral— rather than a metaphor of the touchy-feely crowd or an academic concept in sociobiology. It's what you sense when you look at your dog *hard* and watch her looking back at you, or lean against a tree and realize you're part of it. "Psychedelics opened that channel to many people," Mushroom says. Mescaline and LSD, in particular, made it easier to appreciate certain facts; namely, "The universe is alive. The rocks are alive. . . . This is an animal, and this is a plant, and this is dead, and this is alive. That whole fabric . . ."

By the late '60s, we radicals had set out to explore the Third World. Early in 1967, during the height of the air war, I traveled with a Bertrand Russell War Crimes Tribunal investigating team through the bombed hamlets of North Vietnam. Later that year, I joined a group of American antiwar and civil rights activists who met with North Vietnamese and National Liberation Front delegations in Bratislava, Czechoslovakia. In the fall of 1969, when the mass media was brimming over with war news, and *Viet-Report* had merged into a broader-based journal called *Leviathan*, I accepted an invitation to visit Cuba. It was an opportunity seized for reasons both personal and political. Cuba, more than Vietnam, would enter the dream life of the movement of which I was a part at precisely the time when radicals seemed to lose their bearings at home.

My parents had honeymooned in Havana in 1939, under the dictator Batista. My father used to vacation there with his mother, which is probably why he chose it for his bride. I was conceived there, in the Hotel Lincoln. When I found the hotel in 1968 in the old quarter, it was surrounded by Cuban soldiers. *¿Qué pasa?* I asked, but no one would say. Afterward, I was told that this was the temporary residence of a collection of black revolutionaries from North America, some of whom had hijacked planes to escape criminal charges and seek asylum in Cuba. Whether the Cuban soldiers were protecting them or holding them hostage wasn't clear.

There was something oddly familiar about Cuba in 1969, and in 1970, when I returned, which was more than the dusty Chevrolets and Cadillacs from the '50s. Nor was it the American-style billboards emblazoned with revolutionary slogans, or the empty tollbooths along the highways leaving Havana. Part of the familiarity, of course, was a Latino flamboyance I knew from New York, which seemed more strenuous in Cuba, where work, being socialized, was for a cause, and play, especially music and dance, had an anarchic, *physical* energy.

For the 1969 trip, I made tapes that included the music of the Rolling Stones, Janis Joplin, the Beatles, Dylan, and the Doors. Everywhere we went—myself, an interpreter, and the driver of the elderly Fleetwood in which we traveled—I was asked to play them. The response was always enthusiastic, especially to Jim Morrison. It was either "Break on Through" or "Light My Fire" that brought a shedful of women cigar workers in Santa Clara to their feet, stomping and clapping. Jerry Garcia, who disdained Morrison for his in-your-face heroics, imitative of Mick Jagger, he thought, would not have been amused.

What really rang a bell in Cuba was what Cubans had that we didn't, and wished we did. Optimism, in a word; a belief in the effectiveness of concerted action to change the way things are. For antiwar activists, it was the endless bloodshed in Vietnam, which now suggested that only fundamental shifts in the distribution of power at home—not just political power but economic power—might reverse the policies that led to war. The freedom to live outside the ventilators of capitalism, for instance; to imagine using your life for something other than getting and spending, much less fighting peasants in a distant land—these were the heresies which had begun to interest us. Vietnam sounded the alarm that put them on the table. Cuba showed us they might work.

For young radicals, hundreds of whom (including me) began traveling south on Cuban freighters from Saint John, New Brunswick, in the winter of 1969–1970 to cut sugarcane with a volunteer organization called the Venceremos Brigade, the political attraction of the "First Free Territory of the Americas" was immense. Here was a socialist country, ninety miles from Florida, which, unlike the dreary Soviet-bloc countries, embraced a vision of human perfectibility altogether missing from the American scene. The vision was embodied in Che Guevara's "New Man," who was driven, in an ideal world, not by material incentives but by moral ones. And while Che was dead, murdered in 1967 by CIA-trained soldiers in Bolivia, here was Fidel Castro, in February 1970, personally exhorting us to remember that "the humanity we have known up until now is a prehistoric humanity, a savage humanity, a humanity full of international crimes, wars, exploitations. . . ." Only with the elimination of these abuses will "the real history of humanity begin. We really hope to have a historic society," Fidel said of Cuba; and he believed Cubans were "on the road. . . . One cannot be a revolutionary if he is not an optimist," he asserted, adding, "If you are a pessimist, you must be a conservative, stand still and defend conservative positions." As for the argument that "men cannot do it," that was "equivalent to renouncing forever, to man, the possibility of moral sentiment, of moral development."

These were powerful words in 1970, especially when spoken in a Cuban cane field where a youthful mix of races, classes, and political factions from the North had defied the American embargo on trade and travel to Cuba to arrive there. With the sons and daughters of bishops, military career officers, college teachers, and white-collar workers swinging machetes alongside black street kids from L.A. and Oakland, *puertoriqueños* from New York, and Chicanos from Texas—with a generous sprinkling of government agents leavening the brew—the second Venceremos Brigade showed us how diverse our movement really was.

Of course, it was a gathering whose center could not hold, and didn't. The formula for a movement's longevity is better set by that first family from the Haight, where all the kids on the block are alike. That is, white, working- to middle-class, deaf to politics, which are perceived as dirty— ordinary Americans (though Deadheads would come to reflect a more diverse social reality). We were the freaks. No sooner were all 590 of us installed in camp in Matanzas Province, and assigned to multiracial work brigades by our Cuban *jefes,* than ethnic-identity politics broke out with a vengeance. Field tents flew the flags of "Third World" caucuses from the States: black, Latin, Asian, Native American. A racial confrontation on the first Brigade led blacks to urge the white majority to hold a "white caucus meeting," which was quickly dubbed the "white citizens' council" by its embarrassed participants. On the second Brigade, white *brigadistas,* with no home of their own, cruised the perimeters of the boisterous "Third World" tents like feral dogs hungry for scraps.

"Third World leadership" was another idea on the table, newer than the anticapitalist one; and it was unleashing havoc in the camp. "Third World leadership" was promoted by the Weatherman faction of SDS, the children of lawyers, businessmen, and utility executives, by and large, who dominated the first Brigade. As the most oppressed and exploited people in the world, "Third World people," the argument ran, would necessarily take the most progressive positions on political issues. For white radicals afflicted with racial guilt, the idea provided a kind of absolution by ideology; though an alternative reading is offered by the essayist George W. S. Trow, which is that " 'white guilt' " or " 'white masochism' " was really "white *euphoria*." "[M]any white children of that day felt the power of their inheritance for the first time in the act of rejecting it," Trow suggests. For Third World people themselves, the concept of leadership based on oppression was at best a theoretical one, and thus had never been practiced. It required a multicultural unity that didn't exist even within individual ethnic groups, whose members had been recruited from all over the United States.

Yet it was out of this crude agglomeration of so-called revolutionaries—"You thought we were perfect, and we thought you were revolutionaries," a Cuban Brigade member, a woman, chuckled at the end—that something unprecedented had emerged. Among blacks, in particular, the most numerous and politically seasoned of the Third World contingents, a kind of bonding was achieved that had not been possible before, ironically because regional antagonisms had prevented it. Thus, former civil rights workers from SNCC, black nationalists allied with the Republic of New Africa, and inner-city cadres close to the Black Panther party could check one another out, and did. By the end of the second Brigade, most blacks had pierced their left ears with an earring to signify a newfound unity.

Whites, who comprised about three-quarters of the Brigade, were less fortunate. Many found it easier to pin "Third World" hopes on Cubans or on the Vietnamese students studying in Havana who visited the camp (among them, Vietnam's current ambassador to the United States, Le Van Bang) than to embrace their Third World American comrades. While most whites, themselves reflecting a diversity of backgrounds and political experiences, left Cuba proclaiming a newfound faith in the power of cooperation, hard work, and the correct analysis of problems, a silent minority probably agreed with the young man who wanted "a collective experience / all by myself / that I won't have to share. . . ."

Black-white relations reached a new low in Cuba, or a new level of candor. "I found myself looking at one of the longhaired white men and having a sheer physical urge to kill him," someone submitted anonymously to the "Book Tent," which served as the collection box for the book that was published the following year about the Venceremos Brigade experience. Whites, meanwhile, learned how close to death black militants lived in the United States when on December 5, 1969, the first Brigade received news of the killing of Fred Hampton and another Black Panther by police in Chicago. On March 11, 1970, the second Brigade was informed of the deaths of SNCC workers Ralph Featherstone and "Che" Payne, who were killed when a car they entered exploded in Bel Air, Maryland. Featherstone had once helped H. Rap Brown fend off a Ku Klux Klan attack on a voter registration project in Lowndes County, Mississippi.

Both murders exacerbated racial tensions in camp, but the confrontations that followed also led to small epiphanies among people who had been at one another's throats: such as the young clergyman (white) who returned to his tent after Featherstone's death to find a black tent mate crying. When he asked what was wrong, he was chewed out for his insensitivity; afterward, though, the young black man began to express sorrow that so much of what happens in the United States caused him to hate all white people. Together, they started using "we" when talking about how they were going to "take care of business" when they got home—a point that was made in the telegram the black caucus sent to SNCC leader James Forman on behalf of the Venceremos Brigade.

At night, after the cane was cut, Third World caucuses organized cultural performances and seminars to acquaint *brigadistas* with the history of their respective struggles for justice and self-determination. But nothing moved the second contingent as much as the address black caucus leader Marty Price delivered after the SNCC deaths. Featherstone was a "full-time revolutionary [who] worked for the full liberation of his people," Price said. "When people live their lives in this manner, they simultaneously decide their death." This was another idea that had tremendous impact on young Americans in Cuba, and on the movement at home. The idea of death. Death and revolution. "Death [that happens] to those we know can only reaffirm our commitment to revolution," a young *machetero* wrote in his journal. "A choice no longer exists. Not for me personally. Not for the movement."

Killings such as these were part of the "Sense of Crisis" that journalist Andy Kopkind wrote about in the spring of 1970. Featherstone's car, "blown to bits by a bomb," was preceded on March 6 by the more widely publicized death of three Weathermen who blew themselves up while making bombs in a Greenwich Village town house. A few days later, grenades went off in several corporate headquarters in New York (harming no one). "[G]uerrilla attacks by the revolutionary left and counterattacks by the extreme right seem almost natural," Kopkind reflected, noting that newspapers had begun calling the current crop of radicals *revolutionaries* without quotation marks and without the skeptical qualifier "self-styled."

On March 16, Mississippi senator William O. Eastland told the U.S. Senate that what had been a "comparative trickle" of Americans visiting Cuba in the 1960s now "threatens to become a flood." It was the sort of charge to which Fidel Castro liked to respond: *"It's true! It's true!"* Eastland called for an investigation; and referring to the Venceremos Brigade, he said:

> We intend to light the shadows that surround this vicious operation—to drive from those shadows the missiles—in human form—which have been fashioned on the Communist island and fired at America. We want our people to be aware of the direct chain which reaches from Cuba to our cities, our campuses, our conventions, our lives—and which threatens the life of this Republic.

Brigade members were receiving guerrilla training in Cuba, he charged. Cane cutting was just a ruse. No one believed that the natives in America could be restless all by themselves.

Driving into Boston on Brigade business in December 1969, to meet an Italian street punk named "Shades," I can remember a moment when suddenly it seemed as if the country had tipped on its axis. Many around my age had this sensation, with or without drugs, when the ordinary ingredients of daily life were scrambled in just such a way that everything looked brand new. Anything seemed possible. Usually, you were far from home, going farther. This was a good thing, not like now, when young people look over their shoulders to make sure home's still there.

Shades, nicknamed for the smoky glasses he wore, was a wiry kid with a black ponytail who hinted at mob connections. He had been recruited to the movement by Weathermen during a sweep of South Boston high schools—"jailbreaks," in Weatherspeak—when these former SDS stalwarts, mostly college graduates, and mainly women, invaded classrooms to lecture students about imperialism, racism, and sexism, and to demonstrate their toughness. When somebody moved to stop them, they fought back, displaying their latest karate chops before melting back into the streets—or being hauled off in a paddy wagon.

That year and the next was when some frustrated veterans of the antiwar movement talked of emulating urban guerrillas, such as the Tupamaros in Uruguay. The "Tupes," as we called them, declared that a "revolutionary movement must prepare itself for the armed struggle at any stage, even when conditions . . . don't exist." Why? Because it might be subject to repression at any time, and must be prepared to defend its very breath. "And because if each and every militant isn't inculcated from the beginning with the thinking of a fighter, what we will create will be . . . a mere movement for others to carry out. . . ."

Needless to say, Weatherman's "jailbreaks"—which were also taking place in Detroit, Pittsburgh, Chicago, and New York—generated more hostility than admiration. One can only guess at the motives of recruits like Shades, who had been integrated into a Boston affinity group and was now the bagman for the Venceremos Brigade's regional organizing committee. As a member of the national committee, I was meeting him to pick up the money he had collected from pledges made at fund-raising events around Cambridge, to be used to cover travel expenses for Brigade volunteers. I was also planning to interview prospective candidates, including Shades, for the second Brigade. Shades, as it happened, made a poor *machetero*. He feigned sunstroke the first week and disappeared into a nearby *ville* to set up a cigar-smuggling operation, was caught and sent home.

I was then living outside Boston with a former *Viet-Report* editor, and lecturing on U.S. foreign policy at Southeastern Massachusetts University. It was a nice break from teaching English, my usual job, but I was not happy away from New York; and the editor and I, who had stumbled into marriage in 1968, were wearing out our welcome mat with each other. When the second Brigade left, I went with it. When I returned from Cuba in April 1970, the country had tilted again. Protests, mainly against the war, had been escalating on campuses all year. The American Council on Education counted 9,408 incidents in 1970 alone, including 731 involving police and arrests, 410 relating to property damage—chiefly ROTC buildings—and 230 involving violence to persons. "Wholly unorganized and utterly undirected, the revolutionary movement exists," Kopkind observed, speaking of a larger unrest that now included several armed undergrounds, "not because the left is strong but because the center is weak."

A breakpoint was reached when Nixon invaded Cambodia on April 30. A few days later, on May 4, with 30 percent of the nation's colleges on strike, National Guardsmen fired M1 rifles at protesting students at Kent State University in Ohio, killing four and wounding nine. On May 14, at Jackson State College in Mississippi, the police fired into a women's dormitory, killing two students. In the first half of May, twenty-one campuses were occupied by the National Guard.

Such was the atmosphere when I decided to move to California in July. But before that, I had another obligation to fulfill with the Venceremos Brigade, which was to coedit the book with Sandra Levinson. A group project, it required setting up the "Book Tent" in New York, in the capacious Riverside Drive apartment of my husband's girlfriend, as it turned out, where Brigade caucuses helped organize the stacks of diaries, poems, manifestos, interviews, photographs, and tapes into the hydra-headed portrait of young Americans in Cuba that is *Venceremos Brigade* (1971).

The years 1967, 1968, 1969, and 1970 were "a cyclone in a wind tunnel," Todd Gitlin reflects in *The Sixties*. Especially was this true of 1970, which had a different feel from the 1960s—wilder, more chaotic. "Reality was reckless, and so there is the temptation to dismiss it," Gitlin says of the year's offtrack political events. Indeed, this is what many commentators have done, especially with the Venceremos Brigade, which enjoys an undeserved obscurity. What happened to all those quarrelsome young radicals who went to Cuba? Where did they come from, and where did they go? Politically, the Venceremos Brigade, which sent other work brigades to Cuba throughout the 1970s, but none as large and obstreperous as the first two, had little influence either on U.S. policy toward Cuba or on the unification of the American Left. And Cuba fell far short of the 10-million-ton sugar harvest slated for 1970. Socially and culturally, however, the Cuba sojourn was of immense significance. One might regard an interlude such as this as the equivalent of improvisation in music. It seems like chaos, but put your ear to the ground, listen closely to the *pulse* of what's happening, and to the aftershocks, and you may catch the rhythms of alternate realities that fell by the wayside after the dominant chords were struck.

For white radicals, Berkeley was our very own Third World; not because it was embattled and impoverished, as parts of nearby Oakland were, but because it appeared to be so precariously anchored to the motherland. A decade of protests and confrontations, some scoring notable successes, and others, like People's Park, ending in bloodshed, had taken its toll of the status quo ante. Behind the red flags flying over other rebel strongholds—in Ann Arbor, Michigan; Madison, Wisconsin; and Austin, Texas—normalcy waited to reassert itself with renewed vigor when the time came. But not in Berkeley. While the big political confrontations were over, and antiwar demonstrations, having become increasingly symbolic, were turning into street theater, Berkeley seemed to be heading into the '70s as a liberated zone.

It was where one repaired to shed an obsolete carapace, as I did, leaving behind magazine work, along with international travel and an itinerant teaching career, for what I saw as "a radically different environment where the job is not to 'reach people' but to *become* people." The '60s had left us in a no-man's-land where official culture and institutions held no power, or so we thought, but where we sorely lacked our own direction. "We didn't really know it but when we were exposing the 'military-academic' complex, indicting the federal war machine . . . we really were tearing down the foundations of the white society which produced us," I wrote in May 1971, reviewing the antiwar years in my journal with that inflated sense of purpose and responsibility that attended the New Left's decline. What had fallen, I believed, was "professionalism, cults of privileged individualism, and monogamy, all those *inner sanctums* which shielded our damaged and alienated egos from the harsh realities of the real 20th-century American world." Like our vision of "Amerika," where

"War and Order" prevailed, and "the State has really become the enemy for millions and millions of Americans," nothing of the sort had actually happened, though it felt as if it had. Such pronouncements were incantations, a rhetoric of desire—or fear maybe, masquerading as desire. The war in Southeast Asia had become our metaphor. Everything we touched was inflamed by its portents, by doom and, strangely, by something like an explorer's thrill at the sighting of a new continent. For what was all the senseless fighting about if our government hadn't encountered in Vietnam a counterforce to its own power, one that even the Soviet Union and China could not control?

This last response to the war—usually overlooked in standard accounts of the antiwar movement—was rare in the counterculture, which turned, often quite consciously, to rock 'n' roll and drugs as antidotes to the nameless horrors Vietnam evoked. Especially for young men who faced the draft alone, without access to academic deferments or underground resistance networks, which were stronger in the East than in the West, did the wildness of the Grateful Dead offer a kind of sanctuary. Sacramento street artist Dan Wilson remembers walking into the cafeteria of San Francisco State University in 1965 when the Dead were playing for an Acid Test, and deciding, then and there, "This is my band!" "They had the place just dancing like crazy," he recalls. "The music they played was so full of fun—*life*! And I was worried already about the army and the Vietnam war, and that was so dreary—it's death. And here was the Grateful Dead, just the opposite."

Vietnam occupies a very different place in the memories of Deadheads than it does in the recollections of many antiwar veterans—as do the upheavals of the 1960s generally. "I don't miss those days," Grateful Dead artist Stanley Mouse says of a time when, for many in the Bay Area, "the war, free-speech demonstrations, drugs, cops, free love, and revolution in the air" ultimately inspired more anxiety than hope. "The war was scary, but the scene was great fun," Mouse adds; so maybe "it all balanced out somehow. The slaughter of our generation and the great joy of the spirit . . ."

For us, Vietnam was a proving ground whose lessons, by the turn of the decade, had acquired a titanic import. After the bland imagery of American power to which we were bred, the spectacle of Goliath in Lilliput was a revelation. Not only the horrors of the war but also the mix of ignorance, arrogance, and deception with which government officials defended it confused us, if the truth be told, and confuses us to this day. Who were those people in whom Americans entrusted such vast power? And still do, decades later, as the widespread anger over Robert McNamara's revelations in *In Retrospect: The Tragedy and Lessons of Vietnam* brought home in 1995.

Vietnam opened up something like the "crack in your mind" that Kesey attributes to a high-octane acid trip. But with the ceaseless escalation, it let in *too much* light, blinding the receiving organism, and returning it willy-nilly to the panicked state one observes in antiwar ranks as the '70s wore on. (The GI movement, just then undertaking national actions, was an exception.) During the 1960s, with our bustling array of underground papers, our fondness for conferencing and flair for infighting, New Left intellectuals were like bright schoolchildren who had raced through an elementary course in opposition politics without leaving the classroom. We knew what Washington was up to in Vietnam when it talked about "nation-building"; and why "New Life" hamlets and "Rural Reconstruction" in South Vietnam in the early '60s posed a more serious threat to the peace than Cold War brinkmanship in Berlin or even Cuba—for with the former, failure was always an argument for further intervention, while the risk of nuclear Armageddon hanging over confrontations in Berlin or Cuba acted as a deterrent.

Some of us could argue these points successfully in public debates with government spokesmen; just as, on occasion, we were able to outfox security forces in the street, or turn a bloated propaganda machine back on itself. But what difference did it all make if we lacked a vision of long-term change, which we did, much less the power and patience to initiate it?

By 1970, like a great many others, I was a burnt-out case, eager to move on to the next stage of what we called the "long march." Berkeley, I wrote in my journal, marked the beginning of "the long march through the psyche and the residues of bourgeois culture. . . ." Thus it behooved me to acquire new skills to replace the obsolete ones of reading and writing and teaching—skills that wouldn't "alienate me from the people," such as house painting, and collecting the town's garbage with my housemates on Stuart Street for an outfit called Ecology Action, which compressed it into bales for delivery to Japan, where it was converted into plywood.

In the Stuart Street commune, where I settled after staying with a friend from the Venceremos Brigade, I was learning to cook for groups, to set a splint and wield a speculum, to load, shoot, and clean a rifle. I was beginning to hitchhike, first around the Bay Area, then down the coast to Santa Barbara. I had become proficient in karate, and in learning from sisters, something I had failed to do as an "anti-imperialist woman." I had entered "a new political geography, where how I was brought up and where I went to school and how I love and work opens up a vast new territory for struggle. . . . Socialism in one life-time," I called it, seeing the farce but not beyond it. A sister on Parker Street, a member of Berkeley's Food Conspiracy with whom I sorted dairy products, had an analogy for this weird apprenticeship to revolution. *"Cheese consciousness,"* she named it: "heavily relating to cheese without tasting it."

San Francisco's hippies were wrong: Berkeley's radicals were not in thrall to the rational mind, not then. Our behavior was quite as fabulous, if less spontaneous, as theirs. Nor could it be fairly said that the Haight's acidheads were dropping out by turning on. The exploration of inner space carried real risks, as one could tell after the first ten minutes of a serious hit, when, as Rock Scully recalls, you "became this polymorphously perverse single-celled *thing* humming with the mad intentionality of DNA," who wondered, "Can't they see we're getting involved at the *molecular* level?"

By 1970, Haight Ashbury's bacchanal was history. Eight months after the Human Be-In, after a wave of senseless murders hit the neighborhoods, the anarchist Diggers, whose sense of theater was rooted in founder Peter Berg's original attachment to the Mime Troupe, had organized the "Death of Hippie" parade. The procession ended with the burial of the Psychedelic Shop's store sign; and while a coffin full of paraphernalia was set afire, a bugler played taps:

Leaving behind the final remains
of "Hippie—the devoted son of
Mass media" . . .
the boundaries are down . . .

Before 1967 was out, the Psychedelic Shop's owners, Ron and Jay Thelin, had left town, followed by Michael Bowen, Digger Emmett

Grogan, and Allen Cohen. The Grateful Dead left not long after. It was as if the neighborhood had been invaded by body snatchers, and the original heads were replaced by teeny pod people driven by the siren songs of *Time/Life/Look* and *Newsweek* to leave the provinces for the Promised Land.

The Straight Theatre was vacant. Its facade was draped with the giant flags of the Democratic Republic of Vietnam, the Republic of New Africa, and the Black Panther party. The Panther banner might have been silkscreened at Stuart Street, which was also known as the Media Collective, where a large hand-cranked press turned out both banners and shrouds for the Panthers in the months I lived there. With the collapse of the hippie invasion, honchos from the Mission, Oakland, and Berkeley had swept unopposed through the forsaken neighborhood, raising their colors before falling back to their own contested zones. Among the survivors—those who hadn't migrated to Big Sur or regrouped in rural communes in northern California and Oregon—many were turning up on Telegraph Avenue, a stone's throw from the University of California's Berkeley campus.

The old gingerbread mansions in the Haight, built by robber barons and railroad magnates in the last century, and tarted up in the '60s in rainbow hues of pink, purple, and green, had largely reverted to tenements. Haight Street itself, once awash with people on weekends, when, thanks in part to the Grateful Dead's negotiations with City Hall, it was closed to traffic, was now a ghost strip. The army-navy store was still open, along with a few head shops that had mutated into bakeries and health-food stores. Some Diggers hung on, operating a free bakery and housing office on Waller Street. But the Haight-Ashbury Clinic, with its ragged line of hollow-eyed clients queued up outside the yellow door, was the quarter's principal point of interest.

Hard drugs had chased out the soft, as they had begun to do inside the Grateful Dead organization. In 1969 and 1970, it became apparent that something was going on with the drug supply, Mountain Girl recalls. Acid was getting harder to get, and there was all this other stuff around. Especially cocaine, which was being touted by doctors, like Dr. Hippocrates (Gene Shoenfeld) in the *Berkeley Free Press*. " 'It's great stuff,' " they'd say. " 'It's pure, and it helps you get through your workday, and there's no hangover.' " And Mountain Girl wants to know: "Where did this cocaine come from? Could we ask this question?"

With Paul Krassner, she believed that cocaine, like heroin—which moved in on the Dead some years later—was "not necessarily coming by donkeyback over the mountains of Mexico from *campesinos* far away. It was coming on 747s from Southeast Asia and South America with the CIA. . . . They were flying it into this country and dropping it off to their informants in the inner cities. And it made its way into our scene right away," she says, "because so much of it went to San Francisco and Berkeley.

And it DESTROYED our scene! she exclaims. *And it destroyed the scene in Berkeley, too. It did its job, boy, and it was like a bullet right at the heart of the whole thing. And it scared the shit out of me. I was sure we were being targeted.*

You probably were, I suggest. *You were a market—druggies, with a public who wanted to do everything you did.*

I never thought about the wider thing, Mountain Girl says. *I only thought about us. I only thought that we were being targeted.*

The "bullet" had struck at the heart of the band's extended family, which in a couple of years would be surrounded by "rich fringies" connected to invisible dealers who "started showing up on our doorstep with big old sacks of this stuff."

"Hey, look what's happening here," Mountain Girl would say. *"Everybody's running off into the bathroom; they're jumping into their car or disappearing. They're not coming home. Dinner doesn't matter. Forget doing anything together. You come home and you're in a terrible shitty mood, coming down from this stuff."*

Mountain Girl has her own take on CIA drug running at the time. She's inclined to think it was for the money—that "it was this little branch that had run amok. . . . They were down tinkering with these little wars in South America, and their agents got into the blow. And they realized they could sell this stuff and make money and fuel their secret wars. In Guatemala and Colombia especially."

Who were the dealers who were showing up on your doorstep? I ask. *Not dealers,* she says. *We never saw the dealers;* or at least she didn't. *You'd hear,* "*Hey, man, wow, this is the new thing!" I tried it and hated it immediately,* she declares. *It made me dislike music; it made me dislike my clothes. . . . It made me dislike people. I didn't want anybody to touch me. It turned me into a horrible whining Nazi bitch, and I decided it was not my drug IMMEDIATELY.*

It must have been terrible for the band's music, I say, because they weren't listening to each other—

But it WASN'T. No . . . They played faster and louder, but it didn't seem to affect the music itself that much. Besides, she says, there were still enough psychedelics around that there was some balance.

For Jerry and Mountain Girl, the arrival of these drugs was the beginning of the end. It was disconcerting, Mountain Girl tells me, to be the only one holding back in a roomful of friends with whom you always used to do things together. All of a sudden she was "the odd guy out," she and Sue Swanson, who didn't like cocaine, either. Sometimes Mountain Girl would stay up all night with Jerry and the others and rap and talk; then the next morning, she would say, "Geez, did anybody say anything worth anything? No, nobody said anything worth *shit*. . . . All this extra powerful conversation led to nothing, led to no insight, led to no improvement in the consciousness of the people involved in it. It was just a bunch of surface crud."

So her half a dozen cocaine experiences ended. She lost many friends, but fortunately she and Jerry were living with Bob Hunter and his girlfriend, Christie Bourne, in a nice house in Larkspur. Annabelle was a little girl and she and Sunshine had a decent home life. Watching the kids play, though, Mountain Girl remembers her spirits sinking. In fact, she hadn't known what was going on at first; just that something awful had happened, and she was powerless to stop it.

"Cocaine is a crystal that wants you to want more of it," Kesey explains. "You can have a hundred dollars' worth of acid in the refrigerator, and a hundred dollars in coke, and you'll use the coke before midnight. You won't use the acid all year. You don't know anybody who's going back and taking these monster trips," he adds, answering a question I've had. Are these old acidheads still dropping 500 micrograms of LSD? The answer is no; though both Mountain Girl and Kesey still dabble with psychedelics. And Kesey regards the right to use such drugs as equivalent to a woman's reproductive rights: "What's going on inside you is your own business." Every Easter, he and his Prankster friends and families drive to the top of the little mountain in front of the Kesey ranch in Pleasant Valley and drop some acid.

Kesey, who believes that the federal government made LSD illegal in 1966 after recognizing how it might threaten the status quo, also believes that the government sent in the "*counter*revolutionary drugs—booze and heroin and coke—" to break up the community. "Everybody who has been through the coke scene knows that all you really care about is yourself," he asserts. You're suspicious of everyone because they're out to get the stash. And he tells me a story about how Hitler and five buddies were into cocaine: When the war was about to start, Hitler was afraid the supply would be cut off, "so he ordered some chemists to come up with a substitute, and the substitute they came up with was methedrine. That's where [meth] came from," Kesey states. "It came from the Nazis. It is a Nazi drug. Everybody has used speed to try to get stuff done," he says, "but if you use it for too long, pretty soon you begin to become violent."

By 1971, meanwhile, meth and cocaine had turned the Haight into a drug ghetto. It had become a teenage slum with a soaring crime rate—something new on the American map, in that its inhabitants were largely white and middle class. Hard times had eaten into the salad days of the mid-'60s, when fifty dollars and a little help from your friends could carry you across the country. Vietnam spending was exacting its toll of the domestic economy, for while the troops had begun to trickle home, the bombing had escalated, and the war had widened. In Berkeley and San Francisco, the curbside free boxes, where almost anything could be found, were emptying. The boom-time surpluses of the 1950s and '60s were drying up.

~CHAPTER~
9

THEIR SUBCULTURE AND MINE: II

All is permitted to the children of panic.

WILLIAM BURROUGHS

AFTER YEARS OF living more or less communally, the Grateful Dead began to flee the overcrowded Haight in 1968 for rural Marin County. Marin reminded Hank Harrison of "the Haight Ashbury with Ferraris." This was an exaggeration, although it's true that many of the tarot readers, astrologists, primal screamers, and drug dealers who crossed the Golden Gate Bridge in the early '70s were drawn by big money. And some of it had already pooled in the hands of rock stars like David Crosby of Crosby, Stills and Nash, who bought a house in Mill Valley and owned both a black Ferrari called "Freebase" and a sixty-foot schooner named *Mayan*.

Most Grateful Dead folk lived more modestly in loose-knit households, like the one Jerry and Mountain Girl and Sunshine and Annabelle shared with Bob Hunter and Christie Bourne in Larkspur. Bob Weir's Rukka Rukka Ranch in Nicasio and the ranch Mickey Hart rented in Novato both sheltered a shifting stream of girlfriends, managers, and roadies—a surprising number of whom still work, with their offspring, for the organization today. Eileen Law, who left San Francisco in 1967 when the band began to travel outside the state, first moved in with Bob Weir and his girlfriend, Frankie Hart, in Nicasio. It was there, after returning in 1970, that she gave birth to a daughter, Cassidy, whose father was Rex Jackson, the Dead's popular Oregon crew member, who died in a car accident in 1976. Cassidy Law is named after Butch in *Butch Cassidy and the*

Sundance Kid, a movie that promoted the outlaw fantasy among young gypsies like Eileen (my crowd, too), as did *Easy Rider.* The Grateful Dead's
song "Cassidy," written by Weir and his school chum John Barlow, was
named for Cassidy Law the week she was born. And Cassidy, who is an all-
American beauty, like her mother was in her twenties, has never gotten
over it—how when she was on stage or out in the crowd, "and all of a sudden they'll play it, and your face just beams, and you get embarrassed, and
you're *oooooh,* you know." She grins. "What a gift—*your own song.*"

When the Grateful Dead went on the road, Eileen took care of the
ranch, as she had in 1969 when she joined the group, mostly women, living at Mickey Hart's (no relation to Frankie, though Frankie was his girlfriend first). At Mickey's ranch, people slept everywhere, including in
stalls and on haystacks in the barn. "You had to have seniority to reach the
bedrooms," Eileen recalls. "I can remember the band all driving off to go
to Woodstock," she adds. "They left and we stayed to look after the
horses." Horses were also part of the scene—Appaloosas, mainly. And
guns, for fun.

For the musicians, the Woodstock festival was not much to write
home about. Torrential rains and technical glitches plagued the Grateful
Dead's set; faulty wiring at one point turned Bob Weir's guitar into an instrument of torture, and brought a helicopter radio in on Phil Lesh's bass
amp before it shut down the PA system altogether. But from August 15 to
18, hundreds of thousands of people had lived side by side in the sucking
mud, sharing food and dope and good vibes while listening to Crosby,
Stills and Nash, Jimi Hendrix, Janis Joplin, the Who, and Country Joe and
the Fish.

The crowd included Candace, not yet working for the Dead, and our
brother, Chris, then twelve. The two had joined Candace's friends from
the Fillmore East crew to help out backstage. When Chris was asked to
guard the access ramp to the stage on the day before the festival, Jerry
Garcia had appeared, probably on a sound check, and Chris, who didn't
know who he was, had stopped him to say the stage was off-limits. "Oh
man, get outta here," Jerry said, laughing, but the little guy in the Woodstock T-shirt wouldn't budge. Garcia yelled for help, and somebody waved
him past. Twenty-five years later, when Chris was working for the Grateful Dead as a set carpenter, they had a chuckle over the incident. "The lit-
tlest security guard" is how Jerry remembered him.

Marin County had been the Grateful Dead's playground before it was home. Scully had rented a place called Rancho Olompali in Novato while the band was still living at 710 Ashbury. A few miles south off Highway 101, Olompali was the party house where San Francisco musicians came to unwind—not just the Dead but also Quicksilver, the Charlatans, Jefferson Airplane, and Big Brother. It was another rental, here today, gone tomorrow. And yet what happened there left its mark on the family history and on the mythology that entwined itself around the Grateful Dead all the more densely after the larger community that had sustained it dispersed. With its ample lawn and pool, rolling hills and creek, its huge outdoor oven, sometimes cranking out bread for the Diggers to distribute in Golden Gate Park, Olompali reminded a visitor of Tara in *Gone With the Wind*.

Today the Novato countryside that once seemed so wild—the house that harbored Hell's Angels, visiting Beats and Pranksters, along with London rockers and fresh-faced kids from the Northwest—has been swallowed up in the suburban sprawl of northern Marin. The VW vans, Beetles, and occasional Ferrari have turned into Hondas, BMWs, and armored Humvees. The faith healers have become naturopaths, aromatherapists, and lawyers. Many of the musicians, however—the Dead, above all—remain musicians.

Rancho Olompali, bobbing in a sea of hallucinogens, embodies a moment that Mountain Girl sums up when she speaks of "the real Bohemians." These were German intellectuals in the seventeenth century "who took off their clothes and danced through the meadows of Bohemia. . . . We were the new Bohemians for sure," she exclaims. "There was this energy that said *out* with convention! *To hell* with foolish sexual mores! Let's take all our clothes off and paint lines on ourselves and dance around in the sunlight," which is what the Pranksters did in their Sherwood Forest at La Honda, and what they all did at Olompali. "It was *very* infectious," she says, so infectious that she is certain it will happen again, even in a culture convinced, as ours is, that it will never happen again.

It is a prospect that poet Gary Snyder anticipated in 1969 when he wrote about "the Great Subculture." Pondering the history of both East and West, he identified a string of small but influential heretical and esoteric movements. Usually suppressed, or diluted and rendered harmless in the societies in which they originated, they sometimes slipped underground for centuries, only to resurface elsewhere and worry "the Civilization Establishment." Peasant witchcraft in Europe, Tantrism in Bengal, Quakers in England, Tachikawa-ryu in Japan, Ch'an in China—all were "outcroppings of the Great Subculture," Snyder proclaimed, which ran "without break from Paleosiberian shamanism and Magdalenian cave-painting; through megaliths and Mysteries, astronomers, ritualists, al-chemists and Albigensians; gnostics and vagantes, right down to Golden Gate Park."

The current manifestation was the "tribe," which in Snyder's vision fa-vors head-trippers for whom "the real question is 'just what is conscious-ness?' " But the tribe—and the term was on everybody's lips—certainly included the new Bohemians, along with the protest movements, which "came from outside the normal political channels," Frances FitzGerald has observed, and "were never wholly absorbed by the usual business of poli-tics and government." The New Left, which "aimed, after all, to end racism and otherwise morally reform the white middle class"—starting with itself—"had some concerns that no government could possibly ad-dress." In any event, as the new decade dawned, the boundaries between the political movement and the counterculture grew less distinct.

An "apocalypse now" mentality gripped all sections of the tribe, a crazy quilt of hope and fear that reflected its precarious power. The rebel influ-ence—a questioning of authority and an embrace of new sensations—had crept into every town and suburb. "During the sixties and early seventies all of these movements put together seemed to be on the verge of effect-ing a major cultural transformation in the country," FitzGerald reflects in *Cities on a Hill,* "changing the whole society radically and at once." Then, suddenly, it was over. Perhaps the worm was in the bud. Long before the Civilization Establishment bounced back, the heretics had commenced their diaspora.

In 1970, the Grateful Dead brought out two new albums whose melan-choly ballads—"folk music that has taken LSD and come out the other side," Rock Scully describes it—marked a significant departure from the long, spaced-out riffs of *Aoxomoxoa* and *Live Dead* (both 1969). For Hunter and Garcia, the simpler vernacular was a return to country and bluegrass motifs first explored in Palo Alto, one that made room for storytelling, and thus for a deeper, more conscious interaction with the audience.

On one level, *Workingman's Dead* and *American Beauty* were part of a general return to the forms of traditional American music that occurred at this time. The sawdust charms of "Friend of the Devil," "Cumberland Blues," "Dire Wolf," and "Casey Jones"—even the grainy sepia-toned cover of *Workingman's Dead* (whose working-class heroes, the band, were posed by Stanley Mouse down by the rendering plants on San Francisco's waterfront in 100° F heat)—were direct descendants of the frontier fantasies of *Crosby, Stills and Nash* and Dylan's *John Wesley Harding.* But in a more personal sense, the albums reflected a shifting consciousness within the band.

Workingman's Dead, according to Hunter, was a conscious reaction against LSD: "Like, hold it, we said. Just a minute now, we're getting off the track here. Let's get back to our roots. Push this acid stuff aside!" When I wonder if the dolorous imagery in the songs also represents a metaphor for what was happening in the band's world, he says yes. "What was my environment?" he exclaims. "It was the Grateful Dead. I was entirely surrounded by it. I lived in that sea, and saw the world in those terms"; though he had "cut adrift from Garcia's crowd" in the mid-'60s. And even after writing the songs for *Aoxomoxoa*—"Saint Stephen," "Dupree's Diamond Blues," "Mountains of the Moon," and "China Cat Sunflower," among them—he "was still very apart. I was a visitor," he says.

It was when he moved in with Garcia and Mountain Girl and wrote the *Workingman's Dead* lyrics that "it was back to roots for me," Hunter explains, pointing out that "roots" for him come "in twenty-year cycles." They're the roots of his consciousness. Then, abruptly, he grows somber. "It was always clear to me what was going on, and what was going to become of the negative machinery [in the band]," he says. "But the loneliness and the lost stuff that so informs these songs," he adds, "that was my life up to that point."

I would like to know more about the "negative machinery," but Hunter only refers me to "Ship of Fools," written in 1973. "The lines speak for themselves," he says; "I would just hope that the people who were performing them would listen to what they were performing." Later, I consult the song, which opens:

> Went to see the captain
> strangest I could find

Laid my proposition down
Laid it on the line;
I won't slave for beggar's pay
likewise gold and jewels
but I would slave to learn the way
to sink your ship of fools

The lines don't speak for themselves, although they remind me of how ambivalent Hunter felt about the Grateful Dead's success as a touring machine, and also how rocky his relations with Jerry could sometimes be. In the "Dear JG" letter he wrote on the first anniversary of Garcia's death, Hunter writes: "Our friendship was testy. I challenged you rather more than you liked. . . . In later years you preferred the company of those capable of keeping it light and non-judgemental. . . . If the truth were known, you were too well loved for your own good. . . ."

What sets the sawdust fantasies of *Workingman's Dead* and *American Beauty* apart from the other western songs of the period is that in the Dead's lyrics, the frontier seems to have closed. The songs are suffused with a sense of loss, of chances missed, decks stacked, lovers left. In the face of trouble—"Trouble ahead / Trouble behind"—the narrator assumes a supine passivity. "Drivin' that train / High on Cocaine / Casey Jones, you better / watch your speed" is as far as he will go to forestall the "end," which is just around the corner. "Dire Wolf," with its "don't murder me" refrain, is typical:

When I awoke the Dire Wolf
Six hundred pounds of sin
Was grinning at my window
All I said was "Come on in"

Don't murder me
I beg of you, don't murder me
Please
don't murder me

The wolf came in, I got my cards
We sat down for a game

I cut my deck to the Queen of Spades
but the cards were all the same

Don't murder me . . .

Songs like this—which sing more sweetly than they read, so sweetly that one can forget one's troubles—were also road songs. The gambler is the tired road warrior who's played too many towns behind too many flashing marquees: "Chicago, New York, Detroit, it's all on the same street / Your typical city involved in a typical daydream. . . ." In "Truckin'," he has played his game:

Truckin'—got my chips cashed in
Keep Truckin' like the doodah man
Together—more or less in line
Just keep Truckin' on

Hunter's roster of working stiffs provided the Dead with the perfect foil for articulating the tensions that arose at this time. For band members, the weariness conveyed by the new lyrics was real; they were stepping into a groove that would dictate the terms of their performing lives for the next twenty-five years. With overhead expenses approaching $100,000 a month, and an annual gross income just topping $1 million by 1970–1971, touring, which accounted for 70 percent of the Dead's earnings, had to expand, and did.

In 1970 alone, the band played 145 gigs, more than ever before—or after, for that matter, though some of these gigs were free. Concerts offered them the only way to earn the money that was needed to maintain the growing venture, which by the early 1970s included thirty people on payroll, rehearsal and equipment space in San Rafael, a home office that oversaw business matters, a publishing company to handle copyrights and songbooks, a booking office, and a travel agency. The famous Wall of Sound, the vast PA system designed and built by Stanley Owsley and Dan Healy, cost $100,000 a month to truck from gig to gig and pay a crew of twenty—a far cry from the single van that carried all the Dead's equipment in 1968.

Office folklore invented a mythical beast, the Ourobourus, to convey the dilemma to the fans. A dragon who eats his tail, the Ourobourus, spinning in place, grows ever larger and more hungry as he devours himself. More gigs led to larger halls, requiring more equipment, which called for a bigger organization, demanding more overhead, which required more gigs. Greed was ignited around this time by the successes the band scored with *Workingman's Dead* and *American Beauty,* which led in turn to heftier bookings. The band went on salaries of three hundred dollars a week, and the pressures kept mounting to increase them as individual musicians began to spend money to expand their home studios. Greed, however, didn't upset the payout plan Garcia endorsed, under which royalties didn't go exclusively to the composer and lyricist, the parties of the "original creative flash," as he put it, but a percentage went to all members of the band to acknowledge their part in the finished version of a song. Still, the royalties didn't begin to match the growing expenses, not to mention the demands of the Candyman. People began to make up little sayings, such as "Cocaine is God's way of telling you that you have too much money," Mountain Girl remembers. "So the money began to vanish, to leak away."

"Cumberland Blues," from *Workingman's Dead,* cast what might have been the devil's bargain of mass entertainment in a folksier context:

> Got to get down to the Cumberland Mine
> That's where I mainly spend my time
> Make good money / five dollars a day
> Made any more I might move away—

Lines like these offered the Grateful Dead an inverted allegory for their new relationship to music. Gone, for the most part, were the spontaneous jams, the voluntary coming together and falling apart that had inspired the core group's original vision of itself—the vision that was born in Palo Alto in 1960–1961, which Alan Trist dubs "the dream of the hippie commune."

Trist remembers a time at his parents' house when he, Jerry, Hunter, Laird Grant, Phil Lesh, Bobby Petersen, and Willy Legate had smoked a lid and talked about how they wanted to bring art and the Beat stuff together. They had designed "an ideal habitation," which was based on the

Chateau, the rambling house, full of weird alcoves and hidden stairs, where most of them rented rooms. What they needed, they said, was "a large central house with a kitchen with a refrigerator full of beer," which was what the Chateau had—although they weren't supposed to touch the beer, being underage. They would all have individual cabins spread around the large grounds, so each could get on with his work, "because we were aware," Trist notes, "that this one was a musician and he was a writer and someone else was a painter. We wanted to come together but we wanted to have our privacy, too. . . . Right then," he says, "we had already taken care of the problems which communes would have. Which was the lack of ability to get away. . . . We designed it right from the beginning so that wouldn't happen."

In a sense, the design had held. With its first-floor nest of cubbies and mailboxes, its busy little kitchen and sitting room, the Dead's office in downtown San Rafael—"the Victorian"—functioned for twenty-seven years as a variation on the Chateau. (Trist, Hunter, and Danny Rifkin still work there.) And the band members' assorted houses and ranches—vast spreads in a few cases—became the "cabins." Jerry Garcia kept his multiple interests going on the side; and as they grew to musical maturity, Bob Weir and Mickey Hart followed suit.

But in a deeper sense, by 1970 the design had collapsed and the dream had begun to unravel, as the Grateful Dead, now a thing in itself, with a will of its own, consumed more energy and time. It was around then that band members increasingly spoke of "the Grateful Dead" as something separate from themselves, an employer or rich uncle, capable of showering them with goodies but subject to fits of selfish unreason. The Grateful Dead was a *thing* that had begun to acquire a mysterious life of its own— as in the old monster movie from the 1950s, where the Thing begins to stir in its cake of ice; a vast golem, Mountain Girl's "juggernaut," awaiting the press of events that would spark the meltdown and bring it terrifyingly to life.

Later on in the '70s, the *thing* reminded bluegrass guitarist Peter Rowan of "being in the engine room of a rocket ship. It was like 'Duck or you'll get stepped on.' . . . [T]hat sense of destiny from the inside must have been fierce," he reflects. And he was shaken one night when he was standing next to Jerry's amp and Garcia looked right through him. "No matter how much you felt a part of his life, when the ship went, he went. The ship," says Rowan, "was the Dead. And if you weren't on that ship," well, then, forget it.

In 1970, meanwhile, the band suffered personal losses, which may have contributed to the music's power to tap a growing disillusion in the air. First, Phil Lesh's father died, then Pigpen's, and then both of Bob Weir's parents in 1971, all within eighteen months. Jerry Garcia's mother was killed in an automobile accident while the band was recording *American Beauty*, and the heartbreak on that record, most evident in "Broke-down Palace," according to Hunter, is traceable to Jerry's sadness.

Not only Garcia's mother's death but his father's, too, is evoked in these lyrics, which reveal Hunter's ability to give form and voice to the depth of feeling Jerry Garcia was able to reach in song. Jerry was five when his father drowned while fishing in the surf at Arcata, not far from San Francisco. He and his mother were picnicking on the beach with uncles and aunts. José Garcia, wearing waders, had suddenly disappeared; swept out to sea by the undertow, his body wasn't found for hours. "River gonna take me / Sing me sweet and sleepy / Sing me sweet and sleepy / all the way back home" begins the fourth stanza of "Broke-down Palace," which was nearly always sung in a lilting whisper, as if by a child who is courting death. "It's a far-gone lullaby sung many years ago Mama, Mama, many worlds I've come / since I first left home."

"When the pathos is there, I've always thought Jerry is the best," Hunter told an interviewer in 1987. The same might be said of the Dead's music as a whole. There is a strange triumph to the drifter's ironic lament that dominates *American Beauty* and *Workingman's Dead*, whose songs comprise the heart of the Grateful Dead canon. Tunes like "Uncle John's Band," "Dire Wolf," "Black Peter," "Casey Jones," "Friend of the Devil," "Sugar Magnolia," "Attics of My Life," and "Ripple" perfectly capture the dreamy introversion of sentiment in the face of adversity that remains the signature of the band.

"Ripple" added another dimension to the Dead's reach. In it, singer and song are one, as in other Hunter/Garcia confections, but here it is the listener, alone with his or her sorrows, lost in a choppy sea of humanity, who is courted. "Ripple," a love song to the lonely, is also a hymn:

Reach out your hand
if your cup be empty
If your cup is full
may it be again
Let it be known
there is a fountain
that was not made
by the hands of men

There is a road
no simple highway
between the dawn
and the dark of night
And if you go
no one may follow
That path is for
your steps alone

Such lyrics had the power to bring a crowded stadium such as the Yale Bowl on July 31, 1971, to its knees. The hush could be palpable, a sucking in of sound rather than its absence. In a song like "Ripple," and, to a lesser degree, in "Attics of My Life"—"Full of cloudy dreams unreal / Full of tastes no tongue can know / And lights no eye can see / When there was no ear to hear / You sang to me"—the Dead tapped a free-floating yearning in its vast audiences to shake off their anonymity; to be loved for themselves alone, for their differentness, the differentness each one felt all the more keenly for being surrounded by people who looked just like them.

By 1970, the Dead were no longer playing for their peers. The audiences were a bit younger, and the nostalgia in the songs suggests that the band ("the oldest juveniles in the state of California," Bill Graham called them in 1969) may have been playing to their younger selves. Scanning the lyrics, one is struck by how finely attuned they are to the fears and hopes of adolescence. And this adds another piece to the puzzle of the Grateful Dead's extraordinary longevity. For many, the music and the crowds were/are stations in the cross of growing up absurd in America.

The 1970 albums outsold the band's previous four recordings by hefty margins. Yet it is surprising to learn that the rehearsals and recording sessions went smoothly; that the musicians sat around together day after day singing the songs and working on the material with unamplified guitars. Phil might say, " 'Why don't we use a G minor there rather than a C,' " Hunter recalls, "and a song would pop a little more into perspective." Despite crises over management and money after Mickey Hart's father had raided the kitty, it was a "magic time," Scully recalls. For the boys, that is; the relationships between the musicians were positive, as if something had jelled. It was around this time that Mountain Girl began to feel "sidelined," when her "energy was no longer important because the energy of the rest of the thing had grown and become so enormous."

Out in the world, Jerry Garcia had gotten a face-lift. In 1969, *Rolling Stone* recast him from the ugly duckling he once was—"lumpy, fat-faced and frizzy-haired"—into something "beautiful, his trimmed hair and beard a dense, black aureole around his beaming eyes. His body has an even grace, his face a restless eagerness," writer Michael Lydon continued, noting that Garcia's "intelligence is quick and precise and he can be devastatingly articulate, his dancing hands playing perfect accompaniment to his words." The now-legendary 710 Ashbury, no longer the O.K. Corral, was remembered as "the Brook Farm for the new transcendentalists." Guitarist Dave Nelson noticed that in addition to growing a beard, Jerry had discarded the funny-looking vests and free-box sweaters for Levi's shirts and ponchos. Nelson thought he looked "beatified . . . like an angel . . . an angel with a bad streak."

The adventures with other musicians, meanwhile, sometimes bubbled up out of the purchase of a new toy, as when Marmaduke Dawson dropped in on Garcia at the Dead's recording studio late in 1969 and Jerry told him he had just bought a brand-new pedal steel guitar. "Can I come over and hear it?" Marmaduke asked, and Jerry said sure; Marmaduke brought his guitar and a few songs, and Jerry jumped right in and started playing pedal steel. "When are we going to do this again?" he asked; and when he heard that Marmaduke had a gig at a Hofbrau House in Menlo Park, he invited himself along to accompany him on pedal steel while people ate their roast beef sandwiches. After a few weeks of packing the place, Dawson and Garcia decided to make a little bar band out of it, like country-and-western guys who play in saloons and have a good time. Dave

Nelson, then living with Jerry and Mountain Girl in Larkspur, was invited to join. Hunter, who lived there, too, had suggested calling it the Riders of the Purple Sage (the alternative was the Murdering Punks), which became *New* Riders after it turned out there was already a band by that name.

As the logistical demands of the Grateful Dead intensified, so had the lure of the extracurricular gigs; and in 1970–1971, Garcia integrated the New Riders of the Purple Sage into the tours. With Marmaduke leading a forty-five-minute set to open a show, Jerry could play pedal steel in somebody else's band, without having to sing. Then he would play the acoustic set with the Dead, followed by the longer electric set. He was on-stage all night for shows that usually ended around 2:00 A.M., but which occasionally continued until six in the morning. It was as if the more he played, the more he *had* to play. Jerry was a "picking junkie" long before he was the other kind, says Dawson. The guitar—"that was his first draw." "A few days without it," Mountain Girl remembers, "and he'd be afraid he'd never be able to play again." When he played bluegrass, it was the same with the banjo. If his picking buddies came to Larkspur to re-hearse, Jerry would open the door, with a banjo banging on his chest, ready to start.

For Garcia, the informal jams satisfied a different hunger from that of the grand tours, but the two reinforced each other. The dream that inspired the Grateful Dead, vaguely messianic, in the manner of the Pranksters, could be kept in check, masked, in effect, by the devotional exercises Jerry performed with his country-music friends. In the "Dear JG" letter, Hunter recalls their long talks about the Grateful Dead "in the old days, trying to suss what kind of a tiger we were riding, where it was going, and how to di-rect it, if possible. . . . [Y]ou admitted you didn't have a clue what to do be-yond composing and playing the best you could. I agreed—put the weight on the music, stay out of politics, and everything else should follow. . . ." It hadn't been so simple. As a musician, Jerry Garcia was usually all business, submitting himself and often his mates to a discipline and attention to de-tail more commonly associated with command of a ship. But more and more, it seemed as if the other side of the discipline, the lightness and open-ness to suggestion that made the experience of playing with him such a pleasure, was better served in the smaller bands.

"If you tickled his fancy," bluegrass guitarist Peter Rowan recalls, "he would just come forth with so much loving energy that everyone would do better." There appeared to be no ego involved in his playing, and the example was catching. There wasn't supposed to be any ego with the Grateful Dead, either, but the unevenness in the group's background created tensions that were missing from the other bands. Thus, a little later in the '70s, in the balancing act Garcia maintained between the big band and the little ones, he began tilting toward acoustic jams with keyboardists Howard Wales and Merle Saunders, bassist John Kahn, drummer Ron Tutt, and mandolinist David Grisman, among others. These were often low-key, jazzlike sessions that fit comfortably inside clubs such as the Matrix in San Francisco and the Keystones in Berkeley and San Francisco. No guards were posted at the doors, and when the other musicians arrived early, there was Jerry with his carton of Camels and his roadie, already noodling on his guitar or picking on his banjo.

"Where's it go from here?" Peter Rowan remembers him saying, when Old & In the Way, the best known of the little bands, besides the Jerry Garcia Band, played bluegrass at the Boarding House. Rowan, Grisman, Kahn, and Vassar Clements couldn't wait to unpack their instruments and jump in. It was in this musicians' world inside the show business world— where nicknames were conferred like badges, as in a tree house or fort run by ten-year-olds—that Jerry seemed to feel most at home. Peter Rowan was "Red" for the song he wrote called "Panama Red"; Grisman got the name "Dog," or "Dawg," at this time from Jerry; and Jerry was "Spud Boy," as in "Hey, Spud, how do you like this?"

In 1970, however, a kind of crossroads had been reached and decisions made—not by thrashing things out, but in one of those telepathic exercises of groupthink for which the Grateful Dead are famous. In 1970, they had elected to renew the vows of chance. Hunter's "Uncle John's Band" (after Jerome John Garcia, not, as legend has it, manager Jon McIntire) sealed the pact. Another road song, it was composed together in a burst of camaraderie:

> Goddamn, well, I declare
> Have you seen the like?
> Their walls are built of cannonballs,
> their motto is "Don't Tread on Me"

Which was the good ol' Grateful Dead in a nutshell.

> I live in a silver mine
> and I call it Beggar's Tomb
> I got me a violin
> and I beg you call the tune
> Anybody's choice
> I can hear your voice
> Whoa-oh, what I want to know,
> how does the song go?

In "Uncle John's Band," tag lines from the old songs Garcia sang with the Black Mountain Boys in Palo Alto—"It's a Buck Dancer's Choice, my friend," and "It's the same story the crow told me"—tied the knot with the past. But the future looked uncertain; and in the sing-along stanza, a new note is sounded:

> Come hear Uncle John's Band
> by the riverside
> Come with me or go alone
> He's come to take his children home

It was an echo of Kesey's "You're either on the bus or off the bus," necessary perhaps because the children had lost their way. Here they were in 1967, filtered through the song Eileen Law heard over and over in the basement leather shop, "The Golden Road (to Unlimited Devotion)":

> Everybody's dancin' in a ring around the sun
> Nobody's finished, we ain't even begun
> So take off your shoes child, and take off your hat
> Try on your wings, and find out where it's at.
> Hey hey, come right away, join the party, party
> everyday.

By 1970, the children had lost their shoes and singed their wings, and Uncle John had come to take them home. In song after song, the Dead extend a hand. "If I knew the way I would take you home" ("Ripple").

"Daddy's here and he never will forget you / I will take you home" ("I Will Take You Home"). This last was keyboardist Brent Mydland's swan song, a lullaby for the 1980s, like "I Need a Miracle." Garcia admired the song's "authentic emotion." Brent, he told an interviewer in 1989, the year before Brent Mydland died of a drug overdose, "has a prosaic earthiness that some of us lack." Jerry himself, by then more like the old lady who lived in a shoe, had tired of all those children, and was content to let this smoky-voiced young daddy from the East Bay take them home.

It wasn't until 1976, however, after folding up the big top for a year in the mid-'70s, that Garcia was finally able to say, "I think the thing I'm most into is the survival of the Grateful Dead."

In our commune on Stuart Street, we listened to *Workingman's Dead,* whose gritty iconography I'm sure we favored over *American Beauty,* with its roseate mandala on the cover, though we listened to both. "Truckin' " is the song I remember best. I associated it with the R. Crumb figures in Head Comix. Crumb's vision of the mutating world outside our windows was closer to my own than the psychedelic divinations of the drug culture, especially "Whiteman," whose angst ("I've tried! God knows I've tried!") was a parody of our own honky guilt. Nothing escaped R. Crumb's attention but hope.

Not that we didn't smoke pot or drop acid on occasion; we did. Or believe "that everything was beginning again," as Robert Stone, who hung out briefly with the Pranksters, says of the time when "everyone really knew . . . that things began again only once, nearly thirty years ago, in the green and golden hills around the Bay Area." We knew that, too. Unlike Stone, however, who goes on to "admit immediately that drugs played their part," we kept the faith with the help of a rarer ether, a vision of revolution that demanded heroic action. Something equal to the horror of the never-ending war; something that might harness the formidable energies that resistance to the war had unleashed in our political generation.

Today such perceptions, if they are cited at all, are peeled away from the events that inspired them, the better to examine them clinically as manifestations of a social pathology or spiritual agitation. Despite a veneer of nostalgia for the idealism of the '60s, a distaste for the messy work of shaking things up is widespread. The conservative's traditional abhorrence for insurgent action has merged with the liberal's unease over any challenge to what is quietly perceived in present-day America as an extremely fragile status quo. And liberals, especially learned ones, have proceeded to switch paradigms: to transfer the smoking testimony of insurgent thought from politics and history to the more temperate departments of culture and religion. Thus, the antiwar movement, in a currently fashionable academic view, is the latest "in a long line of Protestant reform movements stretching back to the American Revolution"—a piece of religious history. As "part of the *American* experience," in another reading, it had little bearing on the outcome of the war, which was a military engagement. Our experience, for what it's worth, was different.

The belief that some sort of revolution was imminent, far-fetched on the face of it, was rooted in the not-unreasonable expectation that the Vietnam War, with its spiraling social and economic costs, would continue to escalate. The spring 1970 invasion of Cambodia portended further expansion of the ground war, and the intensification of the bombing of North Vietnam under Nixon would surely lead to massive civilian casualties, without reversing the steady erosion of support for the U.S.-backed regime in South Vietnam. In this context, the movement's effort to "bring the war home" through increasingly disruptive confrontations was not so far-fetched. It was the thinking behind the May Day demonstrations of 1971, and also behind underground attacks on Army induction centers and selective service offices, namely, that while peaceful protests had helped mobilize public opinion against the war, they had failed to rein in the war party.

We didn't know at the time that Nixon had decided not to move against new targets in North Vietnam—which included, as Seymour Hersh later reported, "the massive bombing of Hanoi [and] Haiphong . . . ; the mining of harbors and rivers; the bombing of the dike system; a ground invasion of North Vietnam; the destruction—*possibly with nuclear devices*—of the main north-south passes along the Ho Chi Minh Trail; and the bombing of North Vietnam's main railroad links with China [italics added]." Limited implementation of the first and last proposals occurred anyway, while there were serious military and political objections to others. But Nixon had also been deterred by what Kissinger described as "the hammer of antiwar pressure."

American opinion was already deeply divided over the war—including, as we know now, at the highest levels of government. But Congress failed to translate escalating antiwar pressures into a vote to discontinue military spending. The closest it came was in June 1970 when the Senate repealed the Tonkin Gulf resolution. As a result, the war didn't end until April 1975, when the North Vietnamese Army drove the Americans from the U.S. embassy in Saigon. It was the swiftness with which the vast edifice of American power in Southeast Asia then collapsed—a swiftness that surprised no one more than the North Vietnamese—that owed itself to the decade of antiwar pressure.

Meanwhile, given the level of government repression at home, even the imagery of "liberated zones" and "armed struggle" that had entered our communications appeared to be plausible pieces of an impending scenario. In Berkeley in 1969, riot police had fired on peaceful demonstrators at People's Park, injuring many and killing one. Later that year, a police occupation of the University of California's Santa Barbara campus had ended in protesters firebombing the local Bank of America. Governor Reagan had called for a "bloodbath" to settle the "student problem" in Santa Barbara and Berkeley; while in Chicago, after Weathermen blew up the statue of the policeman in Haymarket Square during the October 1969 "Days of Rage," the head of the Police Association announced, "We now feel it is kill or be killed." Then there were the shootings at Kent State and Jackson State in May 1970, followed by an attack by construction workers wearing hard hats on antiwar demonstrators in New York, which left seventy wounded.

In October 1970, the Weather Underground announced a "fall offensive" during which "families and tribes will attack the enemy around the country." Weathermen blew up the police statue in Haymarket Square again, then bombed the Marin County Hall of Justice and the Long Island Court House in New York to call attention to the plight of political prisoners. Throughout the fall, allied groups across the country launched attacks at military and police-connected government buildings. By December, 448 colleges were shut down by protests, and underground attacks on government and corporate targets continued. On March 1, 1971, a bomb exploded in the basement of the U.S. Capitol Building. It was another Weatherman action, and, as in three preceding it and three more afterward, care had been taken so that no one was injured. The Capitol bombing was accompanied by a letter explaining that the act was taken in retaliation for Nixon's expansion of the war into Laos. Along with

previous communiqués, it was naturally ignored by the media, thus furthering the sense of random chaos the bombings conveyed.

And yet by the end of 1971, further escalation of civil strife suddenly
seemed unlikely, as if by some instinct for measure and rule both sides
pulled back from the brink. Kissinger was flirting with Chairman Mao.
And despite intervals of terror bombing against North Vietnam, the war
did seem to be winding down.

The threat of repression, however, and the periodic nuisance of wire-
tapping, break-ins of movement offices, infiltration by informers and government provacateurs had only stiffened our resolve and fueled our
revolutionary ardor, which proved perhaps that we were amateurs. Or
lost. Lost children. "Lost in a haunted wood, / Children afraid of the
night / Who have never been happy or good." Not Jerry's children—
W. H. Auden's, as he portrayed them at the end of the 1930s. But not really Auden's, either, for we were not awaiting collection. In Berkeley and
elsewhere, we were busy enacting a revolutionary drama that broke away
from reality sometime in 1971; one that saw us inventing a "liberated"
zone outside society, rather than solidifying our bases within it. We were
more like Dylan's children in "Visions of Johanna":

> We sit here stranded, though
> We all doin' our best to deny it.

By May 1971, when affinity groups from Stuart Street and Parker
Street met to plan their part in the annual mass action, it was with trepi-
dation. We had tried to resist antiwar leader Rennie Davis's pull from May
Day headquarters in Washington, but in the end we had gone along. "All
of our feet stampeding through the streets have raised the dust again," I
noted in a postmortem. But to what purpose? The world wasn't watching
anymore, and least of all was it watching Berkeley. Only the local FBI was
interested—maybe.

As it turned out, we hadn't marched or practiced civil disobedience,
or disrupted traffic (for long), or fought the pigs. "Riding into San Francisco on the 7 A.M. workers' buses to do an 'educational' trip on the war
and a guerrilla theater thing in the terminal was a first," I observed doubt-
fully. Afterward, we had put a "hex" on the Fairmont Hotel, where former
South Vietnamese president Nguyen Cao Ky was the featured guest.

Actions like these were supposed to "teach us a new way to move in the streets." But they had fallen flat. We weren't the Diggers or the San Francisco Mime Troupe (though one of our members performed in the latter). We were loose wigs, however. And it wasn't so important anymore "to get 'high off of' our own trips. . . . We're no longer afraid about causing a 'scene,' " I concluded. "We *are* a scene."

Looking back on that watershed year, the year the Grateful Dead lifted off from the Bay Area for good and went into national orbit, I am struck by the intensity with which the political community set about reinventing itself. It was as if we had climbed a stairway of permissible options: petitioning, marching, committing acts of civil disobedience, even throwing rocks and spiking the tires of patrol cars in the grand tradition of Paris in the spring of 1968, only to reach a wall of clouds where a ladder veered off at crazy Seuss-like angles into a molten sky. "Kids know that the lines are drawn," Weatherman (no longer kids) announced in its last communiqué before going underground early in 1970. "Revolutionary violence is the only way." We were not Weatherpeople; nor was Berkeley, with its own radical traditions, particularly hospitable to Weather politics; but a high pressure front had settled in, creating a climate for emergency actions in which anything seemed possible.

Some of us were veterans of civil rights actions and local organizing projects, as well as of countless antiwar mobilizations. On the other hand, a brother and sister, new to movement politics, had worked in television—the brother for the *Merv Griffin Show,* his sister for Bob Hope in Los Angeles and South Vietnam. My partner, Richard Levy, had dropped out of a graduate program in economics at Wisconsin, before working with a radical research group in Boston. I had originally planned a Ph.D. dissertation on the Melville-based plays of Robert Lowell, until I ran afoul of Professors William Barrett and Sidney Hook at New York University in 1965. (Foolishly, for I had located them on the Left, I asked Sidney Hook to comment on the proposal for *Viet-Report,* then circulating among fellow graduate assistants; and Hook, who questioned my right to dispute government policy, complained to the chairman of the English Department that I was politicking on university time.)

The core of the Stuart Street group, the Media Collective, were youngsters who had dropped out of art school during the upheaval following Kent State and the Cambodian invasion. They silk-screened posters and banners for local movement groups, including the Black Panthers, whose huge stretch-framed panther logo hung on the wall of our dining room print shop. Meanwhile, we all had odd jobs, some odder than others. But our real energies had gone into our rebirth as street fighters and self-defense adepts. And here is where politics had ended and something else began.

We were determined "to get off the bleachers and into the fight," I wrote in my journal; to shuck "our uptight don't-pinch-me individualism which keeps us away from any fight in the first place." We wanted to shake off the burdens of "white-skin privilege," a buzzword at a time when "Third World leadership," another buzzword, was at least a promise on the world stage. Hence, the target practice, martial arts, and first-aid training, and also a midwifery class, in which Richard enrolled.

An interest in guns was much in the air. Even the Grateful Dead had contemplated picturing themselves with pistols in hand on the back cover of *American Beauty,* until Bob Hunter had intervened. Band members used to go out to Mickey Hart's ranch in Novato for target practice, shooting up a gold record on one occasion. There was nothing revolutionary about it, but toting guns on a record jacket in 1970 was something else. These were "incendiary times," Hunter said later, and he didn't want the band to make that kind of statement.

Hunter wanted to "counter the rising violence" and knew that he had a tool to do it. "We just didn't dare go the other way," he said. "Us and the Airplane: We could have been the final match that lit that fuse," which is stretching the point, and speaks volumes about the band's, or Hunter's, sense of mission. But guns in the hands of the Grateful Dead might have indeed enriched the revolutionary mythology, especially since the band, unlike the Jefferson Airplane or the Rolling Stones, didn't toy with the imagery of political violence.

Thus had *Workingman's Dead* been imbued instead with the spirit of old Buck Owens records from Bakersfield, California, and Bob and Jerry returned to something called "basic rock & roll: nice, raw, simple . . . heartland music." After the acid-rock rumbles of *Anthem of the Sun, Aoxomoxoa,* and *Live Dead,* this album represented the band's attempt to say, "We can play this kind of music. . . . It's something we do as well as we do anything." Encoded in Hunter's new lyrics, moreover, and in the Dead's more interactive stagecraft, were alternative ways of receiving the up-against-the-wall signals emanating from places like Berkeley, Detroit, and both the Upper West Side of New York and the East Village.

"Mister Charlie," for instance, offered listeners a light, mocking handle on the constant confrontations with authority. And who knew which side the protagonist was on?

> Chuba-chuba
> Wooley-booley
> Looking high
> Looking low
>
> Gonna scare you up and shoot you
> 'Cause Mister Charlie told me so

But it's in "Playing in the Band," which appeared on *Grateful Dead* (1971), also known as *Skull and Roses,* that one finds the group's coda:

> Some folks look for answers
> Others look for fights
> Some folks up in treetops
> Just look to see the sights

Back in Berkeley, meanwhile, we women resorted to the politics of the deed. "The women are the most fanatic," a visitor to Stuart Street remarked at the time. We reminded him of the women who cry the loudest at Italian funerals for others who cannot be heard. We specialized in hit-and-run actions, such as torching an art-store mannequin on Telegraph Avenue, whose Barbie doll demeanor offended us; and stoning the windows of the Center for International Affairs, after learning that the U.C. Berkeley institute harbored a Vietnam War–related research project. This last move more than any other signaled the change in what political action had come to mean for a not-altogether-lunatic fringe of the movement.

A few years earlier, after confirming the facts in government contract records, *Viet-Report*'s editors would have reported the offending project to the college newspaper, helped organize a teach-in, and invited someone from the institute or department involved to defend the project, which was usually done on academic freedom grounds, even if the sponsor was the Army Research Projects Agency (ARPA). After exposing and isolating the enterprise, we left the mopping-up operation to the students and faculty. It was their turf. At the magazine, where we published a running log of such projects, we had done this half a dozen times. The tainted research might be removed to a more secure facility like Bendix or the Stanford Research Institute, but the campus community was exposed to the workings of the military-academic complex, and a new cadre was developed for future actions. That was antiwar politics.

What was breaking windows at the Center for International Affairs? (One, and a staff car window. Nothing like the rampage Weathermen had gone on at Harvard's Center for International Affairs the year before.) A guerrilla action? The angry outburst of an oppressed minority? A wake-up call for a slumbering campus? Revolution for the hell of it? An eye for an eye? *Women's liberation?* None of the above; it was just us (and others like us) bringing the war home—not to Amerika, its cities and schools, but to our own backyards. Weatherman spelled it out in matchless prose in a communiqué issued before setting up underground bases, called *focos,* in February 1970: "Smashing the pig means smashing the pig inside ourselves, destroying our own honkiness." ("Talkin' bout the enemy inside of me" was the way Neil Young put it in the song "Big Time.") *We* were the enemy. We white folks carried the virus of the old order, of racism and classism, inside us, and now we were trying to stamp it out. We women especially, the bearers of the race, were more fanatic in our efforts to extirpate the past—not only because we had to prove ourselves tougher than the men (who were probably glad to be sitting this episode out) but also because we were driven to separate ourselves from traditional ways of being women.

"We attempted to make a home for ourselves, as revolutionaries in America (no less), out of our felt need to change the quality of our lives," I wrote on my way out of Berkeley in September 1971, speaking of both sexes. Our passion for reinventing ourselves increased in direct proportion to the waning of our belief in changing the world—beginning with the war in Vietnam, whose underlying causes we might have comprehended intellectually, but whose *need to be,* its very *endlessness,* eluded our grasp. Our ability to change ourselves was also negligible, though I, for one, was altered by the Vietnam War. Our ability to adapt to changes outside ourselves, on the other hand, has proved more elastic. We are, after all, our parents' children as well as our children's children.

Berkeley, of course, was the perfect environment for these experiments; just as the Haight, and Robert Stone's "green and gold hills of Marin," provided the Grateful Dead with a vivid setting for the dream of beginning again, of entering a new kingdom of consciousness, "a dream we dreamed / one afternoon long ago." In the weeks before returning east, Berkeley's unreality had become increasingly palpable to Richard and myself. Looking back over his shoulder as we rolled out of town in our VW van, he imagined he saw the shimmering towers of Brigadoon sink into the horizon.

It's like the *après le deluge* perception that Bob Hunter has when he contemplates, in a poem, the dawn of the Grateful Dead's "American Adventure":

> Behold a city half visible along
> the cloud line, studded with
> faraway spires, domes, turrets
> and other paraphernalia with
> which deep-seated yearning
> tends to outfit a horizon.

The passing of the original dream—for the founders, that is; most Deadheads keep the faith—leaves Hunter with a question we might ask ourselves concerning the dream of revolution. Whether

> In retrospect it's fruitless to try to determine
> if it was simply arrogance compounded
> with sensory overload . . . or if we really saw
> something else besides. . . .

> As for entering the cloud-line city,
> indistinct memories tell us
> we did so, although snapshots
> from the era indicate that it
> might have been otherwise.

The inch-thick layer of immaculate
shamrock glass which coated the
pavement is shown, in the photo,
to be only unadorned city concrete
and not all that clean.

There is no evidence of spires . . .

Berkeley, toward the end, kept flashing in and out of focus. Was it a kind of liberated zone, or a holding pen for the exhausted activists of the '60s? Was it a forerunner of the New Age spas along California's north coast, where graying baby boomers repair to refresh their sagging spirits? Or *did something different happen there,* something whose trace materials lie humming deep inside the body politic?

~CHAPTER~
10

THEIR SUBCULTURE AND MINE: III

> The youth of America is their oldest tradition.
> It has been going on now for three hundred years.
>
> OSCAR WILDE

WOODSTOCK PRESENTED YOUNG radicals with a conundrum. In *Woodstock Nation,* Abbie Hoffman celebrated the Festival of Peace and Music as a triumph of the human spirit, a glorious open-air concert, despite the monsoon rains. (Organizers, however, thanked God for the rain, which kept the crowds at bay.) For Abbie, the proximity of 400,000 kindred souls, the "functional anarchy and primitive tribalism," made Woodstock a lodestar in the '60s arcanum. Yet at the time, he was deeply disturbed by the festival. "Were we pilgrims or lemmings?" he wondered elsewhere. "Was this really the beginning of a new civilization or the symptom of a dying one? Were we establishing a liberated zone or entering a detention camp?" The political animal in him suspected Woodstock of being a dead end, and he worried that rock festivals would fetter rather than free the generation whose pied piper he aspired to be. Given the right mix of music, flowers, and dope, in the right outdoor setting, he warned, why would anyone want to protest anything?

A good question, it is echoed by a Deadhead who recalls the Grateful Dead show that took place at Harpur College, in Binghamton, New York, on May 2, 1970, two days before the National Guard fired on students at Kent State. One of the all-time favorites among tapers, the Harpur College concert showcased the new acoustic material from *Workingman's*

Dead. Rumors had the Dead hanging out in a dorm the afternoon before the show, with unspecified people dispensing liquid sunshine from water pistols. Marmaduke Dawson, who played that night with the New Riders of the Purple Sage, remembers that two-thirds of the audience was "stoned out of their minds on LSD. . . . It was their own miniversion of an Acid Test, as close as they could reproduce it." A token of the event is a large photo of Jerry Garcia in the 1971 yearbook, which also pictures a burning effigy of Nixon, who had recently declared war on "bums, radicals, and other criminal elements."

"I always thought that it was an interesting coincidence that Binghamton, a very liberal and progressive school, had a relatively small amount of campus violence around the time of the Kent State killings," Gregg Bucci writes in *DeadBase VI,* "and I often wonder if the Dead's playing there at that time had anything whatsoever to do with that." Four days later, when the band played at MIT immediately following Kent State, the pattern was the same.

Nixon's "incursion" into Cambodia on April 30 had already galvanized campuses, including Kent State's, where students had burned down the ROTC building. By the MIT show, students had boycotted classes across the country, and campuses were seething. Speaking of the tumult immediately following Kent State, *DeadBase* editor John Scott recalls that "it was natural that some of this restless energy collected around the Dead at Kresge Plaza." But after opening the free show with "Dancin' in the Streets," and getting off some lively jams with "Morning Dew" and "Good Lovin'," nothing was heard from the stage except a pitch from Phil Lesh for the official gig at Dupont Gymnasium the following night. Nor did MIT become the site of any serious disruptions in the ensuing weeks.

At Woodstock, Abbie had persuaded concert promoters to give him some space in the festival program. "The revolution is more than digging rock or turning on," he proclaimed in "The Hard Rain's Already Fallin'." "The revolution is about coming together in a struggle for change. It is about the destruction of a system based on bosses and competition and the building of a new community based on people and cooperation." Calling attention to the nine-year prison sentence just meted out to White Panther leader John Sinclair, busted in Detroit for giving two joints to an undercover cop, he said, "The authorities want to destroy our cultural revolution in the same way they want to destroy our political revolution."

Abbie himself ricocheted between both. And at Woodstock, where he worked with Hugh Romney (who got the name Wavy Gravy there) and other members of the northern California commune called the Hog Farm in a makeshift field hospital, the circuits had jammed. The trip wire was the stage, where he wanted to be and wasn't (nor had the pot, hashish, Darvon, and bad acid he consumed helped him keep his head). After hovering backstage with the performers, then moving in closer and sidling up over the edge of the stage, he had suddenly leapt to the front, seized the mike, and began haranguing the audience about John Sinclair while the Who was in full blast. Pete Townshend had "laid him one upside with his guitar," a witness recounted, and Abbie had staggered off.

Another megaevent, like Monterey, that rubbed the Grateful Dead the wrong way, Woodstock reminded Rock Scully of Vietnam. Declared a disaster on the third day, helicopters, sometimes on evacuation missions, flew in and out with food and water. Rations, which included a huge cache of champagne and strawberries that Candace stumbled on the last day, were as unpredictable as the quality of the music.

By the summer of 1969, rock 'n' roll had turned into something other than the vigorous soundtrack of a time of change. With a burgeoning star system now backed by big money ("Center stage turned out to be another drug," Gitlin observes), the musicians had lost the complicit relationship they once enjoyed with their audiences. High-energy rock songs like the Rolling Stones's "Street Fighting Man," Steppenwolf's "Born to Be Wild," and the Doors's "Break on Through" stimulated an *aura* of revolt. Low-energy tunes such as "Hey Jude" *("Take a sad song / and make it better . . ."),* with its reminder of the breakup of the Beatles, came closer to expressing the tenor of the times—as did the current lyrics of the Grateful Dead. Dylan's "My Back Pages" had moved to the top of my song list in the summer of 1970, when Richard and I had visited friends in communes in Vermont before driving west. "Ah, but I was so much older then, / I'm younger than that now," with its overture to a cultural revolution that tired radicals had somehow missed, perfectly embodied the shift in consciousness under way in our circles.

Columbia Records ran an ad campaign for a rock band with the slogan "The Man can't bust our music." "The Revolutionaries are on Columbia" (an allusion to the SDS-led strike at Columbia University in the spring of 1968) was another. The "rock is dead" movement that flared in the red-hot summer of '68 had protested the appropriation of the politicized energy of music by the entrepreneurs of pop culture. It was also a protest against the chemical stew in which the music was consumed. "Are we to follow the double image of music and dope in order to step out of history, to join hands with the eternal wastrels, fops, and dandies?" asked a San Francisco writer in 1968. Were not all these heads just "sitting on the floor collecting highs like so many stockbrokers collecting shares before retirement"? As for acid rock, it had been reduced to a formula—"like television, loud, large television. It was a sensitive trip," Jerry Garcia remarked, "and it's been lost. . . . It hasn't blown a new mind in years."

Earlier in the '60s, it had always seemed to the Warlocks' manager, Hank Harrison, that when the political climate heated up and direct action beckoned, interest in the music waned. "At first the revolution was the music," he suggests. But he remembers how attention was interrupted by the Tonkin Gulf incident in August 1964, which dropped a cloud over the burgeoning music scene in Palo Alto. Later, in the fall of 1967, a mobilization around community welfare issues in the Haight had produced the same dampening effect. In 1968, when Martin Luther King, Jr., and Bobby Kennedy were assassinated within a few months of each other, Bay Area bands played to near-empty houses. "For eleven weeks in a row," according to Ron Rakow, a former business manager of the Grateful Dead, "no dance halls made money."

After Kent State, the Dead played a concert at the Fillmore West that is remembered by a fan from Maine for its furious attempt to lift the spirits of a crowd numbed by the horror of the killings. "The Dead were trying to make people feel better, but they couldn't do it," says Stephen Jane. "The music really got going like an express train roaring, but it couldn't get people *up.*" Jerry's guitar, a "silvery guitar," he calls it, "danced across the torrent of sound," and at one point, in what Jane calls an instance of "unstaged pyrotechnics," a "mushroom of smoke" rose from the amps. "They were playing *too* hard."

By 1969, most rock 'n' roll bands were no longer accountable to a community other than the commercial one, which was booming. The Dead, who were finding a new path for themselves on college campuses after the end of the dance hall concerts, were among the exceptions. At *Rolling Stone,* Jann Wenner excoriated the New Left for espousing "a completely frustrating and pointless exercise of campus politics in a grown-up world." Only rock 'n' roll, he said, possessed "the magic that can set you free." Woodstock showed Wenner just how vast the audience for rock music had become; and no wonder, for by 1969 the rock music industry was a billion-dollar enterprise. Nor did the audiences identify with a larger community of interests beyond the youth-specific ones. You couldn't say anymore that without the music you lose the meaning of the play, as you could when the Bay Area bands had provided the counterculture with its "first deities, the sources of [its] new myths, metaphors, and anecdotes," as a *San Francisco Express Times* reporter wrote in 1966.

Only the Grateful Dead still fit in the old Saturday-night "dropping ritual," which had begun in the morning with "collecting flowers, buying new costumes, buying and selling dope, getting super-stoned and listening to music." It had continued when the revelers crossed

> the magic bridge together in packed cars. Barely able to see, the initial acid waves pressing us against the walls for support, feeling our way up the Fillmore steps. . . . The old Fillmore, as yet undiscovered by . . . *Life* magazine—a thousand stoned, stoned heads, feeling the gestalt of a thousand love vibrations, for many of us our first understanding of a religious feeling.

In embryo, this was the drama that was being reenacted at places like Harpur College, MIT, Stony Brook, and the Capitol Theater in Port Chester when the Grateful Dead came to town. The original energy and idealism surrounding Bay Area music circles had evaporated. The drug scene had turned creepy, and the loose-knit urban communes had broken up and given way to more hierarchical communal structures in the countryside. On the East Coast, the "religious feeling"—"our first"—tolls through accounts of Grateful Dead concerts like a foghorn, warning us away from facile comparisons to Beatlemania, a generational episode kickstarted by the record companies, or to Elvis worship, a subcultural phenomenon of a different order. Behind the Dead's jingle-jangle rhythms—carny music, inflected with Gregorian tones—behind the skeleton who tips his hat, and the dancing bears, straight from the nursery, the collective soul of the band, and its followers, was (and remains) a witching well of mystic yearnings.

"The Dead had set us up like a sculptor working with his clay, and now they were taking us on a trip," René Gandolfi says of a June 24, 1970, show at the Capitol. It began with the drummers pounding out the opening beats of "Not Fade Away" in sync with explosions from behind a wall of amps and speakers. Each flashing white light was followed by a puff of smoke (the "unstaged pyrotechnics" Stephen Jane observed). When the spots hit the band, the audience left its assigned seats and surged forward, filling the aisles from the stage to mid-orchestra for the rest of the night. Behind the amps, forming a second wall, was an arch of humanity: Dead family, friends, about four people deep, all moving and dancing. When a young woman from the audience jumped onstage, a man moved out from the "wall" to dance her backstage. The same happened when a man jumped up, and a woman did the honors. "Everything was so *mellow*" but charged with something "cosmic," says Gandolfi.

The band played "Dark Star" (as it often did at such shows) "with guitar riffs that made you feel like you'd just left this earth and joined the crew of a starship." At the close, "everyone in the theater felt like they knew everyone else. . . . The amps were turned off, the stage doors opened to let the smoke clear, the early stirrings of dawn could be seen, and still," Gandolfi recalls, "the crowd just sat there, stunned." After a while, the band walked back onstage with Dave Nelson and Marmaduke Dawson and sang the traditional folk song "Cold Jordan," a cappella, ending the concert with an odd solemnity. It was the leitmotif of many a program—like closing the Fillmore East with "We Bid You Goodnight," or the annual New Year's Eve shows with "Auld Lang Syne."

"Dark Star," meanwhile, was nearly every Deadhead's favorite liftoff tune. At the Laser Farm in southern Oregon around the same time, Alan Kapuler—Mushroom—remembers how when someone played it, he flipped back on his shoulders in a yoga stand and, cupping his hands into a telescope, fixed his eye on the sky.

And there was a full moon, and I froze on the full moon. And for twenty-five minutes I was frozen in that position on the "dark star," he tells me, and I landed on another star.

What do you mean, I ask, you "landed on another star"?

All I can tell you is that my mind traveled through the light of the moon and I landed. I went and traveled to another star.

Which you saw with your "eye"?

Which I saw with my eyes.

And you were listening to "Dark Star"?

And I was listening to "Dark Star." And I came back into the body and I re-alized I had just actually moved beyond this physical universe and this solar system, through consciousness, to another star in another universe in another solar system.

Such trips have filtered into the popular culture. Here's "Dilbert" on December 31, 1997, the very day I relate Mushroom's story:

> garbage man: "As your consciousness passes through each uni-verse, you tend to follow a line of probability."
>
> Ratbert: "Got it."
>
> garbage man: "And since it's more probable that matter is near other matter, you have the illusion of gravity as your conscious-ness moves toward the norm."
>
> garbage man: "Did you get all that, Ratbert?"
>
> Ratbert: "Hey, I'm not stupid. Does this Norm guy have a last name?"

Mushroom goes farther:

. . . having traveled through space and taken the whole collective mental struc-ture of this world with me, he says, *he has moved humanity to another star.*

"Moved humanity"?

Yes.

Because you were humanity?

That's right. Exactly.

Not that you pulled many people along with you?

No. Because being one of the species—

Because you were part of a collective consciousness—

That's right.

None of the monster festivals had filled the Grateful Dead, and espe-cially Jerry Garcia, with greater horror than Altamont on December 6, 1969. It was Rock Scully who first conveyed the Dead's interest in having the Rolling Stones join them in a free concert at Golden Gate Park in the fall of 1969. The initial plan, promoted by Jerry, was to use the concert as a vehicle for bringing warring street gangs and biker factions together in the Bay Area—something like what had happened in the East Village on

June 1, 1967, when a free Dead show mediated a turf fight among blacks, Latinos, and hippies in Tompkins Square Park.

The Stones, who hired lighting designer Chip Monck to handle stage chores for their 1969 American tour, had agreed to finance the free beer, barbecue, T-shirts, and Tex-Mex food that was to accommodate everyone from Black Panthers to Brown Berets from the Chicano community. According to Scully, it was the Stones's road manager, Sam Cutler, who wanted the Hell's Angels to cover security for the free concert, against the Dead's better judgment. Cutler was apparently under the illusion that the California Angels would behave like the English bikers the Rolling Stones patronized in London, hearty yeoman who gave loyal service to the lords of rock. But at the time, it was widely believed that Scully himself, acting on the suggestion of Digger Emmett Grogan, hatched the idea of hiring the Angels—which was done with five hundred dollars' worth of beer—to keep things in the family. Grogan had first proposed using local chapters to provide a motorized escort in and out of Golden Gate Park, and the security plan had mushroomed from there.

Former Oakland Angel Skip Workman (at fifty-nine, still an honorary member) confirms the last point. "All we were told was to keep a place open down front for the bikes," he says. "After we got there, we were informed that we were 'security police for the concert.' " He remembers dropping acid on top of a school bus the Frisco club had brought, and watching the melee build up around the stage. It wasn't long before the green recruits sent by San Francisco and Oakland, high on Ripple and quaaludes, had begun attacking the freaks who were spinning in their own pools of agitated consciousness. "Prospects," Workman calls the recruits; "not one of those people ever became members," he claims. "But when we saw some club members in a confrontation," he adds, "we had to get involved."

Workman discovered that the black man in the sky blue suit who subsequently died of knife wounds (Meredith Hunter), had a gun, and he took it from him, he tells me in March 1998. We're sitting in the dusky living room of his bungalow in New Harbor, Maine. It's late afternoon, and the goosenecked desk lamp beside the sofa where Workman sits and a fire in a Franklin stove in the corner are the room's only illumination. The lamp lights up the large tattoo on his left forearm. It's the dragon from Workman's acid trips. It was done in the '60s, he says; and details, including two small lightning bolts, were added over the years as he remembered them. No bugle, though. "That would make no sense—a dragon with a bugle?"

The house is crammed with Workman's collection of guns, uniforms, and flags from military campaigns dating back to Bismarck. Lenin stares from a red satin banner trimmed in gold; but most of the military regalia is from the Third Reich. A little room in back where Skip shows me his old dance hall posters, including a tattered silk-screened announcement of a Grateful Dead benefit for the Hell's Angels at the Anderson Theater in New York, is draped with swastikas and the Japanese rising sun. Altamont has crept into the house on little cat's feet.

At some point in the larger fight that ultimately claimed the life of Meredith Hunter, Workman dove under the stage; and there was this guy covered with blood, he says. He didn't know whether the man was dead or alive when he took the gun. He remembers trying to calm the guy's girlfriend, a white girl, who was screaming. In *Gimme Shelter,* the Maysles brothers' documentary about Altamont, you see the fight, and the flash of the knife or knives that killed Hunter; then he's being loaded onto a helicopter, while his girlfriend, who wears a short white lacy dress, as out of place in the Brueghelesque scene as her boyfriend's pale blue zoot suit, shrieks hysterically. It all happens so fast, it's hard to imagine when Meredith Hunter had time to hide beneath the stage where Skip says he found him, but, of course, the footage has been edited.

His Satanic Majesty, Mick Jagger, has stopped singing, and he peers anxiously in the direction of the fray from the edge of a stage that is almost level with the crowd. A couple of Hell's Angels stand guard beside him. He looks like a little boy in a Superman suit. At his feet, two girls gaze up at him, thunderstruck at the wonder of his nearness, oblivious to everything else. The longhaired boys next to them stare at Jagger with naked admiration. A strange tableau. Afterward, a Hell's Angel was tried for the murder of Meredith Hunter, and then acquitted when witnesses failed to step forward. "Everybody was to blame one way or another," Skip assures me.

The Hell's Angels would probably have showed up anyway, as they did at most Bay Area rock concerts—especially since the Rolling Stones supplied them with their favorite tripping music. San Francisco Angels had already been used for security at the Human Be-In, as well as at impromptu Golden Gate shows. If Scully and Grogan lobbied for their use in what they thought would be a park site, they wouldn't have been alone. The question is why, knowing the Angels as they did, they didn't press for a change of course once the hometown venue was lost. Licensing them to maintain order at the Altamont Speedway in Livermore, a desolate place even for the demolition-derby fans who frequented it, was begging for trouble.

In his memoir, Scully claims he had persuaded the Parks Department to issue a permit for Golden Gate that was good as long as nobody announced the location until twenty-four hours before the concert. When Mick Jagger supposedly gave it away in Los Angeles, where the Stones were recording *Let It Bleed,* the permit was canceled. After two alternate sites fell through, and with only a couple of days remaining to set up the stage, lights, and sound system, Altamont had become the only available alternative. Inaccessible by public transportation, it would not be popular with ethnic audiences, but nearly 300,000 people poured in, more than the population of most American cities.

"First Annual Charlie Manson Death Festival," Emmett Grogan tacked on the bulletin board in the Dead's office a few days *before* the concert. That same week, Manson and his "hippie" followers, as the press identified them, were arrested and charged with the grisly murder of Sharon Tate and four friends. (The news made much of the fact that Manson had been a familiar figure in the Haight and had used acid and talked about revolution. He had also been among the first to lay down the ecology message, in 1969, in the *L.A. Free Press.*) Right from the start, it was evident that with Altamont the old formula of music, drugs, crowds, and good vibes had gone bad. A Berkeley activist who dropped acid during the festival told Todd Gitlin (also there) that he had received the insight that "everyone was dead." Not just the Angels of death who were running amok in front of the stage but also the starstruck children of the Lonely Crowd had, in Gitlin's view, "turned on . . . not to the communal possibilities, but to the big prize, the easy-ticket, the 'good trip.' " And Gitlin wondered "whether the youth culture will leave anything behind but a market."

The police had largely stayed away. The few you see in *Gimme Shelter* look like young cadets. "Let those fucking Hell's Angels kill the hippies, the fuck do we care?" Scully imagined the cops chortling "in some redneck bar somewhere. . . ." Peering out at the bedlam from inside their van backstage, the Dead were horrified. "No way am I playing, man, no fucking way am I going out there!" Jerry had exclaimed, shaking with fright. And as dusk fell, and the Stones began their set, they had made their getaway, leaving behind the truck that was to transport their equipment back to Marin, because, says Scully, some Hell's Angels had deposited a body underneath it (the body of Meredith Hunter?). "The fuck do we care?" could apply to the band, too, though it was fear that immobilized the Dead. Looking down at the writhing mass of humanity bottled up in the inverted vault of the speedway, Scully felt (once again) that they had "just caught the last helicopter out of Saigon."

Like pigeons, the band had homed in on the Fillmore West, formerly the Carousel Ballroom, before Bill Graham bought it. Originally, they were to have played a gig there that night, though everyone knew they were going to Altamont, so nobody had showed up. Retiring to a backstage dressing room, they had attached themselves by umbilical hoses to a tank of nitrous oxide—when in burst Graham. "Ranting and raving about Altamont and how the Dead were responsible for all the atrocities there," he had pounced on the group's road manager, yanking him up off the floor and calling him a "fucking murderer." "I've just taken this huge hit," Scully recalls; "the whole band is there, and I'm blown away, pissed off, hurt— and high as a kite. . . . So I, uh, *throw* Bill Graham down the dressing room's stairs."

The scene is as transparent as a fairy tale (though hard to believe a skinny kid from Earlham College threw *Graham* down the stairs). Bill, as usual, is Big Daddy: an empire builder in the early stages of empire, who regards music festivals like Woodstock as "picnics that cost too much." Winterland, he will later claim, was as big as he wanted to go—until demand pushed supply. The Grateful Dead had been one of Graham's first, and, after the Jefferson Airplane (whom he managed), hottest, properties, and by the winter of 1969, he and the band shared a dangerous perception of one another as beneficiaries of the other's emerging power.

Demand had put the Dead on an open road where Bill Graham's two Fillmores, and Winterland, were but way stations. "We didn't need Bill," says Mickey Hart, speaking later. "Everybody needed Bill but us. That's why Bill wanted us so bad." It was time to put "Uncle BoBo," as they called him, in his place; even to humiliate him, as Scully's denouement suggests. For Graham doesn't fall downstairs—he "sails out of that dressing room and lands on his ass in front of everybody sitting in the big hospitality room where all the stagehands hang out with the family and kids."

It's one of those occasions when the Dead's fantasy world and the real world overlap and reinforce each other. The band's fear of massive crowds and of conflict furthers the recourse to drugs. Their sensitivity to the more brutish forms of power enlarges their respect for such power and instructs them in its uses. "Bill was a *New Yorker,*" Jerry Garcia once declared, apropos of Graham's genius for making people do what he wanted. "He was, like, the guy who taught us about that. A lot of us had never been out of California. You know, what else was going on any place else that you even wanted to know about?"

Next to Garcia, there would always be a seat of honor for whoever could throw his weight around in the worlds Jerry knew nothing about. Graham, né Wolfgang Grajonca, a Jewish refugee from Nazi Germany, who served in Korea in an otherwise all-black unit, had introduced a generation of musicians to the one-armed bandit's world of show business: to rock politics, which you could play like a game. He was tough, and Jerry esteemed toughness; as did Steve Gaskin, the hippie patriarch from the Farm, whom Graham once called "a slimy motherfucker" (an epithet duly recorded in *Rolling Stone*). "Bill was a *lot* tougher dude than most of the rest of us," says Gaskin. "Bill put a toughness and a grownupness into our movement that would not have been there without him." "The Godfather of rock 'n' roll," Hart calls him.

Others saw him differently, such as Candace, who worked for Bill Graham at the Fillmore East, and dealt with him later at countless Bill Graham Presents concerts in California. "He didn't seem to want to be around anybody who didn't really worship him, and most people who worked for him did," she recalls. It was a "colony" she disliked. Graham, she says, was "kind of gaga for the whole scene"—less for the music than for the stars, Jimi Hendrix and Jerry Garcia, for example. Garcia, meanwhile, knew that while Bill "loved it when the crowd got off on something," it was only after Mickey Hart's arrival, when the band "started doing things with more exotic flavors," that he took any real interest in their music.

Mickey Hart and Bill Graham had a past. Years before, they had worked at a casino at Atlantic Beach in New Jersey that played Latin

Fidel Castro, meeting with volunteer canecutters in 1970,
wears a hat given him by an American *brigadista*. © *Jerry Berndt*

Vietnamese students studying in Havana visit the Americans at the Brigade camp in 1970. Pictured here, in hat (THIRD FROM LEFT), is Le Van Bang, currently Vietnam's ambassador to the United States. © *Jerry Berndt*

A message to the Movement from Jim Sheldon's Furry Freak Brothers, 1971.
© *Peace Press / A People's Printing Collective*

Mountain Girl and Jerry Garcia, 1968.
© *Herb Greene*

Robert Hunter, around 1975. © *Herb Greene*

Eileen Law with her daughter Cassidy at Bob Weir and Frankie Hart's house in Mill Valley, California, 1972. © *Frankie Hart*

Crew members Steve Parish and Kidd Candelario, on tour in Europe, 1972. © *Mary Ann Mayer*

Jerry Garcia at the Yale Bowl, July 31, 1971, the night New Haven cops tear-gassed demonstrators outside. © *Chuck Pulin*

The Grateful Dead's Wall of Sound. © *Mary Ann Mayer*

Pigpen warming up for the Yale Bowl concert, July 31, 1971. © *Chuck Pulin*

Playing for a SNCC benefit in 1966 (ABOVE) or for the Black Panther Party in 1971 at the Oakland Coliseum (LEFT) took the Dead off rock 'n' roll's beaten track. *Courtesy of Paul Grushkin.*

music. They were Tito Puente fans; and when Puente played in the upstairs ballroom, Hart, a teenager who was stuck downstairs as the short-order cook, got the waiters, Graham included, to sneak him in. Bill Graham was a "mambo king," says Hart. He remembers going to a Latin club in San Francisco in the late '70s, and there was Bill, "writhing with this beautiful woman" on the other side of the room. "We were the only white guys in the place," he says, "and we just smiled at each other."

Candace and Bill had a past, too. "We used to have our times," she admits, when the two of them would raid the "confiscated booze stash" and sit drinking for hours after a New Year's concert, sometimes until daybreak, hashing over the production. Bill would review his midnight entrance at Winterland, the Oakland Coliseum, Henry J. Kaiser Auditorium, or the Cow Palace, when he would fly across the arena on a mirrored ball, dressed as an eagle, or ride in on a giant skull or mushroom or lightning bolt. These performances were very important to him. "We were both into *shows,*" says Candace, "putting on *shows.*"

But a few years before Graham died in a helicopter crash in 1991, they had a showdown that had been a long time coming. It began with runners from Bill's office at Oakland Coliseum telling Candace, not for the first time, to beef up the lights during a New Year's show. Normally, she complied, but this time she really thought it was a bad idea, and she said no, adding that she'd be happy to talk to Graham about it. Finally he came out and angrily waved her over. She left the lighting booth, heard him out, but held her ground. She'd be happy to do anything he wanted for his part of the show, "but really, Bill," she said, "you don't tell a band's lighting designer what to do. . . . And he got madder and madder and I got calmer and calmer," she remembers, until she said, "Oh, Bill, just calm down," while he threw his little fedora on the ground and jumped on it.

She was congratulated by all sorts of people after that incident, including the manager of the Coliseum. But Bill got the last word when, a few months later, in the middle of a show, he walked over and handed her a note. "Nobody has made me lose it like that in ten years, and I've got to hand it to you," he wrote, "you definitely won that round." Candace was impressed. "Wow, what a cool thing," she remembers thinking. It wasn't exactly an apology, but with its nod toward an opponent's negotiating skills, it was more valuable to someone who was a scrapper in her own right.

Bill Graham was vulnerable to charges of financial chicanery: for re-selling tickets to a Grateful Dead concert at Winterland, for example, and pocketing the proceeds. "Money is money," another former Grateful Dead manager, Richard Loren, reflects; and Graham's ability to make sure it came his way was more finely honed than most. Loren, whose job it was to protect the Dead's financial interests later in the '70s, and who may have had more fights with Bill than anybody else, caught him charging the Grateful Dead not only for the free food, calendars, and masks he handed out to audiences at the annual New Year's shows (for which his generos-ity was admired), but also for the gifts he gave the band.

Graham's reputation for moneygrubbing went back to the Acid Tests. "When we did the Trips Festival," Ken Kesey recounts, "you could see Bill Graham's eyes like those little windows in an old-fashioned till, going *'dollar-sign-dollar-sign-dollar-sign.'* " Mountain Girl remembers him guard-ing the door at the Longshoreman's Hall like a "maniac," insisting that everybody buy a ticket. Graham had sniffed out the commercial potential of these events early on, and when the Dead were still the Warlocks, he had tried to pry them loose from the Pranksters. "Graham's the one who put the kibosh on the Acid Test Graduation on that Halloween," Kesey tells me. Why? "He didn't want the band to associate with us at that point because LSD had just been made illegal." Legal defense fees were not part of his game.

Kesey tells a story about the time the Pranksters ran into Graham on their way to the Fillmore Acid Test. "Me and Babbs and Gretch and Cas-sady, we were all decked out and ready for the evening. And Bill Graham moved all the way into the street to not have to confront us," he says. Gra-ham started looking around this way and that, and Neal Cassady said, " 'Look! There's Bill Graham. He's out there checking tire treads to see if one of them picked up a dime!' And Bill says, 'It's all show business, Neal. It's all show business.' And Neal says, 'I worry for your soul, Bill.' He was vulnerable to that," Kesey claims.

"Yet as ornery as he was, everybody knew and he knew that he was part of whatever was happening," Kesey adds. Mountain Girl concurs. "He was like the antagonist for the free trip," she says, "but at the same time he was on our side, working for us." Which of course he was, making "free" pay. Without him, and without managers like Loren, known as "Zippy," who could handle him (Rock and Rifkin were less adept), the Grateful

Dead might not have pulled themselves together as a live act that could
deliver over and over again.

"He was a fighting kind of guy," says Mickey Hart with affection. "The
horror of the Nazis never left him. . . . He was a capitalist. He wanted to
make a lot of money. He was a loner. He was very lonely. He was a sad
kind of guy," and Mickey felt sorry for him because he had no friends.
"Sometimes I'd go home with him to his house, a beautiful, spacious, incredible house, a millionaire's house. All marble, empty. Nobody was
there. He didn't have a wife. The kids were off at boarding school. He was
a workaholic. He was just an animal for this thing—making money and
promoting concerts."

When the bodies were finally counted at Altamont, and blame came the
Dead's way, once again there was the transformative power of song—the
happy ending to the tale. After Ralph Gleason echoed Bill Graham's in-
dictment of the Grateful Dead in his influential column in the *San Francisco
Chronicle,* Bob Hunter responded with "New Speedway Boogie":

> Spent a little time on the mountain
> Spent a little time on the hill
> Things went down we don't understand
> but I think in time we will

For Deadheads, the tune's refrain honors the light at the end of all tunnels:
"One way or another / One way or another / One way or another / this
darkness got to give."

Reading the lyrics in cold print, one is struck by an alternating current
of toughness and worry:

> Please don't dominate the rap, Jack
> if you got nothing new to say
> If you please, don't back up the track
> This train got to run today

"Jack" is Gleason, and it's obvious who's drivin' that train. As for whether
it would have been better to "run away" or "stand still," who's to say? Better run than die?

Now I don't know but I been told
it's hard to run with the weight of gold
Other hand I heard it said
it's just as hard with the weight of lead

As usual, Hunter's lyrics are noncommittal. Jerry's voice is light, almost bouncy, approaching a falsetto in the refrain. The speaker withdraws from judgment and choice, but not from a kind of action, not from truckin' on. Ambiguity is his nectar. And the road that beckons is no ordinary road, but one that leads straight out of this world:

You can't overlook the lack, Jack
of any other highway to ride
It's got no signs or dividing lines
and very few rules to guide

The road the Grateful Dead began to scroll across the American landscape at the start of the 1970s was a fantasy road; a free-fall zone, rich in allusion to invisible things, such as was explored in the nineteenth century by L. Frank Baum, author of *The Wonderful Wizard of Oz,* and by Walt Whitman. Baum's Yellow Brick Road led by a roundabout, adventuresome route to the Emerald City. In "Song of the Open Road," Whitman celebrates another kind of highway, close to the Deadhead's romance:

The earth expanding right hand and left hand,
The picture alive, every part in its best light.
The music falling in where it is wanted, and stopping
    where it is not wanted,
The cheerful voice of the public road, the gay fresh
    sentiment of the road.

Whitman's road knows better than to speak with the voice of a parent or preacher; it's not the voice of Main Street:

O highway I travel, do you say to me, Do not leave me?
Do you say, Venture not—if you leave me you are lost?

Do you say, I am already prepared, I am well-beaten and undenied,
adhere to me?

Certainly not. The "public road," like the Dead's American adventure, seems boundless. It permits of great imaginings:

I think heroic deeds were all conceived in the open air, and all free poems also,
I think I could stop here myself and do miracles,
I think whatever I shall meet on the road I shall like,
   and whoever beholds me shall like me,
I think whoever I see must be happy.

"From this hour," proclaims Whitman, sounding the free man's trumpet, "I ordain myself loos'd of limits and imaginary lines, / Going where I list, my own master total and absolute . . ."

For many, this is what the songs of the Grateful Dead do; although the loosing of limits may last for only the duration of the trip. For the musicians, however, from 1970 on, the highway they trod was a crosshatch of lines, subject to no end of rules. Band members experienced the recurrent sense of dislocation that came from moving from one airport and hotel to another, and from performing in thirteen or fourteen different halls in a single month. After Harpur College, for instance, in May 1970 alone, the Dead played acoustic and electric sets at ten more schools: Wesleyan, Worcester Polytechnic Institute, Temple, Washington University in St. Louis, among them.

Curiously, for a band that had heretofore cultivated a dropout culture, they had learned that colleges and universities were the easiest places to sell a show. By 1971–1972, student associations were eager to get the Grateful Dead on campuses that are remembered today by Mountain Girl as curiously hushed. "The college kids—we felt they were shut-ins," she says, laughing at the memory. The political turbulence had taken its toll of students whose older brothers and sisters might have stopped troop trains, levitated the Pentagon, burned draft cards, stuck flowers in the barrels of soldiers' guns, or cut sugarcane in Cuba, but did not have to cope with the levels of violence that were routine now that the war had come home. "It was like going to institutions and playing at old folks' homes," Mountain Girl recalls of the campus rounds. "They couldn't get out, but we could get in. It was an errand of mercy."

On May 24, 1970, the Dead had flown to England for their first European performance, in Newcastle-under-Lyme. In June, they returned to the Fillmore West, playing four shows, after which the band flew directly to Oahu, Hawaii, where they shared a two-day billing with Quicksilver Messenger Service. Then back to Berkeley for an American Indian benefit before they left for New York again. In New York, they had played multiple gigs at the Capitol Theater; it and the Fillmore East, until the latter closed on June 27, 1971, were the Grateful Dead's East Coast anchors. June 1970 ended with the Trans-Continental Pop Festival in Toronto, where the Dead joined a familiar lineup, which included the Band, Janis Joplin, Traffic, Ian and Sylvia, the Great Speckled Bird, and Tom Rush.

The constant touring, like the burden of knowing exactly where you're going to be most of the time, of having to play whether you want to or not, was transformed, via the magic of song, into the drifter's lament. Out of the grueling routines of the road had come the uncertainty principle celebrated in "High Time," "Dire Wolf," "Black Peter"—"Just want to have / a little peace to die / and a friend or two I love at hand"— "Friend of the Devil," "Broke-down Palace," "Truckin'," and "Box of Rain," which Hunter wrote for Phil Lesh and his dying father:

> Walk out of any doorway
> feel your way, feel your way
> like the day before
> Maybe you'll find direction
> around some corner
> where it's been waiting to meet you—

The appeal of such songs and the force of their sentiment derive in some measure from their denial of the circumstances that inspire them—a denial in which performer and listener conspire. The drifter's refrain feels true, not because the singer, who plays a part, is adrift but because he is not, or at least his body—his *material, historical* self—is not. His dreaming self is howling at the moon or smiling in his sleep. His freedom is a dream. He *dreams* he is free. He labors in the entertainment industry, and his success has made him a star. Working for the Grateful Dead, he is protected by the loyalty of his mates. He won't be pried away—as Janis Joplin was from Big Brother when she went with Clive Davis to Columbia, becoming, partly as a result, an inverted supernova with a heroin-pocked arm. He lives and works in tandem with his band, his family. A drifter is the last thing he will be. "What do you want me to do, / to watch for you while you're sleeping?" asks the speaker in "A Box of Rain." "Well, please don't be surprised / When you find me dreaming, too."

In traditional blues or in the French chanson, the singer addresses the audience directly. Here is where I am. Here is my pain, my sorrow, my joy, my memory. Here is what I know. The Cape Verdean chanteuse Cesaria Evora does this with lyrics composed by her countrymen. The audience *believes;* there is that collusion at the heart of a masterful performance when the audience, whether live or listening to a recording, is invited to play the part, as well. Oddly, the singer who sings from his or her historical self brings the actuality of what he or she knows *home* to the listener, while the singer who invokes a never-never land is more likely to leave the listener in a never-never land, too.

Alternately, when a performer steps aside from his or her character, and renders it *critically*—mocking the lyric, as Mick Jagger ("buzzing better, baby, when your man is gone") does in "King Bee," or German music hall singers once did with "Mack the Knife"—the listener is invited to see the song itself as play. This form of delivery involves a different kind of collaboration, one that sometimes lets the wag out of the bag:

> We're lonely, we're romantic
> and the cider's laced with acid
> and the Holy Spirit's crying, "Where's the beef?"
> And the moon is swimming naked
> and the summer night is fragrant
> with a mighty expectation of relief

Singer/songwriter Leonard Cohen's "Closing Time" couldn't be farther from the holy spirit of the Grateful Dead; though the sacred objects *(acid, spirit, moon)* are all there, if paired with their nemeses. Only "the summer night" of myth is left standing.

"Waiting for the miracle / there's nothing left to do. / I haven't been this happy / since the end of World War II," the refrain of another one of

Cohen's lyrics, could be a send-up of the Dead's "Miracle." But this gravelly-voiced Canadian, the darkness to Neil Young's light, executes romantic parts, too: the lover, "crazy for love," the boxer who will "step into the ring with you." Cohen's dreamer, dreaming "a dream of Hungarian lanterns, / in the mist of some sweet afternoon," wearing "a river's disguise," carrying "my cheap violin and my cross," is a not-so-distant cousin of Hunter's "Saint Stephen with a rose / In and out of the garden he goes."

Both men (Leonard Cohen is also a poet) favor these fleeting phosphorescent images, with their old-world lanterns, garlands and gardens, sacred hearts and violins. The folkish romance with obscurity that invades their songs and poems sometimes slips into a romance with death, as in Cohen's "Take This Waltz," "with its very own breath / of brandy and death, / dragging its tail in the sea." And there's the moral ambiguity of Saint Stephen (said to be inspired by communard Steve Gaskin). Will he survive? "Well he may and he may decline / Did it matter? Does it now? Stephen would answer if he only knew how." And the next stanza: "Wishing well with a golden bell / Bucket hanging clear to Hell . . ."

"Innuendo is our mother tongue," reflects Hunter in a poem called "Holigomena":

> a dialect of denial with
> a hundred words for hunger,
> a hundred words for yearning
> and a hundred words for love.

When words fail, or run against unspeakable truths, poets summon a muse who speaks in tongues, as Hunter does in songs of enchantment such as "Saint Stephen" and "China Cat Sunflower." The latter, with its "Copper dome boddhi drip a silver kimono / like a crazy-quilt star gown / through a dream night wind," is his attempt at getting "the essence of a psychedelic experience." But he agrees with Country Joe, who says, "Drugs don't write songs."

Referring to his muses, those who arrive in threes—"very transparent, very feminine, full of brilliance, very loving and mischievous"— Hunter could be describing the spirits that animate tunes such as these. When he speaks of another, "rather solemn, overriding muse," whose echo I hear when we talk, the wraith of "Holigomena" comes to mind:

Mistress of Mourning
in the Valley of Reptiles,
erupt from some unguarded recess
of our incoherent world to conquer us,
despite reason, as we blunder through
the sophistries of this and other ages

attempting to speak truly
if not
truthfully

about lost things
in lost places
with lost words
in a lost song

and somehow
bring it
to be found.

Leonard Cohen, meanwhile, has placed this baroque dreaming at the
service of a vision of the future that the present hardly understands:

Give me back my broken night
my mirrored room, my secret life
It's lonely here,
there's no one left to torture
Give me absolute control
over every living soul
And lie beside me, baby,
that's an order!

Give me crack and anal sex
Take the only tree that's left
and stuff it up the hole
in your culture
Give me back the Berlin Wall

give me Stalin and St. Paul
I've seen the future, brother:
it is murder.

Weatherman, from Dylan's "You don't need a Weatherman to know which way the wind blows," was always going through changes. Thus it came as not much of a surprise when, in September 1970, instead of denouncing the hippies as "bourgeois," as these former SDS leaders usually did ("Fuck hippie capitalism," Weatherman said of "the Woodstock gentleness freakout"), they wooed them by springing the high priest of the drug culture, Timothy Leary, from a minimum-security prison in San Luis Obispo, California. Leary was serving a ten-year sentence for marijuana possession when some Weathermen cut the juice to a power line, thus permitting him to swing hand over hand across the prison wall. The catch was that there had been two lines, and until he climbed the pole and grabbed the cable, Leary hadn't known for sure which one was hot.

Afterward, Weathermen had arranged his passage to Algiers, where he joined the hornets swarming around Eldridge Cleaver, who was then in hot water with Black Panther leader Huey Newton in Oakland for insubordination and adventurism. In San Francisco, Emmett Grogan heard that it cost Leary $25,000 to get out of jail, and that Cleaver had put him under house arrest in Algiers because he hadn't come up with the ten grand promised him. In any event, Leary made a quick exit from Algiers, and fled to Switzerland where, settling in the resort town of Villars-sur-Ollon, he entered a petition for political asylum. Two years later, he turned up at an airport in Afghanistan, was seized by U.S. agents, and transported back to prison. He was paroled in 1975, after turning evidence against Weatherman. Ideas have consequences, but actions, as any serious student of history knows, only sometimes do.

During my year in Berkeley, the two wings of the Great Subculture groped toward a partnership that never seemed to stick. Weatherman had issued its "New Morning" proclamation, after Dylan's latest album: an overture to "Youth Nation," just as Youth Nation seemed to be slipping into the Pacific. The flower children were merely shedding their hippie skin, just as Berkeley radicals who turned to street fighting and to playing guerrilla war games in the poison oak–infested valleys of Tilden Park (as Stuart Street and another commune, the Red Family, did) were shedding their political radicalism. We were, both wings, rogue members of Baby Boom Land. And all those proclaimers of nationhood—"a new nation has grown inside the robot flesh of the old," declared the organizers of the Human Be-In; *We Are Everywhere,* Jerry Rubin called his second book, dedicated to Weatherman—were, in a way, field-testing a market.

Pointing to the $10 billion annually that young people were already spending on consumer products in the 1960s, it was University of California Chancellor Clark Kerr, of all people, who read the writing on the wall. "The employers will love this generation," he said. "They are going to be easy to handle." The hippie-rock-drug culture may have disturbed the Puritan ethic but it also served as an experimental station for pioneering new products and pleasures that corporate emporiums would harvest later. All those basement leather shops, hippie massage parlors, tie-dye vats, and macramé studios in San Francisco and Berkeley—even Stewart Brand's *Whole Earth Catalog*—were seedbeds for growth industries to come.

In the meantime, the back-and-forth between the politicos and the freaks continued. I remember accompanying a group of White Panthers, working-class kids from Detroit who edited a lively magazine called *Sundance,* on a trip across the Bay Bridge to meet with Lawrence Ferlinghetti in North Beach. Ferlinghetti was one of their heroes, a literary Beat; and the meeting, which took place in a tiny office over City Lights Bookstore, had the feel of an envoi. This cross-pollination with an earlier generation of outlaws was an admirable feature of the youth culture. The older, political people tended to be contemptuous of their elders. Our heroes were mainly in Hanoi and Havana. And yet by 1971, we could be surpassed in our zealotry by our juniors, as in this exchange with the Minister of International Affairs of the White Panther party, Genie Plamondon, and Nancy Rubin of the Youth International Party (Yippies), who visited North Vietnam earlier that summer:

> Q: Is the Vietnamese civilization a high civilization?
>   Nancy: We decided that it was one of the highest.
>   Genie: We told them that they should take over the world. Like it really is a whole new civilization because of the way the people relate to each other. The way they work with each other.
>   Nancy: But they are so civilized that they don't want to take

over the world. They said, "We don't want to take over the world, we only want to unite North and South Vietnam."

In 1971, Weatherman's California *foco,* under Bernadine Dohrn and Jeff Jones, executed another daring action, calculated to win favor with hippies, Yippies, and politicos. This was a midnight raid on the tunnel entrance to Marin County at the western end of the Golden Gate Bridge. Using Day-Glo paint and makeshift rappelling equipment, the commandos sprayed a giant rainbow around the arch. A rainbow bisected by a lightning bolt was the Weather Underground's logo; and the sudden appearance of this colossal image, *on government property,* sent shivers down our spines. The rainbow is still there, its edges neatened up over the years by the state highway authority—whose officials seem to have recognized a California landmark when they saw it.

I met with some Weatherpeople, as they preferred to be called, including Bernadine Dohrn and Jeff Jones, in Golden Gate Park in the summer of 1970, and again in Marin. Wearing beads and headbands and loose-flowing clothes, their hair bleached when it had been brown, or dyed when it had been light, they were bursting with health. When we stopped to eat at a natural-foods restaurant near Bolinas, I was the only one who stepped outside for a cigarette, a detail I remember, while the substance of our conversations—probably about Cuba and Vietnam—has been forgotten.

I hadn't seen any of them since the last NC, as SDS's National Council meetings were called, in Flint, Michigan, at the end of December 1969. This was the "War Council," held in a giant ballroom in a black neighborhood, not far from the Fisher Body plant where the famous 1937 UAW strike took place. I was there on Venceremos Brigade business. Except for the decor, which included semipsychedelic posters of Eldridge Cleaver, Che Guevara, Mao, Malcolm X, Ho Chi Minh, and Fred Hampton, who had been killed in Chicago a few weeks before—and a huge cardboard machine gun labeled PIECE NOW—the Flint hall was not unlike one of the old San Francisco ballrooms or North Beach union halls where the Grateful Dead used to play. Of course, the music was different. To the Beatles' "Nowhere Man," the cadres sang, "He's a real Weatherman, / Ripping up the mother land, / Making all his Weatherplans. . . ." And to "White Christmas" (for it was still the holiday season):

I'm dreaming of a white riot
Just like the one October 8,*
When the pigs take a beating
And things start leading
To armed war against the state.

The Weatherman Songbook also included this riff, adapted from *West Side Story*: "When you're a red you're a red all the way / From your first party cell till your class takes the state . . ."

A lot had happened since the Flint NC, where Tom Hayden, who joined Berkeley's Red Family in 1970, led a karate drill during one of the "Wargasms." The Weather collectives had broken into commando units, then disappeared underground. With the town house explosion on March 6, 1970, not just Weatherman but also the larger movement that followed its gyrations with fascination and horror had suffered its Altamont. In northern California, it seemed as if Weatherpeople were atoning for both the town house and the earlier excesses at Flint, which had included a lurid send-off of the Tate-LaBianca murders in Los Angeles. "Dig it," Bernadine said of the Charles Manson gang: "first they killed those pigs, then they ate dinner in the same room with them, then they even shoved a fork into the victim's stomach. Wild!"

I didn't hear this remark, which took white self-hatred, figuratively speaking, to lunatic lengths, but I saw the new salute: *"Fork you!"* with three fingers raised. It was farce—"up-against-the-wallism," one might have called it then—but the suspension of belief was incomplete. It was a ritual murder of the unrequited hopes of the 1960s. Weathermen, meanwhile, weren't the only changelings to toy with the Manson cult. L.A.'s underground paper, *Tuesday's Child,* once named him Man of the Year. And even after the murders, Jerry Rubin confessed that he was taken by Manson's "cherub face and sparkling eyes" when he saw him on television. Such gestures were not meant to condone murder—even Weatherman made sure its bombs went off in the middle of the night so no one got hurt. They did, however, condone despair.

Years later, I was sometimes reminded of the Weatherman curse—"The Year of the Fork," 1970 was proclaimed—by the plaintive one-finger

*A reference to the October 1969 Days of Rage in Chicago.

salute of Deadheads outside concerts. They were looking for the miracle of a free ticket but also, I came to think, for the lost spirit of the 1960s. This includes the loopy abandon of the Pranksters; the hedonism of the Grateful Dead, with their fondness for risk, at least where drugs and music are concerned, also their genius for teamwork; and the audacity and fierce belief in justice of the New Left at its prime. "I need a miracle" is what you say after your elders have thrown in the towel.

~CHAPTER~
II

Aw, maaan, not that poo-poo again!
JERRY GARCIA, ON BERKELEY'S RADICALISM

I AM STILL SURPRISED when I meet a kindred spirit from my generation who shrank from the political struggles of the 1960s. "The Sixties / were dim, dim and dismal. I graduated dishonored at heart, lost," writes my friend Star Black, a poet and photographer, whose disillusionment is traceable to a family tie. Her father, a psychological operations specialist who was defeated in arguments over the war by his pacifist wife, commanded U.S. support troops in Khorat, Thailand, during the air raids against North Vietnam. The Thai bases were stacked with B-52s, their "down-curved, wicked wings" (Star) darkening the skies over Indochina during years when, for me, it was as if with Vietnam's resistance, a great wind had risen in the East, and, sweeping the West, blew open the doors of change. Khorat's airstrips also crackled with F-105s; their fighter pilots: "rodeo guys who shoot," Star recalls in another poem, flying so low over North Vietnam, "they could see people running. . . ."

I saw people running, too, when wave upon wave of F-105s and F-5 Phantoms struck Thanh Hoa City on January 29, 1967. Hundreds of people fled the burning town, some carrying stretchers, others bent under loads of rolled mats and pots, or trailing oxcarts stacked with bricks, more pots and mats, and the children who hadn't been shipped off to the safer mountainous regions. Winding through the smoky preternatural dusk,

227

they might have been a medieval procession of souls fleeing Hades, or entering Hades.

I was in North Vietnam with the second investigating team of the Bertrand Russell War Crimes Tribunal. When Thanh Hoa was attacked, we were six kilometers from the bombing, awaiting the go-ahead to visit a first-aid station where victims from a previous raid had been assembled for our examination. We were ordered to the shelters, but at the first whine of the planes, the *whoompf* of antiaircraft, the concussive thunder of the bombs, I had ducked back out. What was happening around me made no sense, not really. I was the only American, also the only woman in a group of Europeans and a Pakistani. There was no precedent in my sheltered life for what I saw and heard in North Vietnam in 1967. As an antiwar journalist, I knew some facts; I'd read the literature, debated flacks from the State Department, talked with whistle-blowers, spooks, and soldiers from both sides. I had scanned enough Air Force manuals on "people's war" to know why American war planes might attack a crowded church, school, hospital, or market town—all of which were bombed repeatedly in the provinces I visited—far from the scattered factories, railroad depots, bridges, SAM sites, and petrol dumps that comprised the official targets. In a labor-intensive agricultural economy such as North Vietnam's, these were the strategic targets, whose disruption proved more immobilizing than the loss of a bridge or factory.

What I didn't understand, what stayed locked in the senses, was the connection between the rodeo war, the *whoosh* and the whine, and the smell of burnt straw, the rag-wrapped stumps of missing limbs I saw in a crowd. The thatched roof hanging from the treetop on the road to Thanh Hoa—whose house was that? How many people had slept beneath it? The smashed teacup on the dirt floor of a demolished hut brought tears to my eyes, while a recitation of the dead and wounded, duly recorded in my green notebook, did not. It was the sudden snapping of life from the root that stunned me. Who possessed this power to wipe out whole families and villages, to obliterate their histories? To what end?

I didn't think about Vietnam that way then, from the ground. Real thought had ceased, as it does when there's something awful you can't think about. Feeling had gone with it. Political analysis had taken its place, ideologically driven analyses of the behavior of classes, empires, markets, which tidied up the battlefield and soothed the mind.

Occasionally, as on the morning of January twenty-ninth, when we were ordered to our bunker, I recorded the sensations of thought, aiming my microphone at the sky to catch the anxious twittering of the birds, the children's voices crying *"John-son! John-son!"* and *"Mai bai my! Mai bai my!"* (meaning "American planes") as the bombers drew near, and also the muffled thunder that sounded vaguely familiar—and *was* familiar. Earlier generations of F-5s had lifted off from Glenview Naval Air Station, not far from the Chicago suburb where I grew up. The Phantoms were hometown planes; the rodeo pilots, some, anyway, might have been hometown boys. Behind them sat Defense Secretary Robert McNamara in Washington, but then what did McNamara know? Very little about Vietnam or its people and history, he later announced. What could he know about the half-dozen victims of an earlier bombing who were killed that afternoon while they waited for us in the first-aid station? We never even knew their names.

Star Black was a student at Wellesley around this time when her father arrived on campus in his "whites" to lecture a dubious throng on South Vietnam's "inherent right to independence." He brought slides to display the fruits of America's largesse in the Mekong Delta: a cropped countryside, unpocked by war; new bridges, highways, schools. "No one but a librarian from Newton believed him," she writes. It was terrible, the filial shame. She couldn't act. "Loyalty understands nothing." Hers; his. Star and I are war babies. What we share is a fascination with the banality of the evils we grew up with; or with the menace of banality, an evil compounded of thoughtlessness and power.

Vietnam is conspicuous by its absence from the annals of the Grateful Dead. To speak of the war in an inquiry into the Dead's place in American culture is like dragging an unkempt guest to table, one whose manners may not be reliable. But the Grateful Dead's aloofness from the storms swirling around them was no offhand thing: the usual indifference of musicians, especially stoned musicians, to the political world. Rather, the Dead's detachment—Jerry Garcia's and Bob Hunter's, in particular—reflected an aversion to the radical movements of these years that would, in fact, pan into gold when the doors of change began to slam shut.

Consider the ditty called "Cream Puff War" that Garcia wrote and recorded in the mid-'60s, about the radicals across the Bay: "Your constant battles are getting to be a bore / Go somewhere else and continue your cream puff war . . ." "Garcia had no truck with the literal agenda of Berkeley's ideologues," Rock Scully relates in his memoir. "The very mention of the B word set him off." Only reluctantly would he join Santana and Jefferson Airplane at a bail-fund benefit at Winterland for 450 people arrested during the turf fight over People's Park in Berkeley in May 1969. Nor did he play very well that night, bogging down in "new tangles of bumpy rhythms and dislocated melodies," a *Rolling Stone* reporter noted. All these benefits to bail out the politicos who, in Garcia's opinion, were hung up on confrontations with the cops, with throwing bricks and staging noisy TV interviews—though at People's Park, Alameda sheriffs fired point-blank at demonstrators, killing one—seemed to bring out the worst in the band musically. Jerry even derived a certain satisfaction from the fact.

"I can get behind falling to pieces before an audience sometimes. We're not *performers,*" he told a reporter afterward. Such slippage was an instance of how good and evil "exist together in their little game, each with its special place and special humors. I dig 'em both. What is life but being conscious?" he wondered, warming to the theme that was dear to his heart—one, moreover, that set him safely outside a confrontation with political authority, and which helps illuminate his indifference to the war. "Good and evil are manifestations of consciousness. If you reject one, you're not getting the whole thing that's there to be had. So I had a good time last night," Garcia said. "Getting in trouble can be a trip, too."

Berkeley was seen as dorms and lecture halls and cafeterias by a group who, except for Phil Lesh, hadn't been to college. Garcia, who joined the Army to get out of high school, had taken only a few courses at the San Francisco Art Institute. In the early '60s, Stanford's dorms, cafeterias, and coffeehouses had formed the backdrop to his initial forays into folk music, but even in Palo Alto he had cultivated a persona first honed on the streets of Menlo Park with his childhood buddy Laird Grant, that of the outsider "surrounded by straight geeks." As a teenager he went to "razor totin' schools," he told an interviewer, "where either you were a hoodlum or a puddle." In Berkeley and Palo Alto, the students were the geeks. Jerry's gang were the outlaws, the wild ones who copped their drugs on the street, and whose heroes were Hell's Angels and the Beats.

In this, he fell into a California groove, as old as the Gold Rush, in which the frontier ruffians—vaqueros swinging their lariats at wild bulls in vacant fields—arrayed themselves against the city slickers from the East. It didn't matter that the outlaw legend itself was fueled by transplants, like the Indiana-born poet Joaquin Miller, who became a miner in California in the 1860s and fought on the side of the Indians in the Indian Wars before settling down on a fruit ranch. "I don't know why I always encouraged this idea of having been an outlaw," Miller wrote in later life, "but I recall that when Trelawny told me that Byron was more ambitious to be thought the hero of his wildest poems than even to be king of Greece I could not help saying to myself . . . 'We are of accord.' "

For Jerry, the radicals, worse than geeks, were "cream puffs." For Bob Hunter, speaking today, "the [political] movement, being Marxist-based, had a script, and anything that would further that script was allowable, including unethical and immoral actions." Responding to my question, he says the reason the Dead survived for thirty years while the political movement did not is "because we honor American culture, and what we find good in it. We try to give it some hope."

For radicals, "it was verboten to put down anything that was happening in the Soviet Union or anything that Mao did," Hunter informs me, displaying a rather startling ignorance of his New Left contemporaries— one of whom, me, has just relayed enough of my own political experience to disabuse him of such moldy stereotypes. Even the CIA's Clandestine Services found "pacifists and fighters, idealists and materialists, internationalists and isolationists, democrats and totalitarians, conservatives and revolutionaries, capitalists and socialists, patriots and subversives, lawyers and anarchists, Stalinists and Trotskyites, Muscovites and Pekingese, racists and universalists, zealots and nonbelievers, puritans and hippies, do-gooders and evildoers, nonviolent and very violent" in the "peace front." Seeing only Muscovites and Pekingese, Hunter declares, "there was a lie in it that just turned me off, and that," he believes, "was the true source of the collapse of that movement. The Grateful Dead was the opposite of that."

"In the sense that it was open to so many different influences?" I ask. Bob, however, wants to answer a more relevant question. "How were we *not* political?" he states. "Look at who we were. And the masses that were following us and saying, '*Yes,* this is speaking to me!' It wasn't Karl Marx speaking to them; it was something deeper, something American."

We've moved close to an elusive truth about the Grateful Dead, but I'm not ready to nail it down. "When I ask Deadheads what appeals to them most about the Grateful Dead, they often say, 'There was room for everybody.' The Dead seem to encourage *tolerance,* and that," I suggest, "along with the *caring* for one another which the audiences brought to the concerts, is what made the band so appealing to kids when politics got nasty at the end of the '60s. I think it was important that the Dead had an outlaw persona," I add. "It was attractive to young people for whom there was not much action left in the streets——"

"Attractive and *true,*" interjects Hunter, who probably finds these homilies as off-putting as I find his screed on radicalism. With the word *persona,* however, suggesting that the Dead's outlaw status was inauthentic, I've touched a nerve. This outlawry is part of what Hunter finds so "American" about the Grateful Dead; also, I suspect, what makes them "political." How such a stance could survive the ballooning road shows is irrelevant. "We became the victims of largeness," he concedes; "but the thread did persist. Even though it became more and more mythological, yet it had been established."

Hunter tells me he has committed himself to keeping the Grateful Dead's on-line community alive via DeadNet, "to continue that aspect of the thread." But what is this *thread,* which a moment ago I called the "family thread," that one could still see lurking backstage at the blockbuster shows, and which Hunter seems to relate to the outlaw motif? Scully calls it "*the vibe:* that quivering, numinous essence of the Haightgeist, which the Dead had singlehandedly brought with them, like the Ark of the Covenant, out of the sixties." A *haven* from politics, I think, then and now. Essentially prankish, it's what led the band to dose a gray-uniformed brigade of firemen toting buckets of sand at a Grateful Dead concert in Munich, Germany, in the spring of 1972. After drinking the acid-laced beer handed out at intermission, the fire brigade had fallen apart. Shirts loose, hats askew, tears rolled down the men's cheeks as they stumbled about, fraternizing with their shoes.

The "vibe" could be thuggish, as when the Dead's crew stomped back from a Munich whorehouse bearing trophies: chamber pots, lampshades, paintings, a banister rail. All the big guys, Sonny Heard from Pendleton, Oregon, who had come down through the Pranksters, Steve Parish from Queens, and Peter "Craze" Sheridan, marched through the hotel lobby chanting "DON'T FUCK WITH US! WE WON THE WAR!" Would Hunter, I wonder, find this an instance of the Dead's Americanness? Certainly it's an example of how the band flirted with the culture of delinquency, the outlaw edge of the counterculture, where hoods acquire a shadow life as folk heroes. Like the boy at New Trier High School in Winnetka who set up a detour on Sheridan Road in the late '50s, rerouting rush-hour traffic down the long tree-lined driveway of the Distinguished Senator from Illinois, Charles Percy. Scully, meanwhile, settled up for the damages in Munich the following morning, as he would at the Hotel Navarro in New York in years to come.

The crew's natural habitat at home was backstage, where the air was alive with the scents of spilled beer, sweat, and marijuana. Reporters mingled with expectant groupies, people shooting pool and playing video games, drug dealers and hangers-on, lawyers with their clients, caterers, clowns and jugglers from the fraternal commune, the Hog Farm, who worked as baby-sitters. A warehouselike room or tent was roped off for children traveling with the band: Sunshine, Annabelle, and Trixie Garcia, Roger and Ambrosia Healy, Justin Kreutzmann, Steven Hart, Cassidy Law, and a dozen others. "It was like a carny," Cassidy says today. "We were all very close because we all had this one hidden secret," which was the Grateful Dead; "and when we'd go to our schools and hang out with our friends, they had no idea what this world was like."

Talking to second-generation family members, I'm reminded of stories I've heard from red-diaper babies. Living in two different worlds, the secret world at home, the public, prying, hostile world at school—the themes are the same. "Grateful Dead for all of us was voodoo growin' up," Cassidy tells me; "and a lot of us came out pretty much sayin' we had a hard time." At school in the '70s and early '80s, in Marin County, of all places, the Dead were seen as "drug-crazed hippies who would get on the stage every night, take acid and smoke dope. Like, you know, you were filthy, you were rock 'n' roll." No wonder Cassidy was "shy and quiet" at school; and Eileen was sometimes told, "Mom, you have to wait down at the bottom of the hill. I don't want you pickin' me up from school the way you look." But when the bell rang—and back home, when it was show time—"all of a sudden this whole other person would come out," a girl with "a lot of courage and a lot of ambition."

"Inside the organization, we could go, Phew, like we don't have to play this role or say and do things to accommodate [other people's] feelings." And Cassidy, who is twenty-five in 1996 when we talk, remembers how when she was little she would lie about her parents. "[I'd say], 'Oh, they were married and they divorced.' Because to hear that you were an illegitimate child . . ." she pauses. "But around here that's what everyone was doing."

On the road, "we thought we could rule the world," she says; though "some people went the opposite way and didn't ever go to the shows because they were more involved with what they wanted out of school. I enjoyed the band," Cassidy declares. She finds "strength in the organization," and has worked inside it, mainly in the ticket office, since 1986. Among the children of the Dead who went the opposite way are Sunshine, Annabelle, and Trixie, who, starting in the early '80s, refused to go to shows at all. "They could just barely stand to listen to the music, they were so angry," Mountain Girl says. When they were little they could go onstage and play with the mikes and twiddle with the guitars. Sunshine used to sing, but by the mid-'70s that was out. At home Jerry wouldn't let them near his instruments, which is why (in their mother's opinion) none of the girls evinced much interest in music. When Jerry died, Trixie, on the other hand, was studying art at the San Francisco Art Institute, just like her father had when he was nineteen.

It's with Mountain Girl that one gets the sharpest before-and-after picture of the hippie band morphing into something almost monstrous. For her, the turning point was 1972, when she remembers standing in the service elevator of a large hotel, waiting for the door to roll open so she and Jerry could sneak out a back alley. It opened, and twenty pairs of eyes locked onto theirs, and there was nowhere to run. "It scared the hell out of me," she says. Though it wasn't her the fans wanted; it was him. Mountain Girl was "the person who was in the way, the obstruction, the barking dog chained to the gate." It was in 1972, she recalls, "when things just took off."

Backstage in the '70s, a longtime observer relates, was "a convention of brigands." Rex Jackson, Ramrod (another Oregonian), Kidd Candelario, Steve Parish, and Pranksters Page Browning and Ken Babbs, along with a sprinkling of Hell's Angels, made up "a pirate's convention" in which "everybody was illegal somehow; if you didn't have a record or hadn't done time . . . you were ranked lower than whale manure."

Candace tells me that in 1973, when I visited her at Roosevelt Stadium in New Jersey, Steve Parish ordered me off the stage; and that as a result she resigned. Temporarily, I assume; but no, she was gone for two years (including the year the band stopped touring), during which time she worked for Traffic and Blood, Sweat and Tears. I don't remember the Parish incident; and when I tell Bob Hunter, he says the first time he met Parish, "Steve was trying to throw *me* off the stage, but I said, '*Wait a minute, I wrote the words,*' and he said, '*Well, I'm going to go find out about that,*' and I just pushed my way past him."

Still, I don't know how seriously I would take all this swagger if my sister hadn't told me about the time in the '70s when she walked into band manager Sam Cutler's room on the twenty-fifth floor of the Navarro, and a Hell's Angel was dangling a man upside down by his heels from an open window. The fellow had been impersonating Jerry Garcia, and coming on to women, or running some financial scam, she's not sure which. There was no effort to conceal what was happening. "I thought it was a great way to stop this guy. At the same time," she says, "I thought there was something wrong with it."

Scully describes a similar scene involving a promoter in the South who had supposedly used the Dead's ticket money to buy a large quantity of bad cocaine. "Hurd [sic] and Rex pick this guy up and shake him down— literally—in front of the band. Pick him up by his ankles and shake him and money comes pouring out of his pockets, big *rolls* of it that he'd been collecting from the concessions and the head shops." It doesn't add up to the fifteen thousand dollars he owes them, so Ramrod goes to search his desk and returns with another five thousand. Back at the hotel, with the promoter handcuffed to a radiator Mafia-style, they count up the money, take their "nut and give him back a few bucks to spare. Charming," Scully comments.

An element of showmanship in such scenes, which play to an audience, lends them a theatrical air. The crew revels in its reputation for badness. Like the pack of ruffians who follow Prince Hal in *King Henry IV*—Peto, Pistol, and the lot—they mock the exploits of their masters. In the early '70s, Parish, Ramrod, and Rex Jackson teamed up with soundman Dan Healy and another techie, named Sparky (Mark Raizene), to form a fly-by-night band called Sparky and the Ass Bites from Hell. A few years before, when Parish worked at the Capitol Theater in Port Chester with some buddies from Queens, he presided over a club called Milk and Cookies that specialized in comic routines. Candace remembers a funny one in which Parish and sound man Alex Kochan played two old vets in rocking chairs telling World War I stories.

At the same time, the real band delights in mocking itself; as on April Fools' Day 1980, at the Capitol Theater, when the Grateful Dead walked onstage playing one another's instruments in a rendering of Chuck Berry's "Promised Land." In the '70s, when they met up with Andy Warhol's Velvet Underground of leather and whips in New York, they toyed with the idea of recording a song called "Barbed Wire Whipping Party"—thus, in a sense, mocking *their* betters. Warhol was Lord of Misrule in the city that in the beginning had terrified the bandits from the West.

The outlaw persona is layered, like an onion that brings real tears but lacks substance. Here's the gang in 1983:

> Lesh (to Parish): I thought you were an asshole when I first met you, man—
>
> Parish: Right. Well, you always gave me a chance—you never slammed the door.
>
> Lesh: I knew that you were OK, man, because of certain things. . . . [Ellipses in original]
>
> Garcia: It takes a long time to get interested and to like people.
>
> Parish: We were on the road for many years, but you always talked to me. . . .
>
> Lesh: The thing is that once you have tenure—
>
> Parish: You can go to another level of understanding.
>
> Lesh: Then it's automatic. I had a lot of trouble with Kidd.
>
> Parish: Everybody does.

The "time" the pirates serve is mainly for drug busts, none of which were ballyhooed as much as the celebrated pot bust at 710 Ashbury on October 2, 1967. At the press conference that followed the band members' release from jail, a bowl of whipped cream stood at the ready for offending reporters. "We've always figured that if we ever held a press conference, the first reporter who asked a stupid question would get a cream pie in his face, and you're him," said Danny Rifkin after somebody asked him how many years it had taken to grow his hair so long. The reporter cringed and Danny took pity on him; afterward, cookies, coffee, and cake were passed all around.

Generally, the Grateful Dead courted the press, which covered stories like this with a giggle. When fame arrived in the 1980s, publicist Dennis McNally doled out backstage passes and dangled interviews with Jerry Garcia like so many overnights in the Abraham Lincoln Bedroom at the White House—to journalists, that is. More than one writer planning a book was driven away by his refusal to grant access to band members, particularly Jerry. (McNally, whose biography of Jack Kerouac, *Desolate Angel,* impressed Garcia when he read it, is the Dead's "official biographer" and is currently writing a history of the band.) It was hotels and airplanes that the band and crew sometimes trashed, not the press, and those mainly in the late '70s, in a spirit of antiauthoritarianism that Phil Lesh compares to students seizing administration buildings in the '60s but which seems more likely due to too much booze and blow.

The crew's power to intimidate was based on a cult of manual labor that regarded any other kind of work as shirking. Contrary to the Fillmore East's crew, "middle-class people who had a broader knowledge and a wider set of interests," according to Tom Shoesmith, a Fillmore East light show technician who later worked for the Dead, "the Grateful Dead crew was more working-class, with somewhat narrower interests. It's not to say that one is any better than the other," but between the Dead's gang and their counterparts from the East, "there was something less than perfect and immediate understanding. The Dead's crew also had a sort of ideal of toughness that the Fillmore crew never had." And Shoesmith tells me about the "McIntosh Test," which involved the band's huge vacuum-tube amplifiers, a dozen or more, weighing 125 pounds each. "You picked one up and you didn't even think about asking anybody to help you . . . because if you did, you'd never be allowed to forget it."

The Dead's roadies were quick to anger and occasionally threatening, especially Kidd Candelario. "When he saw someone vulnerable, he attacked." Tom grumbles now about a flight home when he was a little drunk and partying with the stewardesses, "and Kidd made it his business to go right to Karen [Tom's first wife] and tell her all about it." Sonny Heard could be the most threatening, but he had a sense of humor. "He'd *pretend* to threaten, like Hulk Hogan, playing the brute"; and Shoesmith, a lean, quick-moving man with a trim mustache, who today works as a computer programmer for Blue Cross/Blue Shield in New York, snarls and waves his arms. He's imitating Sonny Heard stomping and twirling on a box of skimpy White Castle hamburgers that a promoter had sent in place of the Quarter Pounders that were promised. " 'That's what you can do with your burgers!' " he shouts.

Hearing these stories, I wonder how Candace, one of two women laboring in the pit, managed to hold her ground. The second woman was sound engineer Betty Cantor, who recorded concerts and worked as a mixer on Grateful Dead records. The two got on well, and neither was intimidated by the strutting road crew. Other women were employed in the home offices in San Rafael. On tour, there were only wives, girlfriends, and groupies, Candace once told me; but after 1987, when more business was done on the road, friends from Grateful Dead Productions such as Cassidy Law and Monarch Entertainment's Amy Polan worked in the rented trailers that joined the armada of eighteen-wheelers parked behind the venues. To Cassidy, Candace was something of a heroine, admired as much for her lighting as for her ability to stand up to Dan Healy, Steve Parish, and production manager Robbie Taylor. It didn't hurt that she and Jerry Garcia enjoyed each other's company, and that she could match his former obsessiveness for getting the right sound from a guitar, or the right opening rhythm from the drummers, with her own relentless on-tour fussing over a new lighting system.

Jerry had asked Candace if she would be the band's full-time lighting designer after watching her light a John McLaughlin set in Buffalo in January 1972, where Garcia and keyboardist Howard Wales had opened the show. He knew her from the Fillmore East, where she was the house LD, and from the Capitol in Port Chester, where she had designed and installed the lights. Her first assignment with the Grateful Dead, after the Academy of Music shows in March 1972, was to light the band's 1972 European tour, a logistical challenge, since no one, as far as she knew, had taken a lighting system out on the road. Europe '72 was also a crash course in the weirdness of working for the band.

She had hired Ben Haller, a Fillmore East technician then working at the Rainbow Theatre in London, to assist her. In London, she had been given seven thousand dollars for supplies and per diems, and she and

Haller went to work putting together the dimming and control part of the lighting rig with the help of other ex–Fillmore East people working in England. When she returned to New York to assemble it, she discovered that the Grateful Dead thought she had absconded with the money. "I remember being in some hotel and laughing and thinking that was a good one on them," she says, reminding me that she "didn't enter into that thing with any illusions about these guys." If she had, they were disposed of on the eve of departure for the Europe tour when a coke dealer in New York, whose block on Bleecker Street was always jammed with tractor trailors and limos, told her that the Dead's crew had put all their cocaine in her road boxes. "I don't care what you do with it but get it out," she told him. "And it was the last I ever heard of it," she says; "it was gone."

Ben Haller was Candace's right-hand man for the next few years. A Bunyanesque figure who preferred working as a blacksmith at Old Sturbridge as a teenager and restoring eighteenth-century buildings to sitting in classrooms, he had devised a console in London not much larger than a shoe box to control about forty lights. In Europe, Candace put the control box, control cable, and headsets under a seat marked with duct tape, and when the shows were about to start, she came out, sat down, and pulled the console and headsets out from under the chair to run the lighting and cue the follow spots.

The partnership with Haller flourished; and later she took on Shoesmith and Bill Schwarzbach, formerly of the Fillmore's Joshua Light Show (later Joe's Lights) to round out the Grateful Dead's lighting crew. When she quit in 1973 after the fight with Parish, Ben stepped in as lighting designer. When the band took a break from the road in 1974, Haller went to Los Angeles and became a grip. Hollywood is where a number of Fillmore East people ended up. Allan Arkush, who ran the Joshua Light Show, became a filmmaker whose quirky low-budget flicks—like *Rock 'n' Roll High School* (1979) and *Get Crazy* (1983, featuring a lighting designer named Violetta, based on Candace)—kept a bit of the East Village madness alive. Another light show person, Jonathan Kaplan, who directed sixteen movies, including *White Line Fever* (1975), went on to direct *Cheers* and *Moonlighting* for television. Stagehand Jon Davison produced *Airplane!* (1980) and *Airplane II* (1982). John Ford Noonan became a well-known off-Broadway playwright.

By 1972, at twenty-seven, Candace had been lighting stages for nearly five years. During her first rock 'n' roll gig at the Anderson Theater early in 1968, she hadn't known the difference between a dimmer switch and a circuit-breaker lever, and when the music started, she had reached for the latter. The lights came on like a thunderclap. "A coincidence," she says, and a happy one. The event contained the kernel of a sensation she'd have for years, long after the circumstances behind it had vanished. This was to find herself facing a task that seemed way over her head and "to just try to get through it somehow. It never occurred to me that once I took on a job I wouldn't finish it." And so the jobs "would always get done, for better or for worse." It didn't occur to her to ask for help, either, not in this man's world, where, far from being a Wendy, Candace was one of the guys, doing a guy's job (though not until the late '80s would she get a guy's pay). Hauling equipment, scrambling up the rigging to fix a light, she adapted to the "McIntosh Test." It made her tough, not so much with her mates— that came later—but with herself.

Working with Chip Monck at the Anderson, she saw that "you have to be larger than life to do things big and new and powerful and different and be kind of full of piss and vinegar." It was a role as much as an aesthetic, and while she mastered the former, for many years she shrank from the latter. "What I was *doing* was timid," she maintains of her early lighting with the Grateful Dead. But at the time, she muted the lights so as not to distract from music that was rich and diverse enough, she believed, to carry itself. The idea was to maintain a low-key atmosphere onstage, as in a bar or club—whether the band was playing at the Capitol or at civic centers in Des Moines, St. Paul, Hartford, or Portland, Maine. Being "timid" had little to do with it. The Dead's aesthetic was to avoid show-manship—a bad word in conversations with Jerry Garcia—never to be an *act*. An act was Bob Dylan, Robbie Robertson, and Rick Danko opening a number in London in the '70s by facing drummer Mickey Jones, who raised his sticks high, then brought them down with a crash as the three guitarists leapt into the air, kicking off a song as they hit the ground and whirled to face the audience. Or it was Mick Jagger, flinging his long yellow scarf back and forth as he strutted across the stage.

For the Dead on a good night, the music was the act. Especially was this true in the middle '70s, an experimental time for the band, when a certain musical maturity set in and arrangements became more intricate. "Wharf Rat," a sad tune about a poor drunk down by the docks, is a case in point. "All of a sudden it gets all happy and 'gospel' when it reaches the bridge," Deadhead Jamie Janover says of a favorite bootleg tape from 1976. And he sings it: "But I'll get back / on my feet someday / the good Lord willin'." Later, he notes, the tension rises with "I'll get up and fly away-y-y-y," and he sings that, too. "The band echos it with the instruments, and right there is a major chord change. Oh, God," he says, "the way that tune resolves itself! I just see hills and valleys—"

"Do you see a little guy tripping off into the sunset?" I ask. "No, I don't see that," says Janover; and he explains the "dynamic" that draws him to the Grateful Dead or to any band he likes—Phish, for instance. "It's when a song *goes* somewhere. It starts somewhere and then it goes somewhere." "Hills and valleys" are sonic metaphors for variations in the beat.

For the Dead during this period, the visual pageantry was reserved for festival shows, like New Year's concerts at Winterland, when Bill Graham rode out over the audience on a huge joint or a motorcycle. And Hell's Angels roared up a ramp and onto the stage during the Rhythm Devils set. Chinese New Year and Mardi Gras were other occasions for a piling on of lights, banners, and balloons—Trips Festivals writ large. The rest of the year, the action mainly resided in the music, and the audience might supply the glimmer, as when thousands of matches were lit to bring the Grateful Dead back for encores, and the band returned with "Casey Jones" and puffs of smoke from behind the amps, while high above the crowd, Candace's mirrored ball filtered light across the hall.

Looking back on those years, when rock lighting was still mainly strobes and a projection-driven liquid light show, Candace remembers trying to use projectors as light sources. But they weren't bright enough, and she didn't then say, "Well, okay, then we need to build brighter projectors. . . . I didn't understand that if the equipment isn't there, you have to get somebody to build it," she reflects. It would have meant asserting an authority she didn't believe she had, or maybe admitting to some limitation in herself. "The woods are full of people who are ready to invent something when you want it," she says now—one of them being Chris Brightman, who won his spurs as a rigger at eighteen, working alongside Tom Shoesmith at Roosevelt Stadium in New Jersey in 1975. "All I had to say was, 'This is a problem. We need a brighter projector,' and one would have been built at a time when it would have been useful for lights." It might have allowed her to take the technology forward—perhaps to merge stage lighting with light-show technology before the latter fell out of favor, which it did after the early '70s.

During her first decade with the Grateful Dead, Candace was hampered by the band's aversion to spending money on anything other than the sound system, and by a general indifference toward visual production—a concert dimension the musicians never saw. The antishowmanship aesthetic was part rationalization. When automated lighting arrived in 1982—"wiggly lights," she calls them: Panaspots and Varilites—she was eager to try them out. Their advent coincided with an occupational boredom severe enough to galvanize her into action—even *before* she quit drinking, she observes, alluding to a habit she shared with Pigpen, and with Bill Kreutzmann and Brent Mydland. (She stopped drinking in 1983.) The new lights promised release from routines that were becoming stifling. But first, she had to persuade the Dead to pay for them. And this was an organization that wanted to get everything for free, even its LD. When Garcia had first asked her to work for the band and she inquired about the pay, he hesitated, then said, "Well, a lot of people work for us for nothing." Later, when somebody else called to talk terms, she realized that Jerry never dealt with such issues and so hadn't known the answer.

On the job, she didn't feel like a woman, Candace says, when I ask her about this man's world; she felt like a "lighting designer . . . like someone in charge of a crew"—the Dead's lighting crew, which numbered seven people by the end, but also the union crews she dealt with during setups at theaters and arenas. Former manager Richard Loren puts a different spin on it. "She was beyond sex as a person, you know what I mean?" No, I answer. "It wasn't that she wasn't a woman or a man; she was just Candace, the lighting person. She wasn't anybody's old lady on the scene. . . . And another thing—she was Jerry's lighting director. She was somebody whose work Jerry liked, and you don't fuck around with that. She had that talent on her side."

Her ability to work smoothly with union crews—"the most uncooperative group of people on the planet," Rock Scully believes, maybe because it was his job to "grease them"—stood in stark contrast to the tendency of the Dead's roadies and sound crew to get into brawls with them. Especially when exposed to unfamiliar situations on the road did the crew's territorial instincts overtake them, sometimes with disastrous results. Thus, in September 1978, on the eve of the Grateful Dead's departure for the Great Pyramid in Egypt, Steve Parish refused to allow the parents of the piano tuner to come onstage at Roosevelt Stadium. The piano tuner, an airline pilot who loved the Grateful Dead and tuned Keith Godchaux's piano for free, abruptly quit. In Cairo, the piano was out of tune, and so was the band—so badly out of tune that later Garcia wouldn't allow anything they played there ever to be released. As a result, the anticipated three-record album, *The Grateful Dead at the Great Pyramid,* which Zippy Loren hoped would recoup the $400,000 the band had sunk into the Egyptian venture, never happened. The Dead tumbled into a period of chronic indebtedness just when band members (Garcia excluded) were clamoring for more money; and Loren, who took the rap for the belt-tightening that ensued, was fired in 1981.

"Quality terrified them," Candace says of the Dead's roadies, in particular. "They didn't like Bob Bralove or me or the people on my crew, any one of whom might have fixed Jerry's guitar. . . . It was legendary that the Grateful Dead had the worst crew in rock 'n' roll." Scully agrees, calling them "a much more pigheaded, intransigent, willful, and sulky quantity than the band members. . . . The band takes good care of them and the crew just shits on them. They [the musicians] are ruled by a bunch of kids who never got out of high school and have never worked for anyone else in their lives." Candace once asked Jerry at a band meeting why they didn't fire Kidd Candelario, who was sitting a few seats away. "Just don't ask. Just don't ask," he whispered. She always thought Kidd had something on Garcia or the band, but apparently not.

There was a seamy side to the convention of brigands, who often appeared "stuck and stodgy," like tired extras from an action film that had long ago folded its tent. Their abusiveness "hurt your heart with the ugliness of it," says Candace, who remembers what Dan Healy said of a young woman who worshiped him: "If she wasn't so ugly, I'd fuck her brains out." But when Sonny Heard was fired by the band in 1976, Candace hired him on the spot—to get him on her side. "Ben Haller was formidable," she explains, "but Heard was crazy, a violent version of Harpo Marx." She told him, "I want you on our lighting crew. Would you be loyal to us?" And Heard (who died in a shoot-out over drugs in the 1980s) "got it immediately, and grinned," she says. "I knew he respected me," Candace adds, "because I was game, tough. . . . While he was there, it was just heaven. I have always loved chaos," she suddenly remarks. "That's what attracted me to the Grateful Dead."

This is Rhonda Roscolene speaking, a road name (after a term for lighting gels) that originated with Steve Parish, who could be a pal when he wasn't an antagonist. So could Ramrod, Sparky, Robbie Taylor, or Bill Kreutzmann, who was also bullish one moment and then good fun the next. Rhonda Roscolene's flirtation with chaos sometimes went with a black wig, which signified a wildness that made Jerry Garcia laugh as well. "It was a commune on the go," Zippy Loren says of the Grateful Dead during those years. "It wasn't a commune of the '60s. But it was still a family," where anything might happen, and usually did.

When Rhonda Roscolene visited me in Park Slope, Brooklyn, where Richard and I had settled in the fall of 1972, it was often with a flask of Hennessey's in her capacious bag, and a string of road stories that made my hair curl. There were other names that allowed her to step outside herself, like Lotta Lumens and Candela Blondollar. I see them now as Prankster names, like Intrepid Traveler and Gretchen Fetchin', or Hardly Visible (George Walker) and Dis-Mount (Sandy Lehmann-Haupt). They went along with sharp retorts like the response (courtesy Ben Haller) to the question "How do you do the lights?" Answer: "Naked and tripping."

There was another side to Candace, which Tom Shoesmith, who worked with her at the Anderson and the Fillmore East, recalls. At the Fillmore, he worked as a "lumia artist," reflecting lights off shiny surfaces. He also operated an overhead projector behind the rear projection screen, manipulating parallel clock crystals between which a tinted solution of mineral oil and water, when projected on the screen, formed huge undulating Rorschach-like blots. Candace, when she was the house LD, saw his work, but he couldn't see hers. Tom remembers how careful she was that her lights not wash out the screen. "She was easy to work with," he says. "She was almost overly humble," he adds, identifying a trait that ran like an alternating current alongside the brashness.

Shoesmith tells me that the Fillmore's old follow spots, called "supertroopers," were carbon arc spots. About five feet long, they originated in the 1880s, when Thomas Edison proposed illuminating the new Brooklyn Bridge with lights very much like them. When Candace worked for promoter Howard Stein in 1970–1971, and later toured with the Jerry Garcia Band, she came upon them in industrial towns whose music halls always seemed to be named the Capitol or the Palace. With their "long skinny snoots" and drawstring controls, the follow spots reminded her of cannons. The union men who ran them, "wizened old men" with whom she loved to talk, had used them to light vaudeville shows in the 1920s and '30s.

Soundman Dan Healy had a parallel experience. The PA systems he encountered in halls across the United States dated back to his parents' generation and before, when the groove was Tommy Dorsey or Benny Goodman. But he found the union men horrified with the mountain of scaffolding the Grateful Dead erected for the Wall of Sound. It was like " 'Fuck you, you long-haired punks!' " until they saw an audience of two thousand people "all stop, stand dead still . . . in a little old theater, not flinching, not moving a muscle because what was going on was so electrifying."

Cuing the spot operators on antiquated headsets exactly like the ones telephone operators wore in old movies, Candace experienced a time warp. It was the same with the huge black microphone at Madison Square Garden in 1970, which was the microphone Walter Winchell had used. "Stand by to bump to red, ready and GO," she'd say. "Stand by to pick up lead guitar. . . . Stand by to fade out." The heat-generating "piano boards" in the music halls were also relics of vaudeville. The whole scene made her think that traveling with a band "wasn't all that new. It had been done before with the same kind of lunacy. I'm sure all those people got really drunk and stoned," she says, imagining the old entertainers; "only there was probably more drinking, whereas this time there were more drugs. But they lived the same wild life." Rock on the road, she decides, "was vaudeville in the '70s."

⤜∽⤛

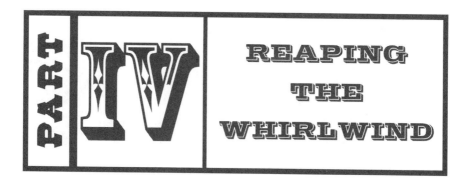

PART IV

REAPING THE WHIRLWIND

~CHAPTER~ 12

THE HOUSE THAT JERRY BUILT

Small wheel turn by the fire and rod
Big wheel turn by the grace of God
ROBERT HUNTER, "THE WHEEL"

T HE GRATEFUL DEAD, of course, were not outlaws. Nor was 710 Ashbury, as *Rolling Stone* reported, ever a latter-day Brook Farm. Appearances deceive, which is why appearances are so revealing. Take "Danny the Riff," as Digger Emmett Grogan remembers Rifkin when he was the twenty-four-year-old comanager of the Grateful Dead. It was the spring of 1970, and Grogan had run into him in the BOAC office on Fifth Avenue in New York, where they were each buying tickets to London. They agreed to meet later at the Park Avenue apartment of mutual acquaintances. And Rifkin bounced down the street, "looking real good, dressed in tattered-patched jeans and carrying an attaché case in one hand, a real, made-in-Africa, cast-iron-tipped spear in the other, and an enormous, kinky, Afro-like hairdo flopping all over his head, covering up most of his gentle Moroccan-Jewish face." Grogan watched him trip past Saint Patrick's Cathedral, "freaking everybody out, stopping them in their tracks and forcing them to turn their heads to get a better look at this costumed monster who was one of their children. He was a peaceful, gentle guy who never intentionally hurt anyone," Grogan reflects, "a sweet cat."

What made the Dead seem like outlaws was their immunity to the entrepreneurs of popular culture, who cruise the fringes of society looking for the far-out, the hip, the weird in order to freshen up the product line. Today when you ask Deadheads whether they think the Grateful Dead was an outlaw band, many say yes, but what they point to is the Dead's refusal to "go commercial." "They were outlaws musically, certainly," says dulcimer player Jamie Janover. "Everybody else who was successful in the music business was successful due to a record company." The Dead treated Warner's like dirt, Janover observes, and while they hit the jackpot with *In the Dark* (1987), they could go for years before that without a new record and still sell out every show.

To listen to Warner executive Joe Smith recall his adventures with the Grateful Dead in the 1960s and early '70s is to enter a cultural divide between industry and artist that is hard to imagine in the blurred relations of today's marketplace. "They never fired a manager. They never got rid of anybody," Smith says wonderingly. "When we'd have a meeting, sixty people would show up. Mothers nursing babies. Owsley mixing up God knows what on the side." Warner planned to spend thirty thousand dollars on the live album *Grateful Dead,* aka *Skull and Roses,* in 1971. "But with their great indecisiveness," Smith recounts, "with the drugs, and with their running around, three would be straight and two would be stoned, and two would be straight and three would be stoned . . . and then they'd all be stoned," they could end up spending ninety grand. "Which at the time was unheard of. Then they wanted to call the album 'Skull Fuck.'"

A moment came when Phil Lesh said, "I've got a great idea. We'll go to L.A. and we'll record thirty minutes of very heavy air on a smoggy day and then we'll go to the desert where it's clear and record thirty minutes of clear air, and we'll mix it and we'll use that as a pad and we'll record over it." Smith, who later became Warner's CEO and then ran Capitol Records, waited for people to laugh, but nobody did. Thinking fast, he told them that the American Federation of Musicians wouldn't allow it, and so they couldn't do it.

It was Papa Jer who saw that nobody got fired, who shrank from any confrontation with a member of the group that might lead to pain. Joe Smith was right, but he wasn't privy to the abuse Garcia frequently heaped on his mates behind their backs. In 1968, after the release of the single version of "Dark Star" and *Anthem of the Sun,* the Dead's second album with Warner (*Skull and Roses* was the fifth), "the Bobby problem" had surfaced once again. Weir's inability to lay down a solid bedrock of rhythm against which Garcia's solos were free to roam had become an embarrassment in rehearsals at Hamilton Army Air Field in Marin County, where the band was then piecing together its third album, *Aoxomoxoa.*

Bobby, whose tuning and timing were off, was doing too much acid, in Jerry's view. Pigpen was also falling behind. He was drinking more and rehearsing less, and visibly struggling with the huge Hammond organ that had replaced the carry-on keyboard he used to play. Neither musician was keeping up with the new directions the music was taking with "Dark Star" and *Anthem,* and Jerry and Phil were beginning to burn Rock Scully's ears with their impatience. One afternoon after Weir and Pigpen left a recording session, Jerry pulled Rock aside and ordered him to fire them both.

The idea was preposterous, and Scully knew it. You don't fire your partners, or if you do, you do it yourself, and Garcia refused. What was needed was a wake-up call, which is what Weir took away from the botched attempt to oust him at a band meeting in the summer of 1968. Pigpen, whose legend grew as he himself began to dwindle away with liver disease, was a tougher case. He rarely came to band meetings, but he could still work a crowd. As late as 1970–1971, when the Grateful Dead took the college circuit by storm, he was often the star, rapping the blues in a way that drew his student audiences into a magic circle of warmth that left them hungry for more. "We can go on calling ourselves the Grateful Dead but after Pigpen's death," Garcia said at Ron McKernan's funeral in 1973, "we all knew this was the end of the original Grateful Dead."

In 1968, Pigpen was pretty much left alone. Phil and Jerry didn't seem to realize that the gap yawning between the country rhythm and blues and Chuck Berry rock 'n' roll so dear to Pig and Weir (respectively), and the long, spacey jams laced with special effects, was not much more than a growing pain. But they knew enough not to tamper with an icon. With the release of *Workingman's Dead* and *American Beauty* in 1970, the new direction reversed itself. And after 1972, the Dead started assimilating all the disparate strands into a musical tapestry of their own.

Garcia's impatience with Bobby would resurface again over the "sour notes" in Weir's experiments with slide guitar. "You guys are a forgiving lot," David Gans commented in 1981, apropos of Weir's inability to stay in tune or hold a melody line. "Tell me about it," Jerry said, laughing, then added that given such problems, "it's totally amazing that we even have an audience. . . ." But Garcia and Weir had a peculiar relationship, more enduring than any other within the band because of its filial overtones. They were like another set of Frank Baum characters, in *John Dough and the Cherub* (1906). John Dough is a large gingerbread man and his sidekick, Chick the Cherub, is the world's first incubator baby. Their attachment is sealed by their differences.

The Dead's larger family, the Grateful Dead Organization (eventually Grateful Dead Productions) had evolved in a similar manner as the band. In 1971, the business manager was David Parker, who once played washboard and kazoo in Mother McCree's Uptown Jug Champions. His wife, Bonnie, was the bookkeeper. Alan Trist, back from England, ran Ice Nine Publishing, which oversaw copyrights, licensing, and the publication of songbooks, while also serving (for a while) as a holding pen for dependents on the payroll. The band's first roadie, Garcia's childhood pal Laird Grant, was still on board, along with "the first fan," as Sue Swanson calls herself. Sam Cutler, who managed the Rolling Stones on their fateful American tour in 1969, looked after the band's production needs on the road and ran the touring office at home. With the exception of a latecomer like Cutler, they were all "Friends of Jerry." Shares in the Grateful Dead pie were divided equally among the six band members, two managers, and two roadies, Laird and Ramrod.

It was a short step for the Grateful Dead to envision recruiting a larger community of heads and freaks, "a Deadland of airwaves and albums and concerts," which would help the band steer clear of the obstacles in its path. These included the internal problems of uneven talent and colliding musical styles, and more important, the clashes with Warner over the promotion and distribution of their records, not to mention record prices, which the Dead wanted to slash from the levels Warner set. They had succeeded with *Live Dead,* reducing it from twelve dollars to six, and again with *Skull and Roses*—though not without accepting substantial cuts in royalties.

The step that soon sent the Dead off on a separate track from other bands was taken in 1971, when a brief notice was slipped inside the jacket of "Skull Fuck" (as it will always be known by Deadheads). Signed by Jerry Garcia, it read:

DEAD FREAKS UNITE: Who are you? Where are you? How are you? Send us your name and address and we'll keep you informed.

There was no form to fill out or boxes to check, just an invitation to write the Dead and let them know who their fans were. A small gesture, executed with the usual shrug, it was uncommon in the record business—as was the relationship the Grateful Dead had already established with its audiences. And it worked. By 1972, 25,000 letters had rolled in, many illustrated with the dense calligraphy that became a hallmark of Deadhead correspondence.

"You know what this is, man? It's a—*snooooort*—'*mailing list*,' " writes Scully, tapping into the scene, the talk, the drugs, without disclosing the meaning of the play. "We can now contact Deadheads *directly*. Tell 'em where we're playing and shit like when the next album's coming out." And Jerry replies, "Cool, maaaan!" as if the Dead Freaks Unite campaign, which predated the term *Deadhead,* was a happy accident. It was, in fact, the opening salvo in a series of strategic decisions (however haphazardly approached) that the Grateful Dead made between 1971 and 1973 to secure their independence from the record industry.

Speaking of the "army" the band recruited, Mickey Hart puts it most succinctly. "If you only know a band by its records, you wouldn't like the Grateful Dead very much," which is why "we went out and recruited these guys head for head, their fathers and their sisters, and their mothers. We went on a head-hunting mission for twenty-five years," he says; "we went out there and got this army in tow. And said, Okay, you guys are some-*thing;* you are a thing. And they themselves recognized their own identity and grew bigger than we ever could even imagine."

And the Lord spake unto Moses, saying,
Make thee two trumpets of silver; of a whole piece shall thou make them:
that thou mayest use them for the calling of the assembly,
and for the journeying of the camps.

(Something in Hart's words, as I relay them now, leads me to the Bible—not a book I am accustomed to consulting—and it opens to that.)

In 1992, I shared the popular view, furthered by the band itself, that the Grateful Dead's astonishing growth was a sociological phenomenon, in which they themselves were largely bystanders. And by then, to a degree it was. "Where are these people who keep coming to our shows coming from?" Garcia wondered in a *Rolling Stone* interview in 1991. "What do they find so fascinating about these middle-aged bastards playing basically the same thing we've always played?" He can't believe it's because they want to pick up on the '60s, which they missed. "The Sixties were fun, but shit, it's fun being young, you know, nobody really misses out on that. So what is it about the Nineties in America?" And Garcia sets forth the company line, which contains its grain of truth: "There must be a dearth of fun out there in America. Or adventure. Maybe that's it, maybe we're just one of the last adventures in America."

In the takeoff years, however, the Grateful Dead knew what it wanted and went after it with a degree of concentration unmatched by any other American band. "We didn't know how big it would get, of course," says Hart, speaking of the audiences of the late '80s and '90s, "but we knew that if we wanted to go on, we would need an army. . . . We were recruiting." The magnitude of the response to the 1971 mailing surprised the band, but the need to establish its independence from the record industry was well understood. Garcia and Lesh had fretted ever since the release of the Dead's first album, *The Grateful Dead* (1967), over the threat that the companies posed to the band's artistic integrity. ("They hated everybody. They just hated me a little less," says Joe Smith, who as president of Warner Records visited the Dead with bodyguards.) It was more than business, Richard Loren recalls. "It was like, 'Those are the fuckin' *straights,* man. . . . They're all fuckin' crooks, they're all businessmen, they're all out to get what they can get, and you don't trust 'em,' and often justifiably," he adds.

"What you have to understand is that the Dead were a workingman's band," Loren tells me. "They played for the people who gave their dollars to hear them play. When the notes were struck and the lights went down, the only people who had anything were the audience. And the Dead. They played their notes. It was over. They didn't count on the records to make their living. When they played, they got paid. When they didn't play, they didn't care." By 1971, the band had managed to assert its interests with Warner with some success, but this made it no less responsive to the young Wall Street arbitrageur Ron Rakow when he proposed in 1972 that the Grateful Dead form their own record label.

Rakow, who had lent the Dead money for equipment in 1965, worked on and off as a business manager. In 1966–1967, with the Jefferson Airplane, he comanaged the Carousel Ballroom, running it into the ground, in Stanley Owsley's opinion, by charging too little and paying the performers too much. Rakow's initial involvement with the Dead (not unlike Owsley's) has the earmarks of a religious conversion, but it is also tinged with a security investor's romance with chaos. His first Dead show was a benefit for the Mime Troupe at the Fillmore Auditorium in 1965, which Scully had invited him to in order to hit him up for money. Rakow had dropped acid; things got strange; then he went and lay down at Jerry Garcia's feet. The band was playing "Viola Lee Blues," "and it had a chaos section in it," Rakow recalls. "My metaphor for the universe was that life was a dance between order and chaos. I thought, 'Oh, this is it. Chaos is going to win out. It's over.' . . . And then bingo, out of the chaos came the blues."

Afterward, he went backstage, where Garcia was sitting like Buddha, smoking cigarettes. " 'You're heavy,' "he remembers Jerry saying. " 'What do you do besides make money in the real world?' " Later, handing over twelve thousand dollars to Rock and Rifkin, Rakow told them he knew he would never be paid back. Instead, he said (again echoing Owsley), "I'll become a patron and be entitled to respect." Rakow had swiftly passed the unspoken test handed aspiring aides-de-camp—" 'OK man! Show us what you can do for us!' "—with a fistful of do-it-yourself ideas for making the Grateful Dead self-sufficient. The centerpiece was All Our Own Record Company, or Grateful Dead Records; and Rakow's brief—a ninety-three-page warren of financial statements and charts called the "So What Papers"—stroked the sacred cows. "I see that the record industry does nothing for the Grateful Dead. It's the other way round," he argued. "The Grateful Dead should sell its own products through its own fans and make more money and support its own people as opposed to those who don't admire them." And Jerry, "maximally enthused," said, "Do it."

Rakow's scheme was shorn of its more bizarre components, such as declaring the Grateful Dead a "minority" to get funds from the government's Minority Enterprise Small Business Investment Company (MESBIC), and setting up Good Humor–style vending trucks to sell records outside venues. Instead, Grateful Dead Records and Round Records (for experimental and solo projects) were financed by selling foreign manu-facturing and distribution rights to Atlantic Records for $300,000. And First National Bank of Boston was persuaded to underwrite eighteen in-dependent record distributorships chosen throughout the country. In Au-gust 1973, the Dead assembled a record company crew, administered by Rakow, with Steve Brown directing production, and moved into the Record Plant in Sausalito to start work on *Wake of the Flood.* Two more al-bums, *Blues for Allah* (1975) and *Steal Your Face* (1976), would appear be-fore the venture collapsed. With Grateful Dead Records, meanwhile, the original communal partnership among the ten family members of the band was dissolved. The new arrangement was a business partnership be-tween Rakow and the band and, in the case of Round Records and spinoff projects, between Rakow and Garcia.

"Dear Fellow Dead Head," ran a September 1973 letter from Grateful Dead Records (which may be the debut of the term *Deadhead*): "This ad-venture is a jumping off point to get us in a position of greater contact with our people, to put us more in command of our own ship, and for un-spoken potentials for the 'far out.' " It was, in fact, the first time any rock group attempted to control all aspects of its record business: recording, cutting, and pressing; distribution and promotion. And while, by 1976, fi-nancial overextension and poor record sales resulted in its failure, requir-ing a bailout by United Artists, Grateful Dead Records struck a chord in the community that was growing by leaps and bounds around the band.

By the mid-'70s, it was a community largely made up of high school and college students, who saw the Dead as a guerrilla band, tweaking the schoolmarm and outwitting a corrupt establishment. The Grateful Dead were going it alone at a time when dozens of other efforts at countercul-tural autonomy had fallen by the wayside. The idea of running your own show had always been a popular piece of countercultural ideology, among political people, as well. "As long as we are forced to depend on the tra-ditional commercial mechanisms, the Movement is going to find itself used by mass media corporations," editor Mitchell Goodman wrote in an epilogue to *The Movement Toward a New America,* a giant family album of ex-tracts from the underground press. Underground papers and groups like Newsreel (a filmmakers' collective) were a start, Goodman said; now it was time for a "Movement publishing house."

On the Left, nothing of the kind ever happened. Only the women's movement was able to create institutions that lasted into the 1980s and '90s, especially women's health groups such as the Women's Health Collective Clinic in Berkeley, HealthRight in New York, and the successive editions of *Our Bodies, Ourselves* published by the Boston Women's Health Collective.

As for the Grateful Dead's short-lived record business, it was probably doomed by the organization's funky financial practices. Ron Rakow was not alone in running up ten-thousand-dollar balances on his credit cards and then declaring bankruptcy. Money was a free radical whose bonding properties in this group were always uncertain. Throughout the '70s, the Dead's manager routinely gave contract employees lump sums on tour to cover the expenses relating to their services, without expecting or collecting receipts. Thus Candace found herself keeping her own records on napkins and matchbooks as she doled out money for transportation, hotels, and per diems to her crew, along with payouts to lighting companies. In 1976, touring with the Jerry Garcia Band, she remembers being given "a very wrinkled grocery bag" containing "a total of a grand" in five-dollar bills in Madison, Wisconsin. The money, collected from the ticket booth, was to be used to pay the crew she had hired locally.

By 1975, with Grateful Dead Records declaring itself a financial disaster, Ron Rakow cleaned out the Dead's Los Angeles account of nearly a quarter of a million dollars, ostensibly to pay himself off, then dropped out of sight. No one went after him. Rakow was another tough guy who had impressed Garcia with a ferocity of manner Jerry could only dream about. Speaking of Garcia's "dark side," Steve Brown remembers him sitting in the office while Rakow screamed on the phone, "and just . . . loving it." Phil loved it, too, says Rakow, adding that "paranoia about controlling their own material was often the only thing they could agree on."

Zippy Loren, a fast-talking Italian from New York who previously worked for the Doors—a tough guy in his own right—has this to say about Rakow: "I never trusted him from the first day I met him. I think Jerry was very impressed with his mind and with his contacts on Wall Street. He was an action man and a gambler and that appealed to Jerry. Rakow was an outlaw and I don't necessarily say that disparagingly." Nor would Ron Rakow necessarily be offended. "I was the family barracuda," he says. It was always easy to bring Jerry around when Ron went out to visit him in Stinson Beach (where Garcia and Mountain Girl moved in

1972). Why? Because "he liked my desire to have a lot of random events going on."

The band's original successes with Warner are worth mentioning, for their consequences were later felt by other bands, which had no idea who broke the ice. To maintain artistic control over the record jackets, the Dead made sure that their own people—mainly San Francisco poster artists Alton Kelley and Stanley Mouse—designed them, which was easy enough. More difficult was to retain control of the publishing rights to their songs, which they did, as well as to the mechanicals of the albums. Their struggles over royalties, meanwhile, raised the bottom line for rock 'n' roll musicians from 5 percent to 15 percent and more. With the example of Thelonius Monk and Charlie Mingus behind them, the band learned how to break through the pop-music formula, which dictated that artists get paid by the song. Traditionally, this amounted to twelve cents a side, with the standard number of three-minute songs per side being six. Like jazz cuts, Dead songs could run seven, ten, and even eighteen minutes long; Monk and Mingus encouraged them to lobby (successfully) for getting paid not by the cut but by the minute.

Grateful Dead band members, of course, have always served as their own board of directors. Even today, each original member owns an equal share in Grateful Dead Productions and has an equal vote in approving merchandise and business decisions, with Bob Hunter—in effect, standing in for Garcia—having veto power over decisions concerning the use of the music. The Dead were also among the first American rock groups to extend health coverage, pension plans, and other benefits to an extended family of employees.

In 1971, Garcia's and Lesh's most serious worries concerned sales promotion; and here is where their victories with Warner counted the most for the Dead's future. False advertising, they believed, would eventually sink them—not just because of the market-driven convention that relates every new creative phenomenon to something salable from the past, but because they might start believing, or living, the public-relations image created for them. Part of the Dead's aversion to AM radio, and their insistence that Warner cultivate the alternative, FM stations, stemmed from this second fear—though AM radio's aversion to seven-minute songs probably rendered it moot.

The fear of becoming trapped in public-relations images alien to their purposes was shrewd. It happens all the time, but with the Grateful Dead, the image that enfolded them, not alien at all, was one they owed mainly to how they related to their fans. You can hear it on bootleg tapes from the early years, when the musicians were working the audience (something they stopped doing after the mid-'70s). The historic show at Harpur College in Binghamton, New York, in 1970, begins with Pigpen's quizzical voice from the monitors: "How come things are so strange around here?" It's a good concert, one of the top ten among tapers, partly because it showcases the original acoustic versions of *Workingman's Dead.* Midway through the acoustic set, the audience yells for its favorite songs, and Jerry says, "Everybody just relax, man; we have you all night long." Phil adds, "How do you expect us to play music when you're screaming?" And Bobby chimes in: "Cool it, you guys, cool it, cool it. You got to start acting like a mature, responsible audience." Jerry snaps, "Don't listen to him." This was the "good ol' Grateful Dead" talking. Speaking from Boston Music Hall on September 25, 1976, Weir, sounding like Garrison Keillor, gives a "Big ol' hello to all you folks out in radioland" (the concert is being broadcast). "It's Billy's birthday. So if everybody wants to wish a happy birthday to Billy Kreutzmann—" Whereupon the crowd whistles and cheers (an inside joke—Mick Jagger used to play the birthday game to embarrass drummer Charlie Watts).

By 1970, the Dead had convinced Warner, whose lackluster promotion of the early records had smartened up with *American Beauty,* to finance free concerts in cities and towns where the band was playing. This was unprecedented, and local promoters were appalled by the free shows, which were nonetheless a Grateful Dead trademark, having blossomed in Golden Gate Park when *free* was a holy word. The park shows, the promoters feared, would reduce ticket sales for the paid concerts, which generally followed them. But the opposite turned out to be true, especially in the college towns. Giving was getting. The musicians, who were building an audience, and who enjoyed playing the parks, took the long view. The promoters simply wanted to make money, *now.*

Warner paid for the flatbed trucks and sound systems, and the Dead, with considerable experience in such matters, did the rest. They lined up the parks and plazas, secured the permits, designed and distributed the flyers, and sometimes managed the growing crowds with the aid of volunteers from the Hog Farm. Joe Smith draws another picture. "You guys just don't know how to promote the record *[Skull and Roses]*," he recalls the Dead saying. "Set up these cities. We'll send out members of the family and members of the band." But when his promotion people went to meet the planes, he grumbles, the Dead's scouts had either missed them or taken different flights.

Starting in 1970, the Grateful Dead had also persuaded Warner to finance radio simulcasts of live concerts. Again promoters worried that customers would be drawn away from the ticket booths. And again the band's judgment proved to be right. Over time, the radio broadcasts, like playing for free, tolerating tapers, and setting up their own ticket office, established the Grateful Dead outside the commercial arena, allowing their roots to spread unhampered by the built-in inhibitors of the marketplace.

In effect, the Grateful Dead got Warner to finance a recruiting mission for a band that was far more interested in expanding concert audiences than in promoting records. The reasons were many, and the erratic quality of the Dead's studio work was clearly among them, as were spotty sales. With lackluster record receipts holding until *Workingman's Dead,* the musicians had begun to think they were jinxed; in their darker moments they blamed poor sales on Warner. Blaming other organized entities on whom they depended—companies, promoters, unions—came easily to the Dead. And there are insiders who attribute the entire thrust toward independence from the commercial world during this period to the band's effort to shelter itself from scrutiny and criticism.

But there was another reason for skipping the rat race of recording and promotion: the reality that, from the beginning, music making required the presence of live audiences, just as fans needed the tactile presence of the group, not just for "music satisfaction" but for the grand Milky Way of the Grateful Dead Experience to unfold. The records seemed stale to the musicians within months of their release. I forget which band member told me in the mid-'90s that he hadn't listened to either *Aoxomoxoa* or "Skull Fuck" since their release. Touring sometimes grew stale, as well, but at least it produced good road songs—which, like "Truckin'," sound like they've been here forever:

> Truckin'—up to Buffalo
> Been thinkin'—you got to mellow slow

Takes time—you pick a place to go
and just keep Truckin' on

Such tunes carried news of the band's adventures to the folks back home, like the drug bust in New Orleans in 1970:

Busted—down on Bourbon Street
Set up—like a bowling pin
Knocked down—it gets to wearing thin
They just won't let you be

Out on the hustings, the Grateful Dead were making connections that no publicist could concoct. On the jittery campuses of the early 1970s, where the band concentrated its touring efforts, the Dead's deep-seated suspicions of the corporate world, their horror of "selling out," touched a responsive chord. The musicians were not anticapitalist. Their politics, loosely speaking, mirrored the laissez-faire libertarianism that most hippies and students lived day to day, whatever the latter's views on the war in Vietnam, or how to end it. It didn't seem to matter that the Grateful Dead's enemy was the record companies and not the war administration, or the cops and National Guard—whose peacekeeping missions had turned deadly. What mattered was that the aura of antiauthoritarianism surrounding the band came from somewhere. It had a source. It wasn't just a hip attitude that sold tickets.

For students whose political options had shrunk since the late '60s, the arrival of these California freaks was charged with an extramusical gravity from the start. The off-the-street look invited identification, as did the acid and pot, openly consumed at concerts in a rush of togetherness. Antiwar protests, now largely centered in Washington, had begun to resemble touring bands of talking heads whose stages rose higher and higher above their audiences. As the movement lost power over public opinion during the final, confusing years of the war, its demands hollowed out. Like the shrill cry carried through the streets of the capital during the May Day demo in 1971—*If the government doesn't end the war, we'll stop the government!*—the slogans were no longer actionable. Rock concerts, on the other hand, after the mammoth tournaments of life and death at Woodstock and Altamont, had grown more intimate and more numerous. And now these musical events, not just the proliferating campus shows but multiband concerts as well, were blanketing the country.

In the summer of 1970, festivals in Rome, Georgia, Chicago's Grant Park, the Merriweather Post Pavilion in Columbia, Maryland, and on Randalls Island in New York City had acquired a political edge. The underground idea that festivals ought to be "liberated" extended beyond the Grateful Dead. Rock shows, such as the Powder Ridge concert scheduled for August 1–2, 1970, in Middlefield, Connecticut, which had prompted a state superior court judge to issue an injunction banning the affair on the grounds that the festival "would create a public nuisance," were increasingly covered by the national media as civil events, one step removed from street demonstrations. On July 29, 1970, the *Washington Post,* citing a recent history of civil disruptions—police confrontations, property damage to towns, and personal injuries—reported that music festivals set for later that summer faced serious legal hurdles. Court injunctions were pending against concert organizers in Missouri, Iowa, Oklahoma, and New Jersey.

Serious disturbances tended to occur at sites where court orders held firm, and where "hippie-type young people [were] already beginning to assemble in the area," observed the CIA in an assessment of the Powder Ridge dispute, which was included in the agency's "Situation Information Report" of July 30, 1970. The CIA's interest in rock concerts—remarkable, on the face of it—testifies to the significance that any massing of youth now possessed for a government that really did seem to be fighting a war on multiple fronts.

Under Nixon, CIA surveillance of rock 'n' roll went hand in hand with an expanded interest in dissident activities, which targeted GI coffeehouses and former Peace Corps members in the Committee of Returned Volunteers, along with the usual suspects, such as SDS and the Black Panthers. In 1969, the CIA had prepared a report entitled "Restless Youth," which concluded that New Left and black nationalist movements were essentially homegrown phenomena. It wasn't what Nixon wanted to hear, and CIA director Richard Helms had been ordered to expand domestic probes under an Agency-sponsored program called Operation CHAOS. The "national security" rationale, customarily adopted to justify domestic operations, was dispensed with. Even a nationwide women's strike on August 26, 1970, promoted by Betty Friedan, was tagged for surveillance. "[Friedan] is urging women to march, demonstrate, sit-in, rap, stop typing, stop vacuuming, stop buying and, if appropriate, stop making love," huffed the agent who filed this report. "Don't Iron While the Strike Is Hot" was the slogan for the multicity march, which was joined by the National Coalition of Nuns and the League of Women Voters, along with radical groups from whom "some surprises are probably in store."

An item on the return of the second Venceremos Brigade to Saint John, New Brunswick, in which I am quoted as announcing that a third group would leave for Cuba on August 1, 1970, is the reason I have this "Situation Report" in the first place. Concert notes from the CIA were the last thing I expected to see when I filed a Freedom of Information Act (FOIA) request in 1995 for files pertaining to my political activities in the 1960s and early '70s. When 104 pages arrived in May 1996, including postings of rock festivals, along with blacked-out entries relating to the Bertrand Russell War Crimes Tribunal and the Venceremos Brigade (material on *Viet-Report* was missing altogether), I first set them aside as useless.

I had filed my request because of a memoir I was planning on Vietnam. Only later did it dawn on me that another unexpected piece of the puzzle regarding the peculiar relationship between the CIA and the Great Subculture had fallen into my lap. Operation CHAOS, it seems, cut a broader swath through American society than previously reported. It's no mystery when you think about it. If the Clandestine Services, with their historic involvement in drug experimentation, set up listening posts in the Haight in the '60s, why wouldn't they tap rock shows, which had become major depots for drug distribution in the 1970s? At Powder Ridge, where more drugs were sold than at any previous festival, especially LSD and STP, thirty thousand people set up camp to wait for the music that never came. The People's Free Festival of Life, the concert was renamed; signs sprang up lettered ACID ALLEY and HIGH STREET, while volatile drug prices were posted on bulletin boards.

Dr. William Abruzzi, who volunteered his services at Woodstock as well as at Powder Ridge, told reporters that the lack of music there was the main reason why so many young people resorted to drugs. Similarly, the lack of political outlets had opened the door to the glut of music festivals, some of which, like the Summer Peace Festivals in August 1970, were identified in CIA reports as "a new political force that would be an alternative to street action for young people." Among the performers who were said to be donating their talent to a "peace festival" in Philadelphia were Janis Joplin, Country Joe, Dionne Warwick, Judy Collins, Steppenwolf, and the cast of *Hair.* The Grateful Dead kept their distance from such events. "The stage is not a pulpit; the stage is not a pulpit" was their mantra.

The last hurrah for the Dead's festival appearances was Watkins Glen on July 27–28, 1973. There, at the Grand Prix Racecourse in upstate New York, playing with the Allman Brothers and the Band, they piled on the family jewels: Chuck Berry's "Promised Land" and "Johnny B. Goode," Hunter's "Sugaree," "Wharf Rat," "Box of Rain," "Jack Straw," "Playing in the Band," "China Cat Sunflower," "Stella Blue," Barlow and Weir's "Me & My Uncle," and the traditional "I Know You Rider." Donna Godchaux, whose husband, Keith, had started filling in for Pigpen on piano in 1972, sang the old favorites, "Sugar Magnolia," "Truckin'," and "Not Fade Away."

As at Monterey and Woodstock, the performances were mixed, and the Dead refused to consent to an album or to allow the footage that CBS shot to be released commercially. Without full editorial control, they wouldn't join in such projects—a position that perplexed a good many people in the music business, but which, looking back, may be said to have served them well. At Watkins Glen, there was a marked decrease in the use of hard drugs and hallucinogens, although pot was everywhere, and the ground was littered with empty bottles of Jack Daniel's and Southern Comfort. "At times the scene in the moist darkness resembled a Bosch painting," Grace Lichtenstein wrote in the *New York Times,* "half naked bodies coated with brown slime, moving rhythmically to the music and huddled figures curled sleeping in the mud at their feet in barbiturate or alcohol-induced stupors."

Reporters said Watkins Glen showed that the hunger for rock festivals among youth was unabated. They marveled at the power of such gatherings over their audiences, who *had to be there.* But by then the festival fever was over. The crowds only had eyes for the Grateful Dead, whose unbuttoned naturalness, combined with the sense they conveyed of *coming from somewhere else,* somewhere outside the "Procter and Gamble world," endeared them to their fans. "The Dead embodied the whole belief that there's another world, another life, that really matters," says Mushroom from the moist fastness of his orchid nursery in Corvallis, Oregon. "They carry the soul, my soul. I'm glad to have had experiences with fifty thousand people where everybody was in joy, dancing around, feeling good," he says, speaking of later concerts in Eugene and Portland, Oregon, that had the flavor of field days. "It was the only time I knew I could bring my kids into a big, complex mass of people," he says, "and it was absolutely safe, because it was a bunch of telepathic sentients who were paying attention. . . . And the idea was to make it cool."

Nearly twenty-five years later, with more beer in evidence than pot, and with LSD joined by Ecstasy and heroin, the telepathy was still happening. Only the content had changed, along with the context. Watching the Grateful Dead in middle age, "ordinary guys, graying, and miles removed from any glitter," an old San Francisco fan, Bill Barich, could still feel he was watching himself onstage. "That was always part of the band's appeal for my generation: we were them, and they were us." For the young people around him in the Oakland Coliseum in 1993, he reasoned, "the show must have had the texture of a fantasy in which their parents actually listened to them and understood their deepest secrets."

A different fantasy had possessed many of the parents, however: those who caught the act in the early '70s. The overarching one—the sense of separateness from a corrupt society, nourished in the '60s—the secessionist impulse, let's call it—was battered and torn. A fix was needed, some compensation for the retreat of both the drug culture's faith in the transformative power of psychedelics and the political movement's vision of change in the power relations of rich and poor. This last specter, not yet driven from the stage, also came from somewhere. It had been ignited in the streets of Selma, Alabama, and McComb, Mississippi, and, for community organizers among the first generation of SDS, in the ghettos of Cleveland, Chicago, Newark, and Boston. It was still smoldering in the jungles of Vietnam. But now after People's Park, Kent State, and Jackson State, it was evident that concerted political action carried unacceptable risks. The government, for example, might shoot you.

Demonstrations had turned into trashings, which offered the police and the National Guard a pretext for using tear gas and guns. Were protesters now supposed to arm themselves? Should they learn how to make bombs? Were affinity groups supposed to go underground like Weatherman? Or should they demobilize and return to teach-ins, petitions, and marching up and down in front of the White House holding candles? For the vast majority of political organizers, not to mention hundreds of thousands of foot soldiers, these questions were answered in the negative. In time, it was a negative that spread like a slow-growing mold over the once-vibrant culture of political activism. Anger and frustration turned into cynicism, and cynicism, feeding on itself, led to withdrawal.

It was against this background that the nation-state of fans to which the Grateful Dead lays claim began to bulk up and acquire some of its characteristic mating calls. Concerts, like the one at Manhattan Center on April 5, 1971, which ended "with a rhythmic-tribal-howling exchange between the singer [probably Pigpen] and the audience," left people feeling that "the crowd and the band are playing TOGETHER." A new kind of alliance, this one demanded little, and on a good night, like the one Deadhead Dave Levy recounts, it could deliver a lot.

Manhattan Center was Levy's first Grateful Dead show. On the subway coming in from Brooklyn, he asked his friends—who included a girl named Roz, with whom he'd just fallen in love—what the big deal about the Dead was. Nobody would tell him. "You'll see, you'll see. You gotta BE there!" they said. When they arrived, the venue was surrounded by people looking for tickets. Somehow a pair of five-dollar tickets materialized for Roz and Dave; and as they file in, Dave hears "people grumbling about how expensive these shows have gotten and how Dead shows should be free and what a Capitalist-ripoff the whole scene is becoming."

Inside, hundreds of freaks are milling around, and when Dave and Roz find another friend, they settle down on the floor. Looking around, Dave (who refers to himself in the third person) notices that the equipment onstage has had all the speaker grills replaced with colorful tie-dyes. The air is charged with electricity. A friend explains that the New Riders of the Purple Sage will start the show "and to watch for Jerry (whoever that is) on pedal steel. Just before the lights go down, some orange juice is passed around. Dave and Roz are real thirsty and drink some."

> . . . as the New Riders start playing Dave sort of fades out. Seems there are all these lights and things happening behind his eyes. This is pleasant Country-style music (but it DOES have an interesting electric edge to it, doesn't it?) and he sort of drifts through the Riders set, disturbed only by requests to push back (it is VERY

crowded—later, he'll learn that there were many counterfeit tickets sold).

A short break happens during which Dave's friends seem to be oddly concerned over his well-being. Dave can't understand this, as he feels fine (he is sure that he's completely disassociated from his body, however, and his consciousness drifts nearby watching the scene with amusement).

The lights go out again and THIS time things get real different. The whole crowd seems to go crazy. Hootin' and hollerin'. It's contagious. Dave starts yelling too. Meanwhile something is happening on a completely non-verbal level with Roz. Somehow, some sort of bonding seems to be happening. Dave can't recall what NOT being with her is like. . . .

It's during the electric set, when the show's effects wash over him— the "reverb-and-echo-and-guitars-and-lyrics-and-the-crowd and the lights and owowoWOWOWOWOWO!!!!"—that Dave is won over. "These guys just PLAY! No jumping around . . . It's like a classical ensemble performance, or a good jazz group," he decides later. "They just let the music do what it's supposed to do and don't rely on a circus atmosphere to pump up the crowd!" which is what turns him off at most rock 'n' roll concerts.

Searching for the rest rooms downstairs, he finds a crowd huddled in the lounge area, where all you can hear is the bass drum and the electric bass guitar—"THUMP ka-THUMP ka-THUMP ka-THUMP." Everyone looks "zombied-out and they are ALL tapping in rhythm to the THUMP ka-THUMP." Confused, he blunders into the ladies' room and is gently maneuvered out. "No one gets uptight."

Back upstairs, returning to his everyday senses, Dave "is pretty sure that during the first set he managed to completely re-create the evolution of the human mind, starting at some sort of invertebrate flatworm-type creature and evolving, evolving. . . . He chats with friends during the break." He's had a fat trip, fatter than most.

During the second set, third if you count the New Riders, the band breaks into an intense, pounding boogie. "Things begin to flow. The whole audience is dancing together." Dave recognizes "Truckin' " from *American Beauty*. As he listens, the music gets softer and the lights go down. Suddenly, there's an "EXPLOSION of bass notes and all the spotlights focus on this SPARKLEBALL! Spinning lights everywhere, colors!" The guy next to him loses it completely: " 'Holy sh*t! The Sun. The Moon. The Grateful Dead. Oh God! Oh God!' he says, over and over and over."

At the end, "Dave and Roz have somehow become DaveandRoz (later to be known as Swifty Nifty and the Howling Whoopee). They describe a sense of being hermetically sealed together. Welded by the experience." Dave sees his friends from a new perspective. As the little group leaves the ballroom and begins to walk off the effects of the acid before descending to the subway, "a feeling envelops them that something really extraordinary has happened. They are satisfied, content, happy." (In August 1991, around the time Dave Levy penned this account, "DaveandRoz" observed their eighteenth wedding anniversary. Four months earlier, on April fifth, they celebrated their twentieth "unofficial" anniversary.)

The Dave Levys who flocked to Dead shows in the early '70s have left behind some of the better concert notes in an otherwise-tedious oeuvre, mainly because they're about people going through changes, not just song lists and send-offs for this or that "Ripple" or "Dark Star." And sometimes they touch on what is happening outside the halls, if fleetingly. Blair Jackson's account of a Yale Bowl concert on July 31, 1971, is a case in point.

It was one of Jackson's first "Grateful Dead field trips" beyond the safe confines of the Fillmore East and the Capitol Theater; and "like any self-respecting elitist, [he] was horrified at first that [his] beloved cult band would play at a stadium." When he and his friends get inside, however, they're relieved to find that the concert fills only an end zone. Still, it's the largest Dead show he has ever seen. After a spacey interlude in the first set linking "Playing in the Band," "Dark Star," and "Bird Song," two new tunes are introduced: "Sugaree" and "Mister Charlie." The second set includes the "Not Fade Away / GDTRFB / Not Fade Away" sequence that the Grateful Dead played all through 1971. Meanwhile, during a "kick-ass Uncle John's > Johnny B. Goode encore," Jackson notices "clouds of smoke rising from outside the stadium." When the concert ends and he and his friends file out, they learn it was tear gas. "A bunch of Yale radicals, believing that the Dead show should be free, had stormed the gates during the second set and had been beaten back by the police! When we got to the car, our eyes burning, we checked out the tape we'd made [which] sucked, quite frankly." Nothing more about the tear gas or the police.

It's interesting to learn that in 1971 "Yale radicals" stormed the gates of a Grateful Dead concert. Were they fans who had been radicalized by the marches and mass rallies of the year before when Yale students shut down the university for weeks to protest the New Haven trial of Black Panther Bobby Seale? Or were they lefties just looking for some action? New Haven was a minefield in those years. Rolling into town on the weekend of the Panther rally in May 1970, after returning from Cuba, I felt as if something extraordinary had happened. People talked of police agents patrolling airports with walkie-talkies—and here they were in the New Haven train station! A bomb had exploded on campus at Ingalls Rink following a rock concert on Friday (nobody knew who planted it); three fires were set at the Yale Law School during the strike, again anonymously. National Guard tanks lumbered up and down Whitney Avenue. Havana was a sleepy *ville* compared to this.

As for the "Yale radicals," they were probably just that. Had they been Dead freaks, they would have hung around the venue until tickets materialized in their hands. Rarely did Dead fans and political activists overlap. If there is a correlation among the drying up of mass political action, the proliferation of rock festivals in the early '70s, and the growth of Blair Jackson's "beloved cult band," it doesn't include disillusioned leftists turning into rock fans or Deadheads. A good many turned to guruland, alas— including leaders like May Day organizer Rennie Davis, who slipped into the comforting arms of the Perfect Master, the teenage Maharaj Ji. Others became Sufis or took up yoga, or began listening to Baba Ram Dass tapes and dropping copious amounts of LSD. Many women found their bearings in consciousness-raising groups, and in the creation of parallel institutions: women's health clinics and newspapers. A few movement men came out as gay. Women friends became lovers, then parted to marry men they hardly knew.

But most New Leftists, like Richard and myself, retreated into private life, or tried to, and picked up jobs not unlike the ones we'd left behind. Those angry black men in Tent Five on the second Venceremos Brigade were right: When the going got rough, longhaired white men and women could go home again. Our distaste for the devotional ideologies that claimed so many people we knew, however, made us leery of instant communities, especially if they seemed to hinge on the performance, musical or otherwise, of a charismatic figure.

I doubt that I formulated such an idea in March 1972 when I first saw the Grateful Dead, but it might explain the distance I felt from the scene—for the elements of a charismatic community were there. The Dead were still an underground phenomenon, and Jerry Garcia's reputation for being "a sort of spiritual advisor to the whole rock scene," as *The Greening of America* author Charles Reich put it, was still unrecognized outside a relatively narrow tributary of fans. Garcia himself was adept at deflating the overblown imagery. The idea that he was *any* sort of spiritual adviser, he told Reich, was "a crock of shit. I'm one of those guys who's a compulsive question answerer," he said of his obvious relish for discoursing on arcane subjects. "But that doesn't necessarily mean I'm right. It's just something I can do," he added, "like having a trick memory, I can answer any question." It didn't really matter what Jerry Garcia said, however. Whatever he said was filler for fantasies that had already been inscribed in the corner of America's youth culture reserved for saints and sages.

You could hear it in the way a young woman said *"Jerry"* when she approached us at the Academy of Music concert in 1972 to ask if we would deliver a shirt she had made for Garcia. It was spoken with a hush, as if the very name were holy. We were on our way backstage to meet with Candace, and the girl had stopped Richard to give him the package. Backstage looked like a rumpus room for overgrown boys, furnished with hippie mannequins who wandered about in a haze of smoke and patchouli. There was nothing of the electricity that had charged the atmosphere outside during the show—rather, the reverse; one felt a kind of sucking ennui. Richard found Garcia and gave him the shirt, which was accepted with a sheepish shrug.

After a few months of camping in spare rooms in New York, Vermont, and Connecticut, Richard and I had settled outside New Haven. He had picked up a research job at Yale, and I was ghosting chapters for a liberal textbook on American foreign policy. Shortly after we drove back east in the red-and-white VW bus, which kept breaking down, I had become pregnant. The sharpest memory I retain of that first Dead concert is of the unborn child fluttering (happily, I hoped) in utero to the thunderous underbeat of the bass and drums. The music and lights were a blur, or are now, but not the audience, which toward the end fell into the "rhythmic-tribal-howling exchange" that Dave Levy describes. I shrank in my seat,

too close to this stage for comfort. Here was another strange phenomenon of the brave new world into which we were stepping with a caution
altogether unlike us.

A Deadhead from the period tells a story about an encounter at the
Fillmore East between Jerry Garcia and a follower, which perfectly illustrates the intensity of the scene that surrounded the Grateful Dead. It's in
1971, long before Garcia went into hiding, when he could, with a deft
swing of his cape, still take on the pumped-up fans who rushed him. A
young man waits outside the stage door after a concert to reprimand him
for being too hard on a friend who kept shouting, *"Saint Stephen! Saint
Stephen!"* throughout the show. Inside, Garcia had stepped up to the microphone and said, in his high nasal voice, "Hey, man, we did that song last
night. We may well do it tomorrow night. It's on two fine LPs. *But you
ain't gonna hear it tonight!"* And everyone had applauded with relief. Standing outside on Second Avenue afterward, the young man muttered, as if
practicing lines, "I've been with the Dead for a long time, and Jerry was
too harsh on that guy. I've been with the Dead a long time, and Jerry . . ."
When the stage door burst open and Garcia stepped out, carrying his guitar and heading for a VW van, the fan jumped out in front of him. "Jerry?"
he began; and Jerry said, *"Yeah?"* hale and hearty. "Jerry, I've been with the
Dead a long time—" Garcia clapped him on the shoulder and said, *"Yeah?
Well, I've been with them longer,"* and he hopped into the van.

It's this sense of *entitlement,* of ownership even, that sets such fans, then
and now, apart from others. For Deadheads, the feeling of entitlement is
an expression of a deeper sense of communion that binds them to the
band. The obliteration of the subject/object relation, in fact, is the linch-
pin of the Grateful Dead experience—and not just for the audience. It
began with those "flashes of recognition" that Garcia experienced while
playing at the Acid Tests, when "it was like one on one. . . ."

"Anybody who's been on acid and felt Garcia reach in there and touch
them," says Kesey, speaking of the mysterious exchange, "all of a sudden
they realize, 'He's not only moving my mind. My mind is moving him!'
You'd look up there and see Garcia's face light up as he felt that come back
from somebody." That flash. Or if not from "somebody"—for by the '70s,
the one-on-one experience had become one-on-thousands—then it was
the nonverbal energy that was exchanged when he played for large audiences, "for the purpose of reaching some degree of communication and

rapport with that audience," Garcia said in 1971. It is what Martin Buber talks about in *I and Thou,* Kesey maintains; and Garcia understood that "he was in a *relationship* with his audience. He was not playing at them," Kesey adds. "He was playing with them."

In a landscape strewn with the skeletons of abandoned movements, lowered visions, dying dreams, the Grateful Dead—alone among the starter communities of the 1960s—had weathered the storm. Whatever I thought at the time, theirs was not an "instant" community, but one with roots in a dense network of subcultures that preceded the 1960s. In 1972, it was mutating into something else, a frontier culture for postindustrial man; a do-it-yourself-pack-on-your-back *trip,* made with a little help from your friends, and, for the majority of weekend road warriors, with no loss of time from the job.

⌒

~CHAPTER~
13

HEADS AND TALES

I like to find
what's not found
at once, but lies
within something of another nature
in repose, distinct.

DENISE LEVERTOV, "PLEASURES"

PETER WIGLEY WAS twenty-nine when he and four friends started off for Eustace Ridge, high in the western mountains of Maine, on a cool Saturday morning in the summer of 1976. It was Peter's first acid trip, his first encounter with what he calls the "Big Whatever," and it hasn't forgotten him. The leader of the group was a pot dealer he knew from "misfit circles," who had supplied the LSD. "Being a misfit," Peter explains, "is one of the commonalities Deadheads share," not just the feeling but *acceptance* of the feeling. When Bob Weir advanced the concept of "misfit power" around 1978 to account for why the Dead didn't "fit into any standard scheme of things," Peter, who had recently left a long-term job at the state's Department of Human Services to join an upcountry commune near Buckfield, thought, "Oh, yeah, he's talking about me."

On the dealer's advice, they had all eaten a huge breakfast; they weren't going to want to eat for a long time, and their bodies would need the fuel. Then they rode up Route 4 to Eustace, stopping at a place called Cathedral Pines, whose "wonderful, tall-trunked, godlike trees" towered over them as they dropped the acid.

We each swallowed this little piece of toilet paper that had a little piece of colored grain in it, Peter begins, *and we got in this pickup truck and went riding down a dirt road for three or four miles, following alongside a stream, called Alder Stream, at the bottom of a steep canyon. . . . The first realization*

273

I had that anything different was going on was: I was sitting in the back of the
pickup truck, looking at the road, and all of a sudden I realized that the road
was writhing. It was hilarious, and I burst out laughing. About that time, the
others started laughing, too.

They pulled over and parked the truck, then clambered down the
steep bank to the water, "as perfect a mountain stream as you'll ever see,
with places where it would run over rocks and places where it would
widen into pools, some with gigantic rocks in the middle where you could
stand and dive." Some of the rocks were so smooth that you could lie
down in the water and be swept over them, *riding* the rocks, in effect. And
there were little waterfalls you could crouch behind and peer out through
sparkling curtains of water.

The group of men and women took off their clothes and hung
out there naked all day long, "playing in the water, getting out of the
water, sunning ourselves on the rocks." Like grizzly cubs, I think, listening to this big bearlike man with Coke-bottle glasses and flyaway rust-
colored hair tell his tale. The scene composes itself in my mind's eye as a
tableau from Rudyard Kipling's *Just So Stories,* where the animals look up
from their tasks with shrewd button-bright eyes. Wigley's American adventure, for that's what it is, is a New England counterpart to the acid
trips on Mount Tamalpais or out on Limantur Beach that West Coast
heads recount in equally radiant detail. A few weeks after I met with
Peter, his Maine tour buddy from a dozen Grateful Dead concerts, Bob
Schroff, known as "Giant," relates his own "watershed experience," involving footprints in a snowstorm. He, too, "mostly tripped in woods
where you could settle down with something like a jack-in-the-pulpit and
find stories in it."

Peter, who is "Petrovich Wigleymon" in Deadhead circles, is partially
deaf and very nearsighted. At Eustace Ridge, he had to take off his hearing aid and glasses before going in the water. Thus communication with
the others was largely cut off. "I can't see more than a foot away, and I
can't hear anything, so all my senses are kind of *feeling* everything," he recalls, as if he's back in Alder Stream.

I'm feeling the wind, I'm feeling the water, I'm feeling the rocks, I'm feeling
the sun, I'm feeling kind of like a lizard, he says, and I'm also having this ab-
solutely amazing sense of "Oh, I BELONG in this world!" which is part of that
misfit thing. Instead of feeling a bit out of step with the world, sort of as if I'm

just a visitor to this planet, I felt like "Oh, I'm exactly where I need to be, and this is exactly the way things should be. Everything is RIGHT here."

For Wigley, a metaphor emerged from the experience which is a metaphor for life:

The world is like a large bowl of water, and each individual in this world is a drop of water . . . that has somehow gotten away from the big bowl. And that drop of water is doing whatever drops of water do, falling through the air as rain, hitting a leaf, running off the leaf, and eventually what it's doing is making its way back to the big bowl, the ocean, really. . . . Each drop knows that there's something missing, but it doesn't know until it reaches the ocean what it was it was missing. What the metaphor means, of course, is when you die, what happens is you go back to the big—the Big Whatever. What we have been missing all of our lives and searching for all of our lives is there at the end.

Once again, the comics provide an unexpected analogue. In "Off the Mark," a line of peanuts queue up to enter the Peanut Butter Factory. One peanut says to another, "I've heard it's intense in there! Like a religious experience . . . Almost as if everybody becomes one!" It's clever. Cynicism, however, is for the fainthearted, and I'm not taking refuge in it. Wigley's experience of oneness, of course, manifests itself in different forms in most of the world's religions. The question is whether the vision is less valid when it is stimulated by a drug. How can anyone take seriously the product of a chemically induced consciousness? There's no labor in it, for one thing. The very idea of such spontaneous revelations smacks of hokum unless, that is, one extends to mind-altering substances the boundless faith that Americans place in hormone-replacement therapy and immune-system boosters, not to mention the herbal concoctions and vitamins that are consumed by millions of people to ward off cancer, heart attacks, aging, and death. And then the idea acquires a more worrisome aspect, because, of course, people *do* put faith in mind-altering substances—though the majority turn to board-certified healers for their medicaments—when faith is the last thing one should put in a drug.

We are sitting in Wigley's music room, in a rambling Victorian house in Danville Junction, Maine, where Peter, now fifty, lives with his wife, Karen, and teenage stepson, Sean. Both he and Karen, who is not very fond of the Grateful Dead, are social workers employed by the

Department of Human Services in nearby Lewiston. Peter, after years of casework, is a supervisor for Child Protective Services. Karen, who grew up in Topsham, is helping to redesign the agency's software. The music room, packed with Grateful Dead memorabilia—posters, Tars (circular frame drums from North Africa, used by Mickey Hart), a map of the United States, showing the cross-country motorcycle trips Peter has made on his Harley 1340, and floor-to-ceiling shelves stacked with over four hundred concert tapes and CDs—is a trophy room. Peter sits at an old-fashioned oak desk, drinking a beer; his computer stands off to one side. While we talk, I thumb through one of several cartons of R. Crumb and Furry Freak Brothers comic books from the 1960s and '70s, another piece of the archive. "I bet there's nothing else like this in Maine," I exclaim, referring to the entire collection, and he agrees there probably isn't.

I see him as an elder, conserving the tradition, and wonder if he's a resource for younger Deadheads in the region. Peter laughs. "From a lot of young people's perspective, you know, I'm not a real exciting guy," he says. He's happy that Sean, no Deadhead, has asked for a couple of hard-to-find concert tapes for Christmas: July 18, 1976, at the Orpheum in San Francisco, and December 26, 1979, at Oakland Auditorium. The Oakland show, I note later in *DeadBase VI,* marks the reemergence of two classics, "Broke-down Palace" and "Uncle John's Band," which hadn't been played since the middle of 1977—for reasons that are no doubt pondered in Deadhead chat rooms.

Peter, meanwhile, likes the period running from 1973 to 1976, for the "organic, jazzy feel" of the music. There's an incredible energy to the flow, a rhythm to the music during these years, when the Dead almost sound like a swing band, like Tommy Dorsey. "Everybody had to *be there* to make it work," he says; everybody but Bobby Weir perhaps, whom he has trouble picking out. (It's okay with him if he never hears "Me & My Uncle," one of Weir's favorite songs, again.) But Peter remains "a ballad fan," and so he's partial to the second half of the '70s, when the band drew out tunes like "Friend of the Devil" to greater and greater lengths.

The next time we meet, he has gotten Sean's tapes; we listen to them, and I hear what he means, though I think I prefer the Tommy Dorsey years. The slowing down, he suggests, came with the shift in Jerry Garcia's drug use. By then, cocaine was giving way to the more serious addiction to heroin. I make a mental note to examine this question of drugs

The poster announces a 1970 Grateful Dead benefit for the Hell's Angels in New York. *Courtesy of Paul Grushkin.*

ABOVE: Former vice-president of the Oakland club, Skip Workman, visiting his parents in New Harbor, Maine, in 1969. *Courtesy of Skip Workman.*
BELOW: Workman at home in Maine today, surrounded by part of his enormous collection of military regalia. © *Sarabinh Levy-Brightman*

Marcie Lichtenstein and her brother Eric on the California coast, 1993. © *Marcie Lichtenstein*

Tour brethren Giant (Robert Schroff) and Peter Wigley in Danville Junction, Maine, 1996.
© *Carol Brightman*

Alan Kapuler (Mushroom) at a farmer's market in Corvallis, Oregon, 1997. © *Kusra Kapuler*

DEADHEADS

ABOVE, UPPER RIGHT, AND BELOW: Fans at Berkeley's Greek Theater, 1986. LOWER RIGHT: Deadheads converge on Golden Gate Park, August 13, 1995, to memorialize Jerry Garcia.
© Jay Blakesberg

LEFT: At a "Gathering of the Tribe in Soho" in 1996, host Wavy Gravy introduces some of the "Executive Deadheads" modeling Grateful Dead ties. BELOW: David Gans (with unidentified woman) programmed the music for the event, which was sponsored by a neckwear company; Dead fan, ABC anchorman Peter Jennings (with unidentified woman) sports a Grateful Dead tie of his own.
© Linn Sage

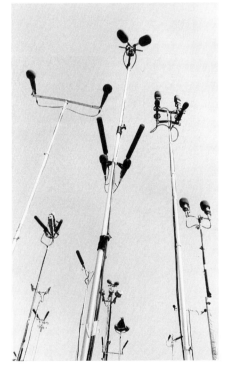

ABOVE: Bootleg tape collectors are all ears, Ventura, California, June 1987.
© Jay Blakesberg

Mickey Hart, Bob Weir, Bob Dylan, and Jerry Garcia, in concert during the
"Alone and Together" tour with Dylan in the summer of 1987. © *Jay Blakesberg*

RIGHT: Candace Brightman launches a fireworks display at Soldier Field, Chicago, on July 9, 1995—closing not just a summer tour, but the Grateful Dead's touring history. © *Jim Anderson*

BELOW: Candace with Chris Brightman dressed as "Mr. Bones" for a highwire prank Chris performed on the last night of the summer 1992 tour. *Courtesy of Chris Brightman,* © *Ed Smythe*

RIGHT: Bill Graham plays the jester on the Golden Gate Bridge float at the New Year's Eve concert in 1987.
© *Mitch Hochman*

FOUNDING FATHERS

Robert Hunter touring alone in 1997.
© *Jay Blakesberg*

Bob Weir, Bill Graham, who died in a helicopter accident in 1991, and Jerry Garcia
at an El Salvador Relief Benefit in Oakland, California, January 1988. © *Jay Blakesberg*

Jerry Garcia, 1987
© *Jay Blakesberg*

and music making more closely, to understand how each member of the Dead's trinity—not just acid but also cocaine and heroin—shaped the product. It's not enough to note that cocaine speeds up the music and heroin slows it down. How do these drugs affect the give-and-take among the musicians, so central to invention? What happens when some members of the band are into blow and the leader is doing smack? Or are such questions academic, a mismating of musicology with "high" theory? Then there is Garcia's own opinion of the decade to ponder. "During the '70s we were experimenting on ourselves, we weren't experimenting with the music," he stated in 1989. "Everybody was off taking their various drugs . . . off on self-destructive paths. Trying stuff out. So for a long time we held together by sheer inertia . . ."

As for whether Peter Wigley's vast collection of sights and sounds from the Dead's arcanum is a resource for others, the answer is no. People may come and "go gaga" over the stuff, Peter remarks, but they don't say, " 'Let's explore this,' or 'Let's look at this from a particular context.' I've been waiting for you now for a long time," he says, grinning at me. Trading tapes on the Internet, he often invites E-mail about other issues, but most of the traders are younger and not into writing. "I tend to be wordy. I want to explain myself," Peter says. "People who use the Internet speak tersely, compactly, concisely." Most Deadheads are only interested in tape collecting—a fact that is confirmed for me by the Webmaster in San Rafael.

"The tape collectors tend to be dominant, very dominant," Bob Hunter reports, which surprises me. The Internet, after all, is one of the last bastions of Deaddom. In the post-Garcia era, one would expect that DeadNet Central, in particular, would be buzzing with reflections about The Meaning Of It All. Hunter, who wishes Deadhead culture would reach out more than it does, sets up sites for the discussion of classical music and poetry, but they're usually empty. "People don't come to Dead-Net to discuss Whitman," he tells me; "they discuss Grateful Dead matters." Not the big questions, but the little ones, or so they seem to me. Such as where and when did this or that song cycle happen for the first time? Or did Phil stop playing "Unbroken Chain" for many years because he believed the band couldn't play his music? The tapes are "their touchstone," Hunter points out. Deadheads, he says, are "like Torah scholars. They want to know if there's a secret code in there."

Speaking of Deadheads' involvement in song selection, writer Jay Stevens, who was visiting with Mickey Hart when we met in Albany, points to another touchstone. "The band is up there saying, We don't know where we're going. . . . But the people on the other end of it, they write it down on their hands, so they can tell their friends—" "I know," I jump in, "it's just the opposite—the need to predict." "No," says Stevens, "they want to know where they *went*. . . . They want to know how they made the trip." And he refers me to the fans who come in late and grab you: "Maybe they'll have the third song, the fifth song, and they'll whisper, 'What's the fourth song?' " And Hart chimes in, "This is their road map."

Something like what Stevens describes happened to me at the Furthur Festival at Old Orchard Beach, Maine, on July 11, 1996. This was the first of the multiband tours coproduced by Grateful Dead Productions with promoter John Scher that have followed the demise of the Grateful Dead. I was standing up front in the mud of a thousand churning feet, swaying to the music and scribbling notes in the dark while Bob Weir sang "Fever" (my favorite song in the summer of 1958, when Peggy Lee sang it), when suddenly a pack of young men closed in on me, wanting to consult my "song list." You see these list collectors swarming like bookies, swapping scraps of paper, outside all Grateful Dead–related events, such as the David Grisman Quintet's concert, which packed the State Street Church in Portland, Maine, in the fall of 1996.

Remembered songs, of course, are repositories for emotions that don't travel well otherwise. Everybody has their personal song list (whose titles are often of dubious taste). Mickey Hart can hear a "Frank Sinatra song or an old Elvis song and remember when [he] was a kid swimming in a pool, or doing something special—music brings that back to you," he says. "There are landmarks in your life, things you can really hold on to. When the music hits you and you're right there in the moment, and the place is right, the person you're with is right, the imprint is indelible."

What, I wonder, are Deadheads embracing with their master lists of songs and dates, cross-referenced into categories that identify every place a given song was played, the number of times each song was played year by year, the "most to least" commonly played songs, songs that were played in a given year but not in the previous or subsequent years, the number of times the Dead played in each state and city in the United

States, along with the dates for every venue? All this and more is the core curriculum of the Deadhead bible, *DeadBase,* and fans are forever exchanging their own compilations.

In part, it is the age-old search for order and pattern in the wilderness of experience—an effort to master the Grateful Dead's arcanum via the voodoo of stats, tables, lists, tape timings, and demographic surveys. *DeadBase VI* even includes anagrams derived from "words pertaining to Grateful Dead culture," thanks to a software package called Ars Magna. *Grateful Dead* produces 1,968 combinations; the song titles "Eyes of the World" and "Scarlet Begonias," 25,717 and 336,854, respectively.

The ordering of such data is like the search for previously undetected patterns lurking inside chaos in chaos mathematics—something Jay Stevens and Mickey Hart are looking at from another angle. They've noticed how "whenever you look at patterns, you look at rhythms. . . . What is chaos mathematics but essentially looking at the rhythm inside of chaos, saying there is a pattern in chaos that we never saw before?" says Stevens. This line of thinking has led them to study rhythmic phenomena such as "entrainment," which is "when you're in rhythm with something," when "you're pulsing exactly with it" and are "unconscious of it. We're *entrained* with American culture," for example, Stevens remarks, and "we're a little bit unconscious of it," which is not the case when you enter another culture. "We've decided that rhythm is a metaphor that almost anything can sit under," he asserts, with that note of triumph one hears when someone has pounced on a single unitary principle, a password to knowledge and control: a *secret code.*

For the tape collectors, the satisfactions are simpler. "At first I wasn't interested in the music," says Andy Graff, a former Deadhead from New Jersey, for whom, in the '80s, the Grateful Dead was mainly a party scene, a place to hang out and get stoned and have weird encounters, such as this one at Giants Stadium: "Walking around one afternoon with a friend, trying to score some weed, we see this black guy who's at least seven feet tall, looking at us, grinning," says Graff, who was a student at Fairleigh Dickinson at the time. "He walks over and gives us a hug and turns around and walks away, and both of us have question marks shooting out of our heads—Hey, what was that about? He was in a good mood, no doubt about that." (He was also one of a tiny minority of black people who attend Grateful Dead concerts—thereby fulfilling the promise of a Dead show, which is to expect the unexpected.)

After a while, Graff, who today works as a purchasing agent at a law firm in Maine, began to collect bootleg tapes and to notice how the "nuance" of a song changed from one concert to another. He's still listening, as are hundreds of thousands of Deadheads who continue to trade bootleg tapes and buy the latest *Dick's Picks* release from Grateful Dead Merchandising. In 1998, after work, he listens to the songs at home. "There's still a mood that Jerry pulls me into when he goes off," he says wistfully. The bootlegs, the bottled music, are mood enhancers.

While Peter Wigley tells me about his first acid trip, he plays a long tape from the famous May 2, 1970, Harpur College concert. He's got it tuned just right, so our voices can be heard but the music snakes in underneath, like the "Phil-bombs" that Lesh occasionally drops with his bass, low-frequency pellets you *feel* rather than hear. Reviewing my interview tape later, I'm struck by how fresh the Harpur College music sounds, especially the acoustic set; probably because the post-1992 concerts I've attended haven't prepared me for the degree of definition the Dead's music attained in smaller halls. For me, the music at the megaevents, including the celebrated fifteenth-anniversary acoustic set at Radio City Music Hall in 1980, lacks the vitality of these early renditions of "Dire Wolf," "Black Peter," "Candyman," "Casey Jones," and "Morning Dew." Hearing the songs pounding under the floorboards as Peter and I speak is like dreaming on the job. It's distracting in a seductive way, and reminds me of what Neal Cassady said about driving through hallucinations.

So I listen carefully to the story Peter tells me, and absorb the set and setting, too. The tale is the granddaddy of the trip stories I've heard. It touches the major chords of the subculture in which Peter himself is a kind of granddaddy. There's the bittersweet feeling of being out of step with the world; the urge to merge with a transcendent entity; a vision of the universe *in the round,* like Jerry Garcia's 360-degree vision of the word *"All,"* or Giant's discovery of "the universal system" in a snowprint. And strangely, there is a romance with death, such as one hears tolling through the lyrics of the Grateful Dead.

Peter tells me that since Eustace Ridge, he has "completely lost any fear of death."

I don't have it to this day. I know that what happens when I die is that I'm going to rejoin, in a very real sense, everything that I've ever missed or lost. I'm not going to rejoin it as a conscious entity called "Peter Wigley." . . . I'm going to be there as part of the Big Whatever. Okay, GOD, he adds, *for want of a better word. We don't have a word for it. How can you have a word for the Unnameable? How can you have a word for something that there's no way for anybody who's alive, who's a separate drop of water, to experience? . . .*

People have been trying to put a name to it and channel it, for better and for worse, for a millennium, I suggest.

Personally, I have no objection to the "Big Whatever," having spent the first nineteen years of my life talking to God and his subalterns, Mary, Jesus, and Jesus' grandmother, my patron saint Ann, until the two-thousand-year-old belief that we were all somehow *personally* related wore thin. It's admirable, I think, that when Deadheads find themselves in the presense of a "big bowl" or a "universal system" in a footprint, or an *"All"* unfurled across the sky, they are not compelled to think they stand in a privileged relation to it, and must therefore march forth to preach the gospel. The Unnameable, remaining unnameable, is free to roam—like the hypothetical "stuff" cosmologists call "quintessence," which fills the nooks and crannies of space. And so, presumably, are they; though it's no surprise that some should want to return, periodically, to dip into the sacred font.

Later in the '70s, a friend who had borrowed Wigley's car (a heap) and trashed it before taking off for San Francisco had made restitution by giving him two sheets of good California blotter acid when he returned. Peter dropped it once a week for about a year. During the first hit, he and some pals watched *The Grateful Dead Movie* in a converted bowling alley in Lewiston, Maine: an amazing experience, he recalls, not for the documentary footage of Winterland in 1974 but for Gary Guttierez's animated sequence that opens the film. Uncle Sam's skeleton roaring for all eternity on a big black chopper was a night tripper's masterpiece.

Surprisingly, or maybe not, at the end of the year, he had agreed to return to the Department of Human Services (DHS) on a temporary basis, commuting from the commune in Buckfield. Gradually, he slipped back into the system. The frontiers of the '60s were a distant memory in the late '70s, more distant even than today, as anyone camping out there will remember. Taking all that acid "was like doing a series of quests," Peter says, and in the course of them he found out more about himself. "When I left my job, I was trying hard to be all things to all people, and not being very successful," he recounts. "Before, the work and I were inseparable." Afterward, he saw himself in relation to something else, to that invisible world, no doubt, of which Kesey and Garcia speak. Hardworking Yankee freeholder that he is ("I try to balance the two," Wigley told me when we first met, "to get things done, and at the same time jump off the bandwagon and see what happens"), he found himself capable of more empathy as well as more objectivity when he returned.

"I can honestly say, on one level, I never *need* to do acid again in my life," he assures me. "But if you asked me do I want to? *Absolutely.*" When was the last time he did it? I ask, expecting to hear that it was some years ago. But it was last summer, with his friend Giant, who was given two hits by a hitchhiker he picked up on the way to the Furthur Festival at Old Orchard Beach in Saco. Giant and Peter were already planning to do mushrooms at the concert, so they put the acid aside for another time, when they could spend the day tripping together. The day came soon enough. The doses are lower now, Peter reports; which is just as well, since he's not sure he could handle the 500 micrograms he thinks he consumed at Eustace Ridge.

Speaking of the revelations from that trip, he finds it "frustrating . . . that organized religion wants to present the illusion that you retain your own consciousness after death. Why would you want to do that?" Why indeed? "Why would you want to be separate?" There's a corollary to Peter's vision: "The minute that the drop of water rejoins this larger drop, the only thing you experience is this unimaginable joy of being reunited. Why would anybody not want that?"

Much of this vision has been confirmed by the Buddhist reading Peter has done since. Specifically, it has made him think about "how all the work we do to maintain our individuality, in fact, prevents us from experiencing a taste of the 'joy' when we're alive." Also, it "somehow keeps us apart from other people." I ask him how this understanding has affected his personal life. It has brought him "a certain serenity" about the future, he replies; "I don't have to spend my time worrying about what's going to happen when I die." At the same time, he wants me to know that "there is absolutely no moral value attached to this. The drop of water is a drop of water. It goes back to the sea no matter whether it was a mass murderer or a saint."

And this shakes me. It's a bit like Jerry Garcia's perception of good and evil as "manifestations of consciousness . . . each with its special place and special humors." Even as the perception of an aesthete, which it is, there is something airless about this vision of "consciousness," which coexists rather too easily, it seems to me, with a sluggish indifference to what's happening to others in a larger society. But Peter is right: No one guards the gates of eternity.

"So the old question of grace versus good works influencing the afterlife doesn't matter?" I ask, recalling (why, I don't know) a point that my sister and I used to debate when we were young. "It doesn't matter in the sense that I'm not building up credits [for an afterlife]," Peter answers. What we do with our lives is for *now*.

Candace had taken the Calvinist position that only the elect were saved, so it didn't really matter what you did with your life. My revolutionary fervor seemed to rattle her. She herself, she insisted, was one of the damned. From this arose her indifference to politics and to the social world, I thought at the time; also perhaps her wildness, which I both worried about and admired. I didn't understand its source. Now I think this fatalism of the middle child was related to alcohol, which was the drug of choice during the first ten years she worked for the Grateful Dead (not that it excluded other drugs). After she stopped drinking, the voice of doom returned to its lunar cave.

I was a recovering Catholic who had embraced the existentialism of Sartre and Simone de Beauvoir, along with a newfound responsibility for opposing public wrongs, especially when they were draped in destiny or promoted as reform, as they were during the nation-building chapter in America's relations with Vietnam. Heaven could take care of itself. It certainly wasn't taking care of the world. Alongside my differences with Candace, of course, subtexts abounded: between the elder daughter with the usual perks (me) and the younger daughter who escaped whipping while her sister did not.

Peter Wigley makes another point. "The reason why we're involved in this journey—the whole reason why there are separate drops of water— is that the Big Whatever wants to know what the world is like, and has no way to know except by these individual drops of water going out and gathering experience, being mass murderers or saints." An arresting thought, it is inspired by an expansive turn of mind, a largeness of spirit, so large that it has reconstructed "God" in its own image. With his original faith in the group process, Jerry Garcia displayed a similar generosity of spirit. When the members of a band were working well together, bringing their *best stuff* to the table, leaving their egos behind, they were, in effect, drawing on qualities Garcia nursed in himself. For Wigley, too, "everything you bring back as you rejoin the Whatever becomes part of it. Obviously, if you spend your life being a mass murderer, that's what you bring back. But would you *want* to bring that back? I certainly don't." *Heaven* needs help, in other words. "So I'm not going to live my life that way," he concludes. "I'm going to live my life in such a way that what I bring back *enriches* the larger thing. And I'm also here to learn, and to experience as much as I can, because that's what I bring back, too, all that experience."

The idea that a good acid trip reveals the face of God is a theme that runs through countless narratives I've recorded over the past six years. It reminds me of the idea, which you still hear, that religion teaches you to be good. Or the contemporary notion that the right kind of therapy will teach you to be happy and productive, while absolving you of the wrongs you have committed and the wrongs you have sustained. Such beliefs, especially the latter, usually collapse under the weight of experience, or when the believer turns elsewhere. However, old hippies, I've noticed, even Hell's Angels like Skip Workman, who was nearly undone by prescription drugs in the 1970s and '80s, and who hasn't been high in seven years, still draw fire from their acid-drenched visions of long ago.

In Workman's case, it's not God, not even Cosmic Forces or Nature with a capital N, that rushes through the cracks that LSD opens in reality's wall. History invades the present in the visions he relates, as it did on a summer night in Maine in the late 1960s when he had done both acid and peyote with some California friends who included the Oakland Angel known as Animal (who appears in *Gimme Shelter* wearing a white wolf's head). They scrambled aboard the *Luther Little,* a derelict schooner rotting in Wiscasset Harbor, a few miles from his folks' place in New Harbor, and when his friends wanted to leave, Skip decided to spend the night alone on the wreck. The town wharves, long gone, rematerialized before his eyes. "I saw sailors rolling barrels, and horses pulling wagons," he says, "and coming down over the hill, I heard 'Rock of Ages.'" It was a hymn he knew from childhood, and after that it joined "Mr. Tambourine Man" from La Honda and the music of the Rolling Stones and Janis Joplin as trip music par excellence.

A few days later, Skip took Animal to the site of a seventeenth-century settlement in Pemaquid to inspect the massive round stone fort. A 1908 replica of the original, which was twice destroyed, first by Indians, then by the pirate Dixie Bull, Fort William Henry was where another vision unfolded. The fort was open, and luckily no tourists were about when Workman and Animal, high on acid, clambered up inside the open tower. "All of a sudden I see the pirate ship out there, and I see cannon balls coming at the fort," Skip exclaims, "and before I knew it I was ducking and getting down. . . . And Animal said, 'What are you doing?' 'I see cannon balls, don't you see them?'" But of course he didn't—"he was seeing other things."

For Jerry Garcia, it was mind, mind, mind that revealed itself on his more memorable trips, most of which took place in the '60s. Asked in 1991 whether the Grateful Dead continued to use psychedelics, Garcia answered, "Oh, yeah. We all touch on them here and there. Mushrooms, things like that. . . . For me, I just like to know they're available, just because I don't think there's anything else in life apart from a near-death experience that shows you how extensive the mind is." With its power to anoint the most familiar objects and encounters with a mysteriousness that suggests another world beyond the quotidian one, LSD was the drug that opened doors for Garcia to the possibility of parallel universes, infinitely more orderly, more *mindful,* than the one he parried day by day.

As for the "value" of such visions, I am reminded of what Mary McCarthy said about religion: namely, that it is *"good for good people. . . ."* She didn't mean this as a paradox, but as a fact she had repeatedly observed. *"Only good people can afford to be religious. For the others, it is too great a temptation—a temptation to the deadly sins of pride and anger, chiefly, but one might also add sloth."* You can say the same, I think, about a fat trip; and while pride and anger are not among its temptations, sloth is. Contrary to what Sony says, fantasy is *not* just another word for fearless. There is that temptation embedded in the richness of the psychedelic vision to substitute the chemically induced experience for the effort to assimilate it and use it long after the drug is gone.

~CHAPTER~
14

JUNKIE DREAMS, ACID RAIN, AND THE RESURRECTION OF THE DEAD

The hippopotamus's day
Is passed in sleep; at night he hunts;
God works in a mysterious way—
The Church can sleep and feed at once.

T. S. ELIOT, "THE HIPPOPOTAMUS"

SOMEHOW IT COMES as no surprise to learn that Petrovich Wigleymon, raised an Episcopalian, has delivered a guest sermon inspired by his spiritual adventures on Eustace Ridge at a Unitarian Church in Lewiston—and that he has drawn on the bowl-of-water vision several times in his professional and personal life. The chemical medium, however, is rarely mentioned. Drugs, even "soft" drugs, might invalidate such a lofty experience. Psychedelics are more problematic today than they were twenty or thirty years ago, and not just because of questions of quality and source.

In many people's minds—former drug users in twelve-step programs, in particular—acid and marijuana are simply links in a chain of "highs" that are bound to ensnare the inebriant in the end. "It's not like it was, you know," says Skip Workman, who is employed part-time as a "patient representative" at the VA hospital in Togus, and volunteers as a drug counselor in Maine schools and prisons. "It's like in the Old West when the guys couldn't wear their guns into town anymore," he reflects; they got trigger-happy. "We're losing the kids," Workman believes, referring to the arrival of crack and heroin in the nooks and crannies of small-town life. "The love of one another for your friends doesn't seem to be there," he adds, speaking of the risks of youthful experimentation; and even if it was, he doesn't think he'd recommend any recreational drug nowadays.

I relay a story Ken Kesey told me about being interviewed for a TV debate on *Nightline* when the Reagan administration's War on Drugs was just beginning. A woman telephoned him to hear what his opening statement would be; what did he advise young people to say when they were offered pot or LSD, for example? "Just say thanks," Kesey answered. The woman was stunned. "What do you mean by that?" she demanded; "*nobody* is for drugs." And Kesey said, "Well, then how can there be a debate? You've never heard anybody put out the positive side of it," he told me. *Nightline,* needless to say, rescinded the invitation.

"It's not good to romanticize drugs, but you gotta tell what happened," Workman concedes. And he's reminded of how when he saw Janis Joplin on a TV documentary recently, he "had this incredible feeling of wantin' to get high." He didn't, being in a twelve-step program himself: "But the *music* and the *memories*—how are you going to tell the kids about that? You can't lie to 'em and say you didn't have a good time." I think about the people I know who hide these experiences, and others who hide their political activism in the '60s and '70s, not only from their kids but from themselves. They're like the frightened ex-Communists of the 1950s who hollowed out their pasts to protect their children, and thereby erased large chunks of the 1930s, leaving their offspring (along with the rest of us) prey to the remodeling of a controversial chapter in American history.

Street drugs have been demonized over the last fifteen years in the United States, in part because of the Just Say No campaign orchestrated by the Reagan White House, which scapegoated drugs, hard and soft (no distinctions made), as the cause of social ills it otherwise chose to ignore—though one must be wary of such generalizations. Reagan's attorney general, Ed Meese, who has since criticized the controversial mandatory minimum sentencing provisions of the 1986 Anti–Drug Abuse Act, claims he argued from the beginning that the sentencing provisions made no sense, but that politically the administration had no choice because so many Democrats were promoting ever-longer sentences for drug trafficking. Congressional leadership for the Anti–Drug Abuse Act, in fact, came from Massachusetts senator Ted Kennedy (who has since withdrawn his support for mandatory minimums).

Meanwhile, during these same Reagan years, American markets were flooded with cocaine and crack from Mexico and Honduras. This was when the contras, led by CIA-trained Cubans from the Bay of Pigs invasion, helped finance their operations in Nicaragua by extending logistical support to drug lords throughout Central America. The rivers of white powder crisscrossing the North sought and found new customers in unlikely places. It was a shocked Grateful Dead fan, "rapping with a fellow Deadhead whom [he] thought was cool," on the Fourth of July, 1986, at Rich Stadium in Buffalo, who was offered a hit of crack. "What th' . . . crack at a Dead show?" he said later, having declined the gift.

The drug scene has changed; and popular attitudes toward drugs have hardened for another, less obvious reason. Under the floorboards of a good many American families lurks a scary battle with addiction. "We're survivors for some reason," says Workman. "The whole culture of the '60s seemed to survive—except for the people that didn't." And he points to "mental institutions that are still full of people who never came down," and prisons crowded with the castaways of a younger generation who use drugs to escape a world they entertain no hope of changing. The prevalence of addiction, with its cloak of secrecy and shame, helps explain, I think, the remarkable tolerance Americans display, first, for antidrug programs such as DARE, which encourages children to inform on their families, and, second, for draconian penal codes like mandatory minimum sentencing for marginal drug offenses.

Imagine, in such an environment, giving public recognition to the spiritual awakening that certain hallucinogens may induce at the right time and place. Imagine this and you sense the delicacy and significance of the Grateful Dead's hold on popular culture during a period when the use of mind-altering substances, apart from the officially prescribed serotonin adjusters, is punished more severely than ever before. Under the Federal Controlled Substances Act of 1991, the manufacture or sale of from one to ten grams of LSD carries a base penalty of from five to forty years in jail. After a California youth was sentenced that year to fifteen years for possession of three grams of LSD carried on a few hundred grams of blotting paper, a suit was filed to challenge the "carrier weight" law, which includes the medium on which LSD is impregnated in weighing the drug. The challenge went all the way to the Supreme Court, and in January 1996, in *Neal vs. U.S.,* the Court ruled unanimously to reaffirm the law. "There may be little logic to defend the statute's treatment of LSD," the justices admitted. "It results in a significant disparity of punishment meted out to LSD offenders relative to other narcotics traffickers." Nevertheless, it is the responsibility of Congress, not the Court, they concluded, "to change statutes that are thought to be unwise or unfair."

For many Grateful Dead fans, a show seemed to provide one of the few spaces in American life where you could exercise your spiritual faculties; where an *inner* world could come *out* without its messages being scrambled. As another of Peter Wigley's tour buddies suggests, this might happen through a kind of divination, employing not just the music, with its chameleonlike lyrics and zigzag riffs, or the drugs, but lights and video projection, as well.

Maggie Motorcycle (née Margaret Terrill) recalls the night she chose to tell her partner, Stephen Jane, that they were going to have a baby. It was February 13, 1986, at Oakland Coliseum—a portentous occasion, three times over. The Dead were celebrating the Chinese New Year and Valentine's Day, and it was also Stephen's birthday. Before she told him, she had focused on the image of a rose that appeared on a screen or scrim, and she watched it change into a skull, and then into something else. "The skull became very small," she relates; "then it turned into a child, then an infant, and then it turned into a fetus." In *reality*? I ask. "In *my* reality," she answers. "And then it materialized as a Down's syndrome baby, which I figured was my fear, and I didn't look away. I went through my fears and came back with the skull and the rose and then the music. And so it was all okay," she decided, "and so then I told him.

"The whole society out there is presenting your fears," Maggie offers, to underscore the importance of the "safe, loving environment" that Dead shows provide their pilgrims. "Asshole consciousness," she calls the fear-mongering mind-set, which is countered by the "camaraderie" you find at a concert, the camaraderie that allows you "to think your thoughts through." Psychedelics, she says, further the process. "The drugs made us aware of the spiritual factor, which we were never exposed to when our parents were raising us," Maggie asserts, relating a basic truth about this movement beyond the spiritual hunger it taps; namely, that it satisfies a longing for an apprenticeship to something or someone who stands *outside society*. Parents made you aware of "different consciousnesses," says Maggie, who works in a Head Start program in Augusta, Maine; "different things you need to worry about," including material things important in their own way; "but they left out the spirit world."

Another "world" they left out, and always will, is the *participation mys-*

tique of the one with the many—what the folklorist Joseph Campbell saw when he attended a Grateful Dead concert: the "loss of self in the larger self of a homogenous community." To Campbell, a Dead show was a Dionysian festival. The powerfully amplified music and the lights sweeping across the upturned faces of the young assured him that Dion spoke through the crowd. It is a theme, this merging of *I* into *It,* and *It* into *Me,* which appears again and again in interviews with band members and Deadheads alike, albeit in different guises, like a folk motif undergoing a shape change to retain its influence.

To the participants, a Grateful Dead tour was an oasis in the parched tarmac of the mainstream habitat, where bodies could come together on the wave of a single thought.

> *At a show, you're all on the same trip, and the trip is connected to the music. There's nothing like it when you hand your ticket to the ticket taker and you get that rush, and everybody's walking in with that smile,* says Marcie Lichtenstein, speaking, in February 1997, in the Deadhead's eternal present.

> *Like you're entering another world,* adds a tour buddy named Todd.

> *And it has this smell to it,* Marcie continues.

> *And when you're on your way out, and you're tripping and somebody smiles at you, it's just like: I KNOW. I never got that anywhere else,* Marcie's older brother Eric declares, rounding out the thought.

But after a while, Marcie didn't care whether she got in or not: *In the end, I just wanted to get high in the parking lot* high on heroin, not acid—*I didn't care.*

We're sitting in her apartment in Santa Fe, New Mexico, eating chicken burritos. Marcie, who grew up in a middle-class household in New Jersey, started hitchhiking around the country in the summers after going to her first Grateful Dead shows in the ninth grade. In the late '80s, she lived in Berkeley for a while, sleeping with friends in People's Park, and then, when the cops chased them out, on Telegraph Avenue. Her wanderlust later took her to a kibbutz in Israel, and to Eastern Europe, where she hitchhiked through Czechoslovakia. She's a true daughter of the Beats, but with a canny, sensible edge that roots her in the present.

The Electric Kool-Aid Acid Test turned Eric on—"I fashioned my acid trips off that book," he says; but *On the Road* was Marcie's bible. "I wanted to live that whole experience," she says; and she read the sacred texts:

Kerouac, Alan Watts, Hunter Thompson, and Ram Dass (Leary's old part-ner, Richard Alpert, who wrote *Be Here Now*); "there was nothing more I wished than to have been born then and been part of it." Eric agrees: "If I could go back in time—and there's a lot of history back there—I would go back to the '60s. I just want to be there when it started. But maybe be-cause I did what I did, I have an idea what it was about," he proposes. "I have more of an idea than people like my parents, who grew up in the '60s and don't have an idea."

I wonder about this, and ask him what his parents, who are in their early fifties, think about the Grateful Dead. They hated the lifestyle, Eric says. When he and Marcie brought friends home, "they'd just flip out. Peo-ple smelled, had dreads." Marcie interjects: "They judged them by their appearance, not by what was inside." "They weren't unique," adds Eric. "When I went over to someone's house, I would get the same looks: Get out of my house."

"So you had the experience of being seen as a dangerous man," I sug-gest, and he nods. He recalls traveling through West Virginia, coming out of the woods "and getting these looks, and it made me feel good," he de-clares. "I was nervous I was going to be beat up. It made me feel good." Not *but* "it made me feel good," just two contradictory sensations rubbing each other the right way. "Because you knew you were different?" "Yeah," he muses, remembering "being in a backwoods general store, and the bells [he wore] would be jingling, and patchouli was stinking up the whole store"—and how good it felt, being way out there.

"At the same time, I think my parents look back and they're almost en-vious," Marcie says suddenly. "They don't know anything about the whole hippie scene, the drug scene," Eric interjects. Their father never knew he "was going with the Dead and taking five hits of acid. He thought I was just going to hear some music." But it's the traveling, the gypsy caravans, that Marcie believes they envy now, if only "in the back of their minds."

Maybe so, I think, remembering all the well-heeled folk, light-years away from jingling bells and patchouli, who have talked excitedly about a son or daughter or grandson or niece who followed/follows the Grateful Dead. Such as Andy Graff's mother in Damariscotta, a handsome woman with cropped iron gray hair who told me, eyes twinkling, about the time (around 1988, when they moved to Maine) that she found a "brick" of marijuana in her son's drawer. Terrified, she marched down Main Street to the Newcastle bridge and dropped it in the river. "You might talk to him," she said. "It was a quarter-pound bag of buds, worth about six hundred dollars," Andy says a year later when I do. "She was beside herself. Of course, I was beside myself because I hadn't paid for it yet. And I screamed at my mom, *'What am I going to do?'* 'That's not my problem,' she said."

Marcie clerks in a bookstore in Santa Fe, and is completing an interrupted education at a local liberal arts college. She's thinking about becoming an art therapist. Todd Marcus, another New Jersey 'head, who graduated from Bard in 1994 after taking a year off on the road, cooks in a restaurant and plays piano and guitar. He's a composer of avant-garde atonal music and would like to go to graduate school. He's not doing drugs now, but he's an occasional drinker. "Yours is not a before-and-after story," I surmise. "No," he says, "it's a continuing journey." Eric, who went to Green Mountain College, is visiting from New Jersey, where he works with his father in the printing business. "A run-of-the-mill drug addict," he calls himself; "a garbagehead," who used to take as much acid, cocaine, Ecstasy, or heroin as he could lay his hands on. "My first bong hit, that was it," he says. Thus he has stayed away from the Grateful Dead over the last few years: "too much temptation."

Both Marcie and Eric have been through rehab. All three used the same drugs in different ways. "Acid, pot, peace, love, looking for something better—" Marcie sometimes talks like a *Time* essay, but without the sarcasm. She started doing heroin in San Francisco in between tours in 1991. Living in the Panhandle, hanging out and partying with Tourheads and Dreadheads, she sold drugs to get drugs, as many did. A San Francisco Department of Public Health study of the Haight's dropout community, which concluded in November 1992 that "for many, homelessness is literally a phase," might have included her. Most "sustain connections to their family and community of origin," the study reported, noting that "for all their pretensions to difference, they are, in fact, quite tied to a set of middle-class values handed down from their parents."

"We'd all go to an apartment," Marcie continues, "about twenty people, and get high."

You can't describe it, she claims, when I ask her to. *You shoot up, and within two seconds you don't have a care in the world. Acid takes you to a different plane. Heroin just takes you to where you don't feel anything. No pain. Nothing matters. You disappear. You just feel—*

Nice. REALLY nice, says Todd.

What are your thoughts? I ask.

Eric: *No thoughts.*

Todd: *Yeah, there are thoughts. It's dreamy, very dreamy.*

Eric: *I never thought about anything.*

Marcie: *You don't think anything consciously. But your mind is some-where else.*

Me: *Are your senses asleep?*

Marcie: *Everything is numb.*

Eric: *When I started doing it, my life was such a wreck. It was just great.*

Marcie: *And then nothing matters but getting drugs. That's why on tour it got really nasty. In the end, people had guns in the parking lot.*

In 1992, Todd remembers looking around at the Boston Garden shows and seeing eighteen- and nineteen-year-old junkies everywhere. He grew cynical, whereas Eric, who did his heroin elsewhere, kept the faith. When he needed a ticket, someone handed it to him; Eric would say, "Are you sure you want to do this?" feeling like "the guy was handing me his life. . . . It makes you feel good to give somebody something," he says to himself. Todd wouldn't pay more than fifteen dollars a ticket. Standing outside, thinking, Where's my fuckin' ticket? he always got it, along with the cus-tomary "miracle tickets." When he didn't, he snuck in, as he did at an RFK show in Washington, D.C., when a crowd of people rushed the gates at in-termission, security backed off, and everyone poured in.

In their mid-twenties, Marcie, Todd, and Eric sound like Province-town's bohemians thirty-seven years ago, bemoaning the corruption of the "scene" by the day-trippers. They deplore the invasion of hucksters and scalpers at concerts in the '90s, along with fifteen-year-old predators scamming for drugs, followed by Drug Enforcement Agency cops trolling for acid, ignoring the smack. The worst newcomers were the last. Under Gene Haislip, the DEA's LSD unit made a career for itself filling the jails with Deadheads, just as in another era on a grander scale, HUAC rode to fame on the backs of the writers it purged from the Screenwriters Guild.

"We've opened a vein here," Haislip told *USA Today* in December 1992. "We're going to mine it until this whole thing turns around." Since 1990, the DEA's LSD squad had tripled spending and personnel; and the number of Deadheads incarcerated for acid rose from fewer than one hundred in 1988 to over two thousand two years later. Today the number may be as high as ten thousand, according to Toni Brown, publisher of the fan magazine *Relix,* who first called public attention to the DEA sweeps in 1993. For Haislip's agents, the fishing grounds grew to immense proportions as the Grateful Dead became, that same year, the most popular live musical act in American history, selling 1.8 million concert tickets and grossing $47 million.

"Acid has been demonized," the Dead's publicist Dennis McNally stated in 1994. "The government doesn't have communism to kick around any more; they have to choose something," so drug users are scapegoated. McNally was appalled by the "McCarthyite" suppression of dialogue on drug issues. But few interested parties were more intimidated by the threatening atmosphere than the Grateful Dead. When the DEA launched its campaign in March 1990 with the arrest of eighty young people in Maryland, not a peep was heard from the band. This was "Operation Deadend," with U.S. Park police posing as fans and infiltrating public campgrounds to make arrests; at the Capital Centre in Landover, where the Dead played, many more people were seized by local police working with DEA agents.

"We made a conscious decision that to lead a political struggle, which we could not win, would only serve to bring more heat on the Deadheads," McNally maintained. But over the next few years, as criticism of mandatory minimums, and the singling out of Grateful Dead fans, spread to journals as dissimilar as *The New Republic* and *Z Magazine,* the Dead failed even to take up the rear. Nor did they exercise the power of the purse. Occasionally, the band expressed its dismay over the use of concerts as "bait" by hippie-looking cops, some of whom worked undercover at Dead shows for years. In 1989, Jerry Garcia complained that every time the Dead played at Nassau Coliseum, the cops busted three or four hundred kids—"so we refused to play there," he told a *Rolling Stone* reporter. "And they said, 'Please come back. We promise we won't bust anybody. Honest to God. Come back.' " So the band returned, but "when we played there," he said, "they did it again"—"they" being an alloy of local police, DEA agents, promoters, and arena managers. The back-and-forth continued, but the Dead never did boycott Nassau Coliseum.

The Grateful Dead always prided themselves on maintaining good relations with the police. In the late '70s and early '80s, when the band regularly hired off-duty cops in New York as limo drivers, the police didn't waste their time busting Deadheads for drugs. After 1986, the climate changed as local police forces were enlisted in the War on Drugs. The band began to clean up its own act, no longer trashing the Navarro Hotel in New York, and moving on to the Four Seasons. But as the heat came down on their audiences, and reports of stepped-up drug raids appeared in the national media, the Grateful Dead kept silent; as if to question a government drug policy run amok, not to mention the persecution of their fans, was to condone drug use—or, worse, to bring the heat down on themselves.

Surprisingly, at least to me, Deadheads have agreed with McNally's assessment of the risks of speaking out. Toni Brown won't criticize the Grateful Dead for their silence, because, she says, "the Dead have always advocated freedom of choice"—hence, "it's their choice." She agrees that to protest the drug busts would bring "more negative light to the whole culture." *Relix,* which regularly runs letters from Deadheads in prison, urges its readers to dispense with Dead stickers on vehicles, especially in the South and Midwest, where they attract law enforcement bounty hunters.

In such a climate of fear, paranoia blooms; and fans have sometimes tortured logic to defend the band's credo of noninvolvement—like the correspondent who informed *Dupree's Diamond News* that band members "are being forced, with the threat of their own incarceration, to keep touring, so the Feds can keep filling their bust quotas." Referring to the DEA's efforts to shut down drug activity at Dead shows by putting even the smallest LSD dealers in jail, Blair Jackson wrote in *The Golden Road:* "It's whacked, of course. But it's reality, and like I've said often in these pages through the years, it's *not our world,* much as we might delude ourselves into thinking that it is during those glorious hours we're in the Grateful Dead show environment." Rather than urge Deadheads to protest the DEA hunting parties, or support the lobbying efforts of advocacy groups such as Families Against Mandatory Minimums, Jackson, like the band, advised people to be "careful, cool and discreet."

If it's not your world, you have no responsibility for what it does—even to you.

. . .

Speaking of the corruption of the tour scene in later years, Marcie Lichtenstein refers to the vending of handmade and mass-produced items on Shakedown Street. "It was hippie capitalism," she says. "You had your dress code, your way to talk. It was just like 'society,' only with long hair and different clothes." People started signing on to make a certain amount of money, made it, then dropped out. The barter economy, which was a feature of earlier tours, was driven to the perimeters. Like the song says: "Nothin' shakin' on Shakedown Street / used to be the heart of town / Don't tell me this town ain't got no heart / You just gotta poke around."

Soon the poking around led restless Deadheads such as Marcie and her friends to reconnoiter the Rainbow Gatherings. There, at the annual reunion of old hippies, one might find the "traditional people," as Bob Dylan called the country musicians of the '20s and '30s. In the '90s, these are hard-core back-to-the-landers from the '60s and '70s, who have assembled every Fourth of July in huge outdoor camps since 1972. For Todd, the Rainbow people were "more spiritual"; the gatherings were "the scene without the capitalism." And it was nice being in the woods, sitting by a fire for days, drinking coffee and smoking cigarettes. "It was much more 'Hi, brother, Hi, sister,' " Eric remarks. "More hippies, more Nature and God," adds Marcie.

"Deadheads aren't hippies," Marcie maintains. The Grateful Dead existed in the middle of society. The shows took place in the middle of towns—and still do, as in the summer of 1998, when a semblance of the band (minus Garcia, Welnick, and Kreutzmann) renamed the Other Ones, hit the road once again on a tour that included shows at the Meadowlands and Nassau Coliseum. Deadheads stayed in hotels, "whereas Rainbow wanted to get away from that," Marcie points out. "Rainbow carried the notion of an alternate place of living," adds Eric, evoking an important fantasy that the Grateful Dead, weighed down by the mammoth touring machine, could no longer sustain.

The term *hippie* has come a long way from being a negative term for high school kids who were "trying too hard to be hip, and wearing the black, and coming on a little too existential," which is how Hunter remembers hippies in Palo Alto. "When it started being applied to us," he says, "we all resented it." Nor is the word any longer encased in the sneering invisible quotes that accompanied its use by the media—at least not for some young people today, for whom it seems to have reemerged as a badge of honor. A blond dreadlocked student at Wheaton College, male, who drives a vintage VW van outfitted with a tiny kitchenette, is called Hippie—not *a* hippie, just Hippie. Alongside legions of young people wearing corporate logos on nearly every body part, such atavistic figures, at the end of the century, evoke a certain wanton freedom from convention. And so the fashion show, which is the politics of *cool,* marches on.

The Rainbow people didn't go to Grateful Dead shows, Todd relates, and they hated it when the shows were over and Deadheads came to the gatherings. "But the Tourheads were respectful," he contends; they camped near the parking lot, not far from the "A" Camp for alcoholics and the Fairie Camp for homosexuals; a few miles away from the circle of tall white tepees where Rainbow Family elders resided. This respectfulness began to slide, however, as acid, normally given away at gatherings, started being sold. And like the Grateful Dead itself, Rainbow Gatherings grew and grew, until in 1995 the reunion in northern New Mexico drew 25,000 people.

Rainbow is an underground, a subculture that harbors its share of fugitives, along with a smattering of ecowarriors, which may explain why when you left camp, you ran a gauntlet of DEA agents, federal, state, and local cops. In 1986, the Rainbow people won the right to organize their gatherings on public lands, which is why they're not bothered in camp, only outside it. Unlike the Grateful Dead, Rainbow has a political edge. "They threaten society, that's for sure," says Marcie, speaking figuratively: Their earth-first principles challenge society's reigning values. To Eric, "the Gathering was really something totally different. That's where you get 'the government this' and 'we shouldn't do this. . . .' Going on the Rainbow trail" was not for him; he was more comfortable at a Dead concert. "I wasn't going there to change government," he says; "I was going there to see the Dead, and get that trip that I wanted."

Unlike Provincetown's Beats, Marcie's trio knows that the glory days of the scenes they cherish didn't begin with them. Their attachment to the '60s—even if it is a hopped-up '60s, mostly devoid of politics—is touching to a veteran like myself. I prefer it to the version promoted in the '80s via movies like *The Big Chill,* where all the action, the boldness, has been leached out and what remains is the fellowship of old boomers who once marched together in a few demos and inhaled pot in the woods off campus. Like Eric, I remember the feeling of being an outlaw as a righteous one. Marcie's, Todd's, and Eric's faith in the Grateful Dead as a carrier of rebel values—a kind of cargo cult, dispensing manna from history via drugs and music—is one I don't share; but I find it significant that, having seen the seamy side of Deadhead culture, they still embrace it.

Ten or fifteen years down the road, how do you think your experience with the Dead will look? I ask.

Marcie: *Awesome.*

Todd: *I'll be very happy. I'll have a large tape collection by then.*

Me: *You'll have stories to tell—*

Eric: *We tell stories all the time.*

Me: *—to your nieces, nephews, children.*

Eric: *Except they won't get it.*

Me: *I'm thinking of people in my generation who hide their pasts from their kids, sometimes because of antidrug programs in the schools. It's pretty deep stuff when the state interferes with relationships between parents and children.*

Todd: *That's depressing. I want to be able to tell my kids.*

Eric: *I'll be able to.*

Marcie: *I will be. I want my kids to know. I want my kids to have an experience like that, if they can. I want them to go out and travel and see things.*

Eric: *It's up to them to listen. They may choose not to listen.* And later: *When I have kids, I would love for them to trip, because it did a whole lot for me. When I was tripping I always found myself saying, Oh my God, I get it. When I wasn't tripping, I didn't get it.*

At a Dead show was the only time Eric was in tune with everybody around him, as at the Deer Creek Music Center in Indiana, when he and a friend dropped LSD together, and the friend "turned around and looked at me, and he didn't even speak, and I knew what he was saying. It was amazing, an amazing thing. But if my kids are anything like me," he says, returning to the present, "one [trip] will be too many."

The pooling of thoughts, with its suggestion of a blood-brother rite, has long been a leitmotif of the acid experience. Andre Bernard, who went to Grateful Dead shows and listened to bootleg tapes when he was a student at Franklin and Marshall College in the middle '70s, recalls speaking without words while tripping with a seminarian friend. "I had a thought and he turned and touched me on the shoulder and said, 'Yeah.' And we got into this amazing back-and-forth conversation without speaking to each other. Our thoughts were jumping from one to the other." Sitting in the office of the charismatic professor who had introduced him to Indian philosophy, and also to dope, Andre flashed on the word *guru;* whereupon the teacher said softly, "I am not your guru."

He recalls these experiences with bemused detachment from his desk in New York, where he works as a trade book editor. In that lushly psychoactive decade, everyone he knew was trying whatever came around: LSD, hash, uppers and downers, speed (snorted), horse tranquilizer (ketamine), which Leary was touting. Andre added opium during his junior year in India; found it wonderful, too wonderful, and stopped. Along with the cornucopia of drugs, the '70s saw the expansion of the consciousness industry, with its parade of devotional ideologies. "Psychic boot camps," FSM veteran Michael Rossman calls them. Arika, est, Scientology, the Maharaji, the Rajneeshee, gestalt, Transcendental Meditation, transpersonal psychology—in one way or another, they taught you how to "stop the world," to live in the present, to forget the past (*time* being but a *construct*), ergo the future, which cannot be imagined outside of history. They were warm-up exercises for the cognitive disciplines that have taught us to regard the world as a *process of interpretation:* just as psychedelic drugs, by heightening *inner* consciousness, were, among other things, a warm-up for the consciousness industry.

The '70s, in their own way, were also years of transformation, stunning to behold. In my circles, after the disintegration of the movement, it was as if a magic wand had swept over our heads, leaving us, in a few years, unrecognizable to one another. In the summer of 1974, when Richard and I were still living together with our little girl on Carroll Street in Brooklyn, one of SDS's founders, Al Haber, turned up on our stoop. Haber, a Ph.D. in sociology, worked as a baker in Berkeley and had embraced the teachings of Baba Ram Dass. Now he had decided to run for president; it was a good way to reconnect with old friends, he said jauntily, referring to his cross-country tour, and beaming at us from the couch like a yellow "Have a nice day" sticker.

Speaking of the decade's rampant drug experimentation, Andre calls it the "tail end, after the *real time*" of the 1960s; "so it was sort of nice." "The drugs," he agrees, "were maybe all that remained of the earlier era." Grateful Dead music was another part of the "tail end," all the more poignant because the "mass commercialization" of culture was closing in. *Working-man's Dead* and *American Beauty* were the "standouts." *From the Mars Hotel* (1974) was very good, Andre suggests, but different from anything the band had done before. "It appeared to be a turning point: the commercialization of the Dead," and he didn't listen to much after that. "It seemed much more glitzy. The sound was fuller, more orchestrated, more *produced.*"

Franklin and Marshall, in Lancaster, Pennsylvania, was one of the colleges that the Grateful Dead had favored with a concert in 1971. It became a nesting ground for Deadheads—among the most devout, the most fearless, being the seminary students. Andre had attended a Dead concert at the Spectrum in Philadelphia with a group of them in April 1977. They had all dropped acid, and when one disappeared and couldn't be found, the others left without him, knowing that he had a car. The next morning, a Sunday, the police found the young man wandering around the arena looking for his car, still tripping, and very anxious because he had to give a sermon at a Lutheran church in Krumsville, Pennsylvania. The police got him to his vehicle, and he made it to Krumsville. He had a prepared text, which he tossed aside, he told Andre afterward, and decided to wing it on the theme of "It doesn't really matter anymore," which was a line from a Grateful Dead song. The congregation was equally divided between those who were awestruck and those who were horrified that this priest, clearly under the influence, was quoting from the Grateful Dead and throwing in some Mick Jagger. You really ought to open your eyes up to other experiences, he urged, adding that drugs may help. "I often wondered what happened to that seminarian," Andre muses.

I wonder what happened to the young attorney from the distinguished law firm of Arnold & Porter in New York, Robert Solow (not his real name), who was retained by the American Psychological Association (APA) in the mid-'60s to establish the legal grounds for ousting Timothy Leary and Richard Alpert for alleged professional misconduct related to their LSD research. The night before the APA meeting in Washington, a colleague from Arnold & Porter had visited Solow on Capitol Hill and suggested they drop acid. "Why not?" said Robert, who had never smoked dope before, much less used LSD. And he proceeded to have a classic trip lasting all night, which plunged him back into a troubled boyhood;

memory's doors flew open, and the family dynamics were revealed with a clarity missing from years of analysis.

Around 6:00 A.M., Robert's wife, Diane, had begun to panic. He was still tripping—"he was fucking *whacked,*" Richard Levy remembers from Solow's account in 1969, when the two of them were in a Washington-based political collective called the High Pressure Front. The APA meeting was scheduled for nine. "Leave me alone; this is the most incredible stuff I've ever been through," Robert told Diane; and at eight, she called the APA to report that her husband had been in an accident while driving their daughter to school and that they should proceed without him. No, the APA representative said; he was too important to the meeting; they'd wait. With no way out, she dragged him into the shower, dressed and shaved him, and drove him to the APA mansion on Sixteenth Street, not far from the White House. Solow sauntered in just as the assembled professors were climbing the spiral staircase to the dining room. He joined them and sat down at a table where, it turned out, Leary, Alpert, and Quinn McNemar, then president of the APA, were also seated. It was all so natural, like going with the flow. Solow asked Leary and Alpert about their work, and about the use of LSD as a therapeutic tool in unblocking memory, in particular. After lunch, when the men rose from the table, he reached over and plucked a sugar cube from the sugar bowl, glanced at Leary, popped it in his mouth, and winked.

Downstairs in the boardroom, the misconduct charges were reviewed, and Solow was invited to present the APA's legal opinion. Standing in front of a huge stack of papers documenting the case for expulsion, he said, "It is the considered opinion of the firm of Arnold & Porter that there is no basis for expelling Drs. Alpert and Leary, and that the APA would be putting itself in a libelous situation if it chose to do so," or words to that effect, and sat down. You could hear a pen drop. Stunned, the APA president called for a motion to ratify the decision of the attorneys, then moved to close the meeting. "One moment, please," said Robert, on his feet again. "With some of the country's most preeminent psychologists seated in this room, wouldn't it be foolish if we did not take this opportunity to hear Leary and Alpert tell us about their discoveries concerning the study of the mind and the formation of personality?" Mr. Solow had a point, the president agreed; if everyone was in favor, they would turn the meeting over to them. And for the next hour and a half, the two miracle workers, recently expelled from Harvard and Mexico, but not yet from the APA, held the floor.

It was when LSD infiltrated professional ranks such as these that the mindful chaos began.

Marcie Lichtenstein believes *The Grateful Dead Movie* (1977) gives the clearest sense of what the Dead were like in their prime: "the glow in their eyes, how happy they are." What a contrast to twenty years later. "At the end, Jerry looked miserable," she says. "He didn't like the Dead. That's not where he felt comfortable musically." Her older brother Eric, who is built like a roadie, and speaks in epigrams like a private eye in a Dashiell Hammett novel, has an interesting habit of pulling the rug out from under a thought to reveal its underside. Thus, Jerry Garcia is no less deserving of sympathy and respect for being, in later years, "real hard to get along with," which he's heard on the grapevine; "Steve Parish was like his bodyguard, kept everyone away and let him do whatever he wanted to do," including procuring drugs from the never-ending supply that awaited him in cities on the road.

"They were all stifled," Marcie continues; but her brother disagrees: "Other band members were not so stifled."

Jerry was pretty miserable. Everybody looked up to him, like the Spinners, who thought he was God. Eric shakes his head. *I never did that. To me, he was like an extraordinary human being, and his music made me feel—I don't have words to say—but I never looked at him as if he wasn't human.*

Marcie: *He'd gone through life with all these people depending on him for the tours—that has to be connected to the drug addiction.*

Eric: *He said in almost every interview I ever read with him that he never wanted to be what he was made out to be. He never wanted to be put up on a pedestal.*

Marcie: *He suffered every day. I look at my heroin addiction, waking up every morning sick—of course, he reacted to it differently than we do.*

Me: *You wake up sick?*

Marcie: *If you don't have it.*

Eric: *Every day when I woke up during my heroin addiction*—pronounced with emphasis, like *my* lower-back pain or *my* midlife crisis— *I felt like a piece of shit. As far as I know, every junkie does, and for, like, Jerry to wake up—*

JERRY WAS A JUNKIE! Marcie exclaims, *in a flash of recognition. Jerry was a junkie.*

Eric: *And he probably thought he was living a lie; people thought he was this great guy, and he was waking up and doing things he didn't want to do.*

The empathy of former addicts is an overflowing cup. So, too, is the empathic power of "the church of love," as Richard Loren calls the larger Grateful Dead community. Eric again: "Imagine how many times a little group of friends sat around and said, 'I wonder what's going to happen when Jerry goes?' They knew it was gonna happen anytime." Indeed they did. "Every time we got on an airplane to travel someplace, you had to be aware of it," the Dead's current manager, Cameron Sears, said a few months after Garcia's death, referring to an in-house sense that all their days were numbered, which first set in when Jerry fell into a diabetic coma in 1986. "It was almost like a Greek drama then," a Hog Farmer named Calico recalls: "The man is down; the man is up. Touch of Grey. He surprised." In the last two years of Garcia's life, the foreboding returned; and Candace would say to me in passing, "If you're planning to interview Jerry, you'd better move fast."

After he died, Candace left me with a moving image from the last tour of Garcia bent over his Power Book in the back of the chartered plane. He's shaking and he holds his head at an odd angle over the brightly winking liquid-crystal screen, which consoles him in his hour of need. He's been touring for years and he's tired and worn. He's drawing, or trying to, having returned to an old flame: art, just as he immersed himself in old-time music between tours. In his affair with Barbara Meier in 1993, and his marriage to Deborah Koons in 1994, he had returned to women with whom he was once footloose and free.

I tell Eric, Marcie, and Todd what I've heard from band members who confronted Garcia several times about his addiction and threatened to pull out, the last time being after he collapsed from "exhaustion" in September 1992. "Go ahead," he'd snap back, "I'll just play with my own band." Or he'd brush them off, saying, in effect, "You know you can't stop. You can't walk out. You need the money." He was right about that; though Richard Loren, for one, believes the musicians should have quit anyway. If they had, if the band had gone off the road for a year or two after they hit the gusher with "Touch of Grey," maybe Jerry Garcia would still be alive.

It's no surprise to Loren that Garcia said no when the band pressed him to clean up his act. Even in the late '70s when the two men worked closely together, Richard remembers Jerry as being unhappy a lot of the time. When he started using more heroin and shutting himself off ("cocooning," Scully calls it), Loren believes it was "because he couldn't say no to the Grateful Dead." Nor could he disappoint the fans—"those people who gave him the opportunity to improve his guitar." Neil Young put it in a song:

> Old man sittin' there
> Touch of grey, but he don't care
> When he hears his children call.

Loren wanted Garcia to follow up the success of *The Grateful Dead Movie,* which Jerry directed, with a film version of Kurt Vonnegut's *The Sirens of Titan.* He saw his boss as a budding cineaste, while Ken Kesey saw him as an intellectual—"the best-read guy this side of Larry McMurtry, an insomniac whose mind was going all the time." It bothered Kesey that at Garcia's funeral, "everybody was hemmed into talking about Jerry and the Grateful Dead as if he was just a guitar player in a band."

In Loren's ideal world, the others would have figured: "We know it's a heavy burden that this god-king Jerry is carrying on his shoulders, and that his responsibility is so great, he can't leave it, because if he leaves it, he thinks he's abandoning the secretaries, he's abandoning the crew, he's abandoning the musicians, he's abandoning the merchandising people. If he stops, they all stop getting paid." And Loren wishes the musicians had said, "Jerry, we're *tired.* We don't need the money. We got our fuckin' houses. We've got our cars. We got our insurance policies. We're gonna take off for a while." But they didn't. "They failed the acid test," he contends, "because they were tempted with the gold. They had the big hit and they went corporate and they pushed the goose. They pushed Jerry to his death." According to Loren, who heard it from friends close to Garcia, Jerry himself shrank from the last tour. "He realized that this was more than he could handle, but the part of him that couldn't say no had let it go after the band overrode him."

No doubt this exaggerates the other musicians' power—certainly it stretches their responsibility—and underestimates the tyranny of inertia over Garcia's life (inertia being the underside of obsessive attachments).

Not surprisingly, Richard Loren's view of the band's culpability is not confirmed by the home office—although Garcia's fatigue and change of heart at the end are. "He was really looking to stop touring and do what he wanted to do," says Sue Stephens, who today serves as the secretary for the Jerry Garcia Estate. "What are we, *broke?*" she remembers Jerry saying at a band meeting early in 1995—meaning, surely we're not working for money.

According to Stephens, a family retainer like Eileen Law, who started cleaning house for Jerry and Mountain Girl in the early 1970s and went on to become Garcia's personal assistant, office manager, and chief financial officer, Jerry dreaded the coming tour—for good reason. A string of disasters included the death of two fans from drug overdoses at a July 5 concert outside St. Louis, and the injury of 150 when an overcrowded platform collapsed at a nearby campground. On June 25, three people were struck by lightning outside RFK Stadium, while at concerts in Indiana and upstate New York, groups of fans angry at drug arrests hurled rocks and bottles at police. A death threat against Garcia at another concert led the band to call in the FBI. "Tensions had reached a peak. The tour was a disaster. And Jerry was looking for a way out," agrees Alan Trist. But so, too, were Bill Kreutzmann and Phil Lesh.

The notion that the band's greed kept the leader in harness rests rather too easily (in my opinion) upon a deification of Jerry Garcia that is by no means restricted to Deadheads. Garcia was an old dog who'd been doing his tricks for too long, with too many bones heaped beside his plate, to summon the energy to walk away. Besides, he was a performer in the archaic sense, who felt he was an instrument of forces outside himself. An ego-driven star would have burned out much sooner. The constant playing was how he justified himself before his gods; made himself a fit instrument, a worthy vessel.

The drugs had always gone hand in hand with the music, more for him than the others. To get high on the Persian, Garcia's opiate of choice, more like morphine than heroin, he might load up on Percodans, then use Demerol or Dilaudid to straighten out for a show, as would the others—keyboardist Keith Godchaux in the mid-'70s, Kreutzmann, Hart, and Brent Mydland later. After ending his cocaine habit in the mid-'80s, Lesh became attached to fine wines; Weir's appetite for LSD leveled out in the 1970s, and never led to the hard stuff. When Jerry ran over his gram-a-day quota of Persian (a gram cost seven hundred dollars), which Rock Scully shipped ahead to the cities they were playing, or when the bundles missed a stop, and he was too "junk-sick" to perform, he might go onstage full of Valium, bumping into the mike, dozing off in the middle of a dirgelike song, losing whole stanzas, even after a TelePrompTer was installed at his feet. For coworkers like Cameron Sears, what was "shocking" and "ironic" about Garcia's death on August 9, 1995, in the drug rehab facility called Serenity Knolls, was that it occurred when "he was taking all the right steps to rectify the past shit he'd been through." But it was "too little too late."

While it embarrassed him to confront the commercial implications of the enormous following he attracted, the truth is that the audiences justified Garcia. "[T]here is that juice when you hit a crowd of eighty thousand people," he said in 1989, "and when you get the *pow,* there's definitely a rush involved." Wake-up juice, one might call it, enough to snap any musician out of the numbing routines of playing night after night, year after year, in one cavernous steel-girdered cage after another. Most of Jerry Garcia's life, by his own account, was spent "seeking the high-energy experience of playing music for large audiences for the purpose of reaching some degree of communication and rapport with that audience."

The songs were the synapses through which energy passed from the band to the audience and back again. Each song was embedded in a web of associations and announced itself with a telltale chord or phrase: this one a little half step, that one a rag or boogie. Another might be a spellbinder, like "Dark Star," with the power to bring a giant stadium to stillness. For Garcia, the songs were the medium through which he chased the "magic moment" when it felt as if the music played *him.* Or the audience played him. "Then you were no longer responsible," he liked to say, referring to "the stuff, the pure gold of the experience"—which confirmed perhaps the transcendent purposefulness of the universe he perceived on acid long ago.

The trip really is "out there, it ain't in here," he insisted, pointing to himself; this was "one of the reasons why you can trust it." It would be "scary if you feel like you're responsible for it," he added; "that's a lot of energy to be responsible for." Luckily, he'd been able to disqualify himself from it, he told David Gans. "I know it's not me, [and] it doesn't really matter what [Deadheads] believe," he said owlishly; "I know by personal subjective testing that it's not the case." Nor was Garcia susceptible to media projections. "The media relationship to reality is almost always wrong," he commented in 1971. "Media in general is never very accurate"; he'd been described "more radically, and also more conservatively" than he really was, so he looked askance at most of what was said about him. Anyway, the kind of fame Garcia was involved in during the early '70s was "low-profile enough" that he wasn't constantly being reminded he was "a big star."

Then and later, he kept the secrets of his heart to himself. When things went right with the music, it was always a "mystery"—the result of "some kind of intuitive thing," which he recognized "phenomenologically" when it was reported from the audience or confirmed in postmortems with the band. "Our best attitude to it," he suggested, was "sort of this stewardship, in which we are the custodians of this thing." It was an artist's stratagem for protecting his muse; and its abandonment usually signaled the downfall of a talent, as it had when Jack Kerouac started babbling on talk shows in the 1950s after the success of *On the Road.* "Tell me, Jack, just exactly what you're looking for"; and Kerouac replied, "I'm waiting for God to show me his face." It was the truth, Joyce Johnson recalls in her memoir, *Minor Characters,* but not for television. When Kerouac failed to protect the "deep visionary part of himself that had to remain in darkness, that would only reveal itself in dreams or books," he crossed a dangerous line.

Garcia knew better how to protect his private myth. "I don't want the fuckin' job," he could say of his fame, and mean it. "I liked it when you could just be a musician . . . an artist and craftsman. . . . [N]obody mobs a cat that makes nice leather clothes or a guy that does woodwork." But when he set forth to explore the shadowy world on the other side of reality's wall with his guitar, he, too, waited for a god (called "It") to show his face. By 1981, however, talking to David Gans and Blair Jackson, and thinking about the public meaning of the Dead's music, Garcia had worried that it was coming "close to being perfect fascism," by which he meant, "close to being perfectly manipulative."

It was a perception Hank Harrison touched on in 1980 when he described how the "lyric images" burned themselves into the suggestible minds of the audiences, turning a "transportive" experience into something "tantamount to a brainwashing session." It made Harrison think of the Dead as "image fascists since the audience was too stoned to resist the suggestions." The traditional "compact" between band and fans thus "became one of abandoned trust; the audience seemed to swoon . . . and would usually default all responsibility to the musicians. . . ."

Garcia was not unaware of this dimension; though when Gans asked him to elaborate, he referred simply to "people who use formula things on the audience . . . show-biz tricks." "But you've used them," Jackson pointed out; and he agreed: "Oh, yeah, a certain amount of it, but our trip is to learn the tricks and then not use them," he said; to discover, " 'Oh, far out, when we do this, look what happens to the audience. Yeah, let's not do that.' We want for the Grateful Dead to be something that isn't the result of tricks." But this was wishful talking.

The actual interaction between the fans and the band was more complex than either Harrison or Garcia suggest. Early on, the Grateful Dead had mastered the central performing trope of the nineteenth-century music hall, which was a kind of *knowingness,* a *collusion* between performer and audience, who constructed each other, in effect. To each according to its wants, from each according to its needs was the formula. In music halls and later in vaudeville, the best performers flattered their audiences' vanities and appeased their hungers, as the Grateful Dead did when they conferred the coveted rank of outlaw, rebel, or misfit on followers who appear for the most part to be relatively placid souls, with unremarkable aspirations for their time and place; a shade more liberal than their peers, more tolerant of differences, sensitive to environmental issues, as was the band. But you won't see Deadheads, who have grown up to include a fair number of elected officials and CEOs, knocking off hats or aiding and abetting insurrection, whether intellectual, political, or moral. They are more likely to be conflict resolvers, which is how the Family Dog's founder, Chet Helms, remembers Jerry Garcia from their time together in the Haight.

By 1982, however, when Garcia told a *Playboy* interviewer that he found "all that ['60s] campus confusion laughable," he could more accurately be described as a scruffian defender of the status quo. "Why enter this closed society and make an effort to liberalize it when that's never been its function?" he declared. "Why not just leave it and go somewhere else? Why not act out your fantasies . . . [instead of] just struggling? . . . [I]t's easy enough to find a place where people will leave you alone." Which is where the Grateful Dead came in, for Garcia and for the legions of Deadheads who made a vast "love scene" of their own out of the music and iconography of the band.

The Grateful Dead, the institution, the True Church that sleeps and feeds at once, is a haven in a heartless world, Maggie Motorcycle's "safe, loving environment." It is the still place at the center of the storm—the "new order," you might say, that emerged from the "formlessness and chaos" of which Garcia spoke in 1972. If Jerry was uniquely sensitive to his audience's hungers, to its spiritual yearnings, loneliness, fear of conflict and, yes, of change—and he was—it was because, to a considerable extent, they mirrored his own.

Jerry Garcia lived in what he once called "the Grateful Dead universe, which has its own parameters, its own goals." It had "a door and you pass through that, then another door, and so on. The doorframe and the wall and the room beyond are the rest of the culture," he explained. "The Grateful Dead is my community, my friends, the people that I care about," he said; and "everything beyond that is some sort of wild rumor you either believe or you don't believe." I have always found this passage immensely affecting; horrifying, in a way, given Garcia's ultimate isolation from the people around him. This included not just the mob with the smiling face, but the Grateful Dead "family," swollen with dependents and subdependents. It was an alienation more or less successfully concealed from the public during his lifetime; although contempt for the idolatry of Deadheads was embedded in the backstage culture by 1992, when I started attending concerts on a regular basis. The mistrust of the fans— whose tie-dyed image, grubbing burritos in the dirt, was served up by local newspapers whenever the Grateful Dead came to town—had merged with a darker mood inside the organization.

A grave uneasiness with the uneven quality of the music afflicted members of both the crew and the band—Phil Lesh, in particular. Visitors foolish enough to praise a set were liable to be scorned, as I sometimes was when my enthusiasm for a triumphant passage from one tune to another overcame me in the lighting booth, my usual perch during the second half of shows. It was as if the music was a ghost of its former self, and a kind of reverse snobbism dictated that insiders who were privy to the grandeur of the original product denounce the watered stock—in part to separate themselves from the uncritical approbation of the masses, who now tipped dangerously toward the MTV generation.

In fact, the band still had its good nights, sometimes producing an entire three-hour concert that rarely flagged, as on a rainy Saturday in June 1993 at Giants Stadium. I remember this show, which *New York Times* critic Peter Watrous singled out as different from the usual fare of "lapidary improvisational moments" surrounded by "hours of swill." It was an occasion, Watrous writes, when "the product of a strange cultural explosion some 30 years ago, playing music more experimental than anything heard on the popular music circuit, suddenly surfaced as something it had been; . . . not the bloated legend it has become [but] a particularly smart, Americanist bar band with imagination."

The moments of brilliance, moreover, lay in the jazzlike transitions, as they had at a Madison Square Garden show on September 12, 1991, also covered by Watrous, when Jerry Garcia treated his fans to one of those breakthroughs prized by aficionados, an "improvisation that began with dark and eerie colors, only to blossom into pastoral harmony." Writing on June 7, 1993, Watrous related the real-time inventiveness to the band's "anti-authoritarianism . . . and the American promise of exploring uncharted terrain. . . . Mr. Garcia, particularly awake," he noted dryly, "matched chromatic and steely runs with wrenching, repeated, lyrical ideas, changing the tempo of his improvisations to give them texture."

After Garcia's death, the *Times*'s pop music critic Jon Pareles summed up the distinctive style of his guitar. "[O]pen and amiable," lacking "bite or cut or scream," the phrasing had "the relaxed tickle of a bluegrass guitarist. . . . He played the way a dolphin swims with its school," Pareles said. "His guitar lines would glide out, shimmer and gambol in the sunlight, then blend into the group as if nothing had happened." It was an apt metaphor for a man who, on vacation, liked nothing more than to swim underwater with the fishes.

Hunter's lyrics—which often included a line Garcia contributed when he sat down to work out the chords and the melody—had the same gamboling quality. They eschewed the emotional heroism of lovers or fighters, rascals or cynics. The Hunter/Garcia voice was never "angry, tortured or self-important," but ruminative, wandering and wondering, in the manner of old ballads and mountain music. It was an unassuming voice, ready to break into an instrumental jam whenever it reached the expressive limits of language, which was often.

Hunter's fondness for tall tales, I believe, allowed Jerry to explore an exotic world that opened up to him when he was a boy, sitting in the sailor's bar his mother ran after his father's death. It was a workingman's bar next door to the merchant marine's union on the corner of First and Harrison in San Francisco. And day after day in the late 1940s, back when "the Orient was still the Orient," Garcia said, he listened to the "incredible stories" the men brought back from the Persian Gulf and the Far East. These and the "weird things" in their seaman's trunks—perfectly tailored double-breasted suits from the 1930s, photographs of square-riggers— gave him "a glimpse into a larger universe that seemed so attractive and fun and, you know, *crazy*." It was one of the reasons he couldn't stay in school, he added; alongside this world, "school was a little too boring."

The incredible stories loom behind the delight Garcia took in playing the roles presented in the songs: the fugitive, the rambling lover, the connoisseur of mystery and magic, the wife-stealing, rockabilly patriot of "U.S. Blues," the survivor of "Touch of Grey"—

> I know the rent is in arrears
> The dog has not been fed in years
> It's even worse than it appears
> but it's all right.

Back in San Rafael, meanwhile, all was not right. The band's failure to stem the downward spiral of Garcia's physical condition, which included his obesity along with diabetes, exacerbated tensions. With a "dysfunctional Dad," as Gans called Jerry, old turf wars flared up between the sound and lighting crews and the riggers and roadies. In 1993, Cameron Sears, who ran a river-rafting operation before he joined the Grateful Dead in his early twenties in 1986, was ordered to fire longtime soundman Dan Healy. Deadheads with backstage passes were rudely chased from hot spots near the stage or the dressing rooms. Around 1994, Grateful Dead ticket manager Steve Marcus, who had an Internet account with the WELL and frequently posted the set-lists from his backstage cubby during encores, was ordered by Steve Parish to stop the practice. Why? I wondered, knowing how eager Deadheads are to know what the band played at every concert. "Basically, it was consorting with the enemy," David Gans suggests, "giving information to *those people.* A bunker mentality," he calls it.

It wasn't rational to turn against the fans, whose devotion put the Grateful Dead over the top, but Gans, who as the "put-it-on-the-radio guy," takes some heat himself, has an explanation. "Everybody who's not getting his needs met has to refer his anger and his frustration and his fear somewhere. You can't go around saying, 'Goddamn that fucking junkie Jerry Garcia! If he wasn't our meal ticket, I'd kick his ass!' " So you pick on others, who—*surprise!*—celebrate Jerry Garcia's benevolence.

For the fans, the Grateful Dead still serve as an underground church, a "church of love" but also a church of fun, which may convene whenever two or more Deadheads get together. Sitting in a frame house under the shadow of the giant crane at Bath Iron Works, Peter Wigley, Maggie Motorcycle, and John Upham, who works at the shipyard, play a pickup game with the songs. Grinning, they toss lines back and forth.

John: *"When life looks like Easy Street / there is danger at your door."*

Peter: *"One way or another / this darkness got to give."* A pause. *"One man gathers what another man spills."*. . . *"Once in awhile / you get shown the light / in the strangest of places . . ."* All join in on that one. This is about Jerry, I realize, a remembrance of things past. The lines are amulets with which they are consoling themselves and reminding themselves of the good times.

John: *"Ashes to ashes / they all fall down."* Everybody laughs.

Peter: *"Politicians throwing stones / the kids they dance and shake their bones"*. . . *"He's gone / and he ain't comin' back."*

Maggie (correcting him): *"Nothing's gonna bring him back."* That can mean almost anything you want it to mean, she says. That's what I listened to when my father died. That's how I was consoled.

I ask for more.

Peter: *"You got two good eyes / you still can't see."*

Me, I think. Maggie laughs.

John: *"Ain't no place I'd rather be."*

Peter: *"Goin' where the weather suits my clothes."*

Now there's a line I haven't heard before. *If it works, it's your line,* Maggie says, *even when you get it wrong. . . . Like "One man gathers up another man's pills,"* intones Peter.

Steve Cornell, who was introduced to Jerry Garcia by Eileen Law when he was a wheelchair-bound kid in the late '70s, says the Grateful Dead gives you clues about life. "The whole thing about life is to be humble and to appreciate what you have and not really look for what you don't have," he maintains. For Cornell, as for other Deadheads I've met, "the Grateful Dead experience is about looking more inward, to try and better yourself to be the kind of person you would want to meet."

This last echoes an AA line; and in some respects the American subculture that is Deaddom is a kissing cousin to the much larger underground church that is the nationwide network of twelve-step recovery programs. They are both mutual-aid societies that hold forth the promise of personal renewal through access to a higher consciousness. They draw their members from the same sunken continent of believers who are ill-served by more hierarchical structures of worship and remediation, and who long for a security that no gated community or reservoir of wealth can assure them. An odd kind of security, it's the sweet oblivion of the road, the music, and the friendship of strangers.

What's special about the Grateful Dead for Eric Lichtenstein is that "they were truly American," another recurrent theme. "That always touched me," he says, speaking of the Dead experience: "It was like *mine*. It was *ours*." And he recalls with pride the time a young man from Germany came to see America through the eyes of the Grateful Dead and latched onto Eric's tour family (which included Marcie and Todd) and traveled all summer with them. Today, Todd (who just got a job with an investment firm in Colorado, and a 1974 BMW to go with it) tells me that what he values most about the Dead is that they introduced him to "the spirit of the country," both through the songs, which are "all about America," and the tours, which showed him the diversity of the people. He doesn't want to sound "like Charles Kuralt" but there was, he says, something "wholesome" about the experience.

Richard Loren sees the Grateful Dead this way: "They waved the flag," he says, paraphrasing "U.S. Blues." "Anarchists that they were, they were *Americans*." Loren himself is "an immigrant kid" from New York whose grandparents were born in Italy, a "Europhile" who now lives part-time in

Rome, teaching English. His surname was originally Giachino. He's "not a meat-and-potatoes guy, not an American flag guy," but a "pasta guy," he tells me, which helps explain the wonder with which he first beheld the Grateful Dead in California, who were "steak and potatoes and guns and acid.

"When I think about the Grateful Dead," he ventures, "I think of a flag and I think of a rose and I think of a steak and I think of a gun. And I think of the West, and I think of consciousness expansion. I think of irreverence and anarchy and I think of something *pure*." Loren speaks softly, almost in a trance. "I think the collective is worthy of it," he says of the purity; "and I think the one individual Jerry Garcia is worthy of it, and I would say the individual Robert Hunter is worthy of it." He catches his breath. "I could be full of shit."

⌁

～NOTES～

Some frequently cited texts are abbreviated after first citation, as follows:

Tom Wolfe, *Electric Kool-Aid Acid Test: EKAT*

David Gans, *Conversations with the Dead: Conversations*

John Marks, *The Search for the "Manchurian Candidate": "Manchurian Candidate"*

Robert Hunter, *A Box of Rain: Box*

Rock Scully with David Dalton, *Living with the Dead: Living*

Jerilyn Lee Brandelius, *Grateful Dead Family Album: GDFA*

Blair Jackson, *Goin' Down the Road: Goin'*

Sandy Troy, *One More Saturday Night: Saturday Night*

Full bibliographical references for all sources are given with first citation. The location and date of interviews and conversations are cited upon first use only, unless more than one interview was conducted with the same person. Interviews are drawn from taped transcripts; conversations from notes.

ix: Robert Hunter, "U.S. Blues," *A Box of Rain* (New York: Viking, 1990), 234.

Introduction

2   "road map": interview with Mickey Hart, Albany, New York, June 12, 1992.

3   Jerry Garcia quoted in *Garcia,* by the Editors of *Rolling Stone* (Boston: Little, Brown/Rolling Stone Press, 1995), 90.

3   "We went on a head-hunting mission": interview with Hart.

3   *Robert Smithson: The Collected Writings,* ed. Jack Flam (Berkeley: University of California Press, 1996), 98.

5   "Room of Great Artists": ibid., 99.

5   helper figure in a fairy tale: See *The Water of Life: A Tale of the Grateful Dead,* retold by Alan Trist (Eugene, Oregon: Hulogosi Press, 1989); and *Grateful Dead Folktales,* ed. Bob Franzosa (Levant, Maine: Zosafarm Publications, 1989).

6   "it all rolls into one": Hunter, "Stella Blue," *Box,* 120–121.

7   Jerry Garcia quoted in Peter Watrous, in "Touch of Gray Matter," *Musician,* December 1989, 40.

7   "It may be that it's": interview with Phil Lesh, San Rafael, California, March 13, 1996.

7   Jerry Garcia quoted in Bill Barich, "Still Truckin' On," *The New Yorker,* October 11, 1993, 99.

8   "When we play": interview with Lesh.

8   Van Wyck Brooks, *The Times of Melville and Whitman* (New York: Dutton, 1947), 103.

Prologue

13   Jerry Garcia quoted in *Garcia,* 95.

13   *"The Captain has just informed me"*: *The Acid Test,* Key-Z Productions, Eugene, Oregon, 1990. Video includes original footage and audio from the January 8, 1966, Acid Test at the Fillmore Auditorium and a February Acid Test in Los Angeles.

14   "ripple in still water": Hunter, "Ripple," *Box,* 185.

14   "The dragon was keeping time": interview with Skip Workman, New Harbor, Maine, March 6, 1998.

15   "love scene": interview with Robert Hunter, San Rafael, California, June 9, 1997.

15   "It was easy": interview with Hunter.

1. The Magic Art of the Great Humbug

17   Kesey quoted in Warren Hinckle, "A Social History of the Hippies," *Ramparts,* March 1967, 11.

17   Kesey quoted in Tom Wolfe, *The Electric Kool-Aid Acid Test* (New York: Bantam, 1968), 8, 55.

17   "Tootling the multitudes" to A VOTE FOR BARRY: Martin A. Lee and Bruce Shalin, *Acid Dreams: The Complete Social History of LSD, the CIA, the Sixties, and Beyond* (New York: Grove Press, 1985), 121.

18   I am indebted to William Blacklock for a background sketch of Neal Cassady, in a letter dated "9/92."

18   "[radical] movement's expressive side": Todd Gitlin, *The Sixties: Years of Hope, Days of Rage* (New York: Bantam, 1987), 162.

19   "the force of acid": Gitlin, *The Sixties,* 209.

19   Oglesby quoted in Lee and Shalin, *Acid Dreams,* 132.

20   Wolfe, *EKAT,* 35.

20   "you're either *on* the bus": Guitarist Mason Williams, speaking on the eve of the bus's April 1997 trip to the Rock and Roll Hall of Fame in Cleveland; in *The Oregonian,* April 21, 1997, C1, 3.

20   " 'Better Living through Chemistry' ": interview with Gene Anthony, Oakland, California, June 9, 1997.

20   "I took these drugs": interview with Ken Kesey, Pleasant Valley, Oregon, March 16, 1996.

20   "more each time": interview with Hunter.

21   "who didn't have the common *balls*": interview with Kesey.

22   background on MK-ULTRA: John Marks, *The Search for the "Manchurian Candidate"* (New York: Times Books, 1979), 56, 119; and Leigh A. Henderson and William J. Glass, eds., *LSD: Still with Us After All These Years* (New York: Lexington Books/Macmillan, 1994), 41.

23   "We were all ringside": Kesey quoted in Rex Weiner, "To Live and Die in L.A.," *The New Yorker,* October 16, 1995, 37.

23   "Ginsberg was one of those little ferrets" to "giggle out of it yourself": interview with Kesey.

23   *"You betcha"*: interview with Hunter.

24   *"Sometimes the light's all shining"*: interview with Kesey.

24   "liberated zone": FSM events from Michael Rossman's *The Wedding Within the War,* cited in Jay Stevens, *Storming Heaven* (New York: Harper & Row, 1987), 295–296.

25   Savio quoted in Gitlin, *The Sixties,* 291n.

25   Kerr on "knowledge factory": Stevens, *Storming Heaven,* 294–295.

25   "frame-breaking experience": Michael Rossman, *New Age Blues: On the Politics of Consciousness* (New York: Dutton, 1979), 64, 61.

26   first cohort of baby boomers: Gitlin reports freshman enrollments jumped 37 percent that year, in *The Sixties,* 163–164.

26   "our little island": interview with Mountain Girl, Pleasant Valley, Oregon, March 15, 1996.

26   "shock workers of the tongue" to *"Fuck it"*: Wolfe, *EKAT,* 195–197.

28   "The whole reason" to "get somethin' *goin'* here": interview with Mountain Girl.

2. Enter Cosmic Forces

31   Allen Ginsberg, "First Party at Ken Kesey's with Hell's Angels," from *Collected Poems: 1947–1980* (New York: HarperCollins, 1988), 375.

32   Interview with Workman.

32   Ginsberg quoted in Stevens, *Storming Heaven,* 308.

33   Sara Ruppenthal quoted in Robert Greenfield, *Dark Star: An Oral Biography of Jerry Garcia* (New York: Morrow, 1996), 72.

33   beatnik to "hit it off": interview with Mountain Girl.

33   Wolfe, *EKAT,* 115.

34   Interview with Mountain Girl.

34   Jerry Garcia's fat trip: Barich, "Still Truckin' On," 101.

34   *"What you're doing"* to *"in a process of discovery"*: interview with Mountain Girl.

35   Wach quoted in Wolfe, *EKAT,* 115.

36   Finney quoted in Page Smith, *The Shaping of America* (New York: McGraw-Hill, 1980), 752.

36   Babbs quoted in Greenfield, *Dark Star,* 73.

36   John Clellon Holmes, "This Is the Beat Generation," *New York Times Magazine,* November 16, 1952, 22.

37   "universes dissolve and reappear" to "it's supposed to be": Jerry Garcia quoted in David Gans, *Conversations with the Dead* (New York: Citadel Underground, 1991), 76–78.

37   "*It was probably*": interview with Mountain Girl.

38   "There's something" to "sophisticated nature, somehow": Jerry Garcia quoted in Gans, *Conversations,* 78–79.

38   "Freewheelin' Frank" quoted by Workman.

38   "Acid made you think" to "part of an acid trip": conversation with Candace Brightman, San Rafael, California, March 10, 1996.

39   Stanislav Grof, *LSD Psychotherapy* (Alameda, California: Hunter House, 1980), 275.

39   "I had to learn" to "over the hill": interview with Mountain Girl.

39   Cowley quoted in Stevens, *Storming Heaven,* 228.

40   "an intellectual companionship" to "a minor note": interview with Mountain Girl.

40   "very connected" to "all the time": Mountain Girl quoted in Cynthia Robins, "She Never Got Off the Bus," *San Francisco Examiner Magazine,* May 25, 1997, 9.

40   "*That's where all*" to "*WOW!*": interview with Mountain Girl.

40   Nelson quoted in Greenfield, *Dark Star,* 57.

40   Huxley quoted in Stevens, *Storming Heaven,* 61.

40   "The Curious Story Behind the New Cary Grant," *Look,* September 20, 1959; quoted in Albert Hofmann, *LSD: My Problem Child,* trans. Jonathan Ott (New York: McGraw-Hill, 1980), 59. Hofmann, who was head of the Pharmaceutical-Chemical Research Laboratories of Sandoz, Ltd., writes that stories like this led the director of the firm to say, "I would rather you had not discovered LSD," 61.

41   Interview with Hunter.

41   L.A. psychiatrists: Stevens, *Storming Heaven,* 64–67.

42   "truly cosmogonic power": Hofmann, *LSD: My Problem Child,* 197.

42   "to be one with the universe": Stevens, *Storming Heaven,* xv.

42   Cohen quoted in Stevens, *Storming Heaven,* 63.

43   Kahn quoted in Lee and Shalin, *Acid Dreams,* 196. The Rand report on LSD recommended obtaining "additional behavioral measurements . . . of the number resigning or becoming [politically] inactive" as a result of frequent LSD use. Kahn's prediction was made in the book he coauthored with Anthony J. Wiener, *The Year 2000* (New York: Macmillan, 1967).

43   Luce cited in Paul Perry, *On the Bus: Complete Guide to the Legendary Trip of Ken Kesey and the Merry Pranksters* (New York: Thunder's Mouth Press, 1990), 6.

43   "every sound generated": Hofmann, *LSD: My Problem Child,* 19.

43   "a deputized minority": Terrance McKenna, *The Archaic Revival: Specula-*

tions on Psychedelic Mushrooms, the Amazon, Virtual Reality, UFOs, Evolution, Shamanism, the Rebirth of the Goddess, and the End of History (San Francisco: Harper, 1991), 82.

43 Kesey quoted in Lee and Shalin, *Acid Dreams,* 29.

43 Wasson trip and CIA: Marks, *"Manchurian Candidate,"* 114.

44 "Pink Party": conversation with Candace Brightman, Kentfield, California, March 13, 1996.

44 Browning quoted in Greenfield, *Dark Star,* 59–60.

45 Leary quoted in Stevens, *Storming Heaven,* 146, 148.

45 "They had a heavy Buddhist": interview with Mountain Girl.

46 Metzner quoted in Stevens, *Storming Heaven,* 264–265.

46 Ruppenthal quoted in Greenfield, *Dark Star,* 57.

46 Kesey quoted in Greenfield, *Dark Star,* 70–71.

47 Clifford Garcia quoted in Greenfield, *Dark Star,* 71.

47 Ruppenthal, Clifford Garcia, and Mountain Girl quoted in Greenfield, *Dark Star,* 71–73.

48 Jerry Garcia quoted in Greenfield, *Dark Star,* 73.

48 Grant quoted in Greenfield, *Dark Star,* 59.

3. Flashes of Recognition

49 "One day the idea": Jerry Garcia quoted in *Garcia,* 61.

49 "The really neat thing": Jerry Garcia quoted by Barich, "Still Truckin' On," 100.

50 "Bring your own gadgets": Gene Anthony, *The Summer of Love: Haight Ashbury at Its Highest* (Millbrae, California: Celestial Arts, 1980), 107.

50 Jerry Garcia quoted in *Garcia,* 61.

50 "It opened the doors" to "more predictable": interview with Lesh.

51 "didn't really catch the flame": Lesh quoted in *Legends,* a documentary film on the Grateful Dead, produced and directed by Jim Berman in 1996.

52 Jerry Garcia quoted in *Garcia,* 61, 64 (emphasis added).

52 Lesh and Jerry Garcia quoted in Gans, *Conversations,* 212.

52 Thompson quoted from *Fear and Loathing in Las Vegas,* in Lee and Shalin, *Acid Dreams,* 163.

52 Interview with Anthony.

53 Grant and Clifford Garcia quoted in Greenfield, *Dark Star,* 7, 8.

54 Marcus quoted in Bruce Shapiro, " 'The Old Weird America' " (review of Marcus's *Invisible Republic: Bob Dylan's Basement Tapes, The Nation,* August 25 / September 1, 1997, 46.

54 Interview with Hunter. The Ramblers included Mike Seeger, Tom Paley, John Cohen, and Eric Thompson.

55 Ruppenthal quoted in Greenfield, *Dark Star,* 29.

55 Meier quoted in Greenfield, *Dark Star,* 17.

55 Ruppenthal quoted in Greenfield, *Dark Star,* 29.

55 Interview with Hunter. According to Alan Trist, Hunter did play the mandolin with the Wildwood Boys; telephone interview, May 19, 1998.

56   Hunter in Scientology movement: Telephone conversation with Sara Ruppenthal, July 8, 1998.

58   "just didn't seem right": Ruppenthal quoted in Greenfield, *Dark Star,* 29.

58   "walk[ing] around the house": Suzy Wood quoted in Greenfield, *Dark Star,* 29.

58   Jerry Garcia quoted in David Shenk and Steve Silberman, *Skeleton Key* (New York: Doubleday, 1994), 101.

58   Kesey quoted in *Garcia: A Grateful Dead Celebration,* presented by *Dupree's Diamond News* (New York: Dupree's Diamond News, Inc., 1995), 30.

60   "Stealin' ": liner notes in *Shady Grove,* acoustic disc produced by Jerry Garcia and David Grisman for Dawg Productions, 1996.

60   Ruppenthal quoted by John Cohen in "The Tradition Lives," liner notes, *Shady Grove.*

60   Marcus and Holmes quoted in Shapiro, " 'The Old Weird America,' " 46.

61   Interview with Hunter.

61   Norman MacPherson Hunter memorial: DeadNet, Robert Hunter/Archive/Journals, January 8, 1996.

61   Hunter, "An Elegy for Jerry," in *Garcia: A Grateful Dead Celebration,* 1.

62   Ruppenthal quoted by Cohen in "The Tradition Lives."

62   Dylan quoted in John Orman, *The Politics of Rock Music* (Chicago: Nelson Hall, 1984), 82.

62   T. S. Eliot, "Tradition and the Individual Talent," in Bradley, Beatty, Long, and Perkins, eds., *The American Tradition in Literature,* vol. 2, 4th ed. (New York: Grosset & Dunlap, 1974), 1168.

63   Thaddeus Golas, *The Lazy Man's Guide to Enlightenment* (Palo Alto, California: The Seed Center, 1971, 1975), 35.

64   Interview with Hunter.

64   "ten thousand got drowneded" to "as-if-by-ear-tradition": Jerry Garcia quoted in Blair Jackson, *Goin' Down the Road: A Grateful Dead Traveling Companion* (New York: Harmony, 1991), 209–210.

65   "The wolf came in": Hunter, "Dire Wolf," *Box,* 58.

65   "Lotta poor man": Hunter, "Cumberland Blues," *Box,* 52.

65   Hunter's compliment: Hunter, *Box,* 52.

65   Interview with Hunter.

66   Van Ronk quoted in Alan Light, "Bob Dylan," in Anthony de Curtis and James Henke, eds., *The Rolling Stone Illustrated History of Rock & Roll,* 3d ed. (New York: Random House/Straight Arrow, 1992), 300.

67   "Just like Jack the Ripper": Hunter, "Ramble on Rose," *Box,* 174.

68   Jerry Garcia quoted in Jackson, *Goin',* 16.

4. How the Balloon Was Launched

69   Hunter, "Cats Under the Stars," *Box,* 33.

69   Weir quoted in Gans, *Conversations,* 191. He mistakenly recalls this as New Year's Eve of 1964.

70   Nelson quoted in Greenfield, *Dark Star,* 48.

70   "I have a band" to "Traitor! Traitor!": conversation with Sue Swanson, Kentfield, California, March 13, 1996.

70   Interview with Mountain Girl.

71   *Help!:* Greenfield, *Dark Star,* 51.

71   Ruppenthal quoted in Greenfield, *Dark Star,* 51.

71   Interview with Hunter.

71   Jerry Garcia quoted in *Garcia,* 193.

72   Conversation with Swanson.

72   *"cry of the ego"* to "baying on cue": Wolfe, *EKAT,* 182–183, 185.

72   "I saw power" to "with the invisible": *A Conversation with Ken Kesey,* a film by Peter Shapiro, ISA Releasing Limited, 1995.

73   "I'd rather do things": Jerry Garcia quoted in Gans, *Conversations,* 244–245.

73   "a surly juvenile delinquent": Rock Scully with David Dalton, *Living with the Dead* (Boston: Little, Brown, 1996), 16.

74   "an arrogant youth": Jerry Garcia quoted by Barich in "Still Truckin' On," 100.

74   Leicester quoted in Greenfield, *Dark Star,* 65.

74   Lesh quoted by McIntire in Greenfield, *Dark Star,* 99.

74   Leicester quoted in Greenfield, *Dark Star,* 65. Garcia simply shifted his students to another store, Guitars Unlimited.

74   Jerry Garcia quoted in Gans, *Conversations,* 244.

75   "Our tribal drum": Scully and Dalton, *Living,* 60.

75   Interview with Lesh.

76   "I've always thought": Lesh quoted by Jerilyn Lee Brandelius in *Grateful Dead Family Album* (New York: Warner Books, 1989), 77.

76   Dawson quoted in Greenfield, *Dark Star,* 65, 67.

77   Jerry Garcia quoted in Scully and Dalton, *Living,* 16.

77   Allen Ginsburg, *Howl* (San Francisco: City Lights Books), 9.

78   Mary Heaton Vorse, *Time and the Town: A Provincetown Chronicle* (New York: Dial Press, 1942), 360.

78   Provincetown Players: Ibid., 120, 207.

79   Interview with Alan Trist, San Rafael, California, March 11, 1996.

79   "having a very psychedelic experience": Trist quoted in Greenfield, *Dark Star,* 17.

79   Interview with Hunter.

80   Meier quoted in Greenfield, *Dark Star,* 16–18.

80   Jerry Garcia quoted in *Garcia,* 61.

81   GRATEFUL DEAD: Shenk and Silberman, *Skeleton Key,* 120. Former manager Jon McIntire reports that it was the *Oxford Companion to Classical Music* that Garcia opened at random to find "grateful dead"—an "English folk song about people who are grateful to be released into death"; Greenfield, *Dark Star,* 104.

81   folk motif of the Grateful Dead: *The Water of Life,* 12, 26.

82   Lesh quoted in Gans, *Conversations,* 104.

82   Jerry Garcia quoted in *Garcia,* 38.

83   Hunter, "What's Become of the Baby?" in *Box,* 242.

84   Interview with Trist.

84   Constanten quoted in Hank Harrison, *The Dead* (Millbrae, California: Celestial Arts, 1980), 71.

86   "Boise was one of us": Harrison, *The Dead,* 60.

86   "big anarchistic family": Stewart Kessler, "Dancing in the Streets," in Greil Marcus, ed., *Rock and Roll Will Stand* (Boston: Beacon Press, 1969), 64. Kessler's story originally appeared in the *San Francisco Express Times* in 1966.

86   "We're a nation of outlaws": Jerry Garcia quoted in Scully and Dalton, *Living,* 131.

5. Courting the Strange

89   Marcus quoted in *Rock and Roll Will Stand,* 70–71.

90   Mountain Girl quoted in Sandy Troy, *One More Saturday Night: Reflections with the Grateful Dead, Dead Family, and Dead Heads* (New York: St. Martin's Press, 1991), 79.

91   Interview with Joel Selvin, San Francisco, July 13, 1993.

91   Gleason quoted in Brandelius, *GDFA,* 42.

92   Jerry Garcia quoted in *Garcia,* 87.

92   bands paid flat fees: Bill Graham and Robert Greenfield, *Bill Graham Presents* (New York: Morrow, 1993), 198.

92   Smith quoted in Greenfield, *Dark Star,* 94.

92   Grateful Dead's equipment: Brandelius, *GDFA,* 138, 119.

93   Haight Ashbury graphics: Anthony, *The Summer of Love,* 37; and Hinckle, "A Social History of the Hippies," 24.

94   "Rockinrifkin": interview with Kesey.

94   "She's an R. Crumb": Scully and Dalton, *Living,* 73.

94   Tangerine and Swanson quoted in Robins, "She Never Got Off the Bus," 21–22.

94   Interview with Mountain Girl.

95   "great big love": Scully quoted in Robins, "She Never Got Off the Bus," 22.

95   "Not at all": Mountain Girl quoted in Robins, "She Never Got Off the Bus," 22.

96   hit record with Cassady: Greenfield, *Dark Star,* 75.

96   Interview with Mountain Girl.

96   McIntire quoted in Robins, "She Never Got Off the Bus," 22.

96   Ruppenthal quoted in Greenfield, *Dark Star,* 47, 61.

96   Annabelle Garcia: memorial service for Jerry Garcia in Golden Gate Park, August 13, 1995.

96   Mountain Girl quoted in Robins, "She Never Got Off the Bus," 22.

97   Mountain Girl quoted in Greenfield, *Dark Star,* 109.

98   Annabelle Garcia quoted in Tim Golden, "Why a Star Is Spinning in the Grave," *New York Times,* January 3, 1997, C14.

98   Koons Garcia quoted from "Garcia v. Garcia: Fighting Over Jerry's Money," Courtroom Television Network, 1997.

98   Andrew Kopkind, *The Thirty Years' Wars: Dispatches and Diversions of a Radical Journalist, 1965–1994* (London: Verso, 1995), 356.

98   Kaukonen quoted in Greenfield, *Dark Star,* 101.

99   Swanson quoted in Greenfield, *Dark Star,* 100.

99   Interview with Mountain Girl.

99   "a world famous dope center": Lee and Shalin, *Acid Dreams,* 148.

100   Sources on Owsley: Gans interview in *Conversations,* 290; Wolfe, *EKAT,* 188; Harrison, *The Dead,* 121; Scully and Dalton, *Living,* 87; and author's interview with Mountain Girl.

100   Interview with Selvin.

101   Owsley in Gans, *Conversations,* 305–306, 294.

102   "vast wisdom" to "powerless dumbshit": Jerry Garcia quoted in Gans, *Conversations,* 79, 80, 78.

102   Ralph Waldo Emerson, "Experience," in Alfred Kazin and Daniel Aaron, eds., *Emerson: A Modern Anthology* (New York: Dell, 1958), 69.

102   Jerry Garcia quoted in Gans, *Conversations,* 80.

102   Owsley cited in Gans, *Conversations,* 303.

103   "Believe it's real": Gans, *Conversations,* 303.

103   Owsley in Gans, *Conversations,* 311.

103   Harrison, *The Dead,* 123.

103   Interview with Cassidy Law, San Rafael, California, March 13, 1996.

103   Interview with Carla Murray, New York, New York, February 10, 1996.

103   "samples": Scully and Dalton, *Living,* 41.

104   Lesh quoted in Gans, *Conversations,* 292.

104   "LSD Madness" stories to Huxley's jingle: Stevens, *Storming Heaven,* 57.

105   LSD unreliable weapon: Lee and Shalin, *Acid Dreams,* 35; see Marks, "*Manchurian Candidate,*" 204, re MK-ULTRA's chief scientist Sidney Gottlieb's own assessment of the shortcomings of the "biological and chemical control of human behavior."

105   *The Dark Side of Camelot* quoted in Barry Bearak, "Book Portrays J.F.K. as Reckless and Immoral," *New York Times,* Sunday, November 9, 1997, 13.

106   CIA listening posts to "fleas on a dog": Lee and Shalin, *Acid Dreams,* 188–189, 296.

106   White quoted in Lee and Shalin, *Acid Dreams,* 32–34. White's letter, dated "November 21, (probably) 1972," originally quoted in Marks, "*Manchurian Candidate,*" 220.

106   "Jolly" West: Lee and Shalin, *Acid Dreams,* 10, 189.

106   Interview with Mountain Girl.

106   "It is, to LSD": Hunter to Terrance McKenna, May 25, 1996, DeadNet, Robert Hunter/Orfeo Files (correspondence with McKenna).

107   Interview with Hunter.

107   Lesh on methedrine: Gans, *Conversations,* 107.

107   Interview with Hunter.

108   Interview with Workman.

108   Burroughs quoted in Lee and Shalin, *Acid Dreams,* 81; "Stay out of the garden": William Burroughs, "Nova Express," in John Calder, ed., *A William Burroughs Reader* (London: Picador, 1982), 203.

108   Interview with Mountain Girl.

109   Interview with Selvin.

110   Hofmann, *LSD: My Problem Child,* 56–57.

111   Capt. Hubbard and CIA LSD factories funded by Mafia, in Lee and Shalin, *Acid Dreams,* 198.

111   Interview with Kesey.

111   Development of STP: Lee and Shalin, *Acid Dreams,* 187.

112   STP and LSD at rock festivals: Robert Santelli, *Aquarius Rising: The Rock Festival Years* (New York: Dell, 1980), 170, 220.

112   BZ victims "won't recall being drugged": *Wall Street Journal,* January 5, 1966; quoted in Carol Brightman, "The Weed Killers," *Viet-Report,* June–July 1966, 41.

112   Battlefield use of BZ: Pierre Darcourt, *"Le temps des massacres," L'Express,* March 13–20, 1966; quoted in Brightman, "The Weed Killers," Table II: Chemical Agents Developed by the U.S. for Use in South Vietnam, 41.

112   BZ use in domestic peacekeeping: Lee and Shalin, *Acid Dreams,* 235.

112   Church committee investigations of CIA to "poor tradecraft": Marks, *"Manchurian Candidate,"* 102–103.

113   Army stockpiled fifty tons: Lee and Shalin, *Acid Dreams,* 235.

113   "a rational approach": Army Research Task Summary, FY 1961, vol. 1, 138; cited in Mickael Klare, "CBW Research Directory," *Viet-Report,* January 1968, 25.

6. Summertime Done Come and Gone

115   Hunter, "Standing on the Moon," *Box,* 208.

115   "in our time" to *"rectification of frontiers":* George Orwell, "Politics and the English Language," *The Norton Reader,* 4th ed., 181.

119   Interview with Peter Wigley, Danville Junction, Maine, November 26, 1996.

120   *Time* quoted in Paul Friedlander, *Rock and Roll: A Social History* (Boulder, Colorado: HarperCollins/Westview Press, 1996), 200.

121   Serra quoted in Troy, *Saturday Night,* 265.

121   "The Hippie Temptation": Telephone interview with Peter Davis, October 27, 1996. The outtake amused the CBS News staff in New York, which included Davis, who later made the documentary *Hearts and Minds*.

121   Nelson's impressions in Greenfield, *Dark Star*, 56.

121   Interview with Lesh.

122   Cohen quoted in Anthony, *The Summer of Love*, 125.

123   Lesh quoted in Scully and Dalton, *Living*, 102.

124   William C. Burton, "Jerry Garcia Remembered," letter to *The New Yorker*, October 2, 1995, 12.

126   McNemar quoted in Smith, *The Shaping of America*, 314.

127   Jerry Garcia quoted in *Garcia*, 95.

127   "Every time the tide turns": the Digger Papers quoted in Lee and Shalin, *Acid Dreams*, 193.

127   Sources for Monterey Pop Festival and impromptu Golden Gate show: Scully and Dalton, *Living*, 101–110; Lee and Shalin, *Acid Dreams*, 177; and interviews with participants.

128   Diggers won't accept money: Santelli, *Aquarius Rising*, 26.

7. Son et Lumière

131   Jazz scene: telephone conversation with Steve Grover, December 19, 1996. Grover is a prizewinning jazz composer and drummer living in Maine.

132   Hart quoted in Gans, *Conversations*, 249–250.

132   Interview with Hart.

132   Oliver Sacks, "The Last Hippie," *The New York Review of Books*, March 26, 1992.

132   Mickey "went tribal": Scully and Dalton, *Living*, 282.

133   "was like the" to "the trinity": Hart quoted in Jackson, *Goin'*, 193, 196–197. *Drumming on the Edge of Magic* was coauthored in 1990 with Jay Stevens.

133   "We've got transformation": Hart quoted in Gans, *Conversations*, 250–251.

134   Interview with Hart.

135   Telephone interview with Jamie Janover, October 19, 1997.

136   Interview with Peter Wigley, Bath, Maine, June 29, 1997.

136   Interview with Hart.

137   Scully and Dawson quoted in Greenfield, *Dark Star*, 81, 125, respectively.

137   Kreutzmann quoted in Jackson, *Goin'*, 152.

138   Interview with Bob Bralove, San Rafael, California, July 17, 1993.

138   Gans, Lesh, and Weir quoted from "The Grateful Dead Hour," #370, produced by David Gans (Oakland, California: Truth and Fun, Inc., 1995).

139   Jackson, *Goin'*, 145–146.

139   Telephone conversation with Grover.

140   Kreutzmann quoted in Jackson, *Goin'*, 151–152.

140   Interview with Hart.

140   Larry Rivers with Carol Brightman, *Drawings and Digressions* (New York: Clarkson Potter, 1979, 1992), 13.

141   Interview with Bralove.

141   Interview with Mountain Girl.

141   Interview with Bralove.

141   Interview with Selvin.

142   Interview with Arthur Mack, Nobleboro, Maine, January 6, 1997.

142   Interview with Selvin.

143   Weir quoted in Gans, *Conversations,* 119–120.

143   Interview with David Gans, Berkeley, California, July 14, 1993.

143   Boston Garden concert: Steve Morse, "Dead Leave Grateful Boston on High Note," *Boston Globe,* October 1, 1993, 62.

144   Interview with Bob Weir, Soldier Field, Chicago, Illinois, June 26, 1993.

145   "I'm the 'Mr. Show-biz' in the group": Weir quoted in Gans, *Conversations,* 118.

145   "When we're up there pumping": Paul Gerald, "Interview with Vince Welnick," *Memphis Flyer,* March 1995.

146   L. Frank Baum, *The Wonderful Wizard of Oz,* illustrated by W. W. Denslow (New York: Dover Publications, 1960—unabridged republication of the first edition published by the George M. Hill Company in 1900), 184, 196, 203.

147   Interview with Weir.

148   Matthew Gilbert, "A Week of Rule-Breaking for the Dead," *Boston Globe,* October 1, 1993, 62.

148   Barlow quoted in Gans, *Conversations,* 176.

149   Telephone conversation with Candace Brightman, October 31, 1997.

150   Interview with Hart.

150   Interview with Bralove.

150   Interview with Weir.

150   Telephone interview with Janover.

8. Their Subculture and Mine: I

155   Hunter, "An American Adventure," 121.

155   Interview with Eileen Law, San Rafael, California, July 15, 1993.

155   "Prophecy of a Declaration": Anthony, *The Summer of Love,* 130.

156   "everyone had looked like diamonds": interview with Eileen Law.

156   Jerry Garcia quoted in Brandelius, *GDFA,* 198.

156   Interview with Eileen Law.

156   Heinlein's *Stranger in a Strange Land* cited in Stevens, *Storming Heaven,* 239.

157   where all the kids are like you: cited by Tom Constanten in Troy, *Saturday Night,* 16

157   "Magic is what we do": interview with Jerry Garcia by Timothy White, taped at Club Front in San Rafael, California, in 1989 and aired on WBLM, October 30, 1996, as "Dead on Arrival."

157   Jerry Garcia in Gans, *Conversations,* 66.

157   Interview with Alan Kapuler ("Mushroom"), Corvallis, Oregon, March 16, 1996.

160   Fidel Castro quoted in Sandra Levinson and Carol Brightman, eds., *The Venceremos Brigade: Young Americans Sharing the Life and Work of Revolutionary Cuba* (New York: Simon & Schuster, 1971), 164.

161   George W. S. Trow, *Within the Context of No Context* (New York: Atlantic Monthly Press, 1981), 50.

161   "You thought we were perfect": Levinson and Brightman, eds., *Venceremos Brigade,* 23.

162   "a collective experience": Joel Sloman, untitled poem, in ibid., 169.

162   "I found myself looking": ibid., 197.

162   Featherstone was a "full-time revolutionary": Black caucus leader Marty Price quoted in ibid., 196.

162   "Death [that happens]": Robert Takagi quoted in ibid., 195.

163   Kopkind, *Thirty Years' Wars,* 211.

163   Eastland quoted in Levinson and Brightman, eds., *Venceremos Brigade,* 17–18.

164   Tupamaro pamphlet quoted in this author's *Berkeley Journal* V, May 5, 1971.

165   protest statistics: Gitlin, *The Sixties,* 409.

165   Kopkind, *Thirty Years' Wars,* 211.

165   Gitlin, *The Sixties,* 242–243.

166   This author's *Berkeley Journal* V, May 19, 1971.

167   Wilson quoted in Linda Kelly, *Deadheads* (New York: Citadel/Carol Publishing, 1995), 5–6.

167   Mouse quoted in Kelly, *Deadheads,* 156.

169   "a new political geography": this author's *Berkeley Journal* V, May 19, 1971.

169   Scully and Dalton, *Living,* 77.

169   "Death of Hippie" parade, etc.: Anthony, *The Summer of Love,* 175; and Lee and Shalin, *Acid Dreams,* 191.

170   Interview with Mountain Girl.

172   Interview with Kesey. The source for the Hitler story is a book on methedrine and the Third Reich, written around 1944, according to Kesey, by a Scandinavian author whose name he's forgotten.

9. Their Subculture and Mine: II

175   Harrison, *The Dead,* 228, 176, 178.

176   Interview with Cassidy Law, San Rafael, California, March 13, 1996.

176   Interview with Eileen Law.

176   Telephone interview with Chris Brightman, August 9, 1997.

177   Interview with Mountain Girl.

177   Gary Snyder, "The Tribe," from *Earth House Old* (New York: New Direc-

tions, 1969); reprinted in Mitchell Goodman, ed., *The Movement Toward a New America* (Pilgrim Press/Knopf: New York, 1970), 662.

178   Frances FitzGerald, *Cities on a Hill: A Journey Through Contemporary American Cultures* (New York: Simon & Schuster, 1981), 18, 19.

179   Interview with Hunter.

179   Hunter, "Ship of Fools," *Box,* 201.

180   Hunter, "Dear JG," DeadNet, Robert Hunter/Archive Journals.

180   Hunter, "Casey Jones" and "Dire Wolf," *Box,* 32, 52.

181   Hunter, "Truckin'," *Box,* 230.

181   overhead expenses, etc.: Brandelius, *GDFA,* 119.

181   Wall of Sound: Scully and Dalton, *Living,* 254.

182   payout plan: ibid., 230.

182   Interview with Mountain Girl.

182   Hunter, "Cumberland Blues," *Box,* 52.

182   Trist quoted in Greenfield, *Dark Star,* 21.

183   Rowan quoted in Greenfield, *Dark Star,* 156.

184   Hunter, "Broke-down Palace," *Box,* 28.

184   Hunter quoted in *Garcia,* 24.

184   Hunter, "Ripple," *Box,* 185.

185   Hunter, "Attics of My Life," *Box,* 12.

185   Graham quoted in Scully and Dalton, *Living,* 162.

186   Hunter quoted in Gans, *Conversations,* 27–28.

186   Interview with Mountain Girl.

186   Michael Lydon, "Dead Zone," *Rolling Stone,* August 23, 1969; reprinted in *Garcia,* 64.

186   Nelson quoted in Greenfield, *Dark Star,* 123.

186   Dawson quoted in Greenfield, *Dark Star,* 120–121, 124.

187   Interview with Mountain Girl.

187   Hunter, "Dear JG," DeadNet, Robert Hunter/Archive Journals.

187   Rowan quoted in Greenfield, *Dark Star,* 154.

188   Hunter, "Uncle John's Band," *Box,* 233.

189   "The Golden Road," in Jamie Jensen, *Grateful Dead: Built to Last: 25th Anniversary Album* (New York: Plume/Penguin, 1990), 20.

190   Jerry Garcia quoted in WBLM interview with White.

190   Jerry Garcia quoted in *Garcia,* 123.

190   Robert Stone, "End of the Beginning," in *Garcia,* 32, 34.

191   "in a long line of Protestant reform movements": Rick Pearlstein, "Who Owns the Sixties?" in *Lingua Franca,* May/June 1996, 33; "part of the American experience": Robert Brigham quoted by Georgette Weir, "Vietnam: What Were the Two Sides Thinking?" in *Vassar Quarterly,* Summer 1996, 13.

191   Hersh quoted in Gitlin, *The Sixties,* 379

191   Kissinger quoted in Lee and Shalin, *Acid Dreams,* 261.

192   "bloodbath" to "kill or be killed": Jack Whalen and Richard Flacks, *Beyond the Barricades: The Sixties Generation Grows Up* (Philadelphia: Temple University Press, 1989), 113.

192   "We now feel": Kirkpatrick Sale, *SDS* (New York: Vintage, 1974), 606.

192   "fall offensive": Sale, *SDS,* 652.

193   "Lost in a haunted wood": W. H. Auden, "September 1, 1939," in Jack Salzman and Barry Wallenstein, eds., *Years of Protest* (New York: Pegasus, 1967), 216.

193   Dylan, "Visions of Johanna," Special Rider Music, Inc.

193   This author's *Berkeley Journal* V, May 6, 1971.

194   Weatherman quoted in Sale, *SDS,* 631–632.

195   This author's *Berkeley Journal* VI, August 3, 1971.

195   Hunter quoted in *Garcia,* 162.

196   Hunter, "Mister Charlie," *Box,* 153.

196   Hunter, "Playing in the Band," *Box,* 170.

197   "Smashing the pig": Sale, *SDS,* 604.

198   "a dream we dreamed": Hunter, "Box of Rain," *Box,* 170.

198   Hunter, "An American Adventure," 122–123.

10. Their Subculture and Mine: III

201   Hoffman quoted in Jonah Raskin, *For the Hell of It: The Life and Times of Abbie Hoffman* (Berkeley: University of California Press, 1997), 193.

202   Dawson quoted in Troy, *Saturday Night,* 173.

202   Gregg Bucci, 5/20/70, Harpur College; and John Scott, 5/6/70, Kresge Plaza, MIT, *DeadBase VI,* 396–397.

202   Hoffman and Townshend quotes in Raskin, *For the Hell of It,* 194–196.

203   "Center stage": Gitlin, *The Sixties,* 407.

203   Columbia Records ad campaign: David Caute, *The Year of the Barricades: A Journey Through 1968* (New York: Harper & Row, 1988), 54.

204   "Are we to follow": Steve Strauss, "A Romance on Either Side of Dada," in Marcus, ed., *Rock and Roll Will Stand,* 134.

204   Jerry Garcia quoted in Lee and Shalin, *Acid Dreams,* 254.

204   "At first the revolution": Harrison, *The Dead,* 7.

204   Rakow quoted in Greenfield, *Dark Star,* 111.

204   "The Dead were trying": Telephone interview with Stephen Jane, March 22, 1997.

204   Wenner quoted in Lee and Shalin, *Acid Dreams,* 253.

205   "first deities": Kessler, "Dancing in the Streets," 64.

205   René Gandolfi, 6/24/70, Capitol Theater, *DeadBase,* 397–398.

206   Interview with Kapuler ("Mushroom").

207   "Dilbert," December 31, 1997, S. Adams, United Features Syndicate, Inc.

207   Interview with Kapuler ("Mushroom").

208   Cutler and Hell's Angels: Scully and Dalton, *Living,* 181.

208   Grogan and Hell's Angels: Santelli, *Aquarius Rising,* 166, 170, 174.

208   Interview with Workman.

210   Manson and the ecology message: Harrison, *The Dead,* 126.

210   Gitlin, *The Sixties,* 406–407.

210   Scully and Dalton, *Living,* 179–182.

211   "picnics that cost too much": Graham and Greenfield, *Bill Graham Presents,* 353.

211   Interview with Hart.

211   "sails out of that dressing room": Scully and Dalton, *Living,* 184.

212   Jerry Garcia quoted in Graham and Greenfield, *Bill Graham Presents,* 200.

212   Gaskin quoted in Graham and Greenfield, *Bill Graham Presents,* 278.

212   Interview with Hart.

212   Interview with Candace Brightman, Damariscotta, Maine, February 13, 1996.

212   Jerry Garcia quoted in Graham and Greenfield, *Bill Graham Presents,* 202.

212   Interview with Hart.

213   Interview with Candace Brightman, February 13, 1996; and conversation, Walpole, Maine, April 15, 1998.

214   reselling tickets: ibid.

214   Interview with Richard Loren, Damariscotta, Maine, November 13, 1997.

214   Interview with Kesey.

214   Mountain Girl quoted in Troy, *Saturday Night,* 78.

215   Interview with Hart.

215   Hunter, "New Speedway Boogie," *Box,* 158.

216   Walt Whitman, "Song of the Open Road," Book VII, *Leaves of Grass* (New York: Modern Library, n.d. [follows arrangement of 1891–1892 edition]), 118–119.

217   Interview with Mountain Girl.

218   Hunter, "Black Peter," *Box,* 18.

218   Hunter, "Box of Rain," *Box,* 26.

219   Leonard Cohen, "Closing Time," "Waiting for the Miracle," "Take This Waltz," *Stranger Music* (New York: Pantheon, 1993), 378, 380, 353.

220   Hunter, "Saint Stephen," *Box,* 195.

220   Hunter, "Holigomena," *Night Cadre* (New York: Penguin, 1991), 93.

221   Cohen, "The Future," *Stranger Music,* 370.

222   "Fuck hippie capitalism": Lee and Shalin, *Acid Dreams,* 253.

222   Leary and the power lines: Interview with Kesey.

222   Emmett Grogan, *Ringolevio: A Life Played for Keeps* (New York: Citadel, 1990), 493.

223   Kerr quoted in Stevens, *Storming Heaven,* ix.

223   "Q: Is the Vietnamese civilization": compiled from Liberation News Service interview and another with Frank Bardacke in Berkeley by *Sundance* (undated clipping in author's collection).

224   "He's a real Weatherman" to "To armed war against the state": Sale, *SDS,* 627.

225   Weatherman Songbook quoted in Harold Jacobs, ed., *Weatherman* (Berkeley, California: Ramparts Press, 1970), 356.

225   Dohrn quoted in Sale, *SDS,* 628.

225   Manson named Man of the Year: Lee and Shalin, *Acid Dreams,* 257.

11. Their Subculture and Mine: IV

227   Jerry Garcia quoted in Scully and Dalton, *Living,* 77.

227   Star Black, "The Fractured Roundeye," unpublished manuscript.

229   Ibid.

229   "Your constant battles": Jerry Garcia, "Cream Puff War," Ice Nine Publishing.

230   Scully and Dalton, *Living,* 77.

230   Jerry Garcia quoted in *Garcia,* 57–58.

230   "surrounded by straight geeks": Grant quoted in Greenfield, *Dark Star,* 10.

230   "razor totin' schools": Jerry Garcia quoted in WBLM interview with White.

231   Miller quoted in Brooks, *The Times of Melville and Whitman,* 114.

231   Interview with Hunter.

231   Central Intelligence Agency, "International Connections of the U.S. Peace Movement," November 15, 1967. Received by author in May 1996 as part of personal FOIA request.

231   Interview with Hunter.

232   Munich whorehouse: Scully and Dalton, *Living,* 245–246, 250.

233   Interview with Cassidy Law.

234   Interview with Mountain Girl.

234   "a convention of brigands": Harrison, *The Dead,* 234.

235   Interview with Hunter.

235   Telephone conversation with Candace Brightman, August 26, 1997.

235   Scully and Dalton, *Living,* 303.

236   Milk and Cookies: Conversation with Candace Brightman, April 15, 1998.

236   Lesh, Parish, and Jerry Garcia quoted in Gans, *Conversations,* 243–244.

236   1967 press conference: Jann S. Wenner, "Busted! The Dead Did Get It," *Rolling Stone,* November 9, 1967; reprinted in *Garcia,* 52.

237   Interview with Tom Shoesmith, New York, New York, February 22, 1997.

238   Interview with Candace Brightman, Damariscotta, Maine, February 13, 1996.

241   Telephone interview with Janover.

241   Interview with Candace Brightman, February 13, 1996.

241   Conversation with Candace Brightman, Bristol Mills, Maine, September 24, 1996; interview with Candace Brightman, February 13, 1996; and telephone conversation with Candace Brightman, February 8, 1998.

241   Interview with Loren.

242   Scully and Dalton, *Living,* 302.

243   Interview with Loren.

243   Telephone interview with Candace Brightman, October 31, 1997.

244   Interview with Loren.

244   Interview with Shoesmith.

245   Healy quoted in Scully and Dalton, *Living,* 213.

245   Interview with Candace Brightman, February 13, 1996.

12. The House That Jerry Built

249   Hunter, "The Wheel," *Box,* 244.

249   Grogan, *Ringolevio,* 419.

250   Telephone interview with Janover.

251   Jerry Garcia quoted in Scully and Dalton, *Living,* 230.

251   Jerry Garcia quoted in Gans, *Conversations,* 39.

252   business profits: Scully and Dalton, *Living,* 230.

252   "a Deadland of airwaves": ibid., 228.

253   Scully and Garcia: ibid., 227.

253   Interview with Hart.

253   "And the Lord spake": Numbers 10:2.

254   Jerry Garcia quoted in James Henke, "Jerry Garcia," *Rolling Stone,* October 31, 1991, 108.

254   Interview with Hart.

254   Smith quoted in *Dark Star,* 128.

254   Interview with Loren.

255   Owsley on Rakow: *Dark Star,* 111.

255   Rakow quoted in Greenfield, *Dark Star,* 78, 79, 142.

255   business deal with Rakow in Scully and Dalton, *Living,* 230.

256   *The Movement Toward a New America: The Beginnings of a Long Revolution,* a collage assembled by Mitchell Goodman (Philadelphia: Pilgrimi Press/Alfred A. Knopf, 1970), 752.

257   Telephone conversation with Candace Brightman, February 22, 1998.

257   Rakow dropped out of sight: Greenfield, *Dark Star,* 177–178; interview with Hart.

257   Loren quoted in Greenfield, *Dark Star,* 144.

257   Rakow quoted in Greenfield, *Dark Star,* 146.

258   getting paid by the cut: Scully and Dalton, *Living,* 65–66.

258   Hunter told me about the veto power in our interview; in a telephone conversation on May 13, 1998, Alan Trist told me that Hunter's voting power applied specifically to music-related decisions.

259   band members quoted in *DeadBase VI,* 395.

260   Smith quoted in Greenfield, *Dark Star,* 128.

260   Hunter, "Truckin'," *Box,* 231.

262   CIA, "Situation Information Report: Calendar of Tentatively Scheduled Activities," July 30, 1970. Received by author in May 1996 as part of personal FOIA request.

263   ACID ALLEY, HIGH STREET, and Dr. William Abruzzi: Santelli, *Aquarius Rising,* 198, 201.

263   CIA, "Situation Information Report," July 30, 1970, 1–5.

264   Lichtenstein quoted in Santelli, *Aquarius Rising,* 253.

264   Interview with Kapuler ("Mushroom").

265   "ordinary guys, graying": Barich, "Still Truckin' On," 97.

266   Dave Levy, 4/5/71, Manhattan Center, *DeadBase VI,* 402.

268   Blair Jackson, 7/31/71, Yale Bowl, *DeadBase VI,* 403–404.

270   "a crock of shit": Jerry Garcia quoted in *Garcia,* 88.

271   Fillmore East story told to David Gans by a Deadhead following Garcia's death, and recorded on "The Grateful Dead Hour," #363.

271   Kesey quoted in Greenfield, *Dark Star,* 76.

271   Jerry Garcia quoted in Harrison, *The Dead,* 76.

272   Kesey quoted in *Dark Star,* 76.

13. Heads and Tales

273   Interview with Wigley, November 26, 1996.

274   Interview with Bob Schroff ("Giant"), Danville Junction, Maine, December 29, 1996.

274   Interview with Wigley, November 26, 1996.

275   "Off the Mark," Mark Parisi, Atlantic Feature, October 24, 1997.

276   Interview with Wigley, November 26, 1996.

277   Garcia quoted in Peter Watrous, "Touch of Gray Matter," *Musician,* December 1989, 44.

277   Interview with Hunter.

278   Jay Stevens sat in on June 12, 1992, interview with Mickey Hart.

278   Interview with Hart.

279   *DeadBase VI,* vi.

279   Interview with Jay Stevens.

279   Telephone interview with Andrew Graff, January 8, 1998.

280   Interview with Wigley, November 26, 1996.

284   Interview with Workman.

285   Jerry Garcia quoted in Henke, "Jerry Garcia," 40.

285   Mary McCarthy, *Memories of a Catholic Girlhood* (New York: Harcourt Brace Jovanovich/Harvest, 1957), 23.

14. Junkie Dreams, Acid Rain, and the Resurrection of the Dead

287   Interview with Workman.

288   Interview with Kesey.

288   Mandatory-minimum sentencing: I am indebted to Julia Stewart, director of Families Against Mandatory Minimums, for this information; telephone interview, March 24, 1998.

288   The contra drug connection is exhaustively documented by Peter Dale Scott and Jonathan Marshall in *Cocaine Politics: Drugs, Armies, and the CIA in Central America* (Berkeley: University of California Press, 1991).

289   "rapping with a fellow Deadhead": John J. Wood, 7/4/86, Rich Stadium, *DeadBase VI,* 460.

289   Interview with Workman.

289   "*Neal vs. U.S.*": Thea Kelley and Dennis Bernstein, "LSD, Deadheads, and the Law," *Z Magazine,* April 1996, 41.

290   Interview with Peter Wigley, Maggie Motorcycle, and John Upham, Bath, Maine, June 29, 1997.

291   Campbell quoted in Brandelius, *GDFA,* 234.

291   Interview with Marcie Lichtenstein, Todd Marcus, and Eric Lichtenstein, Santa Fe, New Mexico, February 17, 1997.

293   Interview with Andrew Graff.

293   Interview with Lichtenstein, Marcus, and Lichtenstein.

294   Dennis Cauchon, "Attack on Deadheads Is No Hallucination," *USA Today,* December 17, 1992, A3; and Dirk Johnson, "For Drug Offenders, How Tough Is Too Tough?" *New York Times,* November 8, 1993, A16.

295   Telephone interview with Toni Brown, March 24, 1998.

295   McNally quoted in Kelley and Bernstein, "LSD, Deadheads, and the Law," 44.

295   "Operation Deadend": Jo-Ann Armao, "80 'Deadheads' Arrested on Drug Charges," *Washington Post,* March 18, 1990.

295   Jerry Garcia quoted in *Garcia,* 173.

296   Telephone interview with Brown.

296   *Dupree's Diamond News* quoted in Frank Smith, "Box of Pain," *The New Republic,* March 21, 1994, 25.

296   Jackson quoted in *The Golden Road,* 1993 Annual, 16.

297   Interview with Lichtenstein, Marcus, and Lichtenstein.

297   Hunter, "Shakedown Street," *Box,* 198.

297   Interview with Hunter.

299   Interview with Andre Bernard, New York, September 25, 1997.

300   Rossman, *New Age Blues,* 65, 117.

301   Telephone interview with Richard Levy, April 3, 1997. For raconteur Andy Kopkind, also a member of the High Pressure Front, this was a favorite story.

303   Interview with Lichtenstein, Marcus, and Lichtenstein.

304   "the church of love": interview with Loren.

304   Interview with Cameron Sears, San Rafael, California, March 13, 1996.

304   Interview with Calico, San Rafael, California, July 15, 1993.

304   Interview with Loren.

305   Young, "You and Me," 1992 Silver Fiddle Music, ASCAP.

305   Interview with Kesey.

306   Telephone interview with Sue Stephens, May 13, 1998.

306   Telephone interview with Alan Trist, May 13, 1998.

306   Garcia's drugs: Scully and Dalton, *Living,* 308, 314, 339.

307   Interview with Sears.

307   "[T]here is that juice": Jerry Garcia quoted in *Garcia,* 174.

307   "seeking the high-energy experience": Jerry Garcia quoted in Harrison, *The Dead,* 76.

307   "magic moment": Jerry Garcia quoted in Gans, *Conversations,* 52–53.

308   "Media in general": Jerry Garcia quoted in Harrison, *The Dead,* 75–76.

308   "mystery . . . some kind of intuitive thing": Jerry Garcia quoted in Gans, *Conversations,* 53.

308   Joyce Johnson, *Minor Characters* (Boston: Houghton Mifflin, 1983), 190–191.

308   "I don't want the fuckin' job": Jerry Garcia quoted in Brandelius, *GDFA,* 83.

308   "close to being perfect fascism": Jerry Garcia quoted in Gans, *Conversations,* 53–54.

308   Harrison, *The Dead,* 225–226.

309   Jerry Garcia's 1982 *Playboy* interview quoted in Brandelius, *GDFA,* 209.

310   Jerry Garcia interviewed by Blair Jackson in *The Golden Road;* quoted in Brandelius, *GDFA,* 244.

311   Peter Watrous, "A Glimpse of the Dead of Old, with Sting," *New York Times,* June 7, 1993.

311   Jon Pareles, *New York Times,* 1995, H26.

312   Jerry Garcia quoted in Henke, "Jerry Garcia," 108.

312   Hunter, "Touch of Grey," *Box,* 228.

312   "dysfunctional Dad"; interview with Gans, March 12, 1996.

313   Interview with Wigley, Maggie Motorcycle, and Upham.

314   Cornell quoted in Troy, *Saturday Night,* 258.

314   Interview with Lichtenstein, Marcus, and Lichtenstein.

314   Telephone interview with Todd Marcus, May 16, 1998.

314   Interview with Loren.

⤚✍⤙

~SELECTED BIBLIOGRAPHY~

Brandelius, Jerilyn Lee. *Grateful Dead Family Album*. New York: Warner Books, 1989.

Cohn, Lawrence, ed. *Nothing But the Blues: The Music and the Musicians*. Introduction by B. B. King. New York: Abbeville Press, 1993.

DeadBase VI: Complete Guide to Grateful Dead Song Lists. Edited by John W. Scott. Hanover, New Hampshire: DeadBase, 1992.

de Curtis, Anthony, and James Henke, eds. *The Rolling Stone Illustrated History of Rock & Roll*. New York: Random House, 1992.

FitzGerald, Frances. *Cities on a Hill: A Journey Through Contemporary American Cultures*. New York: A Touchstone Book/Simon & Schuster, 1987.

Frith, Simon. *Performing Rites: On the Value of Popular Music*. Cambridge, Massachusetts: Harvard University Press, 1996.

Gans, David. *Conversations with the Dead: The Grateful Dead Interview Book*. New York: Citadel Press, 1991.

Garcia. By the editors of *Rolling Stone*. Boston: Little, Brown/Rolling Stone Press, 1995.

Gitlin, Todd. *The Sixties: Years of Hope, Days of Rage*. New York: Bantam Books, 1987.

Greenfield, Robert. *Dark Star: An Oral Biography of Jerry Garcia*. New York: William Morrow, 1996.

Harrison, Hank. *The Dead*. Millbrae, California: Celestial Arts, 1980.

Hofmann, Albert. *LSD: My Problem Child*. Translated by Jonathan Ott. New York: McGraw-Hill, 1980.

Hunter, Robert. *A Box of Rain*. New York: Viking Penguin, 1990.

Jackson, Blair. *Goin' Down the Road: A Grateful Dead Traveling Companion*. New York: Harmony Books, 1992.

Lee, Martin A., and Bruce Shalin. *Acid Dreams: The Complete Social History of LSD*. 2d ed. New York: Grove Press, 1992.

Marcus, Greil, ed. *Rock and Roll Will Stand*. Boston: Beacon Press, 1969.

Marks, John. *The Search for the "Manchurian Candidate."* New York: Times Books, 1979.

Perry, Paul. *On The Bus: Complete Guide to the Legendary Trip of Ken Kesey and the Merry Pranksters*. New York: Thunder's Mouth Press, 1990.

Rossman, Michael. *New Age Blues: On the Politics of Consciousness*. New York: E. P. Dutton, 1979.

Scully, Rock, with David Dalton. *Living With the Dead: Twenty Years on the Bus with Garcia and the Grateful Dead.* Boston: Little, Brown, 1996.

Stevens, Jay. *Storming Heaven: LSD and the American Dream.* New York: Harper & Row/Perennial Library, 1987.

Wolfe, Tom. *The Electric Kool-Aid Acid Test.* New York: Bantam Books, 1969.

~ACKNOWLEDGMENTS~

This is not a book that lay in waiting for its author, as, for instance, the biography of Mary McCarthy, *Writing Dangerously,* did for a long time before I conceived of writing it in 1985. Or, if it did, it has reached me by a more roundabout route, and satisfies a taste for sudden leaps and risky propositions. The germ of the "Their Subculture and Mine" idea appeared in a proposal I submitted for a grant in 1988 called "Period Pieces," a series of reflections on the 1960s, one of which was about the Grateful Dead. It had occurred to me around then that while the fierce attachments of radicals seemed to have melted into air, the fringe group my sister Candace had worked for all these years was turning into something like a national monument.

I didn't get the grant, and it was four more years before I arrived, exhausted, at the end of *Writing Dangerously*. The '60s book had refocused itself on Vietnam and Cuba and their influence on my political generation, a grandiose project that I was in no shape to undertake then. Something simpler was needed to tide me over; something (dare one say?) lighter, which might sell (as in "Sell when you can,/you are not for all markets": Shakespeare, *As You Like It*). And this was when I became the recipient of a bolt from the blue from my agent, Lucy Kroll, who telephoned me excitedly one day in the spring of 1992 to say she had been awakened by a dream the night before in which the idea of my writing about Jerry Garcia appeared vividly before her. "You don't have to say yes," she assured me; for I had fended off other suggestions before. This time though there was a note of elation in her husky voice that made it harder to say no. Yet no it was. The idea of writing a celebrity biography, which is how I saw a book about Jerry Garcia (whose movie interests Lucy represented), appealed to me about as much as reading one.

Still, there was something in the proposal that stirred my fancy and reminded me of that other world I entered whenever I went to see my sister light a Grateful Dead show, a world whose roots lay in a corner of the counterculture remote from my own. So I called Lucy back and talked myself into a book that was to grow immeasurably more complex than either of us imagined, incorporating, in time, even bits of Vietnam and Cuba. Nor would it turn out to be easy to write, or less time-consuming than the biography (or only slightly less so), but was an uphill struggle all the way— for this was unfamiliar turf for me, and to travel it I have had to let go of more familiar preoccupations and slowly, painstakingly, absorb a new arcanum.

Lucy Kroll, whose bolts from the blue were well known in her circle, died at eighty-eight on March 14, 1997. She never saw the fruits of her dream. She is the first of many helpers who stepped out of the woods at a critical juncture to point me down a path I probably wouldn't have found otherwise. And if there were times over the past six years when I came close to cursing her for it, I thank her now. I thank her young successor as well, Barbara Hogenson, who possesses her mentor's unfailing loyalty and generosity of spirit, along with a reservoir of good humor and common sense whose bottom I have never reached.

Candace, meanwhile, was not pleased when I told her in 1992 that I was thinking of writing a book about the Grateful Dead and their place in American culture. It was, after all, an invasion of territory that was embattled enough without the arrival of her big sister, who was quite capable of mistaking the sound booth for the lighting booth. Perhaps the Dead were uneasy, too; for later I would hear from this or that person in the organization that I was writing a book "about Deadheads," when that was not what I had set out in the letter of introduction that publicist Dennis McNally asked me to present. In any event, Candace wasn't unhappy enough to discourage me; and Dennis McNally proved to be very helpful, arranging interviews with everyone I asked for except Jerry Garcia, with whom I wasn't ready to talk formally, in any event, until it was too late. Today I believe the musicians were sincere in their interest in a book about Deadheads, whose motivations and intercommunal life naturally intrigue them.

Candace, of course, had long regaled me with tales from the road, which began to pour forth now that she had a more attentive listener. But her real contribution, less expected, came when she began reading the manuscript with an ear attuned to voice and tone as well as to historical accuracy. "LCD," she signed her communiqués, for the lowest common denominator reader she pretended to be. I was "LB" for Loose Balls, a basketball nickname from high school. (*The Dreadful Great* was my tongue-in-cheek title of an early draft.) Candace and I disagreed at times on points of style and interpretation, and I didn't always follow her suggestions, but when I have, especially on matters of style, I believe the writing is better for it.

Neither Candace nor the many others in and around the Grateful Dead who were interviewed for this book are responsible for errors of fact. Nor are they to blame for the missing players in a narrative that focuses mainly on the band's takeoff years in the late '60s and early '70s—which is when the die was cast, in my view, and also when the political wing of the counterculture, by contrast, faded out. Musicians such as Keith and Donna Godchaux and Brent Mydland, along with Bob Weir's songwriting partner, John Perry Barlow ("the B-Team," Barlow calls the two of them, next to the Hunter/Garcia A-Team), get short shrift in these pages. So, too, do many important songs and landmark shows that the reader will find memorialized in the Deadhead's core curriculum: in *DeadBase, The Grateful Dead Family Album*, and *Grateful Dead: The Official Book of the Deadheads,* together with the fan magazines.

Alongside the interviews I conducted, some of these secondary sources helped fill the gaps in my knowledge of the Grateful Dead's development; among them, David Gans's excellent *Conversations with the Dead*, Robert Greenfield's oral biography of Jerry Garcia, *Dark Star*, and Blair Jackson's *Goin' Down the Road*. Former manager Rock Scully and David Dalton's *Living with the Dead* is the sort of "I can hear it now" narrative one appreciates in projects like this; even if it wallows in the druggy side of the band and leaves out the other managers who helped pilot the Grateful Dead (as if, upon this Rock, Jerry built his Church). The donnish Jon McIntire, for instance, a reader of Hannah Arendt, played as important a role as Scully; as did red diaper baby Danny Rifkin, who still oversees the Dead's charitable arm, the Rex Foundation, from his desk in San Rafael.

After Candace, the principal first-person contributors to the story of the band that emerges here are, among Grateful Dead folk, band members Mickey Hart, Bob Weir, and Phil Lesh, along with electronic sound wizard Bob Bralove and lyricist Robert Hunter; former managers Jon McIntire, Danny Rifkin, and Richard "Zippy" Loren, a fellow bookworm whom I stumbled on in the Skidompha Library in Damariscotta, Maine; and current manager Cameron Sears. Alan Trist, who runs Ice Nine Publishing, and

Eileen Law, who handles public relations, have continued to answer questions (especially Alan) and point me in new directions since our initial interviews. My thanks extend to others who have shared organizational and personal experiences: Eileen's daughter Cassidy Law, Sue Swanson, the self-styled "first fan" from Grateful Dead Merchandising, and Sue Stephens, another old family friend, who helps administer the Jerry Garcia Estate; also former ticket manager Steve Marcus and current manager Frankie Acardie, who were joined during a 1993 interview in San Rafael by Calico from the Hog Farm, who oversaw Grateful Dead security before it became a police function administered by promoters and arenas.

Joel Selvin, for years the music critic for the *San Francisco Chronicle*, opened up his files on the Grateful Dead to give me a sense of the band's history, at a time (1993) when this kind of help was invaluable. Photographer Gene Anthony, who covered the Trips Festival and the Summer of Love for *Newsweek,* was another veteran of the period who made his personal and professional experiences available.

I'm grateful to my brother Chris Brightman—who has worked as a set carpenter for the Dead and continues to fabricate design elements and trusses for the Furthur festivals—for bringing the technical side of touring into focus. The sense of craft one gets from people like Chris (whose sense of the ridiculous is just as useful)—and former light show technician and rigger Tom Shoesmith—provides an invisible scaffolding for a book whose métier, at bottom, is theater.

I benefited from a similar kind of technical virtuosity when I talked about the Dead's music with musically sophisticated Deadheads such as Jamie Janover and Peter Wigley. What makes them such good teachers is their ability to relate the satisfaction they take in the effects of music with a practical knowledge of how the effects are produced and a familiarity with the origins of the songs.

The great storytellers to whom I am indebted are Ken Kesey and Mountain Girl, neighbors in southern Oregon as they were forty-four years ago in Palo Alto. When we met in 1996, Kesey told me a story that was never far from my mind while I was writing this book. Years ago, he and Pranksters Ken Babbs and Gretchen Fetchin' went down to a Fourth of July parade in Santa Cruz, high on acid, "and dressed up in nice red, white, and blue stripey things. And these soldiers came marching by and they would look at us on the street corner. And we began to laugh, and the more we laughed the more they fell out of step. One person laughing on a street corner," Kesey assured me, "can fuck up a huge army."

Mountain Girl, oddly enough, reminds me of Mary McCarthy. She has the same flair for dramatizing an idea in conversation (including the idea of "Mountain Girl") and the same sensitivity to language and talent for extravagant expression. She also possesses a shrewd overview of the Grateful Dead that has helped me interpret the clashing voices I often heard when pursuing a controversial question. "Each of us on our own little journey sees the same landscape from a completely different quadrant," she told me, referring to Rock Scully's book; but the same applied to the Dead, which was, she said, "like a big chess game going on all the time....Sometimes I'd get pushed around," she ventured, "and every once in a while I'd get right in there and play." It worked like a Ouija board, when "four people put their hands together, and the thing kind of moves around. So people who want to go to the letter 'I' have to push pretty hard to get all three other hands to sort of soften up."

"But they can't just *push*," I interject.

"Well, yes, they can, if they want to cheat," she says, adding that "as you go through the game you become aware of being moved and that's when you suddenly become aware of the game."

"That you, too, can move?"

Mountain Girl nods—an old pro, getting ready, in 1996, to go back out on the big board, this time in a courtroom with Deborah Koons Garcia. "Then you, too, gain the powers to move."

Deadheads, needless to say, were often the most generous helpers of all. Especially were they helpful in groups, when the group spirit rose up like a wind full of weather, stormy or bright, sweeping us this way and that; and I got a taste of what Jerry Garcia must have meant when he spoke wonderingly of the "group mind." It happened like that when Peter Wigley introduced me to his tour buddies, first Giant, then Maggie Motorcycle and John Upham; and when my daughter Sarabinh (no Deadhead) introduced me to her friend in Santa Fe, Marcie Lichtenstein, who invited two Deadheads from her tour family, Todd Marcus and her brother Eric, over to talk. Group interviews with Deadheads became occasions for reunions, for bringing out photo albums and power objects, listening to tapes, passing the pipe.

One-on-one exchanges with Arthur Mack, Andy Graff, Alan Kapuler (Mushroom), and Andre Bernard—whose Deadhead years are long past, but whose fat trips seem eternal—were informative in a different way. The same power of recall, where LSD and DMT is concerned, was demonstrated by Skip Workman, the former Hell's Angel from Oakland and a vigorous storyteller in his own right. George Freeman, Pat Ginnerty, Maggi Uhl Samoore, Scott and Jane Schmidt, Gail and Elizabeth Guillet, Georgia West, Glen Douglas, Carla Murray, and others whom I met at Grateful Dead concerts between 1992 and 1995 in Albany, Buffalo, Chicago, New Jersey, New York, Boston, San Francisco, and Highgate, Vermont, all contributed their experiences to this portrait of a subculture that won't go away.

Among Deadheads, no one did a longer piece of the road with me in the early years of the project than David Gans, who seemed to sense exactly what I needed even when I did not. Thus, during visits to the Bay Area, I found myself sitting in on his syndicated radio show, "The Grateful Dead Hour," surfing a Deadhead conference on the WELL in his Oakland studio, and taping interviews with him, which might well have been the seedbed for the hoped-for book "about Deadheads"—if it confronted the dilemma of Deadheads like himself, "who need to traffic in that magic to earn a living," a "magic" that, musically speaking, Gans informed me, had been slipping for years. Gans was equally candid in describing the psychological war games that characterized his relations with the band. And then, so that I might keep first things first, he sent me home in the spring of 1996 with a bagful of "Grateful Dead Hour" tapes containing some of the best live concert music I've ever heard (much of it from the late 1960s and early '70s).

As the editor of *The Official Book of the Deadheads*, Paul Grushkin is another professional Deadhead, one who used to help Eileen Law answer fan mail in the 1970s and now occupies an intermediate zone between the fans and the band. I was introduced to Grushkin by Eileen rather late in the game, but he has made up for lost time by jumping in as an adviser in the selection of photographs and graphic images for the book.

The last group of helpers are the bookmakers—the editors, copy editors, volunteer readers, and researchers who sometimes seemed to me, during the long, lean years of writing and rewriting, to be the only readers I might ever have. The bookies start with the three Carols—myself, editor Carol Southern, and copy editor Carol Edwards—who produced *Writing*

Dangerously together, while Carol Southern and I go back to *Larry Rivers: Drawings and Digressions* (1979, 1995). Time has seasoned our collaboration, and I still count on Carol Southern to steer me away from cryptic conversations with myself and to be both flexible and firm, so that she knows when to back off on a point she wants to change and I don't, and I know when her persistence signals a point well taken. I count on her to keep after me to meet deadlines, and then to mediate if I fail to make them, which I usually do. I depend on Carol Edwards, an excellent copy editor, to know the proper spelling of *amyl nitrate* and why thoughts are not quoted, and also to tolerate my sudden shifts in tense and to bend when she hears *a pen drop* instead of *a pin drop*.

I am grateful to Clarkson Potter's editorial director, Lauren Shakely, for shepherding the book through the publication process with such enthusiasm; to her assistant, Kathryn Crosby, for attending to endless chores with patience and finesse; and to production editor Camille Smith, whose life wasn't made any easier by the missed deadlines. At Potter, I have art director MarySarah Quinn and designer Lauren Monchik to thank for their sensitive attention to the design; and Annie Cutler out in California, a talented graphic artist who freelances for the Dead, who worked on the jacket. Here in Maine, I am indebted to Brenda Madore at the Skidompha Public Library for never giving up on hard-to-find books.

Volunteers who have read the entire manuscript and provided feedback are Richard Levy, my companion-in-arms in the early 1970s, our daughter Sarabinh Levy-Brightman, and Jill Schultz, of the Maine Writers and Publishers Alliance. Schultz also volunteered her services as a research assistant, monitoring the Grateful Dead's website and printing out excerpts from Robert Hunter's online journals. Richard helped me bring the Berkeley period into focus and was a source of quiet and steady encouragement. Sarabinh was a severe reader, whose scholarly training was occasionally offended by sweeping generalizations; but she was provoked by the ideas in this book, and our discussions about the extramusical functions of the Grateful Dead, and the etherealization of drugs, were immensely useful.

Others who were kind enough to read and respond to early chapters in the larval stage were Alison Ford, Dan Rosen, and Gordon Quinn (who fed the musical stream coming my way by taping a four-hour Miles Davis retrospective in Chicago, Miles being in the Dead's firmament). Star Black joined me at the Meadowlands and kept tossing poems and memoranda my way pertaining to the strange trip on which I had embarked, when it seemed that nobody I knew in New York could possibly be interested. But this isn't fair; friends from my old writers' group in the city kept me supplied with clippings and tips, especially Cate Breslin, but also Robin Reisig, Ann Banks, and Marilyn Webb. And anyway, I'm the one who dropped out, and even at home in Maine, fighting for time and space to tame the savage beast (*Sweet Chaos*), and also attend an ailing parent, I had to be caught running backward from everyone.

Walpole, Maine
June 1998

~INDEX~